EYEWITNESS TRAVEL

HUNGARY

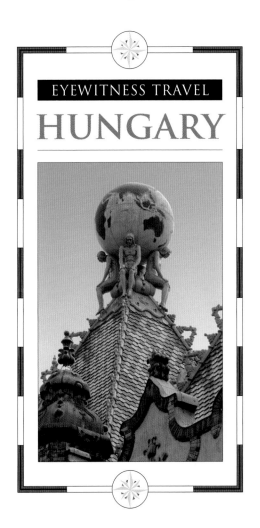

EYEWITNESS TRAVEL

HUNGARY

MAIN CONTRIBUTORS: BARBARA OLSZAŃSKA, TADEUSZ
OLSZAŃSKI, CRAIG TURP

DK

LONDON, NEW YORK,
MELBOURNE, MUNICH AND DELHI
www.dk.com

Produced by Hachette Livre Polska Sp. z o.o.

SENIOR GRAPHIC DESIGNER Paweł Pasternak
GRAPHIC DESIGNERS Paweł Pasternak, Paweł Kamiński
SENIOR EDITOR Agnieszka Trzebska-Cwalina

PHOTOGRAPHERS
Gábor Barka, Dorota and Mariusz Jarymowicz, Krzysztof Kur

ILLUSTRATORS
Michał Burkiewicz, Gary Cross, Dorota Jarymowicz,
Paweł Marczak

CARTOGRAPHERS
Barbara and Jacek Gawrysiuk, Magda Polak

Reproduced in Singapore by Colourscan
Printed and bound by L. Rex Printing Company Limited, China

First American Edition, 2007
13 14 15 16 10 9 8 7 6 5 4 3 2 1

Published in the United States by Dorling Kindersley Publishing.
375 Hudson Street, New York, New York 10014

Reprinted with revisions 2010, 2013

Copyright © 2007, 2013 Dorling Kindersley Limited, London
A Penguin Company

Published in Great Britain by Dorling Kindersley Limited.

A CATALOGING IN PUBLICATION RECORD IS
AVAILABLE FROM THE LIBRARY OF CONGRESS.

ISSN 1542-1554
ISBN 978-0-75669-511-8

FLOORS ARE REFERRED TO THROUGHOUT IN ACCORDANCE WITH
UK USAGE; IE THE "FIRST FLOOR" IS THE FLOOR ABOVE GROUND LEVEL.

Front cover main image: Chain Bridge over the Danube River, Budapest

MIX
Paper from
responsible sources
FSC
www.fsc.org   FSC™ C018179

**The information in this
DK Eyewitness Travel Guide is checked regularly.**
Every effort has been made to ensure that this book is as up-to-date
as possible at the time of going to press. Some details, however,
such as telephone numbers, opening hours, prices, gallery hanging
arrangements and travel information are liable to change. The
publishers cannot accept responsibility for any consequences arising
from the use of this book, nor for any material on third-party
websites, and cannot guarantee that any website address in this
book will be a suitable source of travel information. We value the
views and suggestions of our readers very highly. Please write to:
Publisher, DK Eyewitness Travel Guides, Dorling Kindersley,
80 Strand, London, Great Britain WC2R 0RL,
or email travelguides@dk.com.

◁ **The superb mosaic roof of the Museum of Applied Arts, Budapest**

CONTENTS

Renaissance Storno House and
Firewatch Tower, Sopron

INTRODUCING
HUNGARY

BUDAPEST
AREA BY AREA

A detail on the opulent Esterházy
Palace, in Fertőd

The majestic Chain Bridge, linking Buda and Pest

Sailing on Lake Balaton, Hungary's largest freshwater lake

HUNGARY REGION BY REGION

TRAVELLERS' NEEDS

SURVIVAL GUIDE

Pottery on display at a house in the Open-Air Museum, Tihany

Esztergom Basilica, Hungary's foremost Catholic church

HOW TO USE THIS GUIDE

This travel guide helps you get the most from your visit to Hungary, providing detailed practical information as well as expert recommendations. *Introducing Hungary* maps the whole country and sets it in its historical and cultural context. The first section, on *Budapest*, gives an overview of the capital's main attractions. Hungary's regions are charted in the *Region by Region* section, which covers all the important towns, cities and places around the country, with photographs, maps and illustrations. Details of hotels, restaurants, shops and markets, entertainment and sports are found in *Travellers' Needs*, while the *Survival Guide* contains advice on everything from medical services and public transport to personal safety.

BUDAPEST AREA BY AREA

Budapest has been divided into four central areas and a Further Afield section. Each area is described in an individual section, giving the names of all main sights and attractions. The sights are numbered on the area map.

Sights at a glance lists the buildings in a particular area by category.

1 Area Map
For easy reference, the sights in each area are numbered and plotted on a map. Sights in the city centre are also shown on the Budapest Street Finder *on pages 118–23.*

A locator map shows at a glance where you are in relation to the city plan.

A suggested route for a walk is shown in red.

2 Street-by-Street map
This bird's-eye view shows the heart of each sightseeing area. The sights carry the same numbers here as on the area map and the fuller description on subsequent pages.

Stars indicate the sights that no visitor should miss.

3 Detailed information
All the important sights in Budapest are described individually. Practical information includes a map reference, opening hours and telephone numbers. The key to the symbols used can be found on the back flap.

AROUND BUDAPEST

1 Introduction
The landscape, history and character of each region are portrayed here, with a description of how the area has developed over the centuries and what it offers the visitor today.

HUNGARY REGION BY REGION

The coloured areas shown on the map on the book's inside front cover show the five main sightseeing region into which Hungary has been divided. Each is covered in a full chapter in *Hungary Region by Region (see pp124–255)*. The most interesting towns and places to visit have been numbered on *Regional Maps* throughout the book.

2 Regional Map
This shows the road network and gives an illustrated overview of the whole region. All interesting places to visit are numbered and there are also useful tips on getting around the region by car and train.

Each region of Hungary can be quickly identified by the colour coding on the inside front cover.

3 Detailed information
All the important towns and other places to visit are described individually. They are listed in order, following the numbering on the Regional Map. Each entry has details of the main sights.

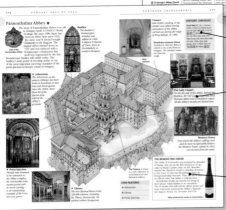

The Visitors' Checklist gives all the practical information needed to plan your visit.

4 Major sights
Historic buildings are dissected to reveal their interiors; museums and galleries have colour-coded floorplans to help you find the most important exhibits.

Story boxes highlight specific aspects relating to a top sight and explore these in more depth.

Ede Heinrich, *The Coronation of Franz Joseph I on 8 June 1867*

INTRODUCING HUNGARY

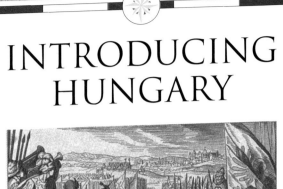

DISCOVERING HUNGARY

Hungary can be divided into six regions, each one defined as much by landscape as by history. The capital, Budapest, is at heart of the Danube Bend and further north are the castle towns that once guarded that very bend. The Northern Highlands arc their

Onion dome, Buda's Old Town Hall

way east, forming natural frontiers. The Great Plain, a vast swathe of flat grassland, covers a third of the country, and the gentle hills and vineyards of Transdanubia, in the west, are split in two by Lake Balaton. Below is an overview of the highlights of each region.

Cruise boats gliding up and down the Danube river, Budapest

BUDAPEST

- Enchanting Castle District
- Majestic architecture
- Fascinating museums

Hungary's capital is renowned for its size, imperial elegance and modern exuberance. Until 1873, Budapest was two separate cities: Buda, the regal centre on the Danube's west bank, and Pest, the commercial capital on the east bank.

The two cities retain their uniqueness today. Buda is a mellow, relaxing place, especially in the **Castle District** (see pp52–65) where cars are few and history is visible on every corner. Two days are needed to explore the area, including the **National Gallery** (see pp58–9), **Mátyás Church** (see pp62–3) and the streets of old Buda. North of the Castle District is the Roman remains of **Aquincum** (see p110), and to the south is the town of **Tabán** (see p74) and Gellért Hill with its magnificent **Gellért Hotel and Baths Complex** (see pp70–71). Leave time to visit the **Buda Hills** (see p111), a green oasis where natural caves, a nature

reserve and steam trains vie for attention.

Pest can be hot and overcrowded in the summer, but its riches outweigh such bothers. The **Hungarian National Museum** (see pp98–9) and the **Ethnographical Museum** (see pp82) are full of wonderful treasures. Its **Opera House** (see pp88–9) is one of the most ostentatious in Europe, and its grandiose **Parliament** (see pp80–81) is a must-see. Allow two days to do central Pest justice, and another one to enjoy its opportunities for repose in **Városliget** (see p107), the city's tranquil park.

The dense woodland of Bakony Forest, Northern Transdanubia

AROUND BUDAPEST

- Danube cruises
- Charming Szentendre
- Palaces and ruined castles

The most serene way to arrive in any of the historic towns along the Danube Bend is by boat from Budapest. Perfect for a day out is **Esztergom** (see pp142–5), with its striking basilica towering above the Danube, while the ruined castle at **Visegrád** (see p141) and the quiet splendour of **Vác** (see p133) are also worth a trip. **Szentendre** (see pp142–5), with its Baroque architecture and maze of cobblestoned streets is both a visitor's and artist's delight. The enchanting Royal Palace at **Gödöllő** (see pp134–5), the botanical gardens of **Vácrátót** (see p133), and the nature reserve at **Ócsa** (see p132) should not be missed.

NORTHERN TRANSDANUBIA

- Pannonhalma Abbey
- Medieval Sopron
- Forests, vineyards and spas

Stretching from Budapest to the Austrian border, Northern Transdanubia possesses many delights for the visitor. Few places in Hungary come close to matching the sombre elegance of **Pannonhalma Abbey** (see pp176–7), a UNESCO World Heritage Site. **Sopron** (see pp168–9) has a fine medieval old town, and despite Austrian influences remains proudly Hungarian. **Fertő-Hanság National Park**

The historic town of Eger, set in Hungary's Northern Highlands

(see p166) is popular with bird-watchers and sports enthusiasts. The hills, forests and vineyards around **Bakony** (see pp156–7), **Pápa** (see p151) and **Sárvár** (see p162–3) are ideal to explore by car, while **Bükfürdő** (see p163), with its thermal waters, is the ideal place to unwind.

SOUTHERN TRANSDANUBIA

- **Resorts of Lake Balaton**
- **Herend and its fine porcelain**
- **Medieval Veszprém**

Central Europe's largest lake, **Balaton** (see pp194–5) has been the playground of Hungarians for centuries. With its warm water and many resorts, it has something for everyone. Siófok has a lively nightlife and attracts a young crowd, while Balatonfüred offers more refined delights with its pretty promenade. The Balaton area makes a great base for exploring, so stay a week and wander the streets of **Keszthely** (see pp196–7) and its Neo-Baroque **Festetics Palace** (see pp198–9). Take in **Herend** (see p203), famous for porcelain, and the old town of **Veszprém** (see pp204–5). Plunging deeper into Southern Transdanubia, **Pécs** (see pp186–9) is home to early Christian burial chambers and an imposing former mosque, and the vineyards that line the route from **Siklós** to **Villány** (see p184) warrant a stop-off.

THE NORTHERN HIGHLANDS

- **The traditions of Hollókő**
- **Eger and its legends**
- **Excellent wineries**

The mountainous region of Hungary's Northern Highlands has been defined over the years by its resistance to invaders. Even today a car is needed to access the more remote parts. Living testimony to the area's sense of preservation is the village of **Hollókő** (see pp214–5), where Palóc traditions are still maintained. **Eger** (see pp216–9), the castle town in the foothills of the **Mátra Mountains** (see p213), draws visitors for the legend surrounding its siege of 1552. Some of Hungary's best vineyards are also in this region, most notably **Tokaj** (see p228). Active visitors should head for **Bükk National Park** (see pp220–21), where hiking trails and dramatic caves await.

THE GREAT PLAIN

- **Secessionist masterpieces**
- **Pretty Lake Tisza**
- **Calvinist strongholds**

The Great Plain covers a third of Hungary, and its vast, often barren land has only occasional delights. Careful planning is needed to ensure that full days are not lost travelling between sights.

The Great Plain can be divided into three areas. The first follows the right bank of the Danube and includes the splendid towns of **Kecskemét** (see pp236–9) and **Kiskunfélegyháza** (see p241). Both are home to fine Secessionist architecture and pretty squares, and make good bases for exploring **Kiskunság National Park** (see p235). Farmsteads and equestrian centres are located throughout the park, and it's here that the **Puszta Fiver** (see p235), a stunning display of horsemanship, takes place. Further south is the cosmopolitan city of **Szeged** (see pp242–3).

The second area is the central Great Plain, which takes in the castles of **Szolnok** (see p241) and **Gyula** (see p241), as well as **Lake Tisza** (see pp248–9), the country's second largest lake, and the Calvinist stronghold of **Debrecen** (see pp250–51) – Hungary's second city. Plenty of good restaurants and hotels and an excellent thermal bath complex can be found here.

The third area covers the northeast, and includes **Nyíregyháza** (see p252), another seat of Hungarian Calvinism, and the historic villages of **Csaroda** and **Szatmárcseke** (see p253).

Sun-kissed vineyards at the edge of Lake Balaton, Southern Transdanubia

Putting Hungary on the Map

The Republic of Hungary is one of the smallest states in Europe, with an area of 93,031 sq km (35,919 sq miles). From west to east it is 528 km (328 miles) at its widest point and from north to south is just 268 km (167 miles). Hungary has borders with Slovakia to the north, the Ukraine to the northeast, Romania to the southeast, Serbia and Croatia to the south and Slovenia and Austria to the west. Entirely landlocked, it is split into three by the rivers Danube (Duna) and Tisa (Tisza), which traverse it from north to south. Lake Balaton, the main geographical feature, is central Europe's largest lake.

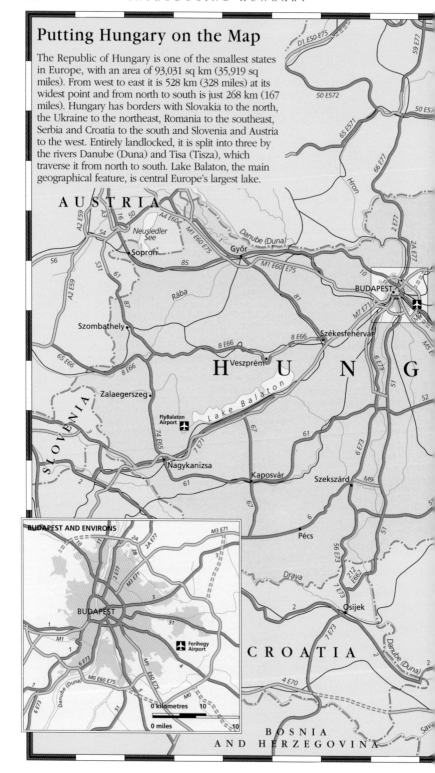

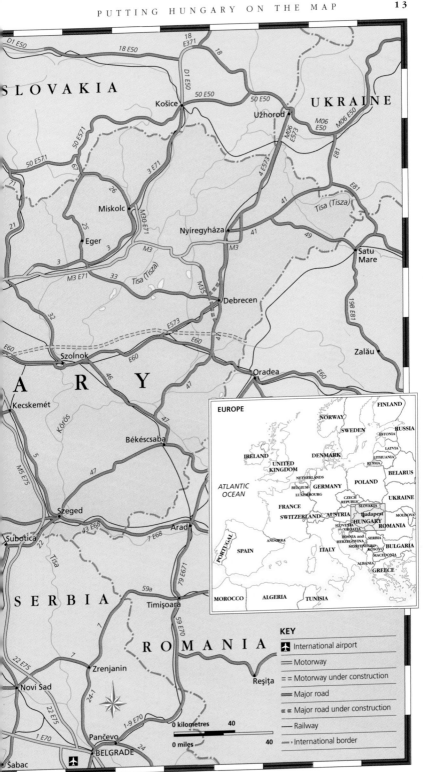

SLOVAKIA

D1 E50
18 E50
18 E371
18
D1 E50
Košice
50 E50
50 E50
Užhorod
M06 E50
UKRAINE
50 E571
50 E571
M06 E573
4 E573
E81
3 E71
26
Miskolc
M30 E71
41
Tisa (Tisza)
E81
25
Nyíregyháza
41
49
Eger
3
M3
Satu Mare
M3 E71
33
Tisa (Tisza)
M35
Debrecen
19B E81
32
E573
Szolnok
E60
E60
41
Zalău
A
R
Y
46
Oradea
E60
Kecskemét
47
Körös
47
Békéscsaba
M5 E75
5
47
Szeged
43 E68
Arad
7 E68
Subotica
22
Tisa
7 E79
59a
S E R B I A
Timişoara
59 E70
7
R O M A N I A
Reşiţa
22 E75
7
Zrenjanin
24-1
Novi Sad
22 E75
1-9 E70
Pančevo
1 E70
24
BELGRADE
Šabac

EUROPE

ATLANTIC OCEAN

FINLAND
NORWAY
SWEDEN
ESTONIA
RUSSIA
LATVIA
IRELAND
DENMARK
LITHUANIA
UNITED KINGDOM
RUSSIA
NETHERLANDS
BELARUS
BELGIUM
GERMANY
POLAND
LUXEMBOURG
FRANCE
CZECH REPUBLIC
SLOVAKIA
UKRAINE
SWITZERLAND
AUSTRIA
Budapest
MOLDOVA
SLOVENIA
HUNGARY
ROMANIA
CROATIA
SERBIA
ANDORRA
BOSNIA and HERZEGOVINA
ITALY
MONTENEGRO
BULGARIA
KOSOVO
PORTUGAL
SPAIN
MACEDONIA
ALBANIA
GREECE
MOROCCO
ALGERIA
TUNISIA

KEY

✈ International airport
═══ Motorway
= = Motorway under construction
━━━ Major road
≈ ≈ Major road under construction
──── Railway
─ ─ › International border

0 kilometres   40

0 miles   40

A PORTRAIT OF HUNGARY

*S*ituated in the heart of Europe, at the centre of the continent, Hungary is a land with a rich history, a charming people and a culture that encompasses music, art and wine. Outside the romantic capital, Budapest, is a diverse landscape of lakes, forests and mountains, with enticing medieval cities and historic castles.

On paper Hungary's physical attractions look less than overwhelming; the tallest peak reaches just over 1,000 m (3,280 ft) and there is no sea coast. But it has got Balaton, Europe's largest lake outside Scandinavia and the nation's very own "inland sea", as well as the mighty Danube river, which makes a dramatic turn south before splitting Budapest in two. Furthermore, there is the endless *Puszta*, or Great Plain, where *Csikósok* – Hungary's sturdy cowboys – still ride. In addition, there are the ancient castles, fascinating churches and cathedrals, historic bath houses, and numerous cities that can boast some of the finest Gothic, Baroque and Secessionist (Art Nouveau) architecture in Europe.

The flag of Hungary

Hungary has been at the crossroads of both trade and cultures for as long as the continent has been inhabited. Many of the country's most enduring traditions predate the arrival of the Magyars in the Carpathian Basin in AD 896, and these are upheld and preserved in the hundreds of lively festivals held in towns and villages around the country each year.

Hungary remains the land of the Magyars nevertheless, a proud people and a nation that has spent more

Hungary's vast Great Plain, covering one-third of the country and famous for its highly skilled cowboys

The ruins of Csesznek castle, Bakony Mountains

than a millennium both welcoming outsiders as well as fending off invaders. History has not always been kind to this land, but Hungary's historical legacy is rich and very well preserved.

Since abandoning Communism in 1989, the country has experienced rapid change and (often uneven) economic growth. But while the scars of state socialism remain – most notably in the bland apartment blocks

that encircle most cities – Hungarians are largely more affluent and optimistic than ever.

NATIONAL ORIGINS

Most modern Hungarians trace their ancestry to the Magyars, an Asiatic people of relatively obscure origins who arrived in the region shortly before the start of the 10th century. Despite centuries of war, occupation and the ever-present fear of being swallowed up by its neighbours, Hungary and the Magyars survived and even flourished. Contemporary Hungarians remain extremely proud of their roots in the steppes of Asia, and they go to great lengths to preserve their traditions. The dramatic displays of horsemanship that take place on the Puszta may be primarily for the benefit of visitors but they also help retain a link with the past, as does the enormous panoramic painting that fills the replica tribal chieftain's tent at Ópusztaszer, near Szeged, commemorating the arrival of the Magyars. The painting is dismissed by some as kitsch and unworthy of our time, yet it plays

Young dancers in traditional folk costume performing at one of Hungary's many festivals

an important role in preserving the spirit and memory of the nomadic Magyar. For better or worse, it is Hungarian nationalism that has kept the nation and the culture alive.

CULTURE AND SOCIETY

Hungarians are very polite, formal people. Older men still kiss women's hands on meeting and even close friends shake hands when they get together. But while all this civility may help to oil

The indoor pool at Gellért Hotel and Baths complex

the wheels that turn a sometimes difficult society, it can be interpreted as aloofness, a desire to keep "outsiders" (foreigners and other Hungarians) at a distance. This is not really the case; Hungarians simply need a while to make up their minds about people. There is also the language issue: Hungarian does not belong to the Indo-European language family, meaning that Russian and Hindi are closer to English than Magyar is. It is part of the Finno-Ugric group, and due to millennia of separation it is not even mutually intelligible with its closest cousins, Finnish and Estonian. As a result, visitors will recognize few words, and trying to order a glass of *vino* in a bar gets you nowhere; the word for wine is *bor*. But while few foreigners ever master Hungarian completely, even after years of patient study, Hungarians themselves are not particularly gifted linguists. A study conducted by the European Union in 2006 found young Hungarians to be the most monolingual in Europe.

The Magyars are not the only people to have left their mark or helped form modern Hungarian society. Germans and Slovaks settled here as long ago as the reign of King Stephen I (István) from AD 1000

to 1038, and on the Great Plain Balkan influences in the form of the region's lively markets can still be seen. There are also Turkish footprints to be found too, most strikingly in the mosque at Pécs, now recycled as a Christian church, and in the towering minaret at Eger, as well as in the handful of wonderfully preserved 16th-century thermal bath houses in Budapest. Hungary also once had a thriving Jewish population, but it was decimated during World War II when all Jews were shipped off to concentration camps. Neglected synagogues still found in many of Hungary's cities and towns are a testament to the numbers who died.

Most Hungarians who profess any religion at all say they are Roman Catholic (52%). But religion in Hungary has often been a question of expediency. Under King Stephen I Catholicism, as opposed to Orthodoxy, was introduced to the country and, while the majority of Hungarians were quite happily Calvinists by the end of the 16th century, many

The symphony orchestra and state choir, Budapest

A market stall selling fresh and dried produce

donned a new mantle during the Counter-Reformation under the Habsburgs. As a result of these swings, Hungarians tend to have a pragmatic view of religion and there is very little bigotry. Today, however, both Catholicism and Calvinism appear to be in terminal decline as the country becomes more and more secular.

Sunflowers cultivated throughout Hungary

POLITICS AND ECONOMICS

The social dislocation inherent in many other post-Soviet societies has been avoided by an often shaky but steady consensus among the political parties as to what Hungary needed in the wake of Communism's collapse. A top priority was membership in the EU, for even the former Communists who initially opposed the idea realized that to remain outside Europe would be ruinous both politically and economically. In 2004 Hungary achieved its goal and was accepted into the EU. The EU nations got a scare during the Budapest street riots of late 2006, which ironically came about through the admission of Prime Minister Ferenc Gyurcsány that Hungary could not keep running on borrowed money and that many of his election promises would not be fulfilled. The fact that the protests ended peacefully after demonstrators realized they could remove Gyurcsány at the next general election was clear evidence of a politically stable, functioning democracy.

Economically Hungary is in the doldrums, its dream of adopting the euro as its national currency by 2012 shattered. Hungary's economy grew less than 4% in 2006, among the slowest growth rates of all the ten Eastern European states to join the EU in 2004.

But Hungary has a very long history of innovation and discovery and boasts an enviable list of world-class scientists, engineers and inventors. Vitamin C, the biro, the safety match and the world-renowned Rubik's Cube, to name a few inventions, all originated here. Hungarians continue to tread new paths, and since 1989 the country has developed as a centre of scientific research; indeed, governments of all political persuasions have

The ornate interior of a Budapest coffee house

A grape-picker with grapes ready for making into Tokaji wine

put vast efforts into promoting their country as a knowledge-based economy. At the same time exports of such quality produce as Tokaji wine and *foie gras* have provided a boom for parts of the agricultural sector in recent years.

MODERN LIFE

Although Hungary can still sometimes find it difficult to shake off the image of a bleak country stuck unwillingly behind the Iron Curtain, and the protests of 2006 did nothing for the its image abroad, such incidents are easily forgotten when walking along the delightful streets of Budapest, Kecskemét and Debrecen. Here, the riotous colours of Secessionist-style buildings are a reminder that this has always been an enlightened, dynamic and forward-looking country.

If modern Hungary has one drawback, though, it is the dependence on the capital for everything. To borrow an old French expression about Paris, many people here believe that "when Budapest sneezes, Hungary catches cold". Although the country's geography may dictate in some ways that all roads lead to Budapest, it is often frustrating when the only way of travelling from one place to another is via the capital. Provincial Hungarians find it particularly galling and a constant reminder that their own cities, towns and villages owe everything to Budapest. The imperial majesty of the capital is captivating but the rest of Hungary also has a wealth of history, character and architecture to offer.

Outdoor dining at one of Szentendre's restaurants

Landscape and Wildlife of Hungary

Poppies – found wild in Hungary

The Great Plain, a rich and fertile land and one of the first in Europe to be cultivated, covers almost half of Hungary. It is traversed by two major rivers: the Tisza in the east, and the majestic Danube (Duna) in the west. The gentle but scenic mountains of the Mátra range mark the nation's northern borders, while the forests of Transdanubia and the great lakes of Balaton and Fertő enhance what is – for a relatively small country – a varied and attractive landscape.

The Danube river, Hungary's defining natural feature

THE GREAT PLAIN

Grassland covers 12 per cent of Hungary, and almost all of it is in the treeless Great Plain. Modern irrigation has enabled much of the original plain to become agricultural land, but in the protected areas of Hortobágy and Kiskunság the pale green vegetation of the region is preserved.

LAKES AND RIVERS

The Danube is greater, but for many Hungarians the Tisza river is more important. All of the country's other rivers are tributaries of these two. Hungary's abundance of lakes makes it a favoured destination of migrating birds. In the northwest, Lake Fertő is also popular with bird-watchers.

Herds of horses *define the Great Plain and are regarded as a sacred part of the nation's soul. Hungarians have traditionally made great horsemen and cowboys or Csikósok still exist.*

The great bustard *is Europe's largest land bird, with males weighing up to 14 kg (31 lb). It is found throughout Hungary and is especially common around the Tisza lake. Catching sight of its intricate spring courtship ritual is a favourite with bird-watchers.*

Racka sheep *are bred for their milk, wool and sometimes their meat, and are unique to the Great Plain region of Hungary. They are characterized by their long, thin, corkscrew-like horns.*

The Hungarian iris *or iris variegata is fond of damp soil and marsh land and thrives on the flood plains of the Danube.*

Mangalica pigs *are hairy, almost sheep-like and are bred for their meat. Look out for sausages made from Mangalica pork.*

Night herons *are particularly active in the evening, when they leave their woodland nests to feed. Thick billed, and with shorter legs than typical herons, the birds are found most commonly in Northern Transdanubia, close to the Danube river.*

HUNGARIAN CONSERVATION

Magyars were once considered one of the great hunting peoples of Europe, but in recent times their efforts have been directed into conservation. As a result, all sorts of species that were once teetering on the brink of extinction are being preserved. Deer, wild boar, wolves and lynxes are again commonly spotted in the Northern Mountains. The National Forest Plantation Programme of 1997 has enhanced the spread of forests and the saving of vulnerable wild flowers. Hungary's wetlands are a preferred destination for migrating birds and the protection of their habitat has become a source of national pride.

The lynx, inhabitant of the Northern Mountains of Hungary

THE NORTHERN MOUNTAINS

Three different mountain ranges, the Mátra, Bükk and Zemplén, are usually grouped together as the Northern Mountains. As the only alpine region in Hungary, they are home to some unique species. In the Mátra range, the country's highest peaks reach a meagre height of 1,015 m (3,330 ft).

FORESTS

A fifth of Hungary is covered in forest, and is set to increase by 2035. The country's existing forests, of which the main areas are the Northern Mountains, the Buda Hills *(see p111)* and the Bakony Forest *(see pp156–7)* are increasingly protected by conservationist legislation.

Browns bears *are commonly found in the Carpathian arc that stretches from northern Hungary to Romania.*

The dolomite flax, *once Hungary's common national flower, survives today only in the forests of the Buda Hills around the capital. Both the flower and its habitat are fiercely protected.*

Horned eagle owls *are one of the largest owl species, often measuring 70 cm (28 in) in height. A superb predator, they feed mostly on rodents and rabbits, though they occasionally devour game birds.*

Lesser purple butterflies *emerge from a deep green chrysalis at the beginning of every July. Widespread in forested areas, they spend much of their time on tree tops defending their territory against unwelcome rivals.*

Great spotted woodpeckers *are a frequent sight in the gardens, parks and woodlands of northern Hungary. They are one of nine woodpecker species native to the country.*

The black stork *stands about 1 m (3 ft) tall. Mainly black, it has a white spot on its stomach and a red bill and legs. This long-distance migrant winters in southern Africa.*

Thermal Springs and Baths

Hungary has been one of Europe's great spa destinations for hundreds of years. Natural hot springs pour out over 80 million litres (18 million gallons) of richly mineralized water every day. There are more than 1,300 hot springs in the country, of which 300 are used for bathing and medicinal purposes. A third of these are in Budapest, which has the greatest concentration of natural springs. Baths have existed since Roman times but it was the Turks who exploited the natural waters for healing all sorts of ailments.

Ornamental detail typical of bath spas

BEST THERMAL BATHS

• Aquaticum *see p251*
• Bükfürdő *see p163*
• Gellért Hotel and Baths Complex *see pp70–71*
• Hajdúszoboszló Medicinal Spa *see p252*
• Lake Hévíz *see p200*
• Miskolc-Tapolca *see p225*
• Nagyatád *see p190*
• Parádfürdő *see p213*
• Sárvár Spa *see p163*
• Széchenyi Baths *see p107*

A VISIT TO THE BATHS

The Széchenyi Baths complex in Budapest (illustrated here) is in many ways the archetypal classic Hungarian bath house, from the complicated pricing system to the vast network of indoor and outdoor baths. Built on the site of a thermal spring first discovered in 1879, Széchenyi is as popular with locals as it is with visitors.

Unisex changing rooms make the baths ideal for families. An attendant provides a locker key and towel, and expects a tip.

The ticket office displays every conceivable price on a board.

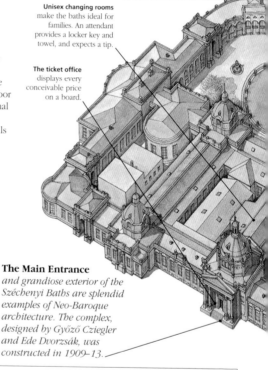

The Main Entrance
and grandiose exterior of the Széchenyi Baths are splendid examples of Neo-Baroque architecture. The complex, designed by Győző Cziegler and Ede Dvorzsák, was constructed in 1909–13.

WELLNESS HOTELS

Wellness centres, dedicated to finding a healthy balance of mind and body, have had a long history in Hungary, ever since, in fact, the discovery of the healing properties of thermal waters. While the roots of the wellness movement lie in alternative medicine, modern wellness centres are based around large, often luxury which, besides thermal spas, offer a wide range of medical, dietary and even psychiatric treatment. Massage, mud packs and electrotherapy may also be available. Some of the best wellness hotels have golf courses attached, such as the Radisson at Bükfürdő *(see p268)*. Arthritis, rheumatism and skin disorders are a few ailments that wellness centres claim to cure, and as such attract a large number of visitors who return year after year.

Bathing in the healing waters of a heated outdoor pool

Outdoor Pools
are open all year round, even in the depths of winter. Taking a bath in the steaming water when the air temperature is below zero is a unique experience. In summer, the outdoor pools can get very busy.

The terrace at the rear of Széchenyi Baths serves refreshing cold drinks to bathers.

Chess being played
is a common sight at baths in Hungary. Matches take place at outdoor pools all year round, even when there is snow on the ground.

Saunas and steam rooms
are used by bathers after taking a hot bath, before bathing again in cooler water.

The spacious and elegant interior
of the Széchenyi entrance hall, like that of many baths in Hungary, is in stark contrast to the changing rooms, which can be a little cramped.

At pools used for medicinal purposes
water temperatures are clearly displayed at the edge of the pool. The hotter the water, it is said, the stronger its healing powers.

Hungarian Architecture

It is difficult to separate the development of Hungarian architecture from the country's history. Of the Romanesque and Gothic constructions built during the reign of the first Magyar kings, little survived the Mongol invasion of the 13th century. Of the Renaissance era, only remnants and reconstructions remain, though there is more of the Baroque period to admire. The Secession (the struggle for a national style at the end of the 19th century) mirrored the nation's political fight for independence. After World War II, Soviet utilitarianism took over, and surrounded fine cities with its unsightly apartment blocks.

Budapest's Secession Post Office Savings Bank

ROMAN (AD 200–450)

The first master builders in Hungary were the Romans, much of whose capital, Aquincum, in the suburbs of present day Budapest, survives. Amphitheatres, fortifications and giant statues were erected making use of *opus cimenticum* (concrete), a Roman invention that enabled great loads to be supported by giant pillars.

Aquincum, *originally a heavily fortified military base, was home to as many as 40,000 people in its heyday at the end of the 2nd century.*

Heavy granite stone was used in the construction of round arches.

The use of stone to reinforce concrete walls lent an aesthetic quality to Roman constructions. Ceramic tiles were also used to decorate concrete walls.

Colonnades *were often used to mask heavy, load-bearing walls.*

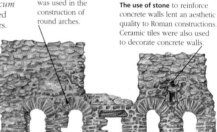

ROMANESQUE AND GOTHIC (1000–1450)

Also referred to as Norman architecture, the Romanesque period was one of the most energetic phases of church building ever witnessed in Europe. On becoming king of Hungary, István ordered a church to be built for every ten villages in the land. Many followed the same construction model, with a large single nave supported by round arches known as piers – the medieval equivalent of Roman columns. Towers did not become commonplace until the 12th century, as superior masonry facilitated their construction. Romanesque façades were usually simple, and it was only as architects became more confident in the 13th century that more decorative elements, such as rose and stained-glass windows, flying buttresses and gargoyles appeared, creating a new style that would become known as Gothic. The 13th-century church at Ják, with its exquisite *porta speciosa* (a stepped portal of rounded, barrel and pointed arches) is one of the finest remaining examples of medieval architecture in Europe, and marks the transition from Romanesque style to Gothic.

A classic *porta speciosa*, at Ják

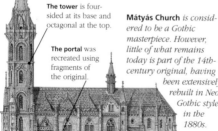

The tower is four-sided at its base and octagonal at the top.

The portal was recreated using fragments of the original.

Mátyás Church *is considered to be a Gothic masterpiece. However, little of what remains today is part of the 14th-century original, having been extensively rebuilt in Neo-Gothic style in the 1880s.*

Gothic arches *precede cross-ribbed vaults in Esztergom cathedral.*

RENAISSANCE AND BAROQUE (1450–1800)

Renaissance architecture was a successful attempt to incorporate the grandeur of Rome into the contemporary world. Led by Italians Brunelleschi and Bramante, the concept of art for art's sake became paramount, with buildings being designed around their façades. In Hungary the movement found royal favour from King Mátyás, who was greatly influenced by his Italian wife, Beatrice. The Hungarian Renaissance was brought to an end by the Turks, who destroyed many of its greatest achievements. After they were expelled from Hungary in 1690, the Baroque era began, characterized by grand designs which reflected a shift away from the proto-humanism of the Renaissance. Most Baroque mansions were built to showcase the wealth of their patrons.

Sarospatak Castle's *15th-century Renaissance tower is a copy of Palazzo Vecchio in Florence.*

The elaborate Bishop's Palace *in Szekesfehérvár is representative of Baroque style.*

NEO-CLASSICAL (1800–90)

In Hungary, the Neo-Classical movement was considered a statement of intent: that this was a heroic nation worthy of statehood. The National Museum *(see pp98–9)* and the Opera House *(see pp88–9)* were built with independence in mind.

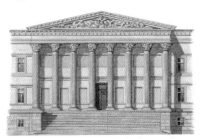

Budapest's National Museum, *built to signify national consciousness, is where Sándor Petőfi read* National Song *and sparked the 1848 Revolution.*

SECESSION (1890–1930)

The Secessionist era saw an ornamental style of art (also known as Art Nouveau) flourish in Europe at the end of the 19th century. In architecture, the movement initially made use of elaborate ironwork, tiles and bright colours to decorate linear buildings, while in the latter part of the Secession period, ever more daring architects created curving, bulbous and organic constructions.

The Cifra Palota, Kecskemét, *is typical of Secession design, with a curved, tiled roof, ironwork balconies and intricate arabesque decoration.*

UTILITARIAN (1950–90)

At the end of World War II, art was relegated to a distant second behind necessity, as Hungary's Communist regime set about constructing hundreds of thousands of new homes on the outskirts of the country's cities. Designed to accommodate the workers taking part in Hungary's massive industrialization programme, vast estates of identical high-rise apartment blocks were rapidly built. Though generally very small and by no means luxurious, the apartments all came with central heating, running water and electricity, which was a first for many of the occupants who were allocated one.

Prefabrication facilitated the swift building of many apartment blocks.

Access to apartments was often via a long balcony.

Built in haste *and at low cost, most Communist-era apartment blocks are still in excellent condition, though they are somewhat bleak-looking.*

Famous Hungarians

For a relatively small nation, a surprisingly large number of Hungarians have made a name for themselves worldwide. They include inventor László Bíró, who gave the world the ballpoint pen, and composer Ferenc Liszt, a Hungarian so famous that it was once quipped "he must be Austrian". His namesake, the late Ferenc Puskás, remains the country's greatest sports star, revered by football fans. In recent years, numerous Hungarian sports stars, inventors, actors and artists have received international acclaim.

Statue of Ferenc Liszt

MUSIC AND LITERATURE

In music, the most prominent Hungarian is Ferenc (Franz) Liszt, born in 1811. His repertoire of beautiful yet technically complicated melodies betray his first love: playing the piano. While Liszt is regarded by most Hungarians as a composer first and foremost, outside Hungary he is known simply as the greatest pianist of all time. After spending much of his life touring France, Germany, Austria and Britain, Liszt retired at the age of 50 to Rome, where he joined the Franciscan Order and spent the rest of his life teaching the piano. He died in 1896, while in Germany attending the Bayreuth Music Festival.

Liszt was succeeded as Hungary's finest musician by a man whom he inspired from afar: Béla Bartók. Born in 1881, Bartók was one of the founders of ethnomusicology, the study of the ethnography of music, as well as being a pianist and composer. Less celebrated internationally is the work of Ferenc Erkel, who wrote *Bánk Bán* (1861), Hungary's rarely performed national opera. It was made into a film in 2002, and featured Éva Márton, Hungary's highly acclaimed soprano. Márton achieved fame at Budapest's State Opera in the

Soprano Éva Márton

1970s before embarking on a sensational international career. She regularly headlines at the opera houses of London and New York and often performed under the baton of Budapest-born Sir Georg Solti, one of the greatest operatic conductors of the 20th century, until his death in 1997.

Hungarian literature has barely made an impression on the world, a result of its often impenetrable language. Although 19th-century poets Mihály Vörösmarty and Sándor Petőfi are celebrated figures, it is more for their activity as revolutionaries than for their poetry. Of the 20th-century literary figures, only Ferenc Molnár, whose work *Liliom* (1909) was translated and adapted into the musical *Carousel* (1945), has achieved anything resembling worldwide fame.

Ferenc Molnár, Hungary's best-known novelist

FILM AND VISUAL ARTS

Hollywood has been a successful stamping ground for Hungarians since before the advent of the talking picture. Indeed, two of the great pioneers of cinema were both born and raised in Budapest.

Tony Curtis playing escapologist Harry Houdini in the 1953 film

Adolph Zukor founded Paramount Pictures and produced the first full-length feature film, *The Prisoner of Zenda* (1937), and Vilmos Fried fled Hungary for Hollywood, changed his name to William Fox and founded Fox Studios. Silver-screen heroes Johnny Weissmuller, the first cinematic Tarzan; Béla Lugosi, the original screen Dracula, and Leslie Howard, whose most renowned role was his portrayal of Ashley Wilkes in *Gone with the Wind* (1939), all had Hungarian roots to one degree or another. So too did the late Hollywood legend Tony Curtis. One of Curtis's best remembered films is *Houdini* (1953), a biopic of another Hungarian, escapologist Harry Houdini. Arguably the greatest Hungarian in Hollywood, however, was Manó Kertész Kaminer, who, under the anglicized name Michael Curtiz, directed the legendary *Casablanca* (1942), a film in which Peter Lorre, master of the sinister and another Hungarian, played a film-stealing cameo. Less celebrated for their work, but notorious for their countless marriages to leading

Hollywood men are Zsa Zsa Gábor and her late sister Éva.

Other Hungarian film stars have also found international fame. István Szabó, who has spent his entire career living and working in Hungary, resisting the lure of Hollywood, won an Oscar for his film *Mephisto* (1981).

Hungarian visual artists have often attracted international acclaim, from architects Miklós Ybl and Imre Steindl – responsible for Budapest's stunning Opera House *(see pp88–9)* and Parliament *(see pp80–81)* respectively – to the trio of Secessionist painters Lajos Gulácsy, János Vaszary and József Rippl-Rónai, whose works inspired a generation of Post-Impressionists worldwide. More latterly, contemporary painters Margit Anna, Lajos Sváby, Tibor Palkó and Zoltán Szabó have been making waves on the international art scene.

SPORT

For a period in the 1950s Hungary was the greatest footballing nation on earth, although it never actually won the World Cup. Defeat in the 1954 final to West Germany remains a national tragedy. The team captain was the legendary Ferenc Puskás, nicknamed "the Galloping Major". Officially an amateur, he had the rank of major in the Hungarian army and possessed a prolific left foot. His

Ferenc Puskás, the greatest Hungarian footballer of all time

three goals against England at Wembley in 1953 were crucial to his side's 6–3 win – the first defeat suffered by England to a foreign team. Puskás was on a tour of Spain with Honvéd football club during the 1956 revolution *(see p45)* and refused to go back to Hungary. He signed for Real Madrid, and led it to three European Cup triumphs. He became a Spanish national and played a number of international matches for Spain.

Before football brought Hungary to the world's attention, athlete Alfréd Hajós had been the country's finest sporting ambassador. Hajós won Hungary's first-ever modern Olympic gold medal for swimming at the 1908 Olympic Games in London. Several swimming pools and thermal baths in Hungary are named after him. More recently, Krisztina Egerszegi has excelled in swimming for

Chess champion, Judit Polgár

her country, winning five Olympic gold medals between 1988 and 1996.

László Papp was the first boxer to win gold medals at three consecutive Olympic Games, a feat he achieved from 1948 to 1956. In 1965 Papp was on the verge of competing for the world middleweight title when the Communist government revoked his permit to travel abroad, thus ending his career.

Hungary has a long history of chess champions. The most recent is the prodigious Judit Polgár who, aged 15, became a grandmaster in 1982.

Polgár is the highest-rated female chess player in the world (a title once held by her sister Zsuzsa). She beat Anatoly Karpov in a speed-chess tournament in 1992, an achievement that makes her the only female ever to defeat a reigning world champion.

HUNGARIAN INVENTORS

The colourful Rubik's Cube puzzle, renowned the world over

It is perhaps in science and technology where Hungarians have most excelled and the ballpoint pen (invented in 1938) is probably the best-known of their inventions. Known as the biro, the pen was named after its inventor, László Bíró. A more controversial inventor was John von Neumann, a child genius who worked as a binary theoretician before becoming a member of the US government's atomic bomb programme, the Manhattan Project. The mathematical projections von Neumann computed with another Hungarian, Edward Teller, were crucial in the development of the hydrogen bomb. A third project member, John Kemény, was co-inventor of BASIC computer language. Other Hungarian inventors include Tivadar Puskás, who built the first European telephone exchange and Ernő Rubik, who in 1977 gave the world the fiendish Rubik's Cube.

The Wines of Hungary

With warm, dry summers and highly fertile soil, Hungary has the ideal conditions for wine-making. It has produced wine since the 3rd century BC, although its industry was badly neglected during the Communist regime. Large-scale private investment has recently revived wine-production in some areas, most notably in Tokaj, which is famous for its wines. Quality reds and whites, as well as sparkling wines, are produced all over the country. In Aszú, the golden wine of Tokaj, Hungary has one of the world's most fêted dessert wines; in Bull's Blood – a full-bodied red from Eger – it has one of the most legendary *(see p219).*

Volcanic red soil *typical of the Balatonfüred-Csopak vineyards gives the wines made here – especially the world-class Pinot Gris – a unique flavour with a hint of vanilla.*

The wines of northwestern *Hungary are characterized by their rich and vivid colours. The dessert wines of the Sopron region are light and refreshing and the relatively high humidity of Aszár-Neszmély is perfect for growing Chardonnay and Sauvignon Blanc grapes.*

Villány-Siklós *is dotted with cellars and wine-press houses, many of which date back to the end of the 18th century.*

Kiskunság specializes in fine table whites made from Chardonnay and Sauvignon Blanc grapes.

TOKAJ WINE REGION

Immigrant Italian farmers introduced viticulture to the Tokaj-Hegyalja region in the 12th century, after finding out-standing conditions for growing grapes on the slopes of Mount Tokaj. The golden Aszú wine that made the area famous was first produced in the 16th century, using overripe grapes infected with *Botrytis cinerea* (noble rot). After pressing, the wine is left to ferment slowly over several years, producing an intensely sweet taste.

Tokaj's landscape – ideal for wine-making

Overripe grapes with noble rot, used to make Aszú

Tokaji Azsú wine *is available in four* puttonyos *(types). The word comes from* puttony, *meaning the barrel in which the wine ferments. A three* puttonyos *wine is the least concentrated and least sweet; the dense seven* puttonyos, *or* escenzia *wine, is the sweetest. Most restaurants serve Aszú by the glass, so try a four or five* puttonyos *first.*

Sweet, aromatic white wines have been produced in Mátraalja since the 14th century.

Miskolc • ⑫
Nyíregyháza •
⑩ ⑪
⑨
M3
Tisa (Tisza)
Debrecen •
• Szolnok
• Kecskemét
M5
⑭
• Szeged

The first vineyards were planted in Bükkalja in the 1960s, making it Hungary's newest wine region.

0 kilometres 50
0 miles 50

Grape-picking *in Hungary is considered an art, and many families have long, proud traditions of serving vineyard owners for generations. Although days are long during the harvest, pickers are among the highest paid agricultural workers in the country.*

Aszú ageing for several years in barrels in cellars

HUNGARIAN SPARKLING WINE

Much as Reims competes with Epernay, so the wineries of Pécs and Etyek-Buda vie for the title of best Hungarian *Méthode Champenoise*. Sparkling wine was first made in Hungary in 1859 at the Pannonia winery in Pécs. Three of its brands – Pannonia, Hungaria and Törley (perhaps the best known) – offer a broad range of excellent sparkling wines, including extra-dry, semi-sweet and rosé. Hungary's sparkling wine is today widely regarded as one of the finest non-vintages produced outside the Champagne region in France.

Hungarian Grande Cuvée sparkling wine

HUNGARY THROUGH THE YEAR

Hungary is subject to climate extremes, with winters usually bitterly cold and summers stiflingly hot. This does have its advantages – Christmas is invariably white, while summer evenings are long, sunny and warm. Spring and autumn too have their charms: spring is welcomed by bathers, who beset the country's out-

Easter is the climax of the religious year

door pools, beaches and thermal baths as soon as the bitter cold makes way for spring. Autumn is the favourite season of bird-watchers, who flock to Hungary to observe the southward migration of the birds, while the late-summer harvest is a popular time for festivals in many towns, especially on the Great Plain, as winter preparations are made.

SPRING

Spring Festivals, often musical events, take place in almost every town and city, to celebrate the passing of winter. Often coinciding with Easter, these festivals offer a chance to taste the many sweet treats – such as gingerbread – that Hungarians prepare in spring.

MARCH

Budapest Spring Festival
(end Mar–Apr), various venues, Budapest. Hungary's cultural year starts with this celebration of classical music. For more than two weeks, renowned performers from the world of opera, music and dance converge on various venues in Budapest, including the State Opera House *(see pp88–9)*.
Pécs Spring Festival
(mid-Mar–Apr), Pécs. Symphonic and chamber concerts, theatre and literary

evenings, folklore shows, exhibitions and craft markets make this the largest Spring festival outside Budapest.
Revolution Day *(15 Mar)*
The anniversary of the revolution of 1848, and the beginning of the revolt against the Habsburgs, is commemorated with a re-enactment of Sándor Petőfi's reading of the Twelve Points on the steps of the National Museum in Budapest.

APRIL

Easter is a major event in devoutly Catholic Hungary, and a large number of people attend Easter Mass. Palm Sunday services, too, are interesting events as people take bright flowers to church to be blessed. Visitors should also make sure they do not miss the brightly decorated gingerbread that can be found in sweet shops and supermarkets all over Hungary in the run-up to Easter.

Boys throwing water over the girls at the Hollókő Easter Festival

Hollókő Easter Festival
(Easter Sun & Mon)
The World Heritage village of Hollókő *(see pp214–15)* showcases Palóc traditional crafts, including fine, delicately painted Easter eggs and tasty gingerbread.

MAY

Gizella Days *(first/second weekend)*, Veszprém.
The May Bank Holiday sees Veszprém honour Gizella of Bavaria, St István's wife, with a colourful procession led through the heart of the city's Old Town.
Sailing Day *(first/second weekend)*, Balatonfüred.
The opening of the sailing season on Lake Balaton is marked with a colourful regatta of thousands of sailing boats. Sailing Day has been celebrated since 1935 and continues to grow in size. Supporting events include exhibitions, concerts, street parties and firework displays.

The Budapest Spring Festival, ringing in the festive year

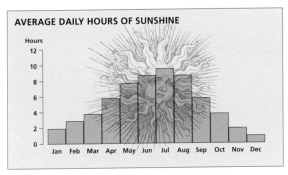

AVERAGE DAILY HOURS OF SUNSHINE

Hours

12 —
10 —
8 —
6 —
4 —
2 —
0 —

Jan Feb Mar Apr May Jun Jul Aug Sep Oct Nov Dec

Sunshine Chart
Hungary enjoys most of its sunshine hours in July and August, although September and even October can often still be very sunny. The southwest of the country sees the most sunshine, the town of Pécs being officially Hungary's sunniest city.

SUMMER

Summer is the most enjoyable season, and every town and village has its festival week. Lake Balaton comes alive, when the entire country seems to decamp here, while folklore, music and artistic events tempt tempt visitors (and residents) to stay in the capital.

JUNE

Miskolc Opera Festival *(mid-Jun)*, National Theatre, Miskolc *(see p225)*. Hungary's premier opera festival is held for a week in June. Each year, one or more Hungarian operas and the work of one great foreign composer are performed at the festival.
Danube and Chain Bridge Carnival *(throughout Jun)*, Budapest. The completion of Chain Bridge is celebrated in a number of river-based activities, which climax in the powerboat races on the final Sunday. There are also

concerts and street performances, many of which take place on Chain Bridge itself.
Sopron Festival Weeks *(mid-Jun–mid-Jul)*, Sopron. Hungary's largest town festival outside Budapest showcases everything from gastronomy and architecture to classical music and children's theatre. The Early Music Days at the end of June are a highlight.
Hortobágy Equestrian Days *(late June)*, Hortobágy National Park. Equestrian pursuits include competitions in carriage-driving and horse-herding, displays of horsemanship, and a large market selling equestrian goods.

JULY

Visegrád Palace Games *(end Jul–Aug)*. Hungary's best castle festival, with jousting contests, archery displays, mock battles and a festival of medieval arts to be enjoyed.
Sziget Festival *(end July)*, Budapest. The biggest music festival in central Europe, the

three-day event on a Danube island attracts the very biggest names in pop and rock.

AUGUST

Hungarian Grand Prix Formula 1 *(Aug)*, Budapest. Hungary has hosted motor races since the 1920s. For three days the F1 circus rolls into Mogyoród.

A flower-covered float at the Debrecen Flower Carnival

Borfalu *(International Wine Festival, 16–20 Aug)*, Royal Palace, Budapest. Hungary's largest wine festival features more than 100 marquees, many of them offering a chance to sample the best Hungarian wines, from all of the country's wine-producing regions.
Flower Carnival, Debrecen *(Virágkarnevál, 20 Aug)*, Debrecen. St István's Day is celebrated in Debrecen by decorating the entire city centre with flowers. A large flower market takes place on Piac utca, and flower-bedecked floats parade through the city's streets. In the evening there is a free pop concert that is usually well attended.

Formula 1 race at the Hungarian Grand Prix, Mogyoród near Budapest

AVERAGE MONTHLY RAINFALL

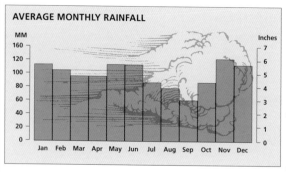

Rainfall Chart
Hungary has only moderate rainfall. It tends to occur in spring and autumn, with November being the wettest month, followed by January, May and June. The country's northern mountains receive the highest amounts of precipitation.

AUTUMN

Harvest fruits dominate the calendar in autumn, with wine and food festivals taking centre stage. Many of the towns along the Danube and Tisza hold fish soup festivals, the largest in Baja. The capital, meanwhile, attracts runners and sports enthusiasts for the Budapest Marathon.

SEPTEMBER

Jazz Days *(mid-Sep)*, Debrecen. Attracting world-renowned jazz musicians, this is the most important jazz event in the country. Running now for more than 30 years, it brings together a range of jazz styles.
Pécs Days *(mid-Sep)*, Pécs. Brass band concerts and wine tastings are the highlights of this week-long festival.
Wine Festivals *(end of Sep)* Major wine harvest festivals are held in all of Hungary's wine-producing regions *(see pp28–9)*, with the largest being those in the Badacsony, and at Eger, Balatonfüred and Sopron. A festival of vintage wines takes place at Szekszárd on 14 Sep.
Goulash Festival *(second Sun of Sep)*, Szolnok. Hungary's national dish *(see pp278–9)* is the centrepiece of this one-day festival. There are goulash cooking competitions, traditional handicraft fairs and recitals of poetry dedicated to the national dish. Most years there is also an attempt to break the "world's largest goulash" record, with the end product shared freely among all.
Wine and Song Festival *(end of Sep)*, Pécs. Wine-makers in Pécs and on the Villány-Siklós wine road celebrate the harvest by bringing in the best choirs in Hungary for ten days of wine and song. There are concerts all along the wine road, with the biggest and best those held in the main square in Pécs.

The Budapest Marathon, one of the largest in Europe

OCTOBER

Budapest Marathon *(first Sun in Oct)*, Budapest. Taking in the city's main sights, including Buda Castle, Margaret Island and Chain Bridge, on its 42-km (26-mile) route, the Budapest Marathon has been run every year since 1985. The start is in Hösök tere, and the finish in City Park *(see p107)*.
Gödöllő Harp Festival *(mid-Oct)*, Royal Palace, Gödöllő. Every year Baroque musicians from all over the world converge on the perfect setting of Gödöllő Royal Palace *(see pp134–5)* for this renowned series of chamber concerts.

NOVEMBER

Szombathely St Martin Week *(first week Nov)*, Szombathely. The town celebrates its patron saint, St Martin of Tours, with a variety of musical and theatrical events.

Music and dance, at the Tihany Wine Festival

AVERAGE MONTHLY TEMPERATURE

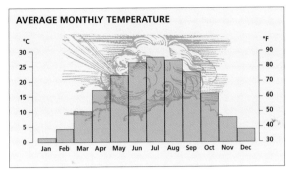

Temperature Chart
July and August can boast up to ten hours of warm sunshine per day, with average summer temperatures a comfortable 22 °C (71.6 °F). Winters are cold, especially on the Great Plain where bitter winds tend to blow in from the east.

WINTER

Snows can arrive as early as November, and by Christmas the country is often covered in a blanket of snow. The big freeze does not, however, stop the outdoor fun, and natural ice rinks, such as that in Városliget, Budapest *(see p107)* are very popular.

DECEMBER

Winter Parliament Concerts *(Dec & Jan)*, Parliament, Budapest. Every Friday evening, this superb building hosts a classical concert by the Hungarian Virtuoso Chamber orchestra. Concerts are followed by a tour of Parliament *(see pp80–81)*.
Mikulás *(6 Dec)*. As in many countries in central Europe, Mikulás (aka St Nicholas or Santa Claus) visits children on this day. Traditional presents given on St Nicholas' Day tend to be of the edible and sugary variety, with larger toys now reserved for Christmas Day.

Christmas Gift Market, Budapest

Christmas Gift Markets *(Dec)*, Sopron and Budapest. Throughout December, Fő tér in Old Sopron and Vörösmarty tér in Budapest are the enchanting settings for Christmas Gift Markets, attracting shoppers from afar as well as locals. Budapest also boasts a giant Advent Calendar.

JANUARY

Szilveszter *(New Year's Eve)* New Year's Eve in Hungary is traditionally celebrated on the streets. People eat early, grab a bottle of sparkling wine and head for the free concerts in most city centres. The largest is in Vörösmarty tér, Budapest, while there is also a massive street festival in Szentendre.

FEBRUARY

Kapos Carnival Days *(early Feb)*, Kaposvár. The whole of Kaposvár *(see p185)* appears to take part in this festival of Kapos culture, the highlight of which is the parade of costumed stilt-walkers.
Renaissance Carnival Gyula *(second weekend of Feb)*, Gyula. The grounds of Gyula Castle *(see p241)* play host to this medieval-style pageant yearly.
Busójárás Carnival *(26 Feb)*, Mohács. During the occupation of Mohács by the Turks the citizens would dress in menacing masks and costumes in an attempt to

Revellers in menacing costumes at the Busójárás Carnival, Mohács

frighten the occupiers away. Today, people still dress up in spooky outfits for the Busójárás Carnival, though it is now a far wider event, featuring performers of both traditional and modern music alongside the costume parade.

PUBLIC HOLIDAYS

New Year's Day (1 Jan)

Anniversary of the Revolution of 1848 (15 Mar)

Easter Monday (Mar/Apr)

Whit Monday (May/June)

May Day (1 May)

National Day (St István's Day) (20 Aug)

Anniversary of the 1956 Hungarian Uprising and the proclamation of Hungary's democratic constitution in 1989 (23 Oct)

All Saints' Day (1 Nov)

Christmas (25–26 Dec)

THE HISTORY OF HUNGARY

Most modern histories give little space to pre-Magyar Hungary but, given the importance of the region both then and now, this is a shame. Hungary's geographical location, at the heart of the European continent, has always made it pivotal in invasions and empire-building from a time long before the notion of Europe – or Hungary – had ever been contemplated.

There is evidence that the Great Plain has been inhabited since the Bronze Age. Horsemen from the steppes eventually destroyed the existing culture in the 13th century BC. Celts later occupied parts of the land, and in AD 10 to 35, in its final push for expansion, Rome conquered Transdanubia, renaming it Pannonia, and later adding Dacia.

Silver Celtic coin from the 4th century BC

The Romans developed an urban infrastructure, including paved roads, city forums, stadiums and baths, in northern Transdanubia, still visible today in the ruins of Aquincum, Obuda, Szombatheley and Sopron.

Barbarian tribes finally put an end to the rule of Rome. In 271 Dacia was abandoned as too expensive and troublesome to defend; Pannonia was similarly left to its fate in 403; Gothic, Hun, Avar and Slav tribes by turns filled the void. Indeed, the Hun king Attila ran his powerful but short-lived empire from here.

THE MAGYARS

The Magyars, a nomadic, pagan, Finno-Ugric tribe whose ancient homeland is thought to have been an area east of the Urals, rolled into the region in 895 or 896. It was at this time that Hungarian history first became entangled in conflict. The Magyars claim to have arrived in a desolate, sparsely populated land (the Slavs having moved south into the Balkans at the end of the 8th century); meanwhile, Romanian historians – to support their claim on Transylvania – insist that the Carpathian basin was in fact inhabited by direct descendants of the Romans.

The Magyars first settled on Csepel Island, in the middle of the Danube just south of present-day Budapest, before quickly occupying much of the surrounding area. Tradition holds that once the entire Carpathian basin had been occupied – and what little resistance there was had been quelled – the Magyar clan leaders chose a chieftain named Árpád to lead them, and that they swore an oath by sipping from a cup of their mixed blood to accept Árpád's male descendants as the Magyars' hereditary chieftains. Estimates suggest that Árpád ruled over c.400,000 people, made up of seven Magyar, one Kabar, and other smaller tribes.

TIMELINE

500,000 BC	10,000 BC	5,000 BC	AD	850 AD
500,000 BC Traces of hunters living at Vértesszőlős near Tata in 500,000 BC, who made and used tools, were found in 1965.		**5,000 BC** Stone Age settlements in Talxina and along the Danube.	**c.10 AD** Romans invade Transdanubia, incorporating it into Pannonia.	**895–6** Magyars migrate west into the Danube-Tisza Basin. Árpád is chosen as their chieftain.
c.10,000 BC Remains dating from the Paleolithic era indicate settlements near present-day Buda.		*Carving of the Sun God Mithras*	**c.50 BC** Celtic Eravi settlements on Gellért Hill, Buda. **800 BC** Tombs with Iron Age urns at Pünkösdfürdő.	**895** Magyars join Byzantine armies to fight the Bulgars.

◁ **Gyula Benczúr's *The Baptism of Vajk*, in the Hungarian National Gallery**

Altarpiece with Saints István, Imre and Gellért

THE BIRTH OF THE HUNGARIAN KINGDOM

Europe in the 10th century was weak and Magyar bands roamed the land and looted the towns for decades. They were routed in the west in 955 by King Otto I, and in the east in 970 by the Byzantines. Chieftain Géza (972–97), Árpád's great-grandson, was baptized into the Christian Church, and missionaries began the process of converting the Magyars. Géza established a strong central authority.

ISTVÁN I

Géza's son, István (Stephen, 997–1038), was baptized as a child and educated in Prague. In 996 he married Gisela, a Bavarian princess and sister of Emperor Henry II. István became chieftain when Géza died. He ousted rival clan chiefs, confiscating their lands. István then asked Pope Sylvester II to recognize him as king of Hungary. The pope agreed, and – with a crown sent by the Pope himself –

Holy Crown of Hungary, or Crown of St István

István was crowned on Christmas Day 1000. István now held absolute power. He ordered that every tenth village build a church and donated land to bishoprics and monasteries. He required all persons – whether Christian or pagan, but not the clergy – to marry. Foreign monks worked as teachers and introduced Western agricultural methods.

ISTVÁN'S SUCCESSORS

István died in 1038 and was canonized in 1083. Hungary continued to grow stronger, having conquered Transylvania in 997–1006. In 1090 Lászlo I (1077–95) occupied Slavonia and Kalman I (1095–1116) became King of Croatia in 1103. Under Béla III (1173–96) Hungary dominated in southeastern Europe.

The good times came to an end with King András II (1205–35). A big spender on foreign military adventures and domestic luxuries, he gave huge land grants to friendly foreign nobles. They soon made up a class of magnates whose wealth was far greater than that of the Magyar lesser nobles. When he tried to raise taxes, the people rebelled. In 1222 he was forced to sign the Golden Bull, limiting his power and leading to the creation of parliament.

Béla IV (1235–70), András's son, tried with little success to regain lost crown lands in order to reestablish royal preeminence, but instead this created a rift between king and nobles just as the Mongols were sweeping towards Europe. He ordered his armies to mobilize, but few did, and the Mongols routed Béla's army at Mohi

---

TIMELINE

King Géza I, father of King István

972–97 Chieftain Géza becomes king. He is baptized as a Christian in 975.

1090 Lászlo I (1077–95) occupies Slavonia.

1103 Kálmán I (1095–1116) takes the title of King of Croatia.

900	950	1000	1050	1100	1150

997 István I (997–1038) succeeds his father Géza; Pope Sylvester II recognizes him as King of Hungary.

1077–95 Latin alphabet adapted for Hungarian. Magyars occupy Transylvania.
10th-century Magyar belt buckle

1173–96 Under Béla III Hungary becomes a leading power in southeastern Europe

on 11 April 1241. Béla fled to Austria. The Mongols utterly destroyed Hungary, killing half the population. After the mysterious death of their leader in 1242, however, the superstitious Mongols withdrew.

RENAISSANCE

On his return to power, Béla transformed royal castles into towns, encouraging Germans, Italians and Jews to populate them. Mining restarted, farming methods improved, and crafts and commerce flourished. Béla died in 1270, and the Árpád line expired in 1301 when András III died without a male heir.

Confronted by succession disputes, Hungary's nobles chose foreign kings. These, Charles I (1309–42) and his son and successor Louis I (1342–82), both from the House of Anjou, ruled during a time of peace. Louis I confirmed the Golden Bull again in 1351, and in 1367 founded Hungary's first university at Pécs. However, he also fought costly wars, becoming king of Poland in 1370. During one of his foreign excursions the Turks made their first

Árpád, sculpture in Mátyás Church, Budapest

inroads into the Balkans. After Louis's death in 1382, Sigismund of Luxemburg bankrupted the country, amid the expansion of the Ottoman empire. Sigismund led a crusade against the Turks in 1396, but was routed at Nicopolis. He died in 1437, and his successors, Albrecht V of Austria (1437–9) and Władysław III of Poland (1439–44), known in Hungary as Ulászló I, both died during campaigns against the Turks.

Hungary's noblemen now chose the infant king László V and appointed a regent, János Hunyadi, to run the country. Hunyadi was a gifted warrior, defeating the Ottomans in Transylvania in 1442 and in the Battle of Belgrade in 1456 but he died of the plague soon after, and after two years of struggle for the succession, his son Mátyás was proclaimed king.

KING MÁTYÁS

Mátyás enlisted 30,000 foreign mercenaries and built fortresses along the southern frontier, but instead of a direct anti-Turkish policy, he launched attacks on Bohemia, Poland and Austria, hoping to forge a unified front against the Turks. Mátyás was a modernizer, reforming the legal system and promoting development. A Renaissance man, he made his court a centre of humanism; under his rule Hungary began printing and established a second university. However, he failed in his quest for a Western alliance and, with it, the Holy Roman crown.

The Renaissance main altar in Mátyás Church, Budapest

1200	1250	1300	1350	1400	1450	
14th-century ciborium		**1309** Charles Robert becomes King Charles I. Marriages link Hungary to Naples and Poland.		**1456** Hunyadi defeats the Turks in the Battle of Belgrade. Hunyadi dies of plague.		**1458** Hunyadi's son, Mátyás (1458–90) crowned king.
1222 Nobles force András II (1205–35) to sign Golden Bull limiting crown's power.				**1367** Hungary's first university is founded at Pécs.		
1241 Mongols rout the Hungarian army at Mohi.	**1242** The Mongols withdraw from Hungary.	**1301** Death of András III, last of the Árpád kings.	**1351** Louis I (1342–82) reconfirms Golden Bull.	**1442** Hunyadi defeats the Turks in Transylvania.		**1490** Mátyás dies while visiting Vienna.

Mátyás Corvinus and the Hungarian Renaissance

Although St Stephen (István) is Hungary's patron saint, Mátyás Corvinus had a much greater impact on the country, and is generally far more celebrated than his canonized ancestor. Mátyás was one of the original Renaissance men: at once a king, military leader, warrior and patron of the arts. During his epic 32-year reign from 1458 to 1490 and at his often brutal behest, Hungary evolved rapidly from its feudal past to become the greatest kingdom in Middle Europe. Much of this progress came from the influence of Mátyás's equally visionary second wife, Queen Beatrice, daughter of the King of Naples. Her powers of persuasion over Mátyás, and subsequently on Hungary, should not be underestimated.

Gold seals *were indicative of the affluence enjoyed by Hungary while Mátyás was on the throne.*

This illuminated letter from the Philostratus Codex *formed part of the* Codex Heroica, *the most valuable volume in Mátyás's library. It featured tracts by the Athenian philosopher Philostratus, and was translated into Latin by humanist Antonio Bonfini in 1497. It is housed at the Széchenyi National Library (see p56).*

KING MATTHIAS AND THE DAUGHTER OF THE MAYOR OF BRESLAU

Painted by Mihály Kovács, this famous 19th-century work depicts a carousing Mátyás wooing Barbara Krebs, the daughter of the Mayor of Breslau (present-day Wrocław). Mátyás wanted to marry Krebs, but as she was not of noble blood he was not permitted to do so. Instead, Mátyás took Krebs as his mistress. She bore him an illegitimate child, Johannus, who, when Mátyás failed to produce a legitimate son, became his chosen heir, although Władysław II was his successor.

Barbara Krebs was Mátyás's mistress for six years.

These marble engravings of Queen Beatrice and Mátyás, *held at the Hungarian National Museum (see pp98–9), are believed to be the work of Gian Cristoforo Romano, and were probably a wedding gift from a rich courtier.*

Inscribed with the date *1470, the Crest of Mátyás Corvinus commemorates the building of significant additions to Mátyás Church in Budapest (see pp62–3). Originally called the Parish Church of Our Lady Mary, the church was renamed after the king.*

Manuscripts from Mátyás's *library are on display at the Széchenyi Library* (see p56). *Mátyás set up the first national library,* Bibliotheca Corviniana, *and sanctioned the first printing press in the country. The earliest book published in Hungary (written in Latin) was the* Chronica Hungarorum, *printed in Buda in 1473.*

RENAISSANCE HUNGARY

The full bloom of the Renaissance period took place in Hungary in the late 15th and early 16th centuries, having reached the country via a procession of Italian master craftsmen and masons brought by Mátyás's second wife, Queen Beatrice. The Turkish occupation, which changed the course of Hungarian art and history, destroyed much evidence of Renaissance splendour but Sárospatak Castle (*see pp228–9*) is a fine example of the style.

Foot soldiers *in Mátyás's army would have carried shields like this one. It bears part of an early coat of arms of the Hunyadi family, and is exhibited at the Hungarian National Museum* (see pp98–9).

The globe, depicted alongside mathematical instruments, books and a telescope, reinforces the idea of Mátyás as a humanist, scientist and man of the arts.

The southern portal of Mátyás Church (see pp62–3) *is one of a few remaining examples of Renaissance architecture left in Hungary. The Neo-Gothic porch around it was added in the 19th century.*

Representing a *man and woman, these wine cups date from the 16th century and are designed to fit together to form one covered receptacle. The cups would have been used in elaborate wedding celebrations during the Renaissance.*

Mátyás was a generous king, known for his equity and his admiration for the Italian Renaissance.

Győr Cathedral (see p174) *was destroyed by the Mongols in the 13th century, and Mátyás viewed its reconstruction as one of his most sacred and important duties.*

Carved by an unknown *sculptor in 1526, this Madonna and Child marks the zenith of Hungarian Renaissance art. Today it forms part of the Andras Bathory collection at the Hungarian National Museum* (see pp98–9).

Siklos Castle *was first constructed in the late Medieval period (about 1190) but is best known for its Renaissance-era modifications. It hosts a summer Renaissance Arts Festival.*

Austrian Siege of Buda, 1602–3

PARTITION

After Mátyás, oligarchs took control of Hungary, crowning a puppet king, Vladislav Jagiello (known in Hungary as Ulászló II, 1490–1516), to nominally rule the country. In 1492 the Diet once again limited the serfs' freedom of movement, and in 1514 serfs attacked estates across Hungary. The rebellion was brutally crushed.

Shaken by the peasant revolt, the Diet of 1514 passed laws that condemned the serfs to eternal bondage. Corporal punishment became widespread, and one noble even branded his serfs like livestock. The laws were included in the Tripartitum of 1514, a document that gave Hungary's king and nobles, or magnates, equal shares of power: the nobles recognized the king as superior, but in turn they had the power to elect and remove him. The Tripartitum also freed the nobles from taxation, and many of their military obligations.

When Ulászló II died in 1516, his ten-year-old son Louis II (1516–26) became king, though a royal council in effect ruled the country. Endless quarrels among the noblemen of the Diet

weakened the country, however, and the Turkish ruler Sultan Suleyman the Magnificent attacked Hungary in August 1526, annihilating the Hungarian army and Louis II at the Battle of Mohacs *(see p183).*

Rival factions of nobles then elected two kings, Janos Zapolyai (1526–40), supported by eastern nobles and the Turks, and Habsburg king Ferdinand (1526–64), supported by western nobles and the Holy Roman Empire. Hungary's partition became final in 1541, when the Turks put an end to Habsburg attempts at reuniting the throne by occupying Buda and Pest.

THE THREE STATES OF HUNGARY

A 16th-century Ottoman coat

Western Hungary officially became part of the Habsburg Empire. The Austrian king directly controlled Habsburg Hungary's financial, military, and foreign affairs, and imperial troops guarded its borders.

Central Hungary became a province of the Ottoman Empire. The Turks ruling in Buda were interested mainly

The liberation of Buda in 1686, painting by Gyula Benczúr (1896)

TIMELINE

1541 Hungary is partitioned between the Turks and the Habsburgs. Transylvania becomes an Ottoman vassal state.		**1566** Siege of Szigetvar. Ottoman Emperor Suleyman the Magnificent (Suleyman I) is killed.	*Ottoman tablet with calligraphy*		
1500	**1525**	**1550**	**1575**	**1600**	**1625**
1526 Turks defeat weakened Hungary at Mohács.	*Sword of Vladislav (Ulászló) II*	**1591** Habsburgs invade Transylvania.		**1606** Protestants in Transylvania are granted the right to worship.	

in squeezing as much wealth from the land as quickly as possible. However, the Turks practised religious tolerance and gave the Hungarians living within the empire significant autonomy.

Transylvania became an Ottoman vassal state. It functioned as an independent country, ruled by local princes who paid a tribute to the Turks. But the princes' increasing autonomy angered the Turks, who routed their armies in 1660 and took control of Transylvania.

Ottoman Campaign Tent, taken during the Siege of Vienna, 1683

REUNIFICATION

Hungary's aristocracy was increasingly dominated by Protestants and opposition to Catholic Habsburg rule grew. Angered by the persecution of Protestants and insufficient action against the Turks, an outright rebellion in 1664 failed to overthrow the Habsburgs. Instead, Emperor Leopold I suppressed the Hungarian constitution, and ruled Habsburg Hungary from Vienna. Protestantism was viciously repressed. Hungarian discontent deepened still further, until 1681 when Imre Thokoly, a Transylvanian nobleman, led a more successful rebellion against the Habsburgs, forcing Leopold to restore Hungary's constitution. It was during these internal conflicts that the Turks attacked Austria, only to be almost wiped out entirely near Vienna in 1683. A Western campaign then gradually drove the Turks from all of Hungary, and the Ottoman government finally surrendered its Hungarian possessions at the Peace of Karlowitz in 1699.

HABSBURG RULE

After the expulsion of the Turks, the Austrians colonized Hungary with Germans, which led to an anti-Habsburg revolt in 1703–11. It was put down and the leader, Transylvanian prince Ferenc Rákóczi, was forced into exile, yet the Habsburgs guaranteed constitutional independence for Hungary and restored noble privileges.

Peace and prosperity followed, first under Empress Maria Theresa (1740–80) and later her son Joseph II (1780–90). Enlightened absolutists, they strengthened their empire by pursuing a more humane social policy. Maria Theresa had Buda and Pest rebuilt, and built most of the Habsburg Royal Palace (see pp54–5) and a floating yet permanent bridge across the Danube.

Joseph II was even more radical. He curbed the power of the church, disbanding a number of monastic orders, and introduced tax reforms that severely limited the powers of the Hungarian aristocracy. He also made German the official language, but he died young, in 1790, and many of his reforms died with him.

The return of the Crown to Buda (1790)

1650	1675	1700	1725	1750	1775

1664 Habsburgs rout a Turkish army at St Gotthard in Hungary.

1683 Turks attack Habsburgs but are routed near Vienna.

1686 Christian troops enter Buda. Turkish rule in Hungary ends.

Order created by Maria Theresa

1780 Joseph II (1780–90) succeeds his mother Maria Theresa; he enacts further reform.

1681 Hungarians rebel against Habsburg rule.

1684 Start of ultimately successful Siege of Buda by Habsburgs.

1699 Turks lose almost all Hungarian possessions in Peace of Karlowitz, which formally ends partition.

1740 Maria Theresa (1740–80) becomes Habsburg Empress, and institutes social reform.

1792 Coronation of Ferenc I (1792–1835), who repeals many of the reforms carried out by his predecessors.

The Founding of the Academy, **bas-relief by Barnabás Holló**

NATIONAL REVIVAL

Ferenc I (1792–1835) was far more conservative than Joseph II. It was during his reign, however, that the Hungarian aristocracy first began to promote the ideas of liberalism, and with them a national consciousness. Large numbers of noblemen supplemented their income from civil occupations, and formed a genuine political movement. Probably their greatest champion was István Széchenyi, a liberal nobleman who believed that the prime cause of Hungary's relative backwardness was the feudal system rather than subordination to Vienna. In 1802 he donated his entire art collection to the state; the collection forms the basis of the National Museum *(see pp98–9).* Széchenyi was also associated with the foundation of the Hungarian Academy of Sciences, the advent of rail transport and the construction of the first permanent bridge across the Danube, the Chain Bridge. Lajos Kossuth, another outstanding Hungarian of the era, called Széchenyi the greatest Hungarian.

In 1847, Kossuth formally established the Opposition Party, an umbrella organization that sought Hungarian independence. On 15 March 1848, during a tumultuous spring – when the whole of Europe seemed to explode in revolution – Sándor Petőfi, one of the greatest Hungarian poets, read his Twelve Points manifesto for liberal reform from the steps of the National Museum. Vienna initially agreed to talks, but after the Austrians had quelled their own revolt in September, they confronted the Hungarian reformers, and armed conflict lasting almost a year ensued. The fate of the reformers was finally sealed by an alliance between Emperor Franz Joseph I and Russian Tsar Alexander II. A 200,000-strong Russian force quickly defeated the Hungarians, who surrendered on 13 August 1849.

Lajos Kossuth's speech during the revolution of 1848

ABSOLUTISM AND COMPROMISE

Hungary was now entirely subsumed by the Habsburg Empire. The political elite, led by diplomat Ferenc Deák, could offer little more than passive resistance. Deák managed to keep the dialogue with Vienna open. By 1866, when Austria had become isolated internationally after a series of wars, Vienna was ready to talk about some kind of compromise.

Deák led the Hungarian delegation, and the Habsburg Empire agreed to transform itself into a federation. The

TIMELINE

1802 Count István Széchenyi donation forms the basis of the Széchenyi National Library and Hungarian National Museum.	**1847** Lajos Kossuth forms the Opposition Party, which openly calls for independence.	**1867** After defeat by Russia a weak Austria accepts a compromise, and Hungarian independence in the Dual Monarchy.
	1817 The first steamboat sails on the Danube.	**1846** Hungary's first railway links Pest with Vác.	

1800	1825	1850

Poet Sándor Petőfi (1823–49)

1808 The Embellishment Commission is established, led by Governor Archduke Joseph.	**1809** The Habsburg Royal Court moves to Buda as Napoleon advances across Europe. He offers independence but the Hungarians side with Vienna.		**1848** The Hungarian Uprising against the Habsburgs begins on 15 March after poet Sándor Petőfi reads his Twelve Points from the steps of the National Museum.

parts of the federation, Austria and Hungary, would be equal and separate, with the emperor at once Emperor Franz Joseph of Austria, and King Ferenc József of Hungary. Half a century of progress followed, crowned when Budapest hosted the Millennium Exhibition in 1896.

Deportation of Hungarian Jews in World War II

WAR, REGENCY AND HOLOCAUST

In World War I, hundreds of thousands of Hungarians died fighting with the Germans and Austrians. After defeat in 1918, a revolution broke out in Budapest in October. A republic was proclaimed, headed by Count Mihály Károlyi. He was overthrown by Bolsheviks, led by Béla Kun, in March 1919. Kun proclaimed the Communist Hungarian Republic of Councils, and killed all those who opposed its policies. Only the intervention of Romanian troops, led by Hungarian Admiral Miklós Horthy, ended the "Red Terror".

In the Treaty of Trianon in 1920, parts of Hungary were awarded to Romania, the new state of Yugoslavia and Czechoslovakia. Horthy became regent. His two decades in power were marked by economic and social stagnation, as well as fierce anti-Semitism. When war broke out in 1939, Hitler offered Hungary half of

Admiral Miklós Horthy signing the Treaty of Trianon

Transylvania as reward for siding with Germany, and in 1941 Horthy committed forces to the invasion of first Yugoslavia, then the Soviet Union. Many Hungarians were killed on the eastern front. When Horthy tried to negotiate a separate peace with the Allies, Hitler replaced him with the Hungarian Nazi Arrow Cross party.

The first Hungarian Jews had been deported in June 1941, on the orders of prime minister László Bárdossy de Bárdos, who believed that this act would keep German troops out of Hungary. In the summer of 1942, however, Horthy replaced Bárdossy with the less viciously anti-Semitic Miklós Kállay. Kállay did not repeal any of Bárdossy's legislation, but he prevented any further large-scale deportations of Jews. After the German invasion of March 1944, Kállay was himself sent to Dachau concentration camp in one of the last deportations of Jews, Gypsies and political criminals. SS chief Adolf Eichmann oversaw the deportations in Hungary. By August 1944, when Horthy put a stop to them, 440,000 Jews had gone, mainly to Auschwitz, despite the efforts of Raoul Wallenberg (see p75). Indeed, a third of all those killed at Auschwitz throughout the war were Hungarian Jews.

Cardinal Mindszenty accused of treason and espionage

SOVIETIZATION

The parliamentary elections in 1945 were won by the Independent Smallholders' Party, supported by a wide spectrum of Hungarian society. However, the occupying Soviet Union enforced a coalition with the Social Democrats, the National Peasant Party and the Communists. New elections in 1947 were rigged, the Communists claiming a massive victory. By the end of 1948 all other political parties had been outlawed, or forced to merge with the Communists in the Hungarian Workers Party (HWP). In 1949, after an election in which only HWP candidates were allowed, Hungary was declared a People's Republic.

The church became the main source of opposition to the HWP. The government confiscated church property and nationalized church schools. Protestant church leaders reached a compromise with the government, but the head of the Roman Catholic Church, Cardinal József Mindszenty, resisted. The government arrested him in December 1948 and sentenced him to life imprisonment. Shortly after, the regime disbanded most Catholic religious orders and secularized Catholic schools.

Between 1948 and 1953 Mátyás Rákosi led a brutal regime that reorganized the economy. In a campaign reminiscent of the Soviet Union's forced collectivization in the 1930s, the regime compelled most peasants to join collective farms and required them to make deliveries to the government at prices lower than the cost of production. Hundreds of thousands were deported, arrested and executed.

REVOLUTION

The terror eased slightly after Stalin's death in 1953, when Rákosi was ousted and Imre Nagy became prime minister. Nagy embarked on reform until the return of Rákosi in 1955. Rákosi attempted to reinstitute a Red Terror. He was forced to resign in July 1956 and replaced by Ernő Gerő. On 23 October anti-Soviet crowds protested in Budapest. Nagy was reappointed. He dissolved the state security police, abolished the one-party system, and promised free elections. On 1 November Hungary announced neutrality and withdrawal from the Warsaw Pact. On 4 November the Soviet Union invaded and crushed the revolution.

Mátyás Rákosi, Hungarian Prime Minister

TIMELINE

1947 The Communists win rigged elections, and outlaw all other political parties.

1953 The reform-minded Imre Nagy becomes prime minister, but lasts only two years before being dismissed. In November Hungary's football team is the first foreign team to defeat England in London; the score is 6-3.

1955 Hungary is a founding member of the Warsaw Pact.

1957 János Kádár becomes Hungarian leader.

1945

1950

1955

1945 The Germans abandon Hungary to the Russians in April 1945.

Imre Nagy (1896–1958)

1956 Nagy is reinstated. When he announces Hungary's withdrawal from the Warsaw Pact, Soviet forces invade and arrest him. He is executed in 1958.

The 1956 Hungarian Revolution

On the morning of 23 October, students and workers discontent with falling living standards marched on Radio Hungary in Budapest, in a bid to broadcast a list of hastily put together demands, which included the immediate withdrawal of all Soviet troops stationed in Hungary. Actively supported by sections of the Hungarian army, the revolutionaries

Flag with communist emblem removed

attacked the AVH and Soviet soldiers, and the revolt spread nationwide. The Hungarian Communist Party, fearing total collapse, gave in to a number of demands, and on 27 October invited Imre Nagy to form a new government. However, on 4 November, thousands more Soviet troops invaded Hungary and despite fierce resistance, quickly crushed the revolution.

REVOLUTIONARIES WITH CAPTURED SOVIET TANK
For a short time, the revolutionaries unquestionably had the upper hand and initially Soviet troops stationed in Hungary offered little resistance. It is thought that some troops even sided with the revolution. However, when the Soviet army invaded on 4 November, it did so to brutal effect, and an estimated 200,000 Hungarians fled the country as refugees.

The enormous statue of Stalin that stood in the centre of Budapest was iconoclastically torn down on 24 October by revolutionaries and perhaps defines the finest moment of the revolution.

Bronze statue of Imre Nagy, Budapest

IMRE NAGY
Captured by the Russians in World War I, Imre Nagy (1856–1958) fell in with Russian Communists and emigrated to Russia at the war's end. Avoiding Stalin's purges of the 1920s and 1930s, he became a leading figure in the Communist international, the Comintern, and in 1944 was sent to accompany the Red Army as it invaded Hungary. He became the Hungarian prime minister in 1953 and pursued a reformist agenda during his two-year reign. Following the uprising, Nagy briefly returned to office in 1956, but after the Soviet invasion he was betrayed by one of his closest friends, Romanian Communist Walter Roman. He was arrested and taken to Snagov Monastery, near Bucharest in Romania, where he was questioned, tried in camera, and then executed in Budapest in 1958.

Goulash Communism, with limited collectivization

THE LONG, SLOW PROCESS OF REFORM

In 1957 the Soviets appointed nominally hardliner János Kádár as head of the HWP but the experience of the 1956 revolution had convinced Kádár that a return to Rákosi's methods of the early 1950s would be counterproductive. He therefore eased restrictions imposed by the Soviets, announcing an amnesty for political prisoners in 1960 and calling a halt to forced collectivization. The economy was reorganized to accommodate a limited amount of private enterprise, and living standards duly improved. By the end of the 1960s Hungarians enjoyed easily the highest standard of living in the Soviet bloc.

Yet as the Soviet invasion of reformist Czechoslovakia in 1968 demonstrated, there was a limit to the economic and political reforms that Moscow would tolerate. The HWP's monopoly on power, and its subservient relationship with the Soviet Union remained taboo subjects.

The Hungarian road to socialism became known – only slightly tongue-in-cheek – as "Goulash Communism". An increasingly relaxed approach to censorship reduced the number of banned works, and expanded the number of intellectual works that were supported and tolerated. Uniquely among Eastern Europeans, Hungarians were relatively free to travel abroad, though only after thorough background checks. Currency regulations further restricted foreign travel to the privileged.

While the Kádár regime must be given some credit for successfully walking a very thin line between acceptable and unacceptable reform, by the 1980s the limitations of Goulash Communism had become far too apparent. Economic reforms proved insufficient to ensure decent levels of growth, meaning that foreign loans were needed in an attempt to prop up falling living standards.

Reformers in the HWP who believed only further economic reform could preserve its grip on power removed Kádár from office in May 1988. Shortly afterwards, opposition groups that had operated in semi-secrecy for years organized themselves into political parties. In 1989 they organized

Soviet soldiers participating in a ceremony to mark the withdrawal of troops from Hungary

TIMELINE

	1963 Kádár grants freedom to most remaining political prisoners in a widespread amnesty.	1968 Kádár announces formal, limited free-market reform, a policy that becomes known as "Goulash Communism".		1981 Director István Szábo receives an Oscar for his film *Mefisto*.	
1960	**1965**	**1970**	**1975**	**1980**	**1985**
János Kádár (1912–89)		1968 Hungary takes part in the Warsaw Pact invasion of Czechoslovakia.	1974 Economist Nyers is forced out of the Politburo. A return to central planning brings economic disaster, and Nyers is reinstated.	1987 Buda's entire Castle District is placed on UNESCO's list of protected historical monuments.	

Proclamation of the Republic of Hungary in 1989

mass demonstrations throughout the country against the HWP's monopoly on power. Led by the Hungarian Democratic Forum (MDF), the Alliance of Free Democrats (SZDSZ) and the Federation of Young Democrats (FIDESZ), the opposition held talks with the government in March 1989, and although no agreement was reached until autumn, the days of the one-party state were numbered. On 23 October 1989, the country's name was changed from Hungarian People's Republic to the Republic of Hungary, a symbolic move confirming the replacement of the one-party system with a multi-party democracy.

HUNGARY SINCE 1990
Hungary's first post-Communist elections, held in 1990, were won by the MDF. The HWP took part as the Hungarian Socialist Party (MSZP), and became the largest party of opposition. Árpád Göncz, who had been sentenced to death for his part in the 1956 revolution, was elected president; he was to serve two five-year terms.

The 1990–94 government enacted tough economic reform, including a massive privatization programme. Living standards for many people dropped, and unemployment reached almost 16 per cent in early 1994. As a result, the Socialists, promising a less dramatic transition to a market economy, easily won the election in 1994. Since then Hungary has seen its governments yo-yo between left and right. In 1998 FIDESZ replaced the Socialists, only for the latter to return to power in 2002. They narrowly won the 2006 general election, though Prime Minister Ferenc Gyurcsány's admission of lying during the campaign provoked weeks of protests. Gyurcsány refused to resign, however, and the protests eventually died down.

A member of both NATO (2001) and the European Union (2004), the 2008 global financial crisis hit Hungary hard. In 2010, FIDESZ swept to victory with a two-thirds majority – the first party to govern outright since the fall of Communism – and introduced deeply unpopular austerity measures to rescue the ailing economy.

Hungary's accession to the European Union, 2004

Hungarian national emblem after 1989

1988 Kádár is forced to resign by his own party.

2004 Hungary joins the European Union on 1 May.

2006 Gyurcsány and the Socialist Party (MSZP) win the elections.

2010 FIDESZ wins elections with a two-thirds majority in parliament.

2012 A new constitution is introduced on 1 Jan 2012.

1990	1995	2000	2005	2010	2015

1989 In March a series of talks begins that will see the HWP renounce its monopoly in October. On 23 October, the Republic of Hungary becomes the country's official name.

1999 Hungary is admitted to NATO.

2002 Imre Kertész receives a Nobel Prize for Literature.

2009 Ferenc Gyurcsány resigns and Gordon Bajnai becomes prime minister.

Ferenc Gyurcsány

BUDAPEST
AREA BY AREA

Budapest at a Glance

The centre of town includes Buda's Castle Hill (district I) on the western bank of the Danube and districts V, VI, VII, VIII and IX of Pest on the river's eastern bank, bounded by the city's original tram line. The Roman numerals denote the official administrative districts. For the purposes of this guide, the centre of Budapest is divided into four areas. Each area has its own chapter containing a selection of the most interesting sights that convey its character and history. Sights on the outskirts of the city are covered in a separate chapter.

Royal Palace
The Royal Palace has been destroyed and painstakingly rebuilt many times. It was last meticulously reconstructed after World War II, to the form that the Habsburgs had given it (see pp40–41).

Liberation Monument
This statue of a woman holding aloft the palm of victory was created by the Hungarian sculptor Zsigmond Kisfaludi Strobl. Situated in a park on Gellért Hill, the monument is visible from all over the city, and so it has become one of the symbols of Budapest (see p72).

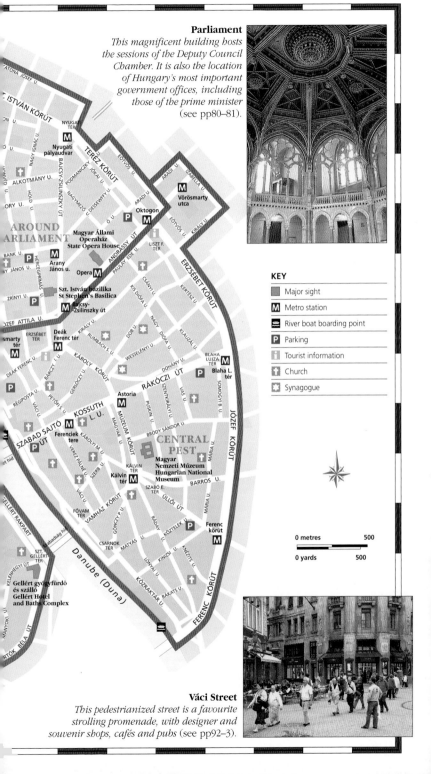

Parliament

*This magnificent building hosts
the sessions of the Deputy Council
Chamber. It is also the location
of Hungary's most important
government offices, including
those of the prime minister
(see pp80–81).*

KEY

▮	Major sight
M	Metro station
⛴	River boat boarding point
P	Parking
ℹ	Tourist information
✝	Church
✡	Synagogue

0 metres   500
0 yards   500

Váci Street

*This pedestrianized street is a favourite
strolling promenade, with designer and
souvenir shops, cafés and pubs (see pp92–3).*

CASTLE DISTRICT

The hill town of Buda grew up around its castle and Mátyás Church from the 13th century onwards. The hill's good strategic position, at 60 m (197 ft) above the Danube, and its natural resources made it a prize site. In the 13th century, a large settlement arose when King Béla IV decided to build his own defensive castle and establish his capital here. The reign of King Mátyás Corvinus in the 15th century was an important

Bas-relief on the Eugene of Savoy monument

period in the evolution of Buda but it was neglected under Turkish rule and then destroyed by Christian troops. Under the Habsburgs, the town was reborn, however, and assumed an important role during the 18th and 19th centuries. By the end of World War II, the Old Town had been almost utterly destroyed and the Royal Palace burnt to the ground. Since the war, both the district and the palace have been restored to their former glory.

SIGHTS AT A GLANCE

Churches
Buda Lutheran Church **17**
Church of St Mary
  Magdalene **18**
Mátyás Church pp62–3 **12**

Museums and Galleries
Budapest History Museum **1**
Golden Eagle Pharmacy
  Museum **8**
Hospital in the Rock **22**
*Hungarian National Gallery
pp58–9* **4**

Museum of Military History **20**
National Széchényi Library **2**
Royal Wine House and Cellar
  Museum **10**

Historic Streets and Squares
András Hess Square **14**
Holy Trinity Square **9**
Lords' Street **21**
Mihály Táncsics Street **15**
Parade Square **7**

Parliament Street **19**
Vienna Gate Square **16**

Palaces, Historic Buildings and Monuments
Fisherman's Bastion **11**
Hilton Budapest Hotel **13**
Mátyás Fountain **3**
Sándor Palace **5**
Tunnel **6**

GETTING THERE
Castle Hill and the Old Town are largely pedestrianized but there are a couple of car parks, from which visitors can walk to the area. Bus 16 runs from Deák tér and from Széll Kálmán tér to Clark Ádám tér and Dísz tér, and a funicular railway (Sikló) connects Clark Ádám tér to Szent György tér. Buses 16a and 116 arrive at this square from Széll Kálmán tér to the north.

| 0 metres | 400 |
| 0 yards | 440 |

KEY

Street-by-Street map
see pp54–5

ℹ️ Tourist information

◁ **Fountain on Tárnok utca in the Old Town**

Street-by-Street: The Royal Palace

The Royal Palace has experienced many incarnations during its long life. Even now it is not known exactly where King Béla IV began building his castle, though it is thought to be nearer the site of Mátyás Church *(see pp62–3)*. The Holy Roman Emperor Sigismund of Luxembourg built a Gothic palace on the present site, from which today's castle began to evolve. In the 18th century, the Habsburgs built their monumental palace here. The current form dates from the rebuilding of the 19th-century palace after its destruction in February 1945. During this work, remains of the 15th-century Gothic palace were exposed and Hungarian archaeologists decided to reveal the recovered defensive walls and royal chambers in the reconstruction.

Sándor Palace ❺

An ornamental gateway, dating from 1903, leads to the Habsburg Steps and the Royal Palace. Nearby, a bronze sculpture of the mythical *turul* bird guards the palace. This statue marked the millennium anniversary of the Magyar conquest in 896.

★ Mátyás Fountain
In the northern courtyard of the Royal Palace stands the Mátyás Fountain. It was designed by Alajos Stróbl in 1904 and depicts King Mátyás Corvinus and his beloved Ilonka ❸

The Lion Gate, leading to a rear courtyard of the Royal Palace, gets its name from the four lions that watch over it. These sculptures were designed by János Fadrusz in 1901.

TIMELINE

1200	1400	1600	1800
1255 First written document, a letter by King Béla IV, refers to building a fortified castle	**c.1400** Sigismund of Luxembourg builds an ambitious Gothic palace on this site	**1541** After capturing Buda, the Turks use the Royal Palace to stable horses and store gunpowder	**1719** The building of a small palace begins on the ruins of the old palace, to a design by Hölbling and Fortunato de Prati	**1881** The architect Miklós Ybl begins programme to rebuild and expand the Royal Palace
c.1356 Louis I builds a royal castle on the southern slopes of Castle Hill		**1686** The assault by Christian soldiers leaves the palace completely razed to the ground	**1849** Royal Palace is destroyed again, during an unsuccessful attack by Hungarian insurgents	
1458 A Renaissance palace evolves under King Mátyás	**1749** Maria Theresa builds a vast palace comprising 203 chambers			

Turul *bird*

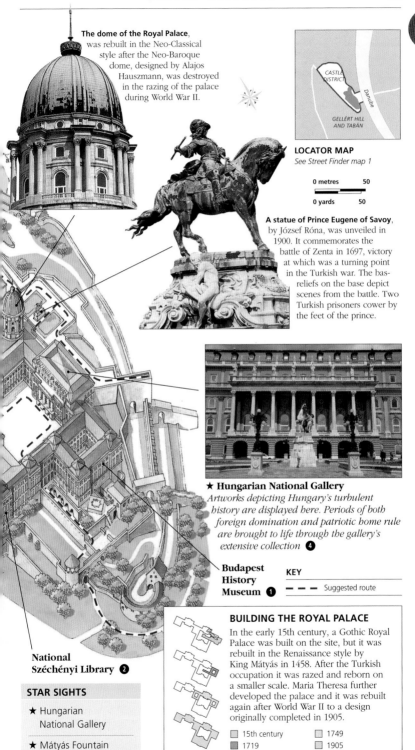

The dome of the Royal Palace, was rebuilt in the Neo-Classical style after the Neo-Baroque dome, designed by Alajos Hauszmann, was destroyed in the razing of the palace during World War II.

LOCATOR MAP
See Street Finder map 1

0 metres	50
0 yards	50

A statue of Prince Eugene of Savoy, by József Róna, was unveiled in 1900. It commemorates the battle of Zenta in 1697, victory at which was a turning point in the Turkish war. The bas-reliefs on the base depict scenes from the battle. Two Turkish prisoners cower by the feet of the prince.

★ Hungarian National Gallery
Artworks depicting Hungary's turbulent history are displayed here. Periods of both foreign domination and patriotic home rule are brought to life through the gallery's extensive collection ❹

Budapest History Museum ❶

KEY

― ― ― Suggested route

National Széchényi Library ❷

STAR SIGHTS

★ Hungarian National Gallery

★ Mátyás Fountain

BUILDING THE ROYAL PALACE

In the early 15th century, a Gothic Royal Palace was built on the site, but it was rebuilt in the Renaissance style by King Mátyás in 1458. After the Turkish occupation it was razed and reborn on a smaller scale. Maria Theresa further developed the palace and it was rebuilt again after World War II to a design originally completed in 1905.

▢ 15th century	▢ 1749
▢ 1719	▢ 1905

Fifteenth-century Renaissance majolica floor, uncovered during excavations on Castle Hill and displayed at the Budapest History Museum

Budapest History Museum **❶**
Budapesti Történeti Múzeum

Szent György tér 2, Royal Palace Building "E". **Map** 3 C1. **Tel** (1) 487 88 71. 16, 16A, 116.
Mar–Oct: 10am–6pm Tue–Sun; Nov–Feb: 10am–4pm Tue–Sun. fee www.btm.hu

Since Budapest's unification in 1873, historic artifacts relating to the city have been collected and many are on show at the Budapest History Museum (or Castle Museum).

During the rebuilding that followed the destruction suffered in World War II, chambers dating from the Middle Ages were uncovered in the south wing (Building "E") of the Royal Palace. They provide an insight into the character of a much earlier castle within today's Habsburg reconstruction.

These rediscovered chambers, including a tiny prison cell and a chapel, were recreated in the basement of the palace. They now house an exhibition, the Royal Palace in Medieval Buda, which displays various interesting items, including authentic weapons, seals, tiles and other early artifacts.

On the ground floor, the display on Budapest in the Middle Ages illustrates the evolution of the town from its Roman origins to a 13th-century Hungarian settlement.

Also on this level are reconstructed defensive walls, gardens, a keep, and Gothic statues from the Royal Palace dating from the 14th and 15th centuries. These were uncovered by chance during major excavations in 1974. On the first floor, Budapest in Modern Times traces the city's history from 1686 to the present.

National Széchényi Library **❷**
Országos Széchényi Könyvtár

Szent György tér 6, Royal Palace Building "F". **Map** 3 C1. **Tel** (1) 224 37 00. 16, 16A, 116.
10am–9pm Tue–Sat. mid-Jul–mid-Aug. www.oszk.hu

A superb collection of books has been housed, since 1985, in the Royal Palace Building "F", built in 1890–1902 by

Corviniani illuminated manuscript in the National Széchényi Library

Alajos Hauszmann and Miklós Ybl (*see p89*). Previously, the library was housed in a part of the Hungarian National Museum (*see pp98–9*).

Among the national library's most precious treasures is the *Corviniani*, a collection of ancient books and manuscripts that originally belonged to King Mátyás Corvinus (*see pp36–7*). His collection was one of the largest Renaissance libraries in Europe. Also of importance are the earliest surviving records in the Hungarian language, dating from the early 13th century.

The library was established by Count Ferenc Széchényi in 1802, who endowed it with 15,000 books and 2,000 manuscripts. The collection now comprises five million items; everything that has been published in Hungary, in Hungarian or that refers to Hungary is represented here.

Crest on the Lion Gate, adjacent to the Mátyás Fountain

Mátyás Fountain **❸**
Mátyás kút

Royal Palace. **Map** 1 B5. 16, 16A, 116.

The ornate fountain in the northernmost courtyard of the Royal Palace (between Buildings "A" and "C") was designed by Alajos Stróbl in 1904. The statue is dedicated to the great Renaissance king, Mátyás, about whom there are many legends and fables.

The Romantic design of the bronze sculptures takes its theme from a 19th-century ballad by the poet Mihály Vörösmarty. According to the tale, King Mátyás, while on a hunting expedition, meets a beautiful peasant girl, Ilonka, who falls in love with him, but their love is doomed. This representation shows King Mátyás disguised as hunter, standing proudly with his kill. He is accompanied by his chief hunter and several hunting dogs in the central part of the fountain. Below the left-hand columns sits Galeotto Marzio, an Italian court poet, and the figure of the young Ilonka is below the columns on the right.

In keeping with the romantic reputation of King Mátyás, a new tradition has grown up concerning this statue. The belief is that anyone wishing to revisit Budapest should throw a coin into the fountain to ensure their safe return.

Hungarian National Gallery ❹
Magyar Nemzeti Galéria

See pp58–9.

Sándor Palace ❺
Sándor-palota

Szent György tér 1–3. **Map** 1 B5.
🚌 16, 16A, 116. ⭘ *3rd weekend of Sep only (National Cultural Heritage Days).* **www**.keh.hu

By the top of the cog-wheel railway stands the grand Neo-Classical mansion, Sándor Palace. It was commissioned in 1806 by Count Vincent Sándor from architects Mihály Pollack and Johann Aman.

The bas-reliefs that decorate the palace are the work of Richárd Török, Miklós Melocco and Tamás Körössényi. The decoration on the western

The imposing entrance to the tunnel on Clark Ádám tér

elevation depicts Greek gods on Mount Olympus. The south side shows Count Sándor being knighted, and the northern façade features a 1934 sculpture of Saint George by Zsigmond Kisfaludi Strobl.

Sándor Palace functioned as the prime minister's official residence from 1867 to 1944, when it was severely damaged in World War II. It has been completely restored and is now the official residence of the President of Hungary.

Tunnel ❻
Alagút

Clark Ádám tér. **Map** 1 C5.
🚌 16, 86.

The Scottish engineer Adam Clark settled in Hungary after completing the Chain Bridge. One of his later projects, in 1853–7, was the construction of the tunnel that runs right through Castle Hill, from Clark Ádám tér to Krisztinaváros. The tunnel is 350 m (1,150 ft) long, 9 m (30 ft) wide and 11 m (36 ft) in height.

The entrance on Clark Ádám tér is flanked by two pairs of Doric columns. The square in front of the tunnel is the city's official centre because of the location here of the Zero Kilometre Stone, from which all distances from Budapest are calculated.

The tunnel's western entrance was originally ornamented with Egyptian motifs. However, it was rebuilt without these details after it was damaged in World War II.

Parade Square ❼
Dísz tér

Map 1 B5. 🚌 16, 16A, 116.

In the past, Parade Square was a market place and a site of execution. It is named after the military parades that were held here in the 19th century. At the northern end of the square is the Honvéd Monument, built in 1893 by György Zala. It honours and commemorates those who died during the recapture of Buda from Austria in the 1848 revolution.

The two-floor Baroque palace at No. 3 was the home of the Batthyány family until 1945. It was built between 1743 and 1748 by József Giessl, and although it has been frequently remodelled, the façade remains intact.

A few houses on Parade Square incorporate medieval remains. Examples can be seen at Nos. 4–5 and No. 11, built by Venerio Ceresola. The former has seat niches dating from the 13th century.

The western elevation of the Neo-Classical Sándor Palace

Hungarian National Gallery ❹

Established in 1957, the Hungarian National Gallery houses a comprehensive collection of Hungarian art from medieval times to the 20th century. Gathered by various groups and institutions since 1839, these works had previously been exhibited at the Hungarian National Museum *(see pp98–9)* and the Museum of Fine Arts *(see pp106–107)*. The collection was moved to the Royal Palace (wings B, C and D) in 1975.

Sisters by Erzsébet Schaár

There are now six permanent exhibitions, which present the most valuable and critically acclaimed Hungarian art in the world.

St Anne Altarpiece
(c.1520)
This elaborately decorated folding altarpiece from Kisszeben is one of the gallery's Gothic highlights.

Madonna of Toporc
(c.1420)
This captivating example of medieval wood sculpture in the Gothic style was originally crafted for a church in Spiz (now part of Slovakia).

First floor

Madonna of Bártfa
(1465–70)
This painting of the Madonna and Child is from a church in Bártfa (now in Slovakia). It is thought to have been painted in Cracow, Poland.

★ **The Visitation** *(1506)*
A delightful example of late Gothic Hungarian art, this painting by Master MS is a fragment of a folding altarpiece from a church in Selmecbánya in modern-day Slovakia.

Ground floor

Main entrance

STAR EXHIBITS

★ Picnic in May

★ The Visitation

KEY

▨	Stone sculptures and artifacts
▨	Gothic works
▨	Late Gothic altarpieces
▨	Renaissance and Baroque works
▨	19th-century works
▨	Early 20th-century works
▨	Temporary exhibitions

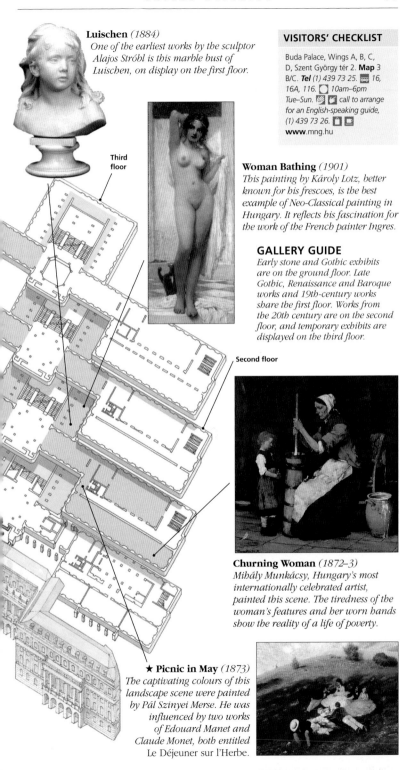

Luischen *(1884)*
One of the earliest works by the sculptor Alajos Stróbl is this marble bust of Luischen, on display on the first floor.

Third floor

Second floor

VISITORS' CHECKLIST

Buda Palace, Wings A, B, C, D, Szent György tér 2. **Map** 3 B/C. **Tel** (1) 439 73 25. 16, 16A, 116. 10am–6pm Tue–Sun. call to arrange for an English-speaking guide, (1) 439 73 26. **www**.mng.hu

Woman Bathing *(1901)*
This painting by Károly Lotz, better known for his frescoes, is the best example of Neo-Classical painting in Hungary. It reflects his fascination for the work of the French painter Ingres.

GALLERY GUIDE
Early stone and Gothic exhibits are on the ground floor. Late Gothic, Renaissance and Baroque works and 19th-century works share the first floor. Works from the 20th century are on the second floor, and temporary exhibits are displayed on the third floor.

Churning Woman *(1872–3)*
Mihály Munkácsy, Hungary's most internationally celebrated artist, painted this scene. The tiredness of the woman's features and her worn hands show the reality of a life of poverty.

★ Picnic in May *(1873)*
The captivating colours of this landscape scene were painted by Pál Szinyei Merse. He was influenced by two works of Edouard Manet and Claude Monet, both entitled Le Déjeuner sur l'Herbe.

Golden Eagle Pharmacy Museum ❽

Arany Sas Patikamúzeum

Tárnok utca 18. **Map** 1 B5. **Tel** (1) 375 97 72. 🚌 16 from Deák tér, 16, 16A & 116 from Széll Kálmán tér. 🕐 mid-Mar–Oct: 10:30am–6pm Tue–Sun; Nov–mid-Mar: 10:30am–4pm Tue–Sun.

This pharmacy was opened in 1688 by Ferenc Ignác Bösinger and traded under the name "The Golden Eagle" from 1740. It moved to this originally Gothic building, with a Baroque interior and Neo-Classical façade, in the 18th century. The museum opened in 1974 and displays pharmaceutical items from the Renaissance and Baroque eras.

Holy Trinity Square ❾

Szentháromság tér

Map 1 B5. 🚌 16 from Deák tér, 16, 16A & 116 from Széll Kálmán tér.

This square is the central point of the Old Town. It takes its name from the Baroque Holy Trinity Column, originally sculpted by Philipp Ungleich in 1710–13, and restored in 1967. The column commemorates the dead of two outbreaks of the plague, which struck the inhabitants of Buda in 1691 and 1709.

The pedestal of the column is decorated with bas-reliefs by Anton Hörger, depicting the horrific fate Buda's citizens suffered during these epidemics. Further up the ornate column are statues of holy figures and at the summit is a magnificent composition of the figures of the Holy Trinity. The central section of the column is decorated with angelic figures surrounded by clouds.

Buda's Old Town Hall, a large Baroque building with two courtyards, was also built on the square at the beginning of the 18th century. It was designed by the imperial court architect, Venerio Ceresola, whose architectural scheme incorporated the remains of medieval houses. In 1770–74 an east wing was built, and bay windows and a stone balustrade with Rococo urns, by Mátyás Nepauer, were also added. The corner niche, opposite Mátyás Church, houses a small statue of the Greek goddess Pallas Athene by Carlo Adami.

Royal Wine House and Cellar Museum ❿

Királyi Borház és Pincemúzeum

Szent György tér, Nyugati sétány. **Map** 1 B5. **Tel** (1) 267 11 00. 🚌 16 from Deák tér, 16, 16A & 116 from Széll Kálmán tér. 🕐 noon–8pm daily. 🌑 Oct–Apr: Mon. 📷 🎫

This intriguing museum, located in historic 14th-century wine cellars under Buda Castle, houses an exhibition on Hungary's wine and drink culture. Learn about the country's various wine regions as well as about medieval crafts and occupations connected with the art of wine making. The museum also hosts Hungarian wine tasting events, festivals and classical music concerts.

A statue of St István in front of the Fisherman's Bastion

Fisherman's Bastion ⓫

Halászbástya

Szentháromság tér. **Map** 1 B5. 🚌 16 from Deák tér, 16, 16A & 116 from Széll Kálmán tér. 🕐 9am–11pm daily. 🎫 Mar–Oct.

Frigyes Schulek designed this Neo-Romanesque monument to the Guild of Fishermen in 1895. It occupies the site of Buda's old defensive walls and a medieval square where fish was once sold. The bastion is a purely aesthetic addition to Castle Hill and boasts fine views of the Danube. In front of it is a statue of St István.

Mátyás Church ⓬

Mátyás templom

See pp62–3.

Buda's Old Town Hall, its clock tower crowned with an onion-shaped dome, on Holy Trinity Square

Bas-relief depicting King Mátyás on the Hilton Budapest Hotel's façade

Hilton Budapest Hotel ⑬

Hilton Szálloda

Hess András tér 1–3. **Map** 1 B4. **Tel** (1) 889 66 00. 16 from Deák tér, 16, 16A & 116 from Széll Kálmán tér.

Built in 1976, the Hilton Budapest Hotel is a rare example of modern architecture in the Old Town. Controversial from the outset, the design by the Hungarian architect Béla Pintér combines the historic remains of the site with contemporary materials and methods.

From 1254 a Dominican church, to which a tower was later added, stood on this site, followed by a late-Baroque Jesuit monastery. The remains of both buildings are incorporated into the new hotel. The ruins of the medieval church, for example, uncovered during excavations in 1902, form part of the Dominican Courtyard, where concerts and operettas are staged in summer.

The main façade comprises part of the façade of the Jesuit monastery. To the left of the entrance is St Nicholas's Tower. In 1930, a replica of a 15th-century German bas-relief of King Mátyás, considered to be his most authentic likeness, was added to this tower.

András Hess Square ⑭

Hess András tér

Map 1 B4. 16 from Deák tér, 16, 16A & 116 from Széll Kálmán tér.

This square is named after the Italian-trained printer who printed the first Hungarian book, *Chronica Hungarorum*, in a printing works at No. 4 in 1473. The house was rebuilt at the end of the 17th century, amalgamating three medieval houses, with quadruple seat niches, barrel-vaulted cellars and ornamental gates.

The former inn at No. 3 was named the Red Hedgehog in 1696. This one-floor building has surviving Gothic and Baroque elements.

The square also features a statue by József Damkó of Pope Innocent XI, who was involved in organizing the armies that recaptured Buda from the Turks. It was built to mark the 250th anniversary of the liberation, in 1936.

Mihály Táncsics Street ⑮

Táncsics Mihály utca

Táncsics Mihály utca 7. **Map** 1 A/B4. 16 from Deák tér, 16, 16A & 116 from Széll Kálmán tér. **Museum of Musical History Tel** (1) 214 67 70. 10am–4pm Tue–Sun. www.zti.hu

Erdődy Palace was built in 1750–69 for the Erdődy family by Mátyás Nepauer, the leading architect of the day. It features outstanding Baroque façades on three sides. Like many

The Museum of Musical History on Mihály Táncsics Street

houses on this street, it was erected on the ruins of medieval houses. In 1800, Ludwig van Beethoven, who was then giving concerts in Budapest, resided here for a short time.

The palace now houses the Museum of Musical History and the Béla Bartók archives. A permanent exhibition illustrates musical life in Budapest from the 18th to 20th centuries, and includes some of the oldest surviving Hungarian musical instruments.

The Royal Mint stood on the site of No. 9 during the Middle Ages, and, in 1810, the Joseph Barracks were built here. These were later used by the Habsburgs to imprison leaders of the 1848–9 rebellion, including Mihály Táncsics.

Relics of Buda's Jewish heritage can be found at Nos. 23 and 26. The remains of a 15th-century synagogue stand in the garden of No. 23. During excavations, tombs and religious items were found in the courtyard of No. 26.

KING ISTVÁN I

Born in Esztergom in 975, Vajk (Hero), the son of Géza, was baptized at the age of 10 and chose the name István (Stephen). He succeeded his father as Prince and in 1000 was crowned Catholic king of Hungary – the Vatican signalled its approval by sending what became known as the crown of St István. A devout man, István set about Christianizing Hungary, founding bishoprics, cathedrals and abbeys. He died in 1038, and was canonized by Pope Gregory VII as St István of Hungary in 1083.

Mátyás Church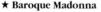

The Parish Church of Our Lady Mary was built on this site between the 13th and 15th centuries. Some of the architectural style dates from the reign of Sigismund of Luxembourg, but the church's name refers to King Mátyás Corvinus, who greatly enlarged and embellished it. Much of the original detail was lost when the Turks converted the church into the Great Mosque in 1541. During the liberation of Buda, Mátyás Church was almost totally destroyed, but was rebuilt in the Baroque style by Franciscan Friars. The church sustained further damage in 1723, and was restored in the Neo-Gothic style by Frigyes Schulek in 1873–96. The crypt houses the Museum of Ecclesiastical Art.

Rose Window
Frigyes Schulek faithfully reproduced the medieval stained-glass window that was in this position during the early Gothic era.

Béla Tower
This tower is named after the church's founder, King Béla IV. It has retained several of its original Gothic features.

★ Baroque Madonna
According to legend, the original statue was set into a wall of the church during the Turkish occupation. When the church was virtually destroyed in 1686, the Madonna miraculously appeared. The Turks took this as an omen of defeat.

Main Portal
Below the arches of the west entrance is a 19th-century bas-relief of the Madonna and Child, seated between two angels. The work is by Lajos Lantai.

STAR FEATURES

- ★ Baroque Madonna
- ★ Mary Portal
- ★ Tomb of King Béla III and Anne de Châtillon

★ Tomb of King Béla III and Anne de Châtillon
The remains of this royal couple were transferred from Székesfehérvár Cathedral to Mátyás Church in 1860. They lie beneath an ornamental stone canopy in the Trinity Chapel.

Pulpit
The richly decorated pulpit includes the carved stone figures of the four Fathers of the Church and the four Evangelists.

The roof is decorated with multicoloured glazed tiles.

The main altar, created by Frigyes Schulek, was based on Gothic triptychs.

Stained-Glass Windows
Three arched windows on the south elevation have beautiful 19th-century stained glass. They were designed by Frigyes Schulek, Bertalan Székely and Károly Lotz.

★ Mary Portal
This depiction of the Assumption of the Blessed Virgin Mary is the most magnificent example of Gothic stone carving in Hungary. Frigyes Schulek reconstructed the portal from fragments.

TIMELINE

c. 1387 Church redesigned as Gothic hall-church by Sigismund of Luxembourg

1458 Thanksgiving mass following the coronation of Mátyás Corvinus

1541 Turks convert church into a mosque

1686 After liberation of Buda from Turkish rule, church is almost destroyed. New church built with a Baroque interior

Holy figures on the pulpit

1250	1350	1450	1550	1650	1750	1850	1950

1309 Coronation of the Angevin king Charles Robert

1255 Church originally founded by King Béla IV after the Mongol invasion

1526 Cathedral burnt in the first attack by Turks

1470 Mátyás Tower is completed after its collapse in 1384

1896 Frigyes Schulek completes the reconstruction of the church in the Neo-Gothic style

1945 Church is severely damaged by German and Russian armies

1970 Final details are completed in post-war rebuilding programme

Vienna Gate, rebuilt in 1936, commemorating the liberation of Buda

Vienna Gate Square ⑯

Bécsi kapu tér

Map 1A4. 🚌 *16 from Széll Kálmán tér, 16, 16A & 116 from Moszkva tér.*

The square takes its name from the gate that once led from the walled town of Buda towards Vienna. After being damaged several times, the old gate was demolished in 1896. The current gate, based on an historic design, was erected in 1936 on the 250th anniversary of the liberation of Buda from the Turks.

The square has a number of interesting houses. Those at Nos. 5, 6, 7 and 8 were built on the ruins of medieval dwellings. They are Baroque and Rococo in design and feature sculptures and bas-reliefs. The façade of No. 7 has medallions with the portraits of Classical philosophers and poets; Thomas Mann, the German novelist, lodged here in 1935–6. No. 8, however, is differentiated by its bay windows, attics and the restored medieval murals on its façade.

On the left-hand side of the square is a vast Neo-Romanesque building with a beautiful multicoloured roof, built in 1913–20 by Samu Pecz. This building houses the National Archive, which holds documents dating from before the battle of Mohács in 1526, and others connected with the Rákóczi and Kossuth uprisings (*see pp38–9*).

Behind the Vienna Gate Square is a monument built in honour of Mihály Táncsics, the leader of the Autumn Uprising. It was unveiled in 1970.

Buda Lutheran Church ⑰

Budavári Evangélikus templom

Táncsics Mihály utca 28. **Map** 1 A4. **Tel** *(1) 356 97 36.* 🚌 *16 from Deák tér, 16, 16A & 116 from Széll Kálmán tér.* ♿

The Neo-Classical Lutheran church was built in 1896 by Mór Kallina. A plaque commemorates the evangelical pastor Gábor Sztéhló, who saved some 2,000 Jewish children and adults during World War II.

At one time, a painting by Bertalan Székely, called *Christ Blessing the Bread,* adorned the altar, but unfortunately it was destroyed during the war.

Church of St Mary Magdalene ⑱

Mária Magdolna templom

Kapisztrán tér 6. **Map** 1 A4. 🚌 *16 from Deák tér, 16, 16A & 116 from Széll Kálmán tér.*

Now in ruins, this church was built in the mid-13th century. During the Middle Ages, Hungarian Christians worshipped here because Mátyás Church was only for use by the town's German population.

The church did not become a mosque until the second half of the Turkish occupation, but it was severely damaged in 1686, during the liberation

The reconstructed Baroque tower of the Church of St Mary Magdalene

of Buda from the Turks. An order of Franciscan monks subsequently took possession and during their time added a Baroque church and a tower.

After suffering serious air-raid damage in World War II, all but the Franciscan tower and gate were pulled down. These now stand in a garden, together with the reconstructed single Gothic window.

Parliament Street ⑲

Országház utca

Map 1 A4.

This street was once inhabited by the Florentine artisans and craftsmen who were working on King Mátyás' Royal Palace (*see pp54–5*), and so it was known for a time as Italian Street. Its present name comes from the building at No. 28, where the Hungarian State Parliament and Budapest High Court met from 1790 to 1807. This building was designed in the 18th century by the architect Franz Anton Hillebrandt as a convent for the Poor Clares. However, Emperor Joseph II dissolved the order before the building was completed. The Great Hall is beautifully restored.

Numerous buildings on Parliament Street have retained Gothic and Baroque features. No. 2 Országház utca, now with a Neo-Classical façade, is the site of the Alabárdos restaurant, but the building's history dates back to the late 13th century. In the 15th century, Sigismund of Luxembourg built a Gothic mansion here and some details, such as the colonnade around the courtyard and the murals on the second floor, have survived until today. The entrance to No. 9 features the Gothic traceried seat niches that were popular in Buda at this time. In front of the Neo-Classical house at No. 21 stands a statue of the famous actor Márton Lendvay (1807–58).

The façade of the Museum of Military History

Museum of Military History ⑳

Hadtörténeti Múzeum

Kapisztrán tér 2–4. **Map** 1 A4. **Tel** (1) 325 16 00. 16 from Deák tér, 16, 16A & 116 from Széll Kálmán tér. 10am–6pm Tue–Sun. www.militaria.hu

The museum is located in a wing of the former Palatine barracks. It houses a wide range of military items relating to the skirmishes and wars that have afflicted Budapest from before the Turkish occupation to the 20th century. Uniforms, flags, weapons, maps and ammunition from as far back as the 11th century give an insight into the long, turbulent history of Budapest.

Of particular interest is the exhibition concerning the 1956 Uprising. Photographs illustrate the demonstrations that ended in a Soviet invasion, the execution of the Prime Minister and a great number of civilian deaths (see pp44–5).

Lords' Street ㉑

Úri utca

Map 1 A4 and 1 B4. 16 from Deák tér, 16, 16A & 116 from Széll Kálmán tér. **Telephone Museum Tel** (1) 201 81 88. 10am–4pm Tue–Sun. www.postamuzeum.hu

The buildings in Lords' Street, or Úri utca, were destroyed first in 1686 and again in 1944. Reconstruction in

1950–60 restored much of their original medieval character. Almost all have some remnant of a Gothic gateway or hall, while the façades are Baroque or Neo-Classical.

An excellent example of a Gothic façade can be seen on Hölbling House at No. 31. Enough of its original features survived the various wars and renovations to enable architects to reconstruct the façade in considerable detail. The first-floor window is a particularly splendid Gothic feature. The houses opposite are also examples of restoration work.

The building at No. 53 was rebuilt between 1701–22 as a Franciscan monastery, but in 1789 it was restyled for use by Emperor Joseph II. In 1795, Hungarian Jacobites, led by Ignác Martinovics, were imprisoned here; a plaque records this event. A well, featuring a copy of a sculpture of Artemis, the Greek goddess of hunting, by Praxiteles, was set in front of the house in 1873.

The **Telephone Museum**, at No. 49, is housed in the city's first telephone exchange, established in 1881. It is an enjoyable interactive museum, centred around a huge switch-board with exhibits on the history of telephony.

Hospital in the Rock ㉒

Sziklakórház

Lovas út 4/c. **Map** 1 B5. **Tel** (36) 707 01 01 01. 16 from Deák tér, 16, 16A & 116 from Széll Kálmán tér. 10am–8pm daily. www.sziklakorhaz.hu

Connected to the network of caves under Buda Castle, the Hospital in the Rock is an atmospheric sight where visitors can learn about the history of Hungary throughout the mid-20th century. In 1944–45 the caves were used as an emergency military hospital and air raid shelter, providing treatment and refuge for thousands of people during the siege of Budapest. During the revolution in 1956 it was again used as a hospital. A nuclear bunker was added during the Cold War, the existence of which was only made public in 2010.

Many pieces of the original medical equipment are on display. There are presentations on the history of the city, information on the 1956 Revolution and the Cold War, along with wax figures, all bringing this unique sight to life. The guided tour (approx 60 mins) is compulsory.

Lords' Street, or Úri utca, which runs the full length of the Old Town

GELLÉRT HILL AND TABÁN

Carving on the altar in the Rock Church

Rising steeply beside the Danube, Gellért Hill is one of the city's most attractive areas. From the top, at a height of 140 m (460 ft), a beautiful view of the whole of Budapest unfolds. The Celtic Eravi, who preceded the Romans, formed their settlement on the hill's northern slope *(see p74)*. Once called simply Old Hill, many superstitions and tales are connected with it. The hill's present name recalls the fate and martyrdom of Bishop Gellért who tried to convert the unwilling locals to Christianity. In 1046, they threw the bishop from the hill to his death in a sealed barrel. Gellért Hill bulges out slightly into the Danube, which narrows at this point. This made the base of the hill a favoured crossing place, and the settlement of Tabán evolved as a result.

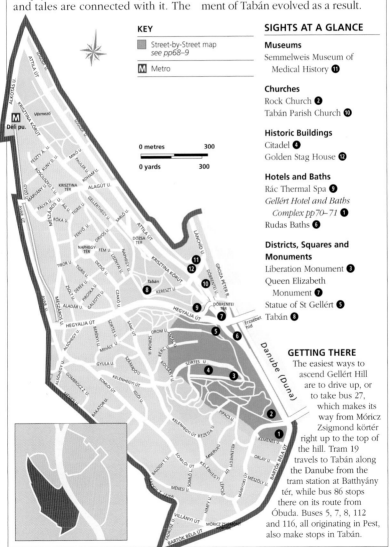

KEY

| | Street-by-Street map *see pp68–9* |
| M | Metro |

0 metres 300
0 yards 300

SIGHTS AT A GLANCE

Museums
Semmelweis Museum of Medical History ⑪

Churches
Rock Church ②
Tabán Parish Church ⑩

Historic Buildings
Citadel ④
Golden Stag House ⑫

Hotels and Baths
Rác Thermal Spa ⑨
Gellért Hotel and Baths Complex pp70–71 ①
Rudas Baths ⑥

Districts, Squares and Monuments
Liberation Monument ③
Queen Elizabeth Monument ⑦
Statue of St Gellért ⑤
Tabán ⑧

GETTING THERE
The easiest ways to ascend Gellért Hill are to drive up, or to take bus 27, which makes its way from Móricz Zsigmond körtér right up to the top of the hill. Tram 19 travels to Tabán along the Danube from the tram station at Batthyány tér, while bus 86 stops there on its route from Óbuda. Buses 5, 7, 8, 112 and 116, all originating in Pest, also make stops in Tabán.

◁ Statue dedicated to the murdered 11th-century bishop St Gellért, patron saint of Budapest

Street-by-Street: Gellért Hill

The hill to the south of Castle Hill was long regarded as a notorious spot. In the 11th century, Prince Vata, brother of King István, incited a heathen rebellion here that resulted in the death of Bishop Gellért. During the Middle Ages, witches were even reputed to celebrate their sabbath here. Under the Turks, a small stronghold was first built on the hill to protect Buda. In 1851, the Austrians placed their own bleak and intimidating Citadel at the summit. Not until the end of the 19th century did the popular image of Gellért Hill begin to change, when it became a venue for picnicking parties. In 1967, the area around the Citadel was made into an attractive park.

Queen Elizabeth Monument
Close to the entrance to Elizabeth Bridge stands this statue of Austrian Emperor Franz Joseph's wife, who was popular with the Hungarians **7**

★ **Statue of St Gellért**
Blessing the city with his uplifted cross, the martyred Bishop Gellért is known as the patron saint of Budapest **5**

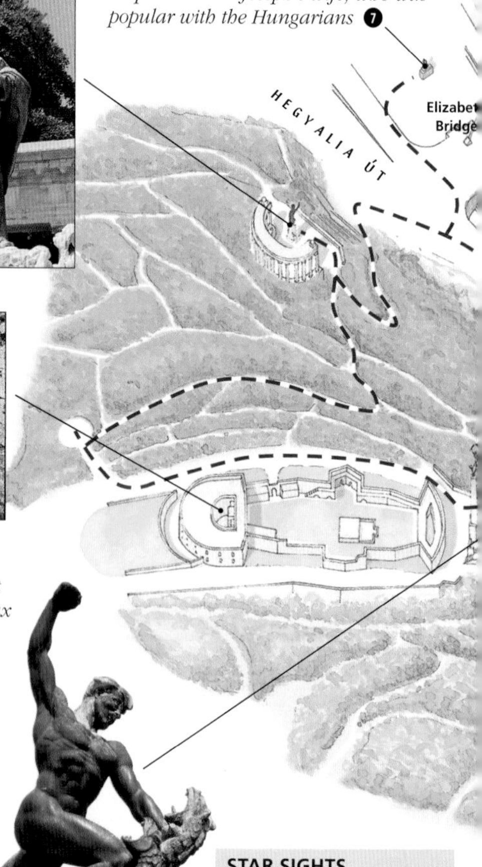

HEGYALIA ÚT

Elizabet Bridge

Citadel
Once a place to inspire terror, the Citadel now hosts a hotel, restaurant and wine bar, where people can relax and enjoy the splendid view **4**

0 metres 500
0 yards 500

KEY

— — — Suggested route

Liberation Monument
At the foot of the Liberation Monument, towering above the city, are two sculptures, one representing the battle with evil **3**

STAR SIGHTS

★ Gellért Hotel and Baths Complex

★ Statue of St Gellért

For hotels and restaurants in this area see pp260–1 and pp282

Rudas Baths

These famous Turkish baths, which date from the 16th century, have a characteristic Ottoman cupola ❻

The observation terraces on Gellért Hill reward those who climb up to them with a beautiful panorama over the southern part of Buda and the whole of Pest.

LOCATOR MAP
See Street Finder map 3

THE RESERVOIR

In 1978, a new reservoir to supply the capital with drinking water was built near the Uránia Observatory to the northwest of Gellért Hill. The surface of the reservoir is covered over and provides a point from which to observe the Royal Palace *(see pp54–5)* to the north. A sculpture by Márta Lesenyei decorates the structure.

Sculpture by Márta Lesenyei on Gellért Hill's reservoir

Rock Church

This church was established in 1926 in a holy grotto. Under the Communists, the Pauline order of monks was forced to abandon the church, but it was reopened in 1989 ❷

SZENT GELLÉRT RAKPART

Liberty Bridge

★ **Gellért Hotel and Baths Complex**
One of a number of bath complexes built at the beginning of the 20th century, this magnificent spa hotel was erected here to exploit the natural hot springs ❶

Gellért Hotel and Baths Complex ❶

Stained-glass window by Bózó Stanisits

Between 1912 and 1918, this hotel and spa was built in the modernist Secession style *(see p83)* at the foot of Gellért Hill. The architects of the hotel were Ármin Hegedűs, Artúr Sebestyén and Izidor Sterk. The earliest reference to the existence of healing waters at this spot dates from the 13th century. During the reign of King András II and in the Middle Ages a hospital stood on the site. Baths built here by the Ottomans were mentioned by the renowned Turkish travel writer of the day, Evliya Çelebi. Destroyed in 1945, the hotel was rebuilt and modernized after World War II. Today it has several restaurants and cafés. The baths complex includes an institute of water therapy, set within Secession interiors but with modern facilities.

Outdoor Wave Pool
An early swimming pool with a wave mechanism, built in 1927, is situated at the back of the complex, looking towards Gellért Hill behind.

★ Baths
Two separate baths, one for men and one for women, are identically arranged. In each there are three plunge pools, with water at different temperatures, a sauna and a steam bath.

Balconies
The balconies fronting the hotel's rooms have fanciful Secession balustrades that are decorated with lyre and bird motifs.

★ Entrance Hall
The interiors of the hotel, like the baths, have kept their original Secession decor, with elaborate mosaics, stained-glass windows and statues.

Sun Terraces
Situated in the sunniest spot, these terraces are a popular place for drying off in summer.

VISITORS' CHECKLIST

Szent Gellért tér. **Map** 4 D3.
Tel (1) 466 61 66. 🚌 7, 7A, 86. 🚎 18, 19, 47, 49. ♿ ⬇
⬛ 🍴 🏊 **Baths** Kelenhegyi út.
⏰ 6am–8pm daily. 📷 🚫 ♿
www.budapestspas.hu

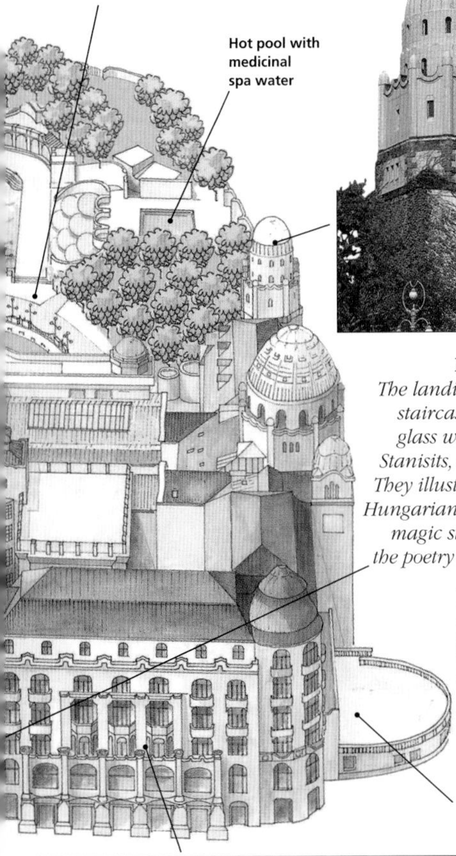

Hot pool with medicinal spa water

Eastern-Style Towers
The architects who designed the hotel gave its towers and turrets a characteristically Oriental cylindrical form.

Main Staircase
The landings of the main staircase have stained-glass windows by Bozó Stanisits, added in 1933. They illustrate an ancient Hungarian legend about a magic stag, recorded in the poetry of János Arany.

Restaurant Terrace
From this first-floor terrace, diners can appreciate a fine view of Pest. On the ground and first floors of the hotel there is a total of four cafés and restaurants.

★ Main Façade
Behind the hotel's imposing façade are attractive recreational facilities and a health spa that is also open to non-guests. The entrance to the baths is around to the right from the main entrance, on Kelenhegyi út.

STAR FEATURES

- ★ Baths
- ★ Entrance Hall
- ★ Main Façade

Entrance to the Rock Church, run by the Pauline order of monks

Rock Church ❷
Sziklatemplom

Szent Gellért rakpart 1. **Map** 4 D3.
Tel *(1) 385 15 29.* ⏱ *9am–8pm daily.*
🚌 *7, 7A, 86.* 🚋 *18, 19, 47, 49.*

Based on Lourdes, this grotto
church on the southern slope
of Gellért Hill was established
in 1926 by Kálmán Lux for the
Pauline order of monks, which
originated in Hungary in the
13th century. The church was
sealed in the late 1950s by the
Communist authorities, but it
and the adjoining monastery
were reopened in 1989, when
a papal blessing was conferred
on its new granite altar.
To the left of the grotto is a
copy of the *Black Madonna of
Czestochowa* and a depiction
of a Polish eagle. A painting
commemorates the Polish
monk St Kolbe, who died
helping inmates at Auschwitz.
At the entrance to the church
stands a statue of St István. In
the monastery, Béli Ferenc's
exquisite wooden sculptures
are worth seeing.

Liberation Monument ❸
Felszabadulási emlékmű

Map 4 D2. 🚌 *27.*

Positioned high on Gellért
Hill, this imposing monument
towers over the rest of the
city. It was designed by the
outstanding Hungarian
sculptor Zsigmond Kisfaludi
Strobl and set up here to
commemorate the liberation
of Budapest by the Russian

army in 1947 *(see pp42–3).*
The monument was originally
intended to honour the
memory of István, son of the
Hungarian Regent Miklós
Horthy, who disappeared in
1943 on the eastern front.
However, after the liberation
of the city by Russian troops,
Marshal Klimient Woroszyłow
spotted the work in the
sculptor's workshop and
reassigned it to this purpose.

The Liberation Monument, standing
at the top of Gellért Hill

The monument's central
figure is a woman on a
pedestal, reaching a height
of 14 m (46 ft). At the base
of the monument there are
two allegorical compositions,
representing progress and
the battle with evil.
The arrival of the Russians
in Budapest was a liberation
but it also signalled the beginning of Soviet rule. After the
fall of Communism, a figure
of a Russian soldier was
removed from the monument
to Statue Park *(see p112).*

Citadel ❹
Citadella

Map 3 C2. 🚌 *27.* **Open-air
Museum Tel** *(1) 466 57 94.*
⏱ *8am–11pm daily.* 🏨 **Hotel
Citadella Tel** *(1) 466 57 94.* ⏱ *daily.*
🍽 **Citadella Restaurant Tel** *(1)
386 48 02.* ⏱ *11am–11pm daily.*
www.citadella.hu

After the suppression of the
uprising of 1848–9 *(see pp40–
41),* the Habsburgs built a
fortification on this strate-
gically important site.
Constructed in 1850–54, the
Citadel housed 60 cannons,
which could, in theory, fire
on the city at any time. In
reality, from its very inception
the Citadel did not fulfil any
real military requirements, but
served rather as a means of
intimidating the population.
The Citadel is some 220 m
(720 ft) long by 60 m (200 ft)
wide, and has 4-m (12-ft)
high walls. After peace was
agreed with the Habsburgs,
Hungarians continually
demanded the destruction of
the Citadel but it was not until

SAINT GELLÉRT

Bishop Gellért was born Giorgio di Sagredo, near Bologna,
Italy, around 980. He became a Benedictine monk and made
a pilgrimage to the Holy Land where he
met the Raslan, Abbot of Pannonhalma
Abbey *(see pp176–7),* who invited him
to Hungary. After a period preaching
in pagan areas of the country, he was
asked by King St István to tutor his
son, Prince Imre. István later made
him a Bishop. Gellért was killed in
1046 during a pagan revolt – sealed in
a barrel, he was thrown off the hill that
today takes his name, Gellért Hill.

**A hotel window
depicting St Gellért**

1897 that the Austrian soldiers left their barracks here and a section of its entrance was symbolically ripped out.

After much debate in the early 1960s, the Citadel became a leisure complex. A restaurant, a hotel and a nightclub now tempt customers up Gellért Hill. From the old walls of the Citadel there are spectacular views of the entire city below.

The main plunge pool at the Rudas Baths, covered by a Turkish cupola

Statue of St Gellért ⑤

Szent Gellért emlékmű

Map 3 C2. 🚌 *27 (and a long walk; go via the steps by Elizabeth Bridge).*

In 1904 a vast monument was established on the spot where, in the 11th century, Bishop Gellért was said to have been thrown off the hill in a sealed barrel, by a mob opposed to the adoption of Christianity. St Gellért holds a cross in his outstretched hand and a Hungarian convert to Christianity kneels at his feet.

The statue was designed by Gyula Jankovits; the semi-circular colonnade behind it is by Imre Francsek. A spring that bubbles up here was used to create the fountain.

Overlooking the Elizabeth Bridge, the larger-than-life monument of the bishop can be seen from all over the city.

Rudas Baths ⑥

Rudas Gyógyfürdő

Döbrentei tér 9. **Map** 3 C2. *Tel* *(1) 356 13 22.* **Spa Baths** ◯ *(men only) 6am–8pm Mon, Wed–Fri; (women only) 6am–8pm Tue; (mixed) 10pm–4am Fri, 6am–8pm & 10pm–4am Sat, 6am–7pm Sun.* **Swimming pool** ◯ *6am–6pm Mon–Fri, 6am–5pm Sat & Sun.* www.spasbudapest.com

Dating originally from 1550, these baths were greatly extended in 1566 by Sokoli Mustafa, an Ottoman pasha. The main part of the baths, which comprises an octagonal plunge pool and four small corner pools with water of varying temperatures, dates from this period.

In recent years the baths have been extensively modernized and now include a covered swimming pool. This pool is for mixed bathing.

Queen Elizabeth Monument ⑦

Erzsébet királyné szobra

Döbrentei tér. **Map** 3 C1/2.

This monument to Queen Elizabeth, wife of Habsburg Emperor Franz Joseph, was created by György Zala.

The statue was erected in its present location in 1986. It stands close to the Elizabeth Bridge, which was also named after the empress, who showed great friendship to the Hungarians. The statue stood on the opposite side of the river from 1932 until 1947, when the Communists ordered it to be taken down.

The landmark Gellért Monument, overlooking the Elizabeth Bridge

Tabán 8

Map 3 B/C1. 18, 19.
5, 112.

The Tabán now consists of a pleasant park and a few historic buildings, but it was once very different. In the early 20th century this district, nestling in between Castle Hill and Gellért Hill, was a slum which was cleared as part of a city improvement programme. Only a few buildings survived, including Tabán Parish Church.

Natural conditions ensured that this was one of the first places in the area where people chose to live. The Celtic Eravi were the first to make a settlement here, while the Romans later built a watchtower from which they could observe people using a nearby crossing point over the river. The first reference to the thermal waters in Tabán dates from the 15th century. The Turks took advantage of this natural asset and built two magnificent baths here, the Rác Baths and the Rudas Baths (see p73). Around them a blossoming town was soon established. Apart from the baths, virtually everything was destroyed in the recapture of Buda in 1686.

In the late 17th century, a large number of Serbs, referred to in Hungarian as Rác, moved into the Tabán after fleeing from the Turks. They were joined by Greeks and Gypsies. Many of the inhabitants of the Tabán at this stage were tanners or made their living on the river. On the hillside above, grapevines were cultivated. In the early 20th century, though picturesque, the district was still without proper sanitation. The old, decaying Tabán, with its bars and gambling dens, was demolished and the present green space established in its place.

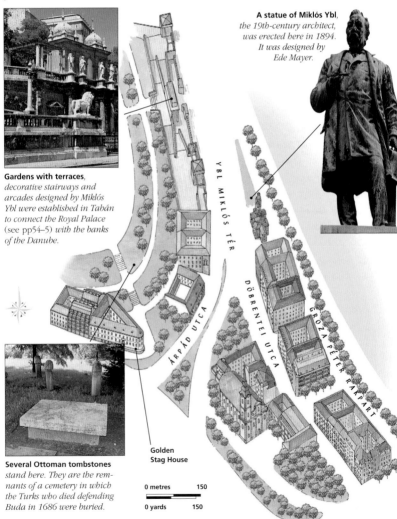

Gardens with terraces, *decorative stairways and arcades designed by Miklós Ybl were established in Tabán to connect the Royal Palace (see pp54–5) with the banks of the Danube.*

A statue of Miklós Ybl, *the 19th-century architect, was erected here in 1894. It was designed by Ede Mayer.*

YBL MIKLÓS TÉR

ÁRPÁD UTCA

DÖBRENTEI UTCA

GROZA PÉTER RAKPART

Several Ottoman tombstones *stand here. They are the remnants of a cemetery in which the Turks who died defending Buda in 1686 were buried.*

Golden Stag House

0 metres   150

0 yards   150

Rác Thermal Spa ❾
Rác Gyógyfürdő

Hadnagy utca 8–10. **Map** 3 C2.
🚋 18, 19. ● *currently closed.*

The Rác Spa dates from 1550 and boasts an original thermal Turkish pool, a hammam bath and a historical dome. This significant piece of heritage is now privately owned, and has been renovated with a five-star luxury hotel adjoining it, with modern facilities for guests and visitors to indulge in the latest spa treatments. Unfortunately, the opening of the hotel and thermal spa complex has been delayed by unresolved financial issues.

Turkish bath area, Rác Thermal Spa

Tabán Parish Church ❿
Tabáni plébánia

Attila út 11. **Map** 3 C1.
Tel (1) 375 54 91. 🚋 18, 19.

A temple is thought to have stood on this site even in the reign of Prince Árpád. In the Middle Ages a church was built here, which was converted to a mosque by the Turks and subsequently destroyed. In 1728–36, after the Habsburgs had taken control of the city, a new church was erected to a design by Keresztély Obergruber. Mátyás Nepauer added the tower in 1750–53. In 1881 the façade was extended and the tower was crowned by a fine Neo-Baroque dome.

Inside the church, on the right-hand side under the choir gallery, is a copy of a 12th-century carving entitled

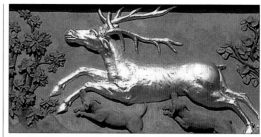

Bas-relief above the entrance to Golden Stag House

Christ of Tabán; the original is now in the Budapest History Museum *(see p56)*. The nave and side chapels are Baroque, the altar, pulpit and several paintings adorning the walls all date from the 19th century. The church hosts regular organ concerts.

Semmelweis Museum of Medical History ⓫
Semmelweis Orvostörténeti Múzeum

Apród utca 1–3. **Map** 3 C1. **Tel** (1) 375 35 33. 🚋 18, 19. ○ Mid-Mar–Oct: 10:30am–6pm Tue–Sun; Sep–mid-Mar: 10:30am–4pm Tue–Sun. 📷 📷 📷 **www**.semmelweis.museum.hu

This museum is located in the 18th-century house where Dr Ignáz Semmelweis was born in 1818. He is renowned for his discovery of the cause and cure for puerperal fever, a fatal condition frequently contracted by women during or shortly after childbirth.

The history of medicine from ancient Egypt onwards is portrayed in the museum, which includes the replica of a 19th-century pharmacy. Semmelweis's surgery can also be seen with its original furniture. In the courtyard stands a monument called *Motherhood* by Miklós Borsos.

Golden Stag House ⓬
Szarvas ház

Szarvas tér 1. **Map** 3 C1.
Tel (1) 375 64 51. 🚋 19.
www.aranyszarvas.hu

Standing at the foot of Castle Hill is this distinctive early 18th-century house. Its name recalls the inn that opened here in 1704, "Under the Golden Stag" (Aranyszarvas) – a bas-relief above the door depicts a golden stag pursued by two hunting dogs. Much reworked over the past three centuries the house today is a classy, whitewashed Neo-Baroque building, as famous for its uniquely slim chimney pots as for its façade. It is now occupied by the Aranyszarvas restaurant, which serves game dishes, and has a popular terrace with a nice view.

RAOUL WALLENBERG

The celebrated Swedish diplomat Raoul Wallenberg saved more than 7,000 Hungarian Jews from deportation. Born in Sweden in 1912, Wallenberg was assigned to the Swedish Embassy in Budapest in 1944 and immediately began certifying Jews threatened with deportation as Swedish subjects awaiting repatriation. Arrested (as a US spy) by the Soviet Army in 1945, Wallenberg was taken to Moscow and probably executed in 1947. He is honoured in Budapest with a statue depicting a man slaying a snake.

Bas-relief of Raoul Wallenberg

AROUND PARLIAMENT

Towards the end of the 18th and throughout the 19th century Pest underwent a series of huge changes. In 1838 a flood destroyed most of the rural dwellings that had occupied the area. The Chain Bridge, the city's first permanent Danube crossing, was built in 1839–49. The unification of Budapest in 1873 and the 1,000-year anniversary, in 1896, of the Magyar conquest also boosted the city's development. The medieval walls that originally marked Pest's limits were crossed as the area expanded and was urbanized. This period produced some of the most important buildings in Hungary, including St Stephen's Basilica, Parliament and the Hungarian Academy of Science. Many Neo-Classical residences were also built, particularly on Nádor utca, Akadémia utca and Október 6 utca.

An ornate lantern on the Parliament

SIGHTS AT A GLANCE

Historic Buildings and Palaces
Drechsler Palace ❿
Gresham Palace ❻
Hungarian Academy
  of Sciences ❼

Ministry of Agriculture ❸
Parliament pp80–81 ❶
Radisson Blu Béke Hotel ⓬

Theatres
Budapest Operetta Theatre ⓫
*State Opera House
  pp88–9* ❾

Museums
Ethnographical
  Museum ❷

Squares
Liberty Square ❹
Roosevelt Square ❺

Churches
*St Stephen's Basilica
  pp86–7* ❽

GETTING THERE
The M2 metro line (red) runs to Kossuth Lajos tér and the M3 metro line (blue) runs to Arany János utca. Tram 2 runs north along the Danube and continues past Parliament, terminating at Margaret Bridge. Trolley buses 70 and 78 also serve this area.

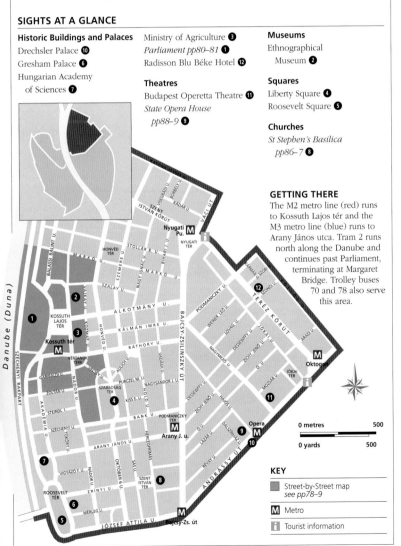

KEY

	Street-by-Street map see pp78–9
M	Metro
ℹ	Tourist information

◁ **Neo-Gothic spires, flying buttresses and stained-glass windows on Hungary's Parliament**

Street-by-Street: Kossuth Square

Brigadier Woroniecki

This square expresses well the pomp and pride with which Pest was developed during the 19th and early 20th centuries. Parliament dominates the square on the Danube side, but equally imposing are the Ministry of Agriculture and the Ethnographical Museum on the opposite side. Several monuments commemorate nationalist leaders and provide a visual record of Hungary's recent political history.

★ **Ethnographical Museum**
Among 170,000 exhibits amassed in the museum's collection is a captivating collection of folk costumes representing the various nationalities and ethnic groups in Hungary ❷

★ **Parliament**
This building has become the recognized symbol of democracy in Hungary, despite the fact that the dome was crowned by a red star during the Communist period ❶

Attila Jòzsef was a radical poet whose work sensitively explored the human condition. In 1937 he committed suicide, aged 32. This statue by László Marton dates from 1980.

LAJOS KOSSUTH (1802–94)

Lajos Kossuth, after whom this square is named, is still immensely popular in Hungary today. Kossuth led the 1848–9 uprising against Austrian rule *(see pp38–9)* and was one of the most outstanding political figures in Hungary. A member of the first democratic government during the uprising, he briefly became its leader before being exiled after the revolt was quashed in 1849. He died in Turin in 1894.

Stained-glass window depicting Lajos Kossuth

| 0 metres | 150 |
| 0 yards | 150 |

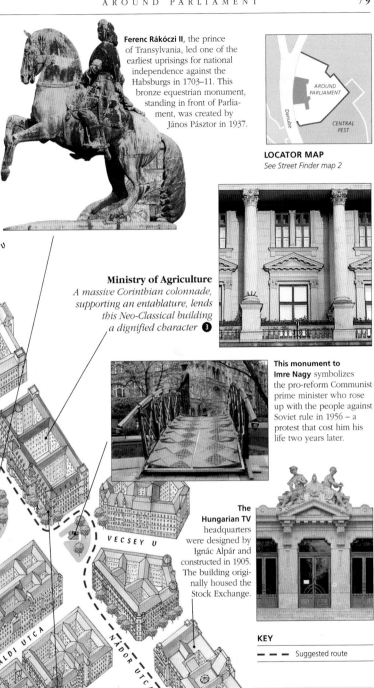

Ferenc Rákóczi II, the prince of Transylvania, led one of the earliest uprisings for national independence against the Habsburgs in 1703–11. This bronze equestrian monument, standing in front of Parliament, was created by János Pásztor in 1937.

LOCATOR MAP
See Street Finder map 2

Ministry of Agriculture
A massive Corinthian colonnade, supporting an entablature, lends this Neo-Classical building a dignified character ❸

This monument to Imre Nagy symbolizes the pro-reform Communist prime minister who rose up with the people against Soviet rule in 1956 – a protest that cost him his life two years later.

The **Hungarian TV** headquarters were designed by Ignác Alpár and constructed in 1905. The building originally housed the Stock Exchange.

VECSEY U

RIBALDI UTCA

NÁDOR UTCA

Plaque commemorating Brigadier Woroniecki, hero of the uprising of 1848–9

KEY

– – – Suggested route

STAR SIGHTS

★ Ethnographical Museum

★ Parliament

Parliament ❶

Hungary's Parliament, the country's largest building, has become a symbol of Budapest. A competition held to choose its design was won by Imre Steindl, who based his plans on the Houses of Parliament in London, built by Charles Barry in 1837–47. Steindl's rich Neo-Gothic masterpiece, constructed between 1885 and 1904, is 268 m (880 ft) long and 96 m (315 ft) high, and comprises 691 rooms.

One of the pair of lions at the main entrance

Aerial View
The magnificent dome marks the central point of the Parliament building. Although the façade is elaborately Neo-Gothic, the ground plan follows Baroque conventions.

★ Domed Hall
Adorning the massive pillars that support Parliament's central dome are figures of some of Hungary's rulers.

Danube façade

★ Deputy Council Chamber
Formerly the lower house, this hall is where the National Assembly convenes now. Two paintings by Zsigmond Vajda, especially commissioned for the building, hang on either side of the Speaker's lectern.

South wing

Gables
Almost every corner of the Parliament building features gables with pinnacles based on Gothic sculptures.

Lobby
Lobbies, the venues for political discussions, are to be found along corridors beneath the stained-glass windows.

Dome
The ceiling of the 96-m (315-ft) high dome is covered in an intricate design of Neo-Gothic gilding combined with heraldic decoration.

VISITORS' CHECKLIST

Kossuth Lajos tér. **Map** 1 C3/4. **Tel** (1) 441 49 04. 🚊 2, 2A. Ⓜ Kossuth tér. 🚌 70, 78. 🏛 *English* 10am, noon, 2pm daily. 🎫 non-EU. 🔌 🖥 www.parlament.hu

Tapestry Hall
This room, on the Danube side of the Domed Hall, has a tapestry depicting Prince Árpád, with seven Magyar leaders under his command, as he signs a peace treaty and takes an oath.

North wing

Old Upper House Hall
This vast hall is virtually a mirror image of the Deputy Council Chamber. Both halls have public galleries running around a horseshoe-shaped interior.

Tickets can be bought at gate 10

The Royal Insignia, excluding the Coronation Mantle (*see p98*), are kept in the Domed Hall.

The main entrance on Kossuth Lajos tér

Main Staircase
The best contemporary artists were invited to decorate the interior. The sumptuous main staircase features ceiling frescoes by Károly Lotz and sculptures by György Kiss.

STAR FEATURES

★ Deputy Council Chamber

★ Domed Hall

The magnificent façade of the
Ethnographical Museum

Ethnographical Museum **❷**

Néprajzi Múzeum

Kossuth Lajos tér 12. **Map** 2 D3.
Tel (1) 473 24 42. 🚎 2, 70.
Ⓜ Kossuth Lajos tér. 🕙 10am–6pm
Tue–Sun. 🎫
📷 www.neprajz.hu

This building, designed by
Alajos Hauszmann and con-
structed between 1893 and
1896, was built as the Palace
of Justice and, until 1945,
served as the Supreme Court.

The building's design links
elements of Renaissance,
Baroque and Classicism.
The façade is dominated by
a vast portico crowned by
two towers. A gable features
the figure of the Roman goddess of justice in a chariot
drawn by three horses, created
by Károly Senyei. The grand
hall inside the main entrance
boasts a marvellous staircase
and frescoes by Károly Lotz.

The building was first used
as a museum in 1957, housing
the Hungarian National Gallery
(see pp58–9), which was later
transferred to the Royal Palace.
The Ethnographical Museum
has been here since 1973.

The museum's collection
was established in 1872, in
the Department of Ethno-
graphy at the Hungarian
National Museum *(see pp98–9)*.
There are now around 170,000
exhibits, although most are
not on display. The collection
includes artifacts reflecting the
rural folk culture of Hungary

from the prehistoric era to the
20th century. A map from
1909 shows the settlement of
the various groups who came
to be included in Hungary.
Ethnic items relating to these
communities, as well as
primitive objects of the
peoples of North and South
America, Africa, Asia and
Australia, can also be seen.

The museum also has two
very informative permanent
displays entitled Traditional
Culture of the Hungarian
Nation and From Primeval
Communities to Civilization.

Ministry of Agriculture **❸**

Földművelésügyi
Minisztérium

Kossuth Lajos tér 11. **Map** 2 D4.
Ⓜ Kossuth Lajos tér.

On the southeast side of
Kossuth Square is a huge
building, bordered by streets
on all four sides, which was
built for the Ministry of Agriculture by Gyula Bukovics at
the end of the 19th century.

The façade is designed
in a typical late-Historicist
style, drawing heavily on Neo-
Classical motifs. The columns
of the colonnade are echoed
in the well-proportioned pedi-
mented windows above.

On the wall to the right of
the building two commemorative plaques can be seen. The
first is dedicated to the com-
manding officer of the Polish
Legion, who was also a hero
of the 1848–9 uprising *(see
pp38–9)*. Brigadier Woroniecki,
who was renowned for his
bravery, was shot down on
this spot by the Austrians in
1849. The second plaque
honours Endre Ságvári,

a Hungarian hero of the
resistance movement, who
died when fighting the
Fascists in 1944.

The two sculptures in front
of the building are by Árpád
Somogyi. The *Reaper Lad*
dates from 1956 and the
Female Agronomist from 1954.

Liberty Square **❹**

Szabadság tér

Map 2 D4. Ⓜ Kossuth Lajos tér,
Arany János utca.

After the demolition of the
Neugebäude Barracks in 1886,
Liberty Square was laid out in
their place. The barracks, built
for the Austrian troops, once
dominated the southern part
of Lipótváros (Leopold Town).
It was here that Hungary's first
independent prime minister,
Count Lajos Batthyány, was
executed on 6 October 1849.
Since 1926, an eternal flame
has been burning at the corner
of Aulich utca, Hold utca and
Báthory utca to honour all who
were executed.

Two impressive buildings by
Ignác Alpár stand on opposite
sides of the square. The former
Stock Exchange, now the
Hungarian TV headquarters
(Magyar Televízió székháza),
dates from 1905 and shows
the influence of the Secession
style. The Hungarian National
Bank (Magyar Nemzeti Bank),
also from 1905, is decorated
in Historicist styles. An
obelisk by Károly Antal at the
northern end of the square
commemorates the Red Army
soldiers who died during the
siege of Budapest in 1944–5.
A second statue honours US
General Harry Hill Bandholtz,
who foiled the looting of the
Hungarian National Museum.

Bas-reliefs on the former Stock Exchange in Liberty Square

Secession Architecture

Visitors to Budapest are often impressed by its wonderful late 19th- and early 20th-century buildings. The majority of these are found in central Pest and around the Városliget district *(see pp106–7)*; Buda was already developed at this stage and so boasts few examples. The Secession Movement started among groups of avant-garde artists in Paris and Vienna, from where the term Secession comes. In Budapest, the Secessionist style was also the inspiration for what would develop into the Hungarian National Style. Secessionist architecture is characterized by decorative forms, glazed ceramics and the artistic implementation of modern technical solutions.

Ödön Lechner (1845–1914), *Hungary's most influential Secessionist architect, combined modern functionalism and characteristically decorative forms.*

The former Post Savings Bank *has a splendid main staircase designed by Ödön Lechner. It is embellished by fine balusters, spherical lamps and decorative window frames.*

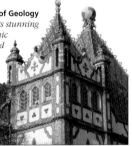

The Institute of Geology *is characterized by its stunning blue Zsolnay ceramic roof tiles. Designed by Ödön Lechner, the building dates from 1898–9. The central pitched roof is topped by three human figures bent under the weight of a large globe.*

This vase by István Sovának *stands in the Museum of Applied Arts. Its plain shape and Oriental flower motif hint at the many Eastern elements that crept into later Secessionist works of art.*

Finely crafted peacocks, *a classic Secession motif, adorn the wrought-iron gates of Gresham Palace. This former office block, now a luxury hotel (see p263), was built by Zsigmond Quittner in 1905–7.*

This window at the Hungarian National Bank *was created by Miksa Róth in 1905. Róth (1865–1944) was Hungary's leading exponent of stained-glass windows. His windows also adorn Budapest's Parliament.*

Reinforced concrete, steel and glass *were often used together to create large, light interiors. The foyer of the Gellért Hotel and Baths Complex is a perfect example of this technique.*

Monument to Ferenc Deák, dating from 1887, in Roosevelt Square

Roosevelt Square ❺
Roosevelt tér

Map 1 C5. 🚊 16. 🚌 2.

Roosevelt Square was known by several different names – Franz Joseph Square and Unloading Square among others – but it received its current title in 1947. It leads into the Pest side of the **Chain Bridge**, which was designed by Englishman William Tierney Clark and built by the Scot, Adam Clark in 1839–49. It was the city's first permanent Danube bridge and a major feat of engineering.

At the beginning of the 20th century the square was lined with hotels, the Diana Baths and the Lloyd Palace designed by József Hild. The only building from the previous century still standing today is the Hungarian Academy of Sciences. All other buildings were demolished and replaced by the Gresham Palace and the Bank of Hungary, on the corner of József Attila utca.

There is a statue to Baron József Eötvös (1813–71), a reformer of public education, in front of the InterContinental Budapest. In the centre of the square are monuments to two politicians with quite different ideologies: Count István Széchenyi (1791–1860), the leading social and political reformer of his age and initiator of the Chain Bridge, and Ferenc Deák (1803–76), who was instrumental in the Compromise of 1867, which led to the Dual Monachy *(see p39)*.

Gresham Palace ❻
Gresham palota

Roosevelt tér 5–7. **Map** 2 D5. **Tel** *(1)* 268 60 00. 🚊 16. 🚌 2. **www**.fourseasons.com/budapest

This Secession palace aroused both controversy and praise from the moment it was built. One of Budapest's most distinctive pieces of architecture, it was commissioned by the London-based Gresham Life Assurance Company from Zsigmond Quittner and the brothers József and László Vágó, and completed in 1907.

The enormous edifice enjoys an imposing location directly opposite the Chain Bridge. The façade features classic Secession motifs *(see p83)*, such as curvilinear forms and organic themes. The ornately carved window surrounds appear as though they are projecting from the walls, blending seamlessly with the architecture. The bust by Ede Telcs, at the top of the façade, is of Sir Thomas Gresham. The founder of the Royal Exchange in London, he came up with Gresham's Law: "bad money drives out good".

On the ground floor of the palace there is a T-shaped arcade, covered by a multi-coloured glazed roof, which is occupied by shops and a restaurant. The entrance to the arcade is marked by a beautiful wrought-iron gate with peacock motifs. Still the original gate, it is widely regarded as one of the most

Bust of Sir Thomas Gresham on the façade of the Gresham Palace

splendid examples of design from the Secession era. Inside the building, the second floor of the Kossuth stairway has a stained-glass window by Miksa Róth, featuring a portrait of Lajos Kossuth *(see p78)*.

In 2004 the palace was restored and re-opened as a Four Seasons Hotel, the second in Central Europe and the first in Hungary. Visitors are welcome to admire its splendours.

Miklós Izsó's sculptures inside the Hungarian Academy of Sciences

Hungarian Academy of Sciences ❼
Magyar Tudományos Akadémia

Széchenyi István tér 9. **Map** 1 C5. **Tel** *(1)* 411 61 00. 🚊 16. **Academy and Collection of Art** ⬜ 11am–4pm Mon–Fri. 🌙 Jun–Aug. **www**.mta.hu

Built in 1862–4, this Neo-Renaissance building was designed by the architect Friedrich August Stüler.

Six statues, representing the disciplines of knowledge – law, history, mathematics, sciences, philosophy and linguistics – and the works of Emil Wolf and Miklós Izsó, adorn the façade. On the Danube side, allegories of poetry, astronomy and archaeology can be seen, while the building's corners have statues of renowned thinkers including Newton and Descartes. Inside, there is a library and the Academy's Collection of Art.

The Neo-Renaissance façade of the Drechsler Palace

St Stephen's Basilica **8**

Szent István bazilika

See pp86–7.

State Opera House **9**

Magyar Állami Operaház

See pp88–9.

Drechsler Palace **10**

Drechsler palota

Andrássy út 25. **Map** 2 E4/5.
M Opera.

Formerly the State Ballet Institute, the Drechsler Palace was originally built as Neo-Renaissance apartments for the Hungarian Railways Pension Fund in 1883. It was designed by Gyula Pártos and Ödön Lechner to harmonize with the façade of the State Opera House (see pp88–9), and is of great architectural importance to the area.

The palace's name derives from the Drechsler Café, which occupied the ground floor towards the end of the 19th and in the early 20th century.

Budapest Operetta Theatre **11**

Budapesti Operettszínház

Nagymező utca 17. **Map** 2 E4.
Tel (1) 472 20 30. M Oktogon.
4, 6, 70. **www**.operettszinhaz.hu

Budapest has long enjoyed a good reputation for musical entertainment, and its operetta scene is over 100 years old.

Operettas were first staged on this site in the Orfeum Theatre, designed in the Neo-Baroque style by the Viennese architects Fellner and Helmer, in 1898. In 1922, the US entrepreneur Ben Blumenthal redeveloped the building and opened the Capital Operetta Theatre, which then specialized in the genre. After 1936, this theatre became the only venue for operetta in Budapest.

The theatre presents light opera by international and Hungarian composers, such as Imre Kálmán, Ferenc Lehár and Pál Ábrahám.

Radisson Blu Béke Hotel **12**

Radisson Blu Béke Hotel

Teréz körút 43. **Map** 2 E3.
Tel (1) 889 39 00. M Oktogon.
www.danubiushotels.com/beke

This elegant, historic hotel was built in 1896 as an apartment building, and in 1912 was restyled by Béla Málnai as the Hotel Brittania. A mosaic of 16th-century general György Szondi was added to the façade at this time.

In 1978 the hotel was taken over by the Radisson group, which restored the rich interiors to their former splendour. Notable features are the fine stained-glass windows and frescoes by Jenő Haranghy in the Szondi Lugas Restaurant, which illustrate the works of Richard Wagner. The Romeo and Juliet Conference Room and the Shakespeare Restaurant are named after the murals that decorate them. The Zsolnay Café serves cake and coffee on porcelain from the Pécs factory (see pp186–9).

Entrance to the Budapest Operetta Theatre on Nagymező utca

St Stephen's Basilica ❽

St István's coronation

Dedicated to St Stephen, or István, the first Hungarian Christian king *(see p61)*, this church was designed by József Hild in the Neo-Classical style, using a Greek cross floor plan. Construction began in 1851 and was taken over in 1867 by Miklós Ybl *(see p89)*, who added the Neo-Renaissance dome after the original one collapsed in 1868. József Kauser completed the church in 1905. It received the title of Basilica Minor in 1938, the 900th anniversary of St István's death.

St Matthew
St Matthew is one of the four Evangelists represented in the niches on the exterior of the dome. They are all the work of the sculptor Leó Feszler.

Dome
Reaching 96 m (315 ft), the dome is visible from all over Budapest.

Observation point

Tower
A bell, weighing 9,144 kg (9 tons) is housed in this tower. It was funded by German Catholics to compensate for the original bell, which was looted by the Nazis in 1944.

Main Portal
The massive door is decorated with carvings depicting the heads of the 12 Apostles.

Mosaics
The dome is decorated with mosaics designed by Károly Lotz.

VISITORS' CHECKLIST

Szent István tér. **Map** 2 D5.
Tel *(1) 338 21 51.* Ⓜ *Deák Ferenc tér.* **Church** ⬤ *9am–5pm Mon–Fri, 9am–1pm Sat, 1–5pm Sun.* 🎫 ♿ ✝

★ Main Altar
In the centre of the altar there is a marble statue of St István by Alajos Stróbl. Scenes from the king's life are depicted behind the altar.

★ Holy Right Hand
Hungary's most unusual relic is the mummified forearm of St István. It is kept in the Chapel of the Holy Right Hand.

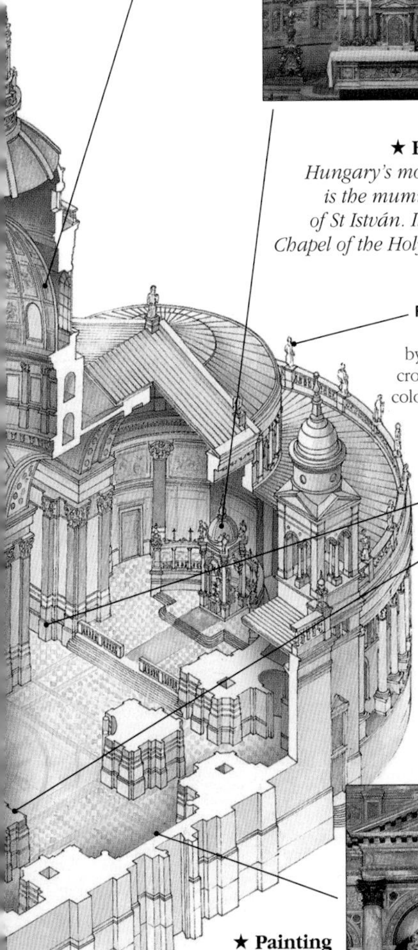

Figures of the 12 Apostles, by Leó Feszler, crown the outer colonnade at the back of the church.

St Gellért and St Emericus
This portrayal of St Gellért and his pupil, St Emericus, is the work of Alajos Stróbl.

★ Painting by Gyula Benczúr
This image shows King István, left without an heir, dedicating Hungary to the Virgin Mary, who became *Patrona Hungariae, the country's patron.*

STAR FEATURES

- ★ Holy Right Hand
- ★ Main Altar
- ★ Painting by Gyula Benczúr

State Opera House ❾

Decorative lamp with putti

Opened in September 1884, the State Opera House in Budapest was built to rival those of Paris, Vienna and Dresden. Its beautiful architecture and interiors were the life's work of the great Hungarian architect, Miklós Ybl. The interior contains ornamentation by Hungarian artists, including Alajos Strobl and Károly Lotz. During its lifetime, the State Opera House has seen some influential music directors, including Ferenc Erkel, composer of the Hungarian opera *Bánk Bán*, Gustav Mahler and Otto Klemperer.

Façade
A musical theme underlies the decoration of the symmetrical façade. In niches on either side of the main entrance there are figures of two of Hungary's most prominent composers, Ferenc Erkel and Ferenc Liszt (Franz Liszt). Both were sculpted by Alajos Stróbl.

Murals
The vaulted ceiling of the foyer is covered in magnificent murals by Bertalan Székely and Mór Than. They depict the nine Muses.

★ Foyer
With its marble columns, gilded vaulted ceiling, murals and chandeliers, the foyer gives the State Opera House a feeling of opulence and grandeur.

Main entrance
Wrought-iron lamps illuminate the wide stone staircase and the main entrance.

★ Main Staircase
Going to the opera was a great social occasion in the 19th century. A vast, sweeping staircase was an important element of the opera house as it allowed ladies to show off their new gowns.

Chandelier

The main hall is decorated with a bronze chandelier that weighs 3,050 kg (3 tons). It illuminates a magnificent fresco by Károly Lotz of the Greek gods on Olympus.

VISITORS' CHECKLIST

Andrássy út 22. **Map** 2 E4.
Tel (1) 332 81 97 or 353 01 70
(box office). ⓂOpera. 🚌 4, 70.
🚊 4, 5, 6. 🕙 ⊘ ♿ 🚻 🎁 📷
3pm & 4pm daily. **www**.opera.hu

Central Stage

This proscenium arch stage employed the most modern technology of the time. It featured a revolving stage and metal hydraulic machinery.

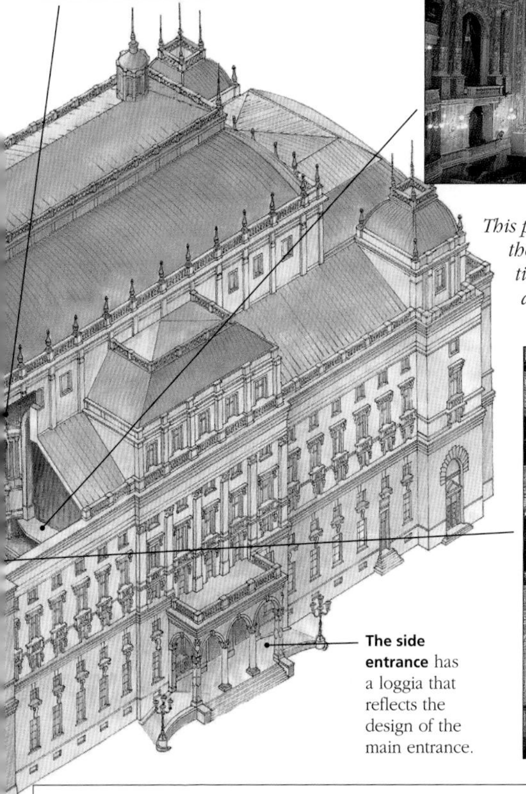

The side entrance has a loggia that reflects the design of the main entrance.

★ Royal Box

Located centrally in the three-storey circle, the royal box is decorated with sculptures symbolizing the four operatic voices – soprano, alto, tenor and bass.

MIKLÓS YBL (1814–91)

The most prominent Hungarian architect of the second half of the 19th century, Miklós Ybl had an enormous influence on the development of Budapest. He was a practitioner of Historicism, and tended to use Neo-Renaissance forms. The State Opera House and the dome of St Stephen's Basilica are examples of his work. Ybl also built apartment buildings and palaces for the aristocracy in this style. A statue of the architect stands on the western bank of the Danube, in Miklós Ybl Square.

Bust of Miklós Ybl

STAR FEATURES

★ Foyer

★ Main Staircase

★ Royal Box

CENTRAL PEST

At the end of the 17th century much of Pest was in ruins and few residents remained. Within the next decades, however, new residential districts were established – today's mid-town suburbs. In the 19th century, redevelopment schemes introduced grand houses and apartment blocks, some

Bas-relief on the façade of the City Council Chamber

with shops and cafés, as well as secular and municipal buildings. Perhaps the most prominent example of this work is the Hungarian National Museum. At this time Pest surpassed Buda as a centre for trade and industry. This was partly due to the Jewish community, who actively helped develop the area.

SIGHTS AT A GLANCE

Museums

House of Terror Museum ⑱
Hungarian National Museum pp98–9 ⑫
Museum of Applied Arts ⑪

Historic Buildings and Monuments

City Council Chamber ⑧
Ervin Szabó Library ⑩
Ferenc Liszt Music Academy ⑯
Klotild Palaces ⑦
New Theatre ⑰
New York Palace ⑮
Pest County Hall ④
Turkish Bank ③

Churches and Synagogues

Great Synagogue ⑬
Inner City Parish Church ⑥
University Church ⑨

Streets and Squares

Jewish Quarter ⑭
Mihály Vörösmarty Square ②
Váci Street ⑤
Vigadó Square ①

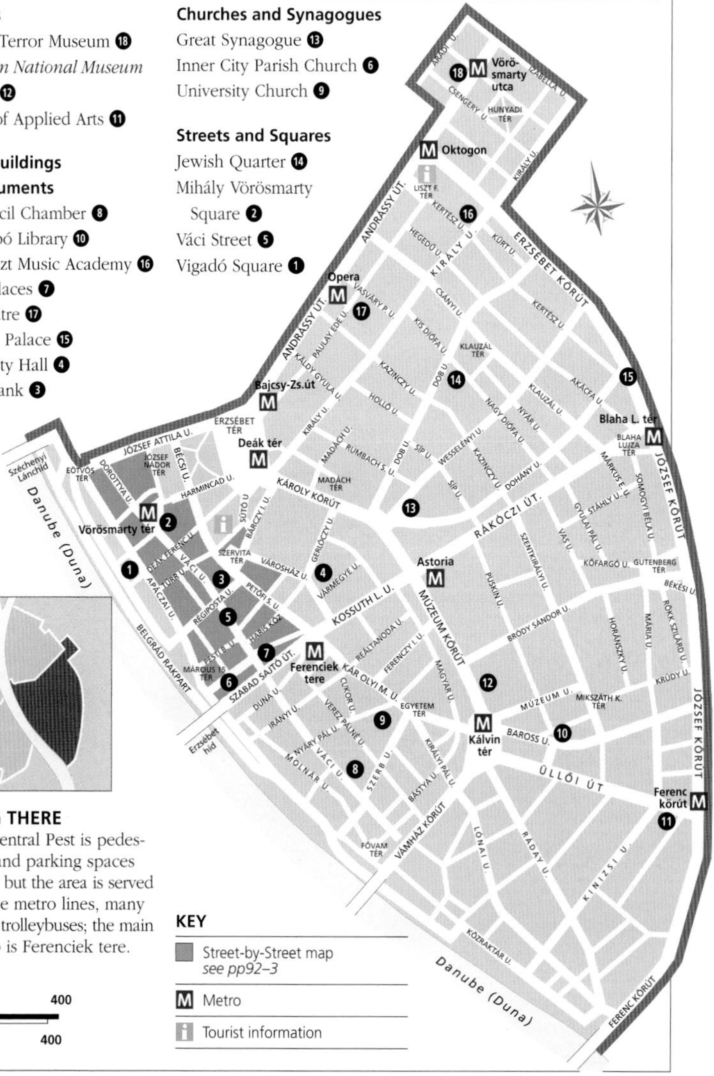

GETTING THERE

Much of central Pest is pedestrianized and parking spaces are scarce, but the area is served by all three metro lines, many buses and trolleybuses; the main traffic hub is Ferenciek tere.

0 metres   400
0 yards   400

KEY

Street-by-Street map *see pp92–3*

Ⓜ Metro

ℹ Tourist information

◁ **Statue of the Danaides, condemned to carry water to a leaking barrel, in Szomory Dezső tér**

Street-by-Street: Around Váci Street

The northern section of Váci Street has been Budapest's
fashionable area for walking, meeting in cafés and
shopping in elegant boutiques since the early 19th
century. Its attractive promenade is an enjoyable place
for a stroll in the evening, when it is stylishly illuminated.

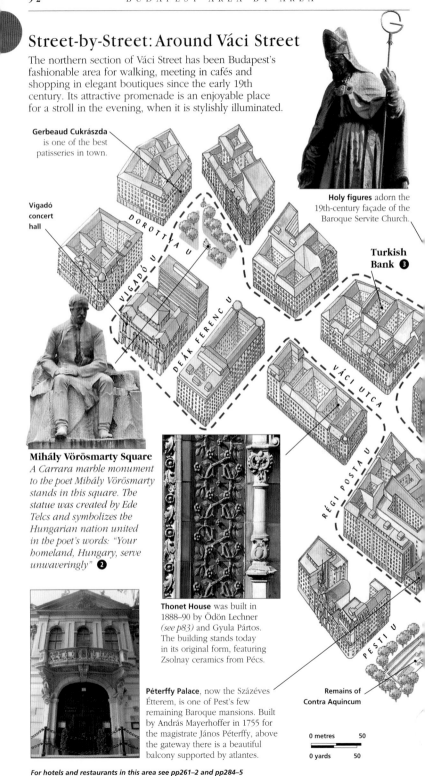

Gerbeaud Cukrászda
is one of the best
patisseries in town.

Vigadó concert hall

Holy figures adorn the
19th-century façade of the
Baroque Servite Church.

Turkish Bank ❸

Mihály Vörösmarty Square
*A Carrara marble monument
to the poet Mihály Vörösmarty
stands in this square. The
statue was created by Ede
Telcs and symbolizes the
Hungarian nation united
in the poet's words: "Your
homeland, Hungary, serve
unwaveringly"* ❷

Thonet House was built in
1888–90 by Ödön Lechner
(see p83) and Gyula Pártos.
The building stands today
in its original form, featuring
Zsolnay ceramics from Pécs.

Péterffy Palace, now the Százéves
Étterem, is one of Pest's few
remaining Baroque mansions. Built
by András Mayerhoffer in 1755 for
the magistrate János Péterffy, above
the gateway there is a beautiful
balcony supported by atlantes.

**Remains of
Contra Aquincum**

0 metres   50

0 yards   50

LOCATOR MAP
See Street Finder map 4

★ **Váci Street**
Budapest's most elegant promenade and shopping area is lined with fashion boutiques, cafés, fountains and statues. Off the street there are old courtyards and shopping arcades **5**

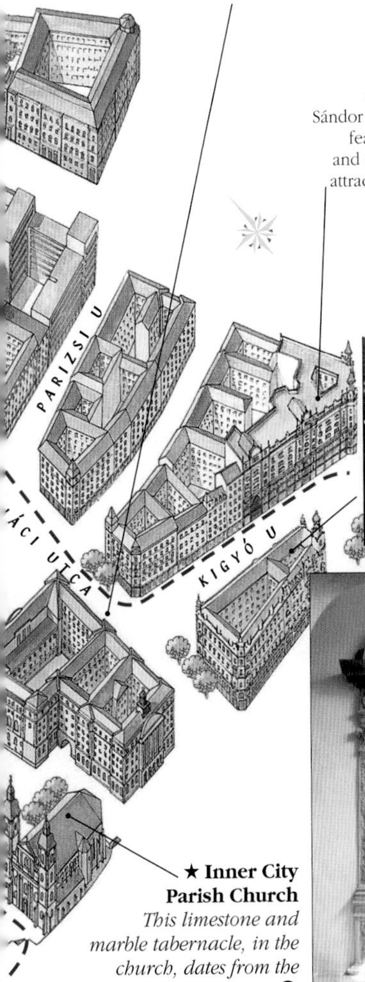

Párizsi Udvar
is found on the corner of Kígyó utca and Petőfi Sándor utca. The arcade, which features shops, bookshops and a café, is decorated with attractive wrought-iron work.

★ **Klotild Palaces**
These beautifully decorated twin buildings together form a magnificent gateway to the Elizabeth Bridge **7**

KEY

— — — Suggested route

★ **Inner City Parish Church**
This limestone and marble tabernacle, in the church, dates from the early 16th century **6**

STAR SIGHTS

★ Inner City Parish Church

★ Klotild Palaces

★ Váci Street

Inside the elegant Gerbeaud patisserie, on Mihály Vörösmarty Square

Vigadó Square ❶
Vigadó tér

Map 4 D1. 2.

The Vigadó concert hall dominates the square with its mix of eclectic forms. Built to designs by Frigyes Feszl from 1859 to 1864, it replaces a predecessor destroyed by fire during the uprising of 1848–9 (*see pp38–9*). The façade has arched windows and includes features such as folk motifs, dancers on columns and busts of former monarchs, rulers and other Hungarian personalities. An old Hungarian coat of arms is also visible in the centre.

The Budapest Marriott Hotel, located on one side of the square, was designed by József Finta in 1969. It was one of the first modern hotels to be built in Budapest.

On the Danube promenade is a statue of a childlike figure sitting on the railings: *Little Princess*, by László Marton. Vigadó Square also has numerous craft stalls, cafés and restaurants.

Mihály Vörösmarty Square ❷
Vörösmarty Mihály tér

Map 2 D5. Ⓜ *Vörösmarty tér.*

In the middle of this splendid pedestrianized square stands a monument depicting the poet Mihály Vörösmarty

(1800–55), after whom the square is named. Unveiled in 1908, it is the work of Ede Telcs. Behind the monument, on the eastern side of the square, is the Luxus department store. It is located in a three-storey corner building dating from 1911 and designed by Kálmán Giergl and Flóris Korb.

The main attraction on the northern side of the square is the renowned patisserie, Gerbeaud Cukrászda, first opened by Henrik Kugler in 1858. It was taken over by his business partner, the Swiss *pâtissier* Emil Gerbeaud, who was responsible for the richly decorated interior which survives to this

day. It features fine woods, marble and bronze; ceiling stucco-work in Louis XIV-style; chandeliers, lamps and Secession-style chairs brought from Paris. A tempting selection of frothy coffee, cakes, pastries and desserts is on offer. In summer, refreshments can be taken on a terrace overlooking the square.

Turkish Bank ❸
Török Bankház

Szervita tér 3. **Map** 4 D1.
Ⓜ *Deák Ferenc tér.*

Dating from 1906 and designed by Henrik Böhm and Ármin Hegedűs, the building that formerly housed the Turkish Bank is a wonderful example of the Secession style.

Modern construction methods were used to create the glass façade, which is set in reinforced concrete. Above the fenestration, in the gable, is a magnificent colourful mosaic created by Miksa Róth. Entitled *Glory to Hungary*, it depicts the country paying homage to the Virgin Mary, its patron saint, *Patrona Hungariae (see p87)*. Angels and shepherds surround the Virgin, along with figures of Hungarian political heroes, such as Prince Ferenc Rákóczi (*see pp38–9*), István Széchenyi (*see pp40–41*) and Lajos Kossuth (*see p78*).

Glory to Hungary, the mosaic on the façade of the Turkish Bank

Pest County Hall ❹
Pest Megyei Önkormányzat

Városház utca 7. **Map** 4 E1. *Tel (1)
485 68 00 or 485 68 26.* Ⓜ *Ferenciek
tere.* ◯ *8am–6pm Mon–Fri.*

Built in several stages, this is
one of Pest's most beautiful,
monumental Neo-Classical
civic buildings. It was erected
during the 19th century, as
part of the plan for the city
drawn up by the Embellish-
ment Commission.

A seat of the Council of Pest
has existed on this site since
the late 17th century. By 1811,
the building comprised two
conference halls, a prison and
a prison chapel. Between 1829
and 1832, a wing designed by
József Hofrichter was added
on Semmelweis utca.

In another development
phase, in 1838–42, Mátyás
Zitterbarth Jr completed the
impressive façade, which
overlooks Városház utca. It
features a portico with six
Corinthian columns supporting a prominent tympanum.

County Hall was rebuilt
and enlarged after destruction
during World War II. Three
internal courtyards were added.
The first of these is surrounded
by cloisters; summer concerts
are often held here.

In the small adjoining street,
Kamermayer Károly tér, stands
an aluminium monument,
designed in 1942 by Béla
Szabados, to Budapest's first
mayor, Károly Kamermayer
(1829–97), who took office
in 1873 after the unification
of Óbuda, Buda and Pest.

Váci Street ❺
Váci utca

Map 4 D1–E2. Ⓜ *Ferenciek tere.*

Once two separate streets,
which were joined at the
beginning of the 18th century,
the two ends of Váci Street
still have distinct characters.
Today, part of the southern
section is open to traffic, but
the northern end is pedestrianized and has long been a
popular commercial centre.
Most of the buildings lining
the street date from the 19th
and early 20th centuries. More

**Thonet House, with Zsolnay tile
decoration, at No. 11 Váci Street**

recently, however, modern
department stores, banks and
shopping arcades have sprung
up along the street among the
older original buildings.

Philantia, a Secession-style
florist's shop
opened in 1905,
now occupies
part of the Neo-
Classical block
at No. 9, built in
1840 by József
Hild. No. 9 also
houses the Pest
Theatre, where
classic plays by
Anton Chekhov,
among others, are
staged. The building was
once occupied by the "Inn of
the Seven Electors", which
had a large ballroom and
concert hall. It was here that
a 12-year-old Ferenc (Franz)
Liszt performed in 1823.

**Crest of Pest in Inner
City Parish Church**

Thonet House, at No. 11, is
most notable for the Zsolnay
tiles from Pécs that adorn its
façade. No. 13 is the oldest
building on Váci Street and
was built in 1805. In contrast,
the post-modern Fontana
department store at No. 16
was built in 1984. Outside
there is a bronze fountain
with a figure of the Greek
god Hermes, dating from the
mid-19th century.

The Nádor Hotel once
stood at No. 20 and featured
a statue of Archduke Palatine
József in front of the entrance.
Today the Taverna Hotel,
designed by József Finta and
opened in 1987, stands here.
It has a popular coffee shop.

In a side street off Váci Street,
at No. 13 Régiposta utca,
stands a Modernist-style
building. An unusual sight in
Pest, this Bauhaus-influenced
building dates from 1937 and
is by Lajos Kozma.

Inner City Parish
Church ❻
Belvárosi Plébánia templom

Március 15 tér 2. **Map** 4 D1.
Tel *(1) 318 31 08.* Ⓜ *Ferenciek tere.*
◯ *9am–7pm daily.* ✝ *daily.*

The oldest building in Pest,
the church was first established during the reign of
St István, on the burial site of
the martyred St Gellért. In the
12th-century it was replaced
by a Romanesque church of
which a wall fragment remains
in the façade of the South
Tower. In the 14th-century
it became a large
Gothic construction,
and subsequently
a mosque; a small
Turkish prayer niche
can be seen beside
the altar. Damaged
by the Great Fire
of 1723, the church
was partly rebuilt
in the Baroque style
by György Paur in
1725–39. The interior
also contains Neo-Classical
elements by János Hild, as
well as some 20th-century
works. The main altar (1948)
is one such piece, replacing
the original. It was painted by
Károly Antal and Pál Molnár.

**The Baroque nave of the Inner City
Parish Church dating from the 1730s**

Klotild Palaces ❼
Klotild paloták

Szabadsajtó út. **Map** 4 D1.
Ⓜ Ferenciek tere.

Flanking Szabadsajtó utca, on the approach to the Elizabeth Bridge, stand two massive apartment blocks built in 1902. The buildings were commissioned by the daughter-in-law of Emperor Franz József, Archduchess Klotild.

The palaces were designed by Flóris Korb and Kálmán Giergl in the Historicist style, with elements of Rococo decoration. Once it was entirely rented apartments, now only the upper floors remain in residential use. The ground floor is occupied by shops, a café and the Budapest Gallery; the right wing of the palace houses the Buddha-Bar Hotel.

One of the twin Klotild Palaces, by the approach to Elizabeth Bridge

City Council Chamber ❽
Új Városháza

Váci utca 62–4. **Map** 4 E2. **Tel** (1) 235 17 00. Ⓜ Deák tér. 📷

This three-storey edifice was built between 1870–75 as offices for the newly unified city of Budapest. Its architect, Imre Steindl, was also responsible for designing the Parliament *(see pp80–81)*.

The building is a mix of styles. The exterior is a Neo-Renaissance design in brick, with grotesques between the windows, while the interior features cast-iron Neo-Gothic

City Council Chamber decorative façade

motifs. The Great Debating Hall is decorated with mosaics designed by Károly Lotz.

Fashionable bars, restaurants and cafés, all assembled along a pedestrianized road, make the area around the Council Chamber a charming part of the city. There are some antiquarian bookshops and galleries located here, as well as fashion boutiques, and high-end designer shops.

University Church ❾
Egyetemi templom

Papnövelde utca 7. **Map** 4 E1/2. **Tel** (1) 318 05 55. Ⓜ Kálvin tér. 🕐 7am–7pm daily.

This single-aisle church is considered one of the most impressive Baroque churches in the city. It was built for the Pauline Order in 1725–42, and was probably designed by András Mayerhoffer. The tower was added in 1771. The Pauline Order, founded in 1263 by Canon Euzebiusz, was the only religious order to be founded in Hungary.

The magnificent exterior features a tympanum and a row of pilasters that divide the façade. Figures of St Paul and St Anthony flank the emblem of the Pauline Order, which crowns the exterior. The carved-wood interior of

the main vestibule is also worth seeing.

Inside the church a row of side chapels stand behind unusual marble pilasters. In 1776 Johann Bergl painted the vaulted ceiling with frescoes depicting scenes from the life of Mary. Sadly, these frescoes are now in poor condition. The main altar dates from 1746, and the carved statues behind it are the work of József Hebenstreit. Above it is a copy of the painting *The Black Madonna of Czestochowa*, which is thought to date from 1720. Much of the Baroque interior is the work of the Pauline monks, for example the balustrade of the organ loft, the confessionals and the carved pulpit on the right.

The church – which is the property of Budapest University's Law Faculty – today often hosts concerts of choral and classical music, to raise funds for a massive programme of renovation.

Magnificent sculptures decorating the pulpit in the University Church

Spiral staircase in one of the rooms of the Ervin Szabó Library

Ervin Szabó Library **⑩**
Fővárosi Szabó Ervin Könyvtár

Reviczky utca 1. **Map** 4 F2. **Tel** (1) 411 50 00. Ⓜ Kálvin tér. ◷ 10am–8pm Mon–Fri, 10am–4pm Sat.

In 1887, the wealthy industrialist Wenckheim family commissioned the architect Artur Meining to build a palace in the Neo-Baroque and Rococo style. The result was Wenckheim Palace, regarded as one of the most beautiful palaces in Budapest.

In 1926, the city council acquired the palace and converted it into a public lending library, which focuses on the city itself and social sciences.

It was named the Ervin Szabó Library after the politician and social reformer Ervin Szabó (1877–1918), who was the library's first director. The library has over a hundred branches throughout Budapest and houses some three million books.

Beautifully renovated, the library boasts one of the most elegant reading rooms anywhere. It features glorious stucco decoration with gold tracery, enormous chandeliers and finely worked wooden staircases. Also worth particular attention are the richly gilded salons on the first floor and the dome above an oval panel of reliefs. Outside, the magnificent wrought-iron gates, dating from 1897, are the work of Gyula Jungfer.

Museum of Applied Arts **⑪**
Iparművészeti Múzeum

Üllői út 33–7. **Map** 4 F2.
Tel (1) 456 51 07. Ⓜ Ferenc körút.
◷ 10am–6pm Tue–Sun. 🎫 📷 📷
www.imm.hu

The Museum of Applied Arts was opened in 1896 by Emperor Franz Joseph as part of the Millennium Celebrations. The collection is housed not within a Neo-Classical building, but within an outstanding Secession building designed by Gyula Pártos and Ödön Lechner. The exterior incorporated elements inspired by the Orient as well as the Zsolnay ceramics characteristic of Lechner's work. Damaged in 1945 and again in 1956, the building has been restored to its original magnificence.

The building is set around a glorious, arcaded courtyard, surrounded by cloisters and designed in an Indian-Oriental style. The museum, established in 1872, comprises many superb examples of arts and crafts workmanship.

Amphitrite and Triton pendant

Among the museum's permanent collections is furniture from the 14th to the 20th centuries, including the furnishings of entire historic buildings in Hungary, fine French pieces and Thonet

A 17th-century dress in the Museum of Applied Arts

bentwood furniture. The fine metalwork collection comprises watches, jewellery and other items made by foreign and Hungarian craftsmen. The large ceramics and glassware collection contains early Haban ware, Bohemian glass, as well as glass-making in Hungary. In the textiles section, superb European silks, including many from the 13th and 14th centuries, can be seen. It also traces the history of Hungarian lacemaking.

The museum holds regular temporary exhibitions. The first-floor library, also dating from 1872, contains around 50,000 books, making it one of the largest in Hungary.

The Oriental-style inner courtyard of the Museum of Applied Arts

Hungarian National Museum ⑫

Seal from Esztergom

The Hungarian National Museum is the country's richest source of art and artifacts relating to its own turbulent history. Founded in 1802, the museum owes its existence to Count Ferenc Széchényi, who bequeathed his collection of coins, books and documents to the nation. The museum's constantly expanding collection of art and documents is exhibited in an impressive Neo-Classical edifice built by Mihály Pollack.

Placing the Cornerstone (1864)
This painting by Miklós Barabás shows the ceremony that marked the beginning of construction of the Chain Bridge in 1842.

Silk Corset of Queen Elisabeth
This black silk corset was worn by Queen Elisabeth of Hungary and still bears the mark of the stab wound that killed her in Geneva on 10 September 1898.

First floor

★ **Funeral Crown**
This magnificent 13th-century golden crown was found in the ruins of the Dominican Church and Convent on Margaret Island in the Danube (see pp108–9).

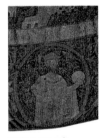

★ **Coronation Mantle**
This textile masterpiece, made of Byzantine silk, was donated to the church in Székesfehérvár by St István in 1031. It became the Coronation Mantle in the 12th century.

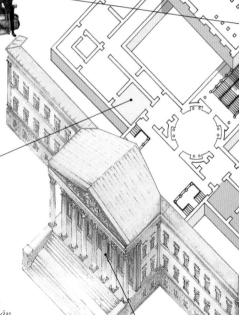

Main entrance

Right Hand of Stalin
This hand is all that remains of the 8 m (26 ft) high statue of Stalin that stood in the Városliget in Budapest. A symbol of the Communist regime, the statue was destroyed in the Hungarian Revolution of 1956.

VISITORS' CHECKLIST

Múzeum körút 14–16. **Map** 4 E1. **Tel** *(1) 338 21 22 (327 77 73 for guided tours in English).*
🚌 47, 49. Ⓜ Kálvin tér, Astória.
🚋 9, 15. ⏱ 10am–6pm Tue–Sun.
📷 ♿ 🛒 🎁 www.hnm.hu

KEY

- ☐ Coronation Mantle
- ▨ Archaeological exhibition
- ▦ 11th- to 17th-century exhibition
- ▤ 18th- to 19th-century exhibition
- ▥ 20th-century exhibition

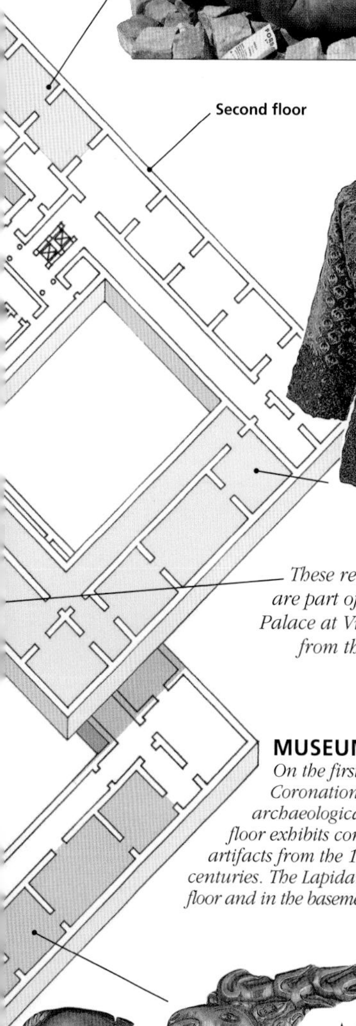

Second floor

Pelisse
This short jacket, dating from around 1620, is typical of Hungarian national costume. It belonged to Gábor Bethlen, a prince of Transylvania.

Gothic Well
These reconstructed fragments are part of a well from the Royal Palace at Visegrád. The well dates from the 14th-century rule of the Angevin dynasty.

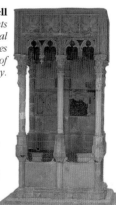

MUSEUM GUIDE
On the first floor is the Coronation Mantle and the archaeological exhibition. Second-floor exhibits comprise Hungarian artifacts from the 11th to the 20th centuries. The Lapidaries are on the ground floor and in the basement.

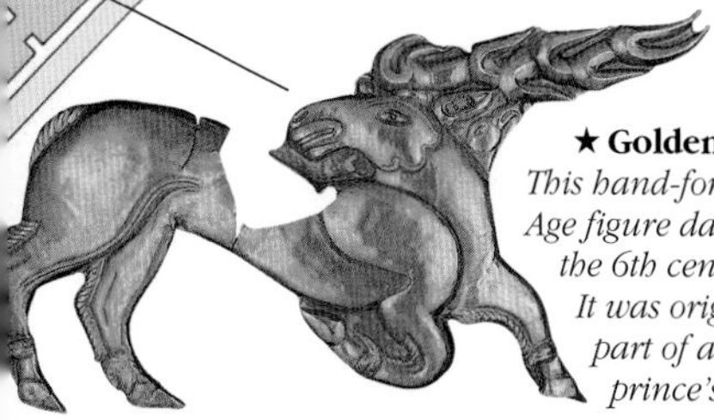

★ Golden Stag
This hand-forged Iron-Age figure dates from the 6th century BC. It was originally part of a Scythian prince's shield.

STAR EXHIBITS

- ★ Coronation Mantle
- ★ Funeral Crown
- ★ Golden Stag

Great Synagogue ⑬
Zsinagóga

Dohány utca 2. **Map** 4 E1.
Tel (1) 342 89 49. Ⓜ *Astoria.* 🚊
74. **Jewish Museum** ☐ *Mar–Oct:
10am–6pm Mon–Thu & Sun, 10am–
4pm Fri; Nov–Feb: 10am–4pm Mon–
Thu & Sun, 10am–3pm Fri.* 📷 ✓

The Great Synagogue is the
largest in Europe. Built in a
Byzantine-Moorish style by
the Viennese architect Ludwig
Förster in 1854–9, it has three
naves and, according to
orthodox tradition, separate
galleries for women. Together
the naves and galleries can
accommodate up to 3,000
worshippers. Some features,
such as the position of the
reading platform, reflect elements of Judaic reform. The
interior has valuable decorative fittings, particularly those
on the Ark of the Law, by
Frigyes Feszl. In 1931, a

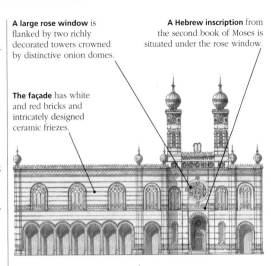

A large rose window is
flanked by two richly
decorated towers crowned
by distinctive onion domes.

A Hebrew inscription from
the second book of Moses is
situated under the rose window.

The façade has white
and red bricks and
intricately designed
ceramic friezes.

museum was established, and
a vast collection of historical
relics, Judaic devotional items
and everyday objects, from
ancient Rome to the present

day, has been assembled. It
includes the book of Chevra
Kadisha from 1792. There is
also a haunting Holocaust
Memorial Room.

Jewish Quarter ⑭
Zsidó Negyed

Király utca, Rumbach Sebestyén utca,
Dohány utca & Akácfa utca. **Map** 2 E5
& 2 F5. Ⓜ *Deák Ferenc tér.*

Jews first came to Hungary in
the 13th century and settled
in Buda and Óbuda. In the
19th century, a larger Jewish
community was established
outside the Pest city boundary,
in a small area of Erzsébetváros.
    In 1251, King Béla IV gave
the Jews of Buda certain priv-
iliges, including freedom of
religion. The Jewish community became well integrated

HOLOCAUST MEMORIAL
Imre Varga's weeping willow sculpture was unveiled in 1991
in the rear courtyard of the Synagogue, in memory of the
600,000 Hungarian Jews killed by the Nazis in World War II.
It was part-funded by the late US-Hungarian actor Tony Curtis.

**Detail of the Orthodox Synagogue,
built in Byzantine-Moorish style**

into Hungarian society until,
in 1941, a series of anti-Semitic
laws was passed by the pro-
Nazi Admiral Horthy, and the
wearing of the Star of David
was made compulsory. In
1944, a ghetto was created in
the area around the Great
Synagogue and the deportation of thousands of Jews to
camps, including Auschwitz,
was implemented. After heavy
fighting between the Russian
and German armies, the Soviet
Red Army liberated the ghetto
on 18 January 1945. In total,
600,000 Hungarian Jews were

victims of the Holocaust. A
plaque on the Orthodox
Synagogue on Rumbach utca
commemorates the thousands
of Jews sent from Budapest.
    In the late 19th century, three
synagogues were built and
many Jewish shops and workshops were established. Kosher
businesses, such as the Hanna
Étterem in the courtyard of the
Orthodox Synagogue, and the
butcher at No. 41 Kazinczy
utca, were a common feature.
Shops, galleries and cafés are
now springing up, attracting
young locals and tourists.

Statue of Ferenc Liszt above the entrance to the Academy of Music

New York Palace
New York palota

Erzsébet körút 9–11. **Map** 2 F5.
Tel (1) 886 61 11. Blaha Lujza tér.
www.newyorkpalace.hu

Built in 1891–5 to a design by the architect Alajos Hausz-mann, the New York Palace was once the offices of an American insurance firm. Today it is a luxurious 5-star hotel. The building displays an eclectic mix of Neo-Baroque and Secession motifs. The decorative sculptures that animate the façade are the work of Károly Senyei.

On the ground floor is the renowned New York Café. Its walls are adorned with paintings by Gusztáv Mann-heimer and Károly Lotz. The beautiful, richly-gilded Neo-Baroque interior, with its grand chandeliers and marble pillars, was once the favourite haunt of literary and artistic circles, though today it tends to attract mainly tourists.

Ferenc Liszt Academy of Music
Liszt Ferenc Zeneművészeti Egyetem

Liszt Ferenc tér 8. **Map** 2 F4. **Tel** (1) 462 46 00. 4, 6 to Király utca. Closed for refurbishment at the time of going to press.

The academy is housed in a late Historicist palace, built in 1904–7 by Kálmán Giergl and Flóris Korb. Above the main entrance there is a statue of Ferenc (Franz) Liszt, by Alajos Stróbl. The six bas-reliefs above its base are by Ede Telcs, and depict the history of music.

The Secession interiors are intact. The *Fount of Youth* fresco, in the first-floor foyer, is by Aladár Körösfői-Kriesch, who was a member of the Gödöllő school. The academy has two auditoria: one featuring allegories of musical movements, the other, chamber music.

New Theatre
Új Színház

Paulay Ede utca 35. **Map** 2 E5.
Tel (1) 269 60 21. Opera.

Originally completed in 1909, this building has undergone many transformations. It was designed by Béla Lajta in the Secession style, and, as the home of the cabaret troupe Parisian Mulató, became a shrine to frivolity.

In 1921 the building was completely restyled by László Vágó, who turned it into a theatre. After World War II, the theatre gained a glass-and-steel façade, and a children's theatre company was based here.

Between 1988 and 1990 the building was returned to its original form, using Lajta's plans. Gilding, stained glass and marble once more adorn this unusual building. Today, Hungary's New Theatre is in residence here.

House of Terror Museum
Terror Háza Múzeum

Andrássy út 60. **Map** 2 F4.
Tel (1) 374 26 00. Vörösmarty utca. 4, 6 to Oktogon. 10am–6pm Tue–Sun. **www**.terrorhaza.hu

The museum records in graphic detail the grim events that took place here from 1936 – when the Arrow Cross (the Hungarian Nazi party) took over the building as its headquarters – until 1956, when it was turned into a club for Young Communists. Set over three floors the most chilling part of the museum is the basement, where the various types of prison cell have been recreated.

The House of Terror Museum, documenting tragic 20th-century events

FURTHER AFIELD

Many of Budapest's greatest treasures are out of the city centre. The city's Art Nouveau zoo is found in the beautiful Varósliget City Park. The vast Heroes' Square opposite has two outstanding art collections: the Museum of Fine Arts and the Műcsarnok Palace of Arts. East of here a new museum honours the victims of Hungary's Holocaust, while to the west Margaret Island makes for

Roman urn from Aquincum

a tranquil day out. North of Buda are the extensive ruins of the Roman city of Aquincum, founded around AD 100. To the west of the city, the beautiful Eagle Hill nature reserve and, further out, the wooded Buda Hills attract nature-lovers. Out to the east of Pest, the Jewish Cemetery is a reminder of the vibrant Jewish community in pre-war Hungary, and the Memento Park to the south is a surreal relic from Soviet days.

SIGHTS AT A GLANCE

Museums

Aquincum **8**
Budapest Holocaust Memorial
　Centre **10**
Museum of Fine Arts **2**
Műcsarnok Palace of Art **3**
Palace of Arts **11**

**Historic Buildings
and Monuments**

Memento Park **14**
Széchenyi Baths **6**
Vajdahunyad Castle **5**

Churches

St Anne's Church **1**

**Parks and Recreation
Areas**

Buda Hills **13**
Eagle Hill Nature Reserve **12**
Margaret Island **7**
Városliget City Park **4**

Cemeteries

Jewish Cemetery **9**

KEY

▨	City centre
▨	Greater Budapest
✈	Airport
🚉	Train station
▬	Motorway
▬	Main road
▭	Other road
—	Railway
---	Narrow-gauge line
+++	COG railway

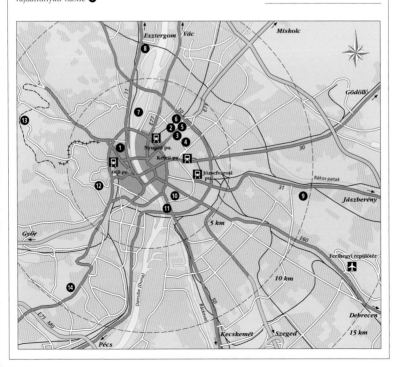

◁ **A peaceful setting in Margaret Island's landscaped Japanese Garden**

Street-by-Street: Around Heroes' Square

Heroes' Square is a relic of a proud era in Hungary's history – it was here that the Millennium Celebrations opened in 1896. A striking example of this national pride is the Millennium Monument. Its colonnades feature statues of renowned Hungarian leaders and politicians, and the grand central column is crowned by a figure of the Archangel Gabriel.

Árpád, leader of the Magyars

Vajdahunyad Castle was built in Városliget, or City Park, adjacent to the square. Probably the most flamboyant expression of the celebrations, it is composed of elements of the finest architectural works found throughout Hungary.

★ **Museum of Fine Arts**
This monumental museum building has an eight-pillared portico supporting a tympanum ❷

Entrance
to the zoo

Millennium Monument
Dominating Heroes' Square, this monument includes a figure of Rydwan, the god of war, by György Zala.

Műcsarnok Palace of Arts
The crest of Hungary decorates the façade of this building – the country's largest venue for artistic exhibitions ❸

Secession pavillon

| 0 metres | | 200 |
| 0 yards | | 200 |

THE HUNGARIAN MILLENNIUM CELEBRATIONS

The Millennium Celebrations in 1896 marked a high point in the development of Budapest and in the history of the Austro-Hungarian monarchy. The city underwent modernization on a scale unknown in Europe at that time. Hundreds of houses, palaces and civic buildings were constructed, gas lighting was introduced and continental Europe's first underground transport system was opened.

Archangel Gabriel

KEY

– – – Suggested route

★ Széchenyi Baths
This is the largest complex of spa baths in Europe. Its hot springs, discovered in 1876, bubble up from a depth of 970 m (3,180 ft) and are reputed to have considerable healing properties ❻

Városliget ❹

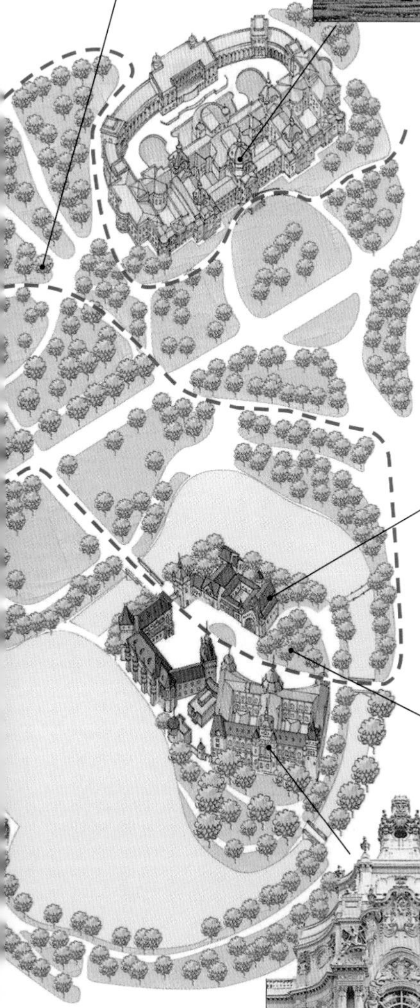

Ják Chapel
This chapel faithfully reproduces the portal of a Benedictine church, dating from 1214, which can be found in the area of Ják *(see p162)*, near the border with Austria. It is part of the Vajdahunyad Castle complex.

Statue of Anonymus
Completed in 1903 by Miklós Ligeti, this is one of Budapest's most famous monuments.

★ Vajdahunyad Castle
This Baroque section of the castle houses the Museum of Agriculture ❺

STAR SIGHTS

★ Museum of Fine Arts

★ Széchenyi Baths

★ Vajdahunyad Castle

St Anne's Church ❶
Szent Anna templom

Batthyány tér 7. **Map** 1 B4.
Tel (1) 201 34 04. Ⓜ Batthyány
tér. ◯ Only for services. ✝ daily.
Angelika Café ◯ 9am–12pm daily.

Budapest is home to many churches, but the twin-towered Baroque parish church of the Víziváros district is one of the finest. Begun in 1740 by Kristóf Hamon and completed after his death by Mátyás Nepauer, it was seriously damaged by an earthquake in 1763. The dissolution of the Jesuit order – which had commissioned it – further delayed completion. It remained unconsecrated until 1805.

The church's façade features Buda's coat of arms on the tympanum, set between the magnificent Baroque spires. Inside, the High Altar (1773) depicts Mary, as a child, with St Anne, her mother.

High Altar in St Anne's Church, one of Károly Bebo's finest works

Museum of Fine Arts ❷
Szépművészeti Múzeum

Dózsa György út 41. **Tel** (1) 469 71 00.
Ⓜ Hősök tere. 🚊 75, 79. 🚌 4, 20, 30, 105. ◯ 10am–5:30pm Tue–Sun.
🎧 ♿ 🎁 🖥 www.szepmuveszeti.hu

The origins of the Museum of Fine Arts' comprehensive collection date from 1870, when the state bought a magnificent collection of paintings from the aristocratic Esterházy family. The museum's collection

A magnificently decorated ceiling at the Museum of Fine Arts

was enriched by donations and acquisitions, and in 1906 it moved to its present location, a stunning Neo-Classical building with Italian Renaissance influences, designed by Fülöp Herzog and Albert Schickedanz. The tympanum crowning the portico is supported by eight Corinthian columns. It depicts the Battle of the Centaurs and Lapiths, and is copied from the Temple of Zeus at Olympia, Greece.

The museum's collection encompasses a wide range of art from antiquity to the 20th century. Among the exhibition of Egyptian artifacts, most of which were unearthed by Hungarian archaeologists during 19th century excavations, the collection of bronze figures from the New Kingdom of Ptolemy is the most fascinating. The collection of Greek vases is the highlight of the classical artifacts, along with the famous Grimani jug, which dates from the 5th century BC.

A small bronze figure by Leonardo da Vinci is the highlight of the sculpture gallery, while the rich collection of Dutch and Flemish art features the sublime *St John the Baptist's Sermon*, painted by Pieter Bruegel the Elder in 1566. Other collections of note include Italian and Spanish art with works by Raphael, El Greco and Goya, drawings and graphics with items by Dürer, and 19th- and 20th-century works by Pablo Picasso as well as gems from the French Impressionists.

Grimani jug, Museum of Fine Arts

Műcsarnok Palace of Art ❸
Műcsarnok

Dózsa György út 37. **Tel** (1) 460 7000.
Ⓜ Hősök tere. ◯ 10am–6pm Tue–Sun, noon–9pm Thu. 🎧 ♿ 🎁
www.mucsarnok.hu

Situated on the southern side of Heroes' Square, opposite the Museum of Fine Arts, is the largest exhibition space in all of Hungary. Temporary exhibitions of mainly contemporary painting and sculpture are held here.

Designed by Albert Schickedanz and Fülöp Herzog in 1895, the imposing Neo-Classical building is fronted by a vast six-columned portico. The mosaic, depicting St István as the patron saint of fine art, was added to the tympanum in 1938–41.

Behind the portico is a fresco by Lajos Deák-Ébner in three parts entitled *The Beginning of Sculpture*, *The Source of Arts* and *The Origins of Painting*.

Városliget ❹
Városliget

Városliget. Ⓜ Hősök tere, Széchenyi fürdő.

Városliget, or City Park, was once an area of marshland used as a royal hunting ground. Drained and planted during the reign of Maria Theresa, the park was designed and laid out in the English style in the late 19th century.

City Park was the centre for the 1896 Millennium Celebrations, when the Museum of Fine Arts, Vajdahunyad Castle and the Heroes' Square Monument were built.

Today, attractions include a lake – an ice rink in winter and a boating lake in summer – overlooked by a Secession Pavilion. The park is also home to the Széchenyi Baths, Budapest's zoo and Gundel Restaurant, which opened in 1910 and where the Gundel palacsinta, a pancake, was invented.

One of the outdoor pools at the beautiful Széchenyi Baths

Vajdahunyad Castle ❺

Vajdahunyadvár

Városliget. **Tel** (1) 363 19 73. Ⓜ Széchenyi fürdő. 🚋 70, 72, 75, 79. 🚌 4, 20, 30. **Museum of Agriculture Tel** (1) 363 11 17. ◻ Mid-Mar–mid-Oct: 10am–5pm Tue–Sun; mid-Oct–mid-Mar: 10am–4pm Tue–Fri, 10am–5pm Sat–Sun. 🎫 ♿ ✔ www.mmgm.hu

This fairytale-like building is located among the trees at the edge of the lake in Városliget. Not a genuine castle but a complex of buildings reflecting various architectural styles, it was designed by Ignác Alpár for the 1896 Millennium Celebrations (see p104).

Alpár's creation illustrated the history of architecture in Hungary. Originally intended as temporary exhibition pavilions, the castle proved so popular with the public that, between 1904 and 1906, it was rebuilt using brick to create a permanent structure.

The pavilions are grouped chronologically by style, with individual styles linked together

to give the impression of a single, cohesive design. Each of the pavilions uses authentic details copied from Hungary's most important historic buildings or is a looser interpretation of a style inspired by a specific architect of that period. The complex reflects more than 20 of Hungary's most renowned buildings. The medieval period, often considered a glorious time in Hungary's history, is emphasized, while the controversial Habsburg era is not.

The Romanesque complex features a copy of the portal from a church in Ják (see p105) as well as a monastic cloister and palace. The details on the Gothic pavilion stem from castles such as that in Segesvár (now in Romania). The architect Fischer von Erlach inspired the Renaissance and Baroque complex. The façade copies part of the Bakócz chapel in the Esztergom cathedral (see pp144–5).

The **Museum of Agriculture**, in the Baroque section, has interesting exhibits on cattle-breeding, wine-making, hunting and fishing.

Széchenyi Baths ❻

Széchenyi Strandfürdő

Állatkerti körút 11. 🚋 72. **Tel** (1) 363 32 10. Ⓜ Széchenyi fürdő. **Swimming pool** ◻ 6am–10pm daily; **Thermal pool** ◻ 6am–7pm daily. 🖼 www.spasbudapest.hu

A statue stands at the main entrance to the Széchenyi Baths, depicting geologist Vilmos Zsigmondy, who discovered a hot spring here while drilling a well in 1879.

The Széchenyi Baths are the deepest and hottest baths in Budapest – the water reaches the surface at a temperature of 74–5 °C (180 °F). The springs, rich in minerals, are known for their alleged healing properties and are recommended for treating rheumatism and disorders of the nervous system, joints and muscles. The spa, housed in a Neo-Baroque building by Győző Czigler and Ede Dvorzsák, was constructed in 1909–13. In 1926, three open-air swimming pools were added. These are popular all year due to their high water temperatures. Bathing caps are required.

View across the lake of the Gothic (left) and Renaissance (right) sections of Vajdahunyad Castle

Margaret Island ❼

Inhabited as far back as Roman times, Margaret Island (Margitsziget) is a car-free, tranquil oasis in the middle of the Danube, a beautiful green space that has been open to the public since 1869. The 2.5-km (2-mile) long island served as a popular hunting ground for medieval kings, while monks were drawn to its peaceful setting. During Turkish rule it was used as a harem. In the 1200s Princess Margaret, daughter of Béla IV, spent most of her life as a recluse in the former convent here, and the island is named after her. Today Margaret Island still offers the perfect escape after sightseeing in the busy city.

Stained-glass window from St Michael's Church

Palatinus Strand
Opened in 1919, this is the largest outdoor swimming pool in Budapest. Its lush, grassy sunbathing areas and playgrounds make it especially popular with families.

Franciscan Church
Little remains of this early 14th-century church, which was abandoned in the 16th century. Yet the ruins, which include a glorious arched window and staircase, hint at its former size.

Hajós Olympic Pool Complex

Margaret Island's Bicycles
There is no better way to explore the car-free island than hiring one of these family-sized bicycles.

★ Centenary Monument
This monument was erected in 1973 to celebrate a century of united Budapest, the cities of Buda, Pest and Óbuda having merged in 1873. It was designed by István Kiss.

Margit Bridge

★ Japanese Garden

One of three landscaped parks on Margaret Island, the Japanese Garden features a wide range of flora as well as ponds and waterfalls, rock gardens and playgrounds.

— **Árpád Bridge**

Bodor Well

This musical well, built in 1936, is a copy of the original which stood in Târgu Mureş (today in Romania). On the hour, it plays gentle music.

St Michael's Church

Danubius Grand Hotel Margitsziget
This plush hotel, built in Neo-Renaissance style to designs by Miklós Ybl, was opened in 1873. For almost four decades it was the most fashionable hotel in the city, attracting aristocracy from all over Europe.

★ Water Tower

This unique 57-m (187-ft) tower was built in 1911 to provide clean water for the island's hotel. Protected by UNESCO, it offers great views from its Lookout Gallery.

```
0 metres        150
0 yards         150
```

STAR FEATURES

★ Centenary Monument

★ Japanese Garden

★ Water Tower

PRINCESS MARGIT

King Béla IV *(see p23)* swore that if he succeeded in repelling the Mongol invasion of 1241, he would offer his daughter to God. He kept his oath, sending his nine-year-old daughter Margaret to the St Michael's Church and convent, which he built on the island. She led a pious and ascetic life and at the age of 29 died on the island, which today carries her name.

The ruin of the 13th-century convent in which Margit spent 20 years of her life is probably the most important monument on the island. A marble plaque in the nave of the convent church ruins marks the spot where she is buried.

St Margit – stained-glass window, Gellért Hotel

View of the excavations of the Roman town Aquincum and the Museum

Aquincum ❽
Aquincum

Szentendrei út 139. **Tel** (1) 250 16
50. 🚇 Aquincum. 🚌 34, 42, 106.
Ruins ○ May–Sep: 9am–6pm Tue–
Sun; Oct & 15–30 Apr: 9am–5pm
Tue–Sun. **Museum** ○ May–Sep:
10am–6pm Tue–Sun; Oct & 15–30
Apr: 10am–5pm Tue–Sun. 🎫 📷
www.aquincum.hu

The remains of the Roman
town of Aquincum were
excavated at the end of the
19th century. Visitors today
are free to stroll along its
streets, viewing the outlines
of temples, baths, shops and
houses, in what was once
the centre of the town.

The civilian town of
Aquincum, capital of the
Roman province of Pannonia
Inferior, was founded at the
beginning of the 2nd century
AD, a couple of decades after
a legionary fortress had been
established to its south. For
centuries, it was the largest
city in Central Europe.

In the centre of the site a
museum is housed in a Neo-
Classical lapidarium displaying
the most valuable Roman
archaeological finds from the
area. The items on display
include weapons and various
inscribed stone monuments.

Only a fraction of the
former town is open to visitors today, but it is nonethe-
less impressive with its
remarkable central heating
system based on hot air circu-
lated under mosaic floors. A
drain cover is evidence that

there was a good water supply and drainage system. The
sanctuaries of goddesses Epona
and Fortuna can also be seen.

On the other side of the
HÉV railway line, the remains
of an amphitheatre are visible,
where the town's inhabitants
once sought entertainment.

Jewish Cemetery ❾
Zsidó temető

Kozma utca 6. 🚌 37.

Next door to the Municipal
Cemetery is the Jewish
Cemetery, opened in 1893.
The many grand tombs here
are a vivid reminder of the
vigour and
success of
Budapest's
pre-war

Schmidl family tomb at the Jewish Cemetery

Jewish community. At the end
of the 19th century, nearly
a quarter of the city's inhabitants were Jewish. Tombs to
look out for as you stroll
among the graves include
that of the Wellisch family,
designed in 1903 by Arthur
Wellisch, and that of Konrád
Polnay, which was designed
five years later by Gyula
Fodor. Perhaps the most eye-
catching of all tombs belongs
to the Schmidl family. The
startlingly flamboyant edifice,
designed in 1903 by Hungary's
prominent architects Ödön
Lechner and Béla Lajta, is
covered in vivid turquoise
ceramic tiles. The central
mosaic in green and gold tiles
represents the Tree of Life.

Budapest Holocaust Memorial Centre ❿
Holokauszt Emlékközpont

Páva utca 39. **Tel** (1) 455 33 33.
Ⓜ Ferenc körút. 🚌 4, 6, 30, 30A.
○ 10am–6pm Tue–Sun.
www.hdke.hu

This outstanding memorial
centre is dedicated to the
tens of thousands of Hun-
garians deported from the
Budapest Ghetto to Ausch-
witz in the latter stages of
World War II. Housed in a
former synagogue, the
exhibition tells of the fate
suffered by Hungarian Jews,
Gypsies and other victims.

The most moving part of
the memorial is the former
main prayer hall, given
over to the photos of
members of the con-
gregation who once
worshipped here.
The 8-m (24-ft) high
glass wall around
the centre, designed
by László Zsótér, is
inscribed with the
names of all Hun-
garians known to
have died in the
Shoah. It allows
new names to
be added; the goal is
one day to have a
complete list of all
who perished in
the Holocaust.

For hotels and restaurants in this area see pp263–5 and pp285–6

Foyer in the Palace of Arts, a multi-arts performance venue

Palace of Arts ⓫
Művészetek Palotája

Komor Marcell utca 1. 🚊 *1, 2, 2A, 24*. **Ticket Office** for all events.
Tel *(1) 555 33 00/33 01* or online.
🕐 *10am–6pm daily.* 📷
www.mupa.hu
Museum of Contemporary Art
Tel *(1) 555 34 44.* 🕐 *10am–8pm Tue–Sun.* **www**.ludwigmuseum.hu

The Palace of Arts, located in the Millennium City Centre on the Pest side of the Danube, between Lágymányos Bridge and the new National Theatre, brings together all the arts under one roof. Permanent residents in the palace include the Ludwig Museum of Contemporary Art, the Béla Bartok National Concert Hall, the Festival Theatre and the National Dance Theatre.

Eagle Hill Nature Reserve ⓬
Sas-hegy Természetvéldelmi Terület

Táják utca 26. **Tel** *(1) 319 67 89.*
🚊 *8, 8A.* 🕐 *Mid-Mar–mid-June & Sep–mid-Oct: 10am–4pm Sat & Sun.*
📷 *compulsory.*

A nature reserve like this that is close to the centre of a large city is a remarkable phenomenon.

Access to the summit of this steep, 266-m (872-ft) high hill to the west of Gellért Hill *(see pp88–9)* is strictly regulated to protect the extremely rare animal and plant species found here. A smart residential quarter of attractive bourgeois villas, which lies on the lower slope of Eagle Hill, extends almost to the fence of the wild and craggy 30-ha (74-acres) reserve that it encloses.

It is worth taking the guided walk in the reserve, particularly in spring or early autumn. Only here is it possible to see *centaurea sadleriana*, a flower that resembles a cornflower but with a much larger flowerhead. The reserve is also home to a type of spider not found elsewhere in the world, as well as to extraordinary, colourful butterflies and a rare lizard.

Buda Hills ⓭
Budai-hegység

Ⓜ *Széll Kálmán tér, then* 🚌 *56, then cog-wheel railway and chair lift.*

To the west of the city centre are the wooded Buda Hills. There are many caves here, including Szemló-hegyi and Pál-völgyi-barlang.

The first station of a cog-wheel railway, built in 1874, is on Szilágyi Erszébet fasor. This runs up Sváb Hill – named after the Germanic Swabians, who settled here under the Habsburgs *(see pp40–41)* – and then Széchenyi Hill.

From Széchenyi Hill a narrow-gauge railway covers a 12-km (7-mile) route to the Hűvös Valley. As in the days of the Soviet Young Pioneers movement, the railway is staffed by children, apart from the adult train drivers. At the top of János Hill stands the Erzsébet Look-Out Tower, designed by Frigyes Schulek in 1910. A chairlift connects János Hill with Zugligeti út and this is a good way of making the descent.

The Erzsébet Look-Out Tower at the summit of János Hill, Buda Hills

Memento Park ⓮

During Communist rule, Socialist Realism was the artistic movement, resulting in some of the most striking sculpture of the 20th century. While most of the other former Soviet-bloc countries iconoclastically toppled their Socialist statuary as soon as they had toppled their Socialist leaders, the more reflective Hungarians decided to preserve these unique public works of art, which until 1989 had stood in the country's major public squares. The propagandist statues, some of which were erected as late as the mid-1980s, are now displayed in this, Europe's most unusual theme park of Communism.

Soldier's statue near the Park's entrance

Béla Kun Memorial
Béla Kun was a Hungarian Communist who briefly ran the country in 1919 after leading a Russian-backed Communist coup. Kun's regime was quickly overthrown by nationalist forces led by Admiral Horthy, however, and Kun fled to Russia.

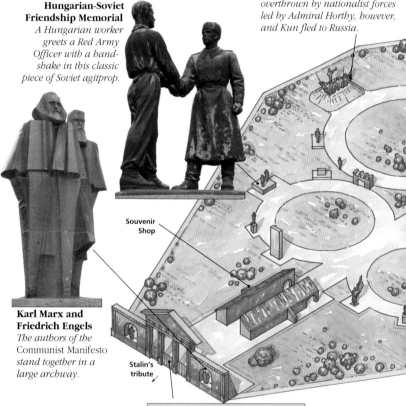

Hungarian-Soviet Friendship Memorial
A Hungarian worker greets a Red Army Officer with a handshake in this classic piece of Soviet agitprop.

Souvenir Shop

Karl Marx and Friedrich Engels
The authors of the Communist Manifesto stand together in a large archway.

Stalin's tribute

STAR FEATURES

★ Main Entrance

★ Republic of Council's Monument

★ Workers' Movement Memorial

★ Main Entrance
The monumental main entrance and the austere wall that surrounds the park are designed to remind visitors of the restrictive nature of the Iron Curtain.

Captain Steinmetz
In December 1944, the Hungarian-born Soviet Red Army Captain Miklós Steinmetz delivered the Ultimátum *with the proposed terms for surrender from the Soviet troops to the Germans occupying Budapest. He was shot while returning to Soviet lines.*

VISITORS' CHECKLIST

Balatoni út & Szabadkai utca, Budapest. **Road Map** D3. **Tel** (1) 424 75 00. from Budapest, Deák tér. Apr–Oct: 10am–dusk daily; Nov–Mar: 10am–4pm daily. www.mementopark.hu

★ **Republic of Council's Monument**
This monument honours the many European revolutionaries of all nationalities who flocked to Spain to fight there in the 1936–9 Civil War.

★ **Workers' Movement Memorial**
Two monstrously large hands are about to clasp a globe, and with it the working class of the world.

SOUVENIR SHOP

There are hawkers and street sellers all over the former Eastern Bloc selling souvenirs of the Communist period and much of this – two decades on – is not likely to be genuine. At the unique Statue Park souvenir shop some original memorabilia of Soviet Hungary, as well as quality reproductions, are on sale. There are Soviet-era flags and banners, excellent Soviet army watches and kitsch Trabant key rings. Also available on CD are the Communist anthem, *The Internationale,* in many languages, as well as recordings of the incomparable Red Army Choir.

Reproduction Soviet flags, on sale in the souvenir shop

Lenin
Vladimir Lenin (1870–1924), leader of the 1917 Revolution and first head of the Soviet state, points the way to a bright Socialist future.

SHOPPING IN BUDAPEST

Shopping in Budapest has changed dramatically in recent years. Despite price rises since the return to a free-market economy, many Hungarian goods still represent good value for visitors. Major shopping streets include elegant pedestrianized Váci Street *(see pp92–3)*, good for folk art, and the less fashionable, but better-value Nagykörút, where locals

Paprika powder, a popular souvenir

do their shopping. For local goods, a visit to one of Budapest's many markets is recommended. These range in style from stunning 19th-century food halls, such as the Great Market Hall (Nagy Vásárcsarnok), to second-hand markets, such as the huge and lively Ecseri Flea Market, where everything from bric-à-brac to furniture and antiques can be found.

OPENING HOURS

Most shops in Budapest open 9am–5:30 or 6pm Monday to Friday, and 9am–1pm on Saturday. Department stores open at 10am, while greengrocers, bakeries and supermarkets are open 7am–8pm. Many shops stay open until 8 or 9pm on Thursday. Indoor markets and department stores open on Sunday, and most cafés also sell milk and bread on Sunday morning. Many small shops, selling groceries, cigarettes and alcohol, are open 24 hours a day.

DEPARTMENT STORES AND SHOPPING CENTRES

Since the late 1990s, 20 department buildings and malls have opened in Budapest. Originally drawing skepticism, department stores have proved popular with the Hungarian populace. Providing a wealth of well established European and internarional brands, the shopping centres normally

Smoked sausages on display at the Central Market Hall

sell elegent men's and women's clothing, accessories and perfumes. **WestEnd City Center**, with over 350 stores, is the best and largest. The stylish **Mammut** on Széll Kálmán tér is frequented by more affluent Buda residents.

MARKETS

Markets are an essential part of life in Budapest. Perhaps the most spectacular are the five cavernous market halls around the city. All were built

in the late 19th century and several are still used as markets. The three-level **Central Market Hall** (Nagy Vásárcsarnok), on Fővám tér is the largest. Here, more than 180 stalls display a huge range of foods under a gleaming roof of coloured Zsolnay tiles. The market opens from 7am–6pm Mon–Fri and 7am–1pm Sat. Other markets to explore are in **Fehérvári út** and in **Fény utca**.

Beginning at 156 Nagykőrösi út in district XIX, tables at the vast outside **Ecseri Flea Market** are covered in Communist artifacts, second-hand clothes and bric-à-brac.

FOOD AND DRINK

Hungarian paprika, a wide variety of spicy salamis and other fine foodstuffs, such as goose liver pâté, are widely available in the city's many lively markets, supermarkets and smaller delicatessens. Visitors wishing to buy – and sample – Hungary's regional wines, including the golden Tokaji, should head for **Borház** in Pest's Jókai tér, **La Boutique des Vins** in József Attila utca or **House of Royal Wines** in Szent György tér, all of which stock a superb selection from all over the country. Hungary's apricot and plum liqueurs and brandy (*pálinka*) can be purchased at **House of Pálinka** in Rákóczi út.

FOLK ART

Hungarian folk art such as embroidered peasant blouses and wooden carvings are still produced in many rural areas and sold in the capital. These

A small wine merchant, selling wines from Hungary's regions

can be found at flea markets around Moszkva tér and Parliament or the top floor of the Central Market Hall. If you are looking for handmade items in particular, head for **Folkart kézműveshár**.

PORCELAIN AND ANTIQUES

Dominated by 18th- and 19th-century pieces in the Habsburg style, the Budapest antiques

Traditional folk costumes, on sale from a street vendor

scene is concentrated in the Castle District, around Falk Miksa utca and on Váci utca (Váci Street, *see pp92–3*). **Moró Antik** is a tiny shop specializing in 18th-century weapons. The huge **Nagyházi Gallery** sells everything from jewellery to furniture. Budapest's flea markets are good places to hunt for collectibles.

If looking to buy genuine **Herend** and **Zsolnay** porcelain, there are several outlets in Budapest. The **Hollóházi** porcelain factory also has a shop.

CLOTHES AND SHOES

Made-to-measure clothes and shoes, as well as ready-made designer clothes, offer some of the best deals to be had in the capital. Clothes can be made up by a local designer in a choice of fabrics – often for a modest fee. At the top end, **Naray Tamas Boutique** is the showcase for one of Hungary's most celebrated designers. Shoemakers **Vass** offer handmade men's shoes, but they are expensive and can take some time to make.

WestEnd City Center, central Europe's largest shopping mall

MUSIC

Hungary's rich musical traditions make for tempting low-priced items to buy. Good quality CDs and vinyl records are widely available. **Rózsavölgyi Zeneműbolt** is a good choice for traditional gypsy and village folk music, as well as orchestral works. In nearby Dob utca, **Concerto Records** specializes in classical and opera. Hungarton, the factory outlet of the label of the same name, sells classical music CDs in Rottenbiller utca.

DIRECTORY

DEPARTMENT STORES AND SHOPPING CENTRES

Arena Plaza
Kerepesi út 9. *Tel* (1) 880 70 01. www.arenaplaza.hu

Mammut I–II Mall
Lövőház utca 2–6. **Map** 1 A3. *Tel* (1) 345 80 20. www.mammut.hu

WestEnd City Center
Váci út 1–3. **Map** 2 E3. *Tel* (1) 238 77 77.

MARKETS

Budapest Flea Market
Zichy Mihály utca 14. *Tel* (20) 933 39 79.

Central Market Hall
Vámház körút 1–3 (Fővám tér). **Map** 4 E2. *Tel* (1) 366 33 00.

Ecseri Flea Market
Nagykőrösi út 156. *Tel* (1) 282 95 63.

Fehérvári út Market
Fehérvári út 20.

Fény utca Market
Near Széll Kálmán tér. **Map** 1 A4.

FOOD & DRINK

Borház
Jókai tér 7. **Map** 2 E4. *Tel* (1) 353 48 49.

La Boutique des Vins
József Attila utca 12. **Map** 2 D5. *Tel* (1) 317 59 19.

House of Pálinka
Rákóczi út 17. **Map** 4 E1/2. *Tel* (1) 338 42 19.

House of Royal Wines
Szent György tér. **Map** 1 B5. *Tel* (1) 267 11 00. www.kiralyiborok.com

FOLK ART

Folkart kézműveshár
Régiposta utca 12. **Map** 4 D1. *Tel* (1) 318 51 43. www.folkartkez muveshaz.hu

PORCELAIN

Herend Shops
József Nádor tér 11. **Map** 2 D5. *Tel* (1) 317 26 22.
Szentháromság utca 5. **Map** 1 B5. *Tel* (1) 225 10 50/51.
Andrássy út 16. **Map** 2 E4. *Tel* (1) 374 00 06.

Hollóházi Shop
Rákóczi út 31. **Map** 4 E1. *Tel* (1) 413 14 63.

Zsolnay Shops
Kossuth Lajos utca 10. **Map** 4 E1. *Tel* (1) 328 08 44.
Kecskeméti utca 14. **Map** 4 E2. *Tel* (1) 318 26 43.

ANTIQUES

Moró Antik
Falk Miksa utca 13. **Map** 2 D3. *Tel* (1) 311 08 14.

Nagyházi Gallery
Balaton utca 8. **Map** 2 D3. *Tel* (1) 475 60 00.

CLOTHES & SHOES

Naray Tamas Boutique
Hajós utca 17. **Map** 2 E4. *Tel* (1) 266 24 73.

Vass Shoes
Haris köz 2. **Map** 4 D1. *Tel* (1) 318 23 75.

MUSIC

Concerto Records
Dob utca 33. **Map** 2 E5. *Tel* (1) 268 96 31.

Rózsavölgyi Zeneműbolt
Szervita tér 5. **Map** 4 D1. *Tel* (1) 318 35 00.

ENTERTAINMENT IN BUDAPEST

Budapest has been known as a city of entertainment since the late 19th century, when people would travel here from Vienna in search of a good time. Its buzzing nightclubs were frequented for their electric atmosphere and the beautiful girls that danced the spirited *csárdás* and the cancan. Between the wars the city was as famous for its glittering society balls as for its more decadent delights. The half-century of Communist rule dampened the revelry, but since 1990 the Budapest music scene has flourished and theatres, cabarets, festivals, cinemas and discotheques are all buzzing.

PRACTICAL INFORMATION AND TICKETS

Two monthly cultural listings magazines, the *Programme* and the *Budapest Panorama*, contain information in English. Both are free and available in hotels and tourist information centres. Pamphlets and bulletins are often issued for festivals and other special events, and it is worth keeping an eye out for the poster pillars throughout the city.

Tickets for plays and concerts can be purchased in advance from the booking offices or the relevant venue. The best way of securing a seat for concerts at the **Ferenc Liszt Academy of Music** (see p101) or major opera productions is via the **Cultur-Comfort Central Ticket Office**.

OPERA, CLASSICAL AND SACRED MUSIC

The standard of opera in Budapest is very high. The **State Opera House** (see pp88–9) has a mainly classical repertoire, sung with Hungarian surtitles. The large hall of the Ferenc Liszt Academy of Music (currently undergoing renovation) is the city's leading venue for classical music. Another venue for concerts and theatre is the **Palace of Art**. Classical concerts may also be held in the domed hall of Parliament (see pp80–81), where the acoustics are excellent. Other important venues for organ or choral music are **Mátyás Church** (see pp62–3), **St Stephen's Basilica** (see pp86–7) and the Great Synagogue (see p100).

JAZZ, TRADITIONAL HUNGARIAN AND ROCK MUSIC

Jazz was very late in reaching Hungary. The best known and revered Hungarian jazz band is the Benkő Dixieland Band, which during Spring

August Rock Festival on Óbudai-sziget

Festivals (see p30) plays in various theatres and large halls. In summer the coolest venue for live jazz is the **Jazz Garden**, a great restaurant.

For traditional Hungarian music and dance, head to the **House of Traditions** where authentic Hungarian dance evenings are held along with lessons for the young and old.

For fans of rock and pop, the biggest event of the year is the three-day **Sziget Festival** in August on Óbudai-sziget. Big names in rock and pop also play at the modern **Papp László Budapest SportArena**. For more live rock, try the party boat **A38** and **Fat Mo's**, a legendary live music venue.

THEATRES AND CINEMA

Budapest has many theatres, which are worth visiting not only for their great repertoires, but also because most are located in beautiful historic buildings. Cinemas show the latest films soon after their world premieres, and most foreign films in Hungary are dubbed and subtitled into Hungarian. Visitors who do not speak Hungarian should choose the *angol nyelvű* (English soundtrack) version.

The main stage at the opulent Opera House, in Budapest

A Budapest casino, one of many gaming establishments in the city

top DJs who play cutting-edge music. A38 also hosts lively club nights.

Budapest's gay scene is legendary. **Action Bar** lives up to its name, with go-go dancing and more, while **Coxx Club** is a huge multi-level place that attracts a more mainstream crowd.

The city is also home to a number of classy **casinos** attracting gamblers from Europe and the Middle East.

Sign for Bahnhof music club

staffed entirely by children. The **War Museum** enthrals older children with weapons, armour and battle scenes.

Most children enjoy the **Zoo**, and this is one of the largest in Europe. The **Great Capital Circus** is another ideal entertainment. Families can also spend many happy hours at the **Vidám Park** funfair at Városliget City Park.

NIGHTLIFE

The dynamic Budapest club scene changes from month to month, often week to week. For a great night with live DJs head to **Corvintető**, a roof garden on top of a 1926 department store. **E-Klub** is a suberb venue notable for its

CHILDREN'S ENTERTAINMENT

The Royal Palace (see pp54–5) and the Castle District generally are good places to start, while a must is the ride up or down Castle Hill by funicular railway. The **Children's Railway** (Gyermekvasút) runs through the woods in Buda Hills and is

Façade of the vast Great Capital Circus building

DIRECTORY

TICKETS

Cultur-Comfort Central Ticket Office
Paulay Ede utca 31. **Map** 2 E5. **Tel** (1) 322 00 00.

Ticket Express
Andrássy út 18. **Map** 2 E4. **Tel** (1) 303 09 99. www.tex.hu

OPERA, CLASSICAL & SACRED MUSIC

Ferenc Liszt Academy
Liszt Ferenc tér 8. **Map** 2 F4. **Tel** (1) 462 46 00.

Mátyás Church
Szentháromság tér 2. **Map** 1 B4. **Tel** (1) 355 56 57.

Palace of Art
Komor Marcell utca 1. **Tel** (1) 555 33 00. www.mupa.hu

St Stephen's Basilica
Szent István tér 2. **Map** 2 D5. **Tel** (1) 317 28 59.

State Opera House
Andrássy út 22. **Map** 2 E4. **Tel** (1) 331 25 50. www.opera.hu

JAZZ, TRADITIONAL & CONTEMPORARY MUSIC

A38
Petőfi híd Budai hidfő. **Tel** (1) 464 39 40. www.a38.hu

Fat Mo's
Nyáry Pál u. 11. **Tel** (1) 267 31 99.

House of Traditions
Corvin tér 8, District 1 (Castle District). **Tel** (1) 225 60 49.

Jazz Garden
Veres Pálné utca 44a. **Map** 4 E1. **Tel** (1) 266 73 64.

Papp László Budapest SportArena
Jfjúság utca 4. Tickets from Ticketa **Tel** (1) 422 26 82. www.budapestarena.hu

Sziget Festival
www.szigetfestival.com

THEATRE & CINEMA

József Katona Theatre
Petőfi Sándor utca 6. **Map** 4 D1. **Tel** (1) 318 65 99.

Margitsziget Openair Stage
Margitsziget Island. **Tel** (1) 340 41 96.

Nemzeti Theatre
Bajor Gizi Park 1. **Tel** (1) 476 68 00.

Palace West End
Váci út 1–3. **Map** 2 E2. **Tel** (1) 238 72 20. www.funzine.hu

CASINOS

Las Vegas Casino
Roosevelt tér 2. **Map** 1 C5. **Tel** (1) 317 60 22. www.lasvegascasino.hu

Tropicana Casino
Vigadó utca 2. **Map** 4 D1. **Tel** (1) 266 30 62. www.tropicanacasino.hu

NIGHTLIFE

Corvintető
Blaha Lujza tér 1–2. **Tel** (20) 772 29 84. www.corvinteto.com

E-Klub
Népliget út 2. **Tel** (1) 263 16 14. www.e-klub.hu

GAY CLUBS

Action Bar
Magyar utca 42. **Map** 4 E1. **Tel** (1) 266 91 48. www.action.gay.hu

Coxx Club
Dohány utca 38. **Map** 2 F5. **Tel** (1) 344 48 84. www.coxx.hu

CHILDREN'S ENTERTAINMENT

Great Capital Circus
Állatkerti körút 7. **Tel** (1) 343 83 00. www.maciva.hu

Children's Railway
Széchenyi-hegy Station. **Tel** (1) 395 54 20. www.gyermekvasut.hu

Vidám Park
Állatkerti körút 14–16. **Tel** (1) 363 83 10. www.vidampark.hu

War Museum
Kapisztrán tér 2–4. **Map** 1 A4. **Tel** (1) 325 16 47.

Zoo
Állatkerti körút 6–12. **Tel** (1) 273 49 00. www.zoobudapest.com

BUDAPEST STREET FINDER

The map references given for all the sights, hotels, bars, restaurants, shops and entertainment venues in Budapest refer to the maps in this section. Opposite is a complete index of street names marked on the maps. The map below shows the area of Budapest covered by the Street Finder; it is colour-coded by area. The Street Finder shows bus and tram routes and major sights together with other useful information listed in the key below. As an aid to navigation, all street names on the Street Finder and in the index are in Hungarian. Terms that may be confusing are: *utca* (often abbreviated to *u*), which means street, and *út* meaning avenue, usually wide, busy roads. Other commonly used terms are *körút* (*krt*, ring road), *tér* (square), *köz* (lane), *körtér* (circus) and *híd* (bridge).

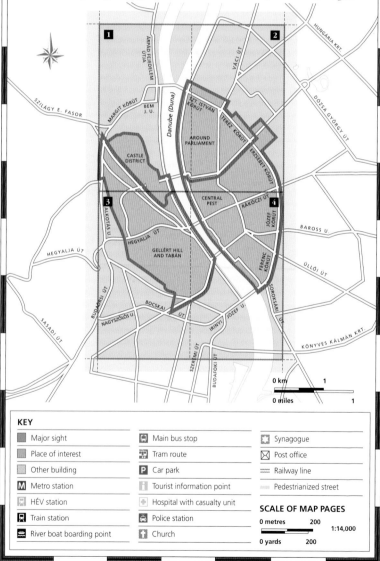

KEY

◼ Major sight	🚌 Main bus stop	✡ Synagogue
◻ Place of interest	🚋 Tram route	⊠ Post office
◻ Other building	🅿 Car park	═ Railway line
Ⓜ Metro station	🛈 Tourist information point	▬ Pedestrianized street
Ⓗ HÉV station	✚ Hospital with casualty unit	
🚆 Train station	🚓 Police station	**SCALE OF MAP PAGES**
River boat boarding point	✝ Church	0 metres 200
		1:14,000
		0 yards 200

Street Finder Index

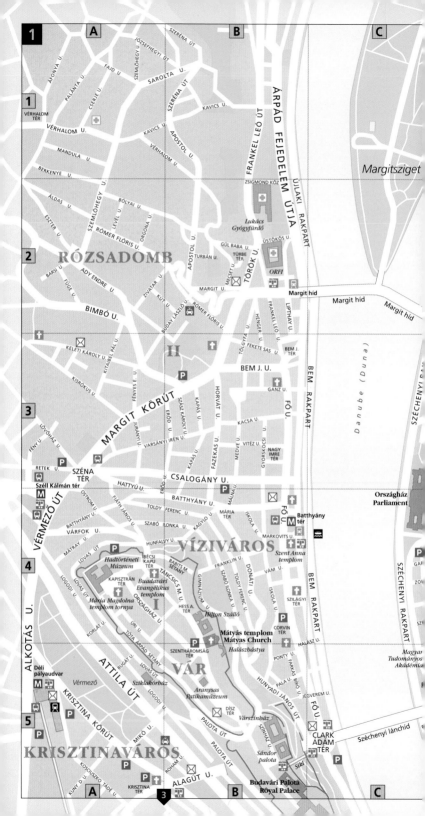

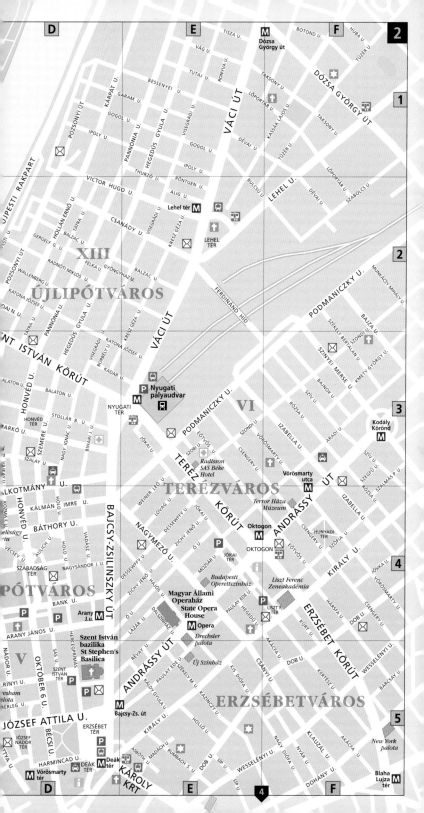

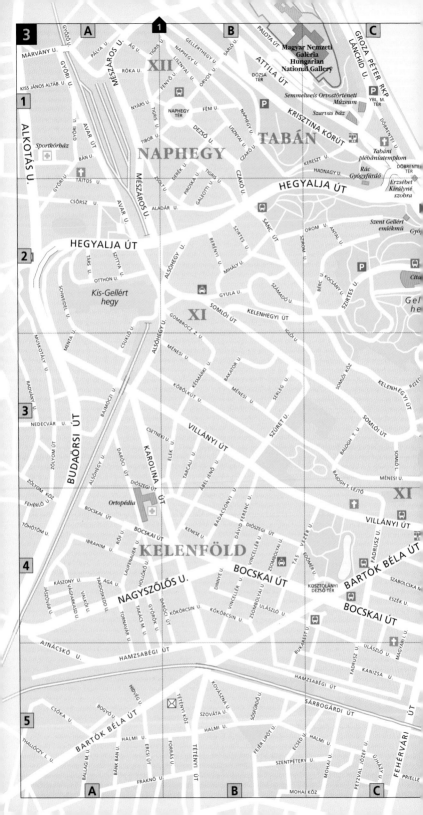

HUNGARY
REGION BY REGION

Hungary at a Glance

Hungary was traditionally divided into four regions –
the Great Plain, the Northern Highlands, Transdanubia and Transylvania – but since 1918, with the
exception of a short period at the beginning of World
War II, Transylvania has been a part of Romania. In
this guide, the vast region of Transdanubia is divided
into a northern and a southern half. While each region
has its own traditions and values, culture and habits,
Hungary is one of the most homogenous countries
in the world. It is also one of the least urban countries
in Europe: outside Budapest no city has more than
200,000 inhabitants. The population is concentrated
in small towns and thousands of villages, and it is
the traditions of these smaller places that give the
country its charm.

Firewatch Tower in Sopron
*Located in the far northwest
of the country, the attractive
town of Sopron has a well
preserved medieval centre.*

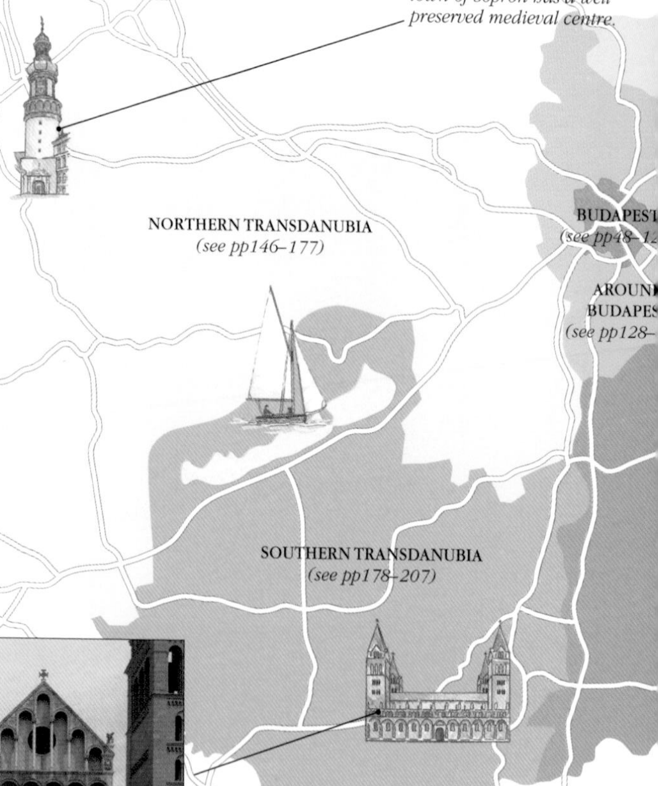

NORTHERN TRANSDANUBIA
(see pp146–177)

BUDAPEST
(see pp48–12...)

**AROUND
BUDAPEST**
(see pp128–...)

SOUTHERN TRANSDANUBIA
(see pp178–207)

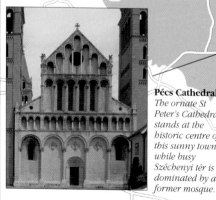

Pécs Cathedral
*The ornate St
Peter's Cathedral
stands at the
historic centre of
this sunny town,
while busy
Széchenyi tér is
dominated by a
former mosque.*

| 0 kilometres | 50 |
| 0 miles | 50 |

Hollókő Church

A museum village devoted to the preservation of the lifestyles and traditions of the Palóc people, Hollókő has been added to the UNESCO World Heritage list. The church here is white-washed, like the village houses.

THE NORTHERN HIGHLANDS
(see pp208–229)

THE GREAT PLAIN
(see pp230–255)

Hortobágy National Park

A UNESCO World Heritage site, the Hortobágy Puszta is famous for its cattle and its horsemen, the Csikós, as well as the national dish of goulash.

Royal Palace of Gödöllő

Emperor Franz Joseph's wife, "Sisi", loved staying here at the Habsburgs' fine summer residence in Gödöllő. The town also has a renowned local artists' colony.

Great Catholic Church in Kecskemét

A centre of the arts and education, Kecskemét boasts some fine architecture, including this large Baroque edifice. Older buildings have been skilfully integrated into the modern cityscape.

AROUND BUDAPEST

*S*trategically sited castles and vast cathedrals, including Hungary's largest, look out over the pleasure boats navigating the Danube Bend. The unique evening sunlight here has always attracted artists to the region, and evidence of a rich cultural heritage is everywhere. Gödöllő boasts the stunning Royal Palace, while the Danube-Ipoly National Park offers a superb habitat for native wildlife.

With its darting twists and turns, steep banks and deep valleys, the Danube Bend has been a site of refuge for almost 2,000 years. Rome built garrisons here, and there are remnants of that great empire everywhere. The natural fortress that is the Danube's west bank was later the chosen site for the construction of the historic towns of Visegrád and Esztergom, both built with protection and defence in mind. Esztergom was the scene of the Hungarian conversion to Christianity, and Visegrád was the impenetrable seat of royal power. Later still came Szentendre which, like Ráckeve to the south of the capital, was founded by Serbs fleeing persecution at home and though few Serbs remain, traces of their culture and their religion are evident everywhere.

Those who come seeking respite today are the thousands of Budapest residents who keep holiday homes in the area, and the legions of visitors on short trips from the capital – a fact that is reflected in local prices.

Over on the east bank the rolling hills of the Börzsöny and the Danube-Ipoly National Park – home to more than half of Hungary's native bird species – make for sensational hiking, walking and bird-watching.

This is perhaps the most cosmopolitan part of Hungary, where visitors can expect warm, welcoming and multi-lingual hosts, but in summer it can be very hot and busy. As autumn usually brings plenty of rain and winter can be very cold, the early spring – March, April and May – may be the best time for exploring these historic places.

Magnificent frescoes in the Serbian Orthodox Church in Ráckeve

◁ **The early 18th-century Víziváros Parish Church, Esztergom**

Exploring Around Budapest

The countryside and villages around Budapest have always been a major draw for visitors to the capital. To the north is the Danube bend (Dunakanyar), and in the middle of it the art-loving village of Szentendre. Further up-river are the Baroque town of Vác and Esztergom, Hungary's most sacred city. Beyond, the Duna-Ipoly National Park offers countless hiking and nature trails. The Royal Mansion in Gödöllő to the east is worth seeing, and south of Budapest are the pretty town of Ráckeve and the Ócsa Nature Reserve, a unique habitat of reedy bogs.

Beautiful waterlilies in the marshes around Ócsa

GETTING AROUND

Budapest has an international airport, and from here destinations such as Szentendre, Gödöllő and Ócsa are best reached by train, on the Budapest suburban rail network (HÉV, see p318). Other sightseeing areas can be visited by train or car. During the summer months, the most relaxing way to reach the Danube bend is by Mahart Passnave motorboat, departing northwards from Vigadó tér in Budapest. Services run to Esztergom and stop at most towns along the way. Other services go to Szentendre and Vác.

Inside Esztergom Basilica, centre of Catholicism in Hungary

SIGHTS AT A GLANCE

The Royal Palace in Gödöllő, built by Count Antal Grassalkovich

SEE ALSO

• **Where to Stay** p265

• **Where to Eat** pp286–7

KEY

═══	Motorway
= =	Motorway under construction
▬▬	Major road
──	Secondary road
⋯⋯	Minor roads
∼∼	Main railway
──	Minor railway
▬▬▬	International border
▬▬▬	Regional border

0 kilometres   10

0 miles   10

**A statue of Justice, crowning the
Baroque Town Hall in Vác**

Magnificent frescoes in the Serbian Orthodox Church in Ráckeve

Ráckeve ●

43 km (27 miles) southwest of Budapest. **Road Map** C4. 🏠 8,500.
� from Budapest. 🚌 from Budapest. 🛈 Tourinform, Eötvös utca 11,
(24) 42 97 47.

The small town of Ráckeve is
built on Csepel Island, which
extends 54 km (34 miles)
south along the middle of
the Danube from Budapest.
Ráckeve (Rác means Serb in
Hungarian) was founded in
the 15th century by Serbs
from Keve, who fled Serbia
after the Turkish invasion.
The oldest building in the
village is the **Serbian Orthodox Church** on Viola utca,
built by some of the first
Serbian refugees to arrive
here. Dating back to 1487,
this is the oldest Orthodox
church in Hungary. Its walls
are covered in well-preserved
frescoes, the first telling the
story of the Nativity and the
last depicting the Resurrection.
The church also boasts a vast,
colourful iconostasis separating the sanctuary from the
nave. The stand-alone belfry
was added in the 16th century.
Ráckeve's peaceful and
convenient situation made it
the country home of one of

Europe's greatest military
strategists, Prince Eugene
of Savoy. Credited with the
expulsion of the Turks at
the end of the 17th century,
Prince Eugene built himself
a country mansion known as
the **Savoy Mansion**, on what
is now Kossuth Lajos utca.
Used as a hotel today, the
interior has been modernized,
but the elegant façade has
been preserved and is well
worth a look. The formal
gardens of the mansion can
be admired from the river.

Ócsa ●

30 km (19 miles) west of Budapest.
Road Map D3. 🏠 8,500. � from
Budapest. 🚌 from Budapest.
🛈 Tourinform, Bajcsy-Zsilinszky utca
2, (29) 57 87 50.

The part-Romanesque, part-
Gothic **Calvinist Church**
at Ócsa was originally built
in the 13th-century by the
Premonstratensian Order,
about whom there is a small
exhibition in one of the
church's side rooms. Used as
a mosque during the Turkish
invasion, it was converted
back into a church during the
18th century, and thorough
restoration in 1920 (after

damage by a fire) has ensured
that this is one of the best-
preserved Romanesque
churches in the country.
Many of the houses that
surround the church date
from the 18th century, and all
are protected buildings. One
contains a small ethnographic
museum, with collections of
folk costumes, tools and dolls.
The house also serves as the
visitors centre for the **Ócsa
Nature Reserve** (Ócsai
Tájvédelmi Körzet), one of
the most accessible nature
reserves in Hungary. The
reserve surrounds the village,
and apart from one small area
visitors can freely explore it.
Much of the reserve consists
of reedy bog or marsh, known
as *turjános*, which once
covered a vast area here.
The marshes are home to
rare plant and animal species
including tortoises, lizards
and a number of birds, such
as harriers and corncrakes.
Guided tours depart from
the visitors' centre.

🦌 **Ócsa Nature Reserve**
Dr. Békési Panyik Andor utca 4–6.
🕐 Mar–Oct: 9am–6pm Tue–Sun.
🎫♿

**Romanesque façade of the Calvinist
Church in Ócsa**

Gödöllő ●

35 km (22 miles) northeast of Budapest. **Road Map** D3. 🏠 29,000.
🚆 HÉV from Budapest. 🛈 Tourinform, Királyi Kastély, (28) 41 54 02.

Gödöllő is most famous for
its restored Baroque palace,
the **Antal Grassalkovich
Mansion** (*see pp134–5*), built

in 1741. Opposite the mansion, on the other side of the railway tracks, is what's left of old Gödöllő, mainly the cluster of buildings around Szabadság tér. At No. 5 is the oldest building in the town, dating from 1661. Once the home of local landowner Ferenc Hamvay, it is today the excellent **Gödöllő Town Museum** (Gödöllő Városi Múzeum). Besides displays telling the story of the town and of its greatest patron, Antal Grassalkovich, there is a colourful exhibition focusing on the works of the Gödöllő Artists' Colony. This group of artists, active between 1901 and 1920, was inspired by William Morris and John Ruskin and pursued ideals of communal rural living. Behind the museum is the Calvinist Church, built here in 1745 with money donated by Grassalkovich, who had demolished the town's original Calvinist church to make way for his palace.

Rock garden, Vácrátót Botanical Gardens

🏛 **Gödöllő Town Museum**
Szabadság tér 5. *Tel (28) 42 20 03.* ◯ *10am–6pm Tue–Sun.* 🔲

Vácrátót ④

35 km (22 miles) from Budapest. **Road Map** D3. 🏚 *1,700.* 🚊 *from Budapest.* 🚌 *from Budapest, Vác.*

The **Vácrátót Botanical Gardens** (Botanikus Kert) are among the oldest in Hungary, and at present the largest. Founded in 1870 by Count Sándor Vigyázó the gardens have been open to the public since 1961. Among the 12,000 different kinds of plant covering over 200 hectares (500 acres) are more than 1,000 species that are native to Hungary, as well as plants of the Russian steppes, Central Asia, the Rocky Mountains in the US, and trees and shrubs from the Far East. Waterfalls, rock gardens, lakes and many statues add to the enjoyment,

while frogs are a frequent sight along the paths and walkways of the gardens.

Inside the greenhouses are a further 2,800 different types of plant and flower, as well as a unique exhibition on the plants of the Bible.

🌿 **Vácrátót Botanical Gardens**
Alkotmány utca 2–4. *Tel (28) 36 01 22.* ◯ **Gardens** *Apr–Oct: 8am–6pm daily; Nov–Mar: 8am–4pm daily.* **Greenhouses** *Apr–Oct: 8am–3:45pm Tue–Sun (to 1:45pm Fri).* 🔲 🚹 🔲

Vác ⑤

40 km (25 miles) north of Budapest. **Road Map** D3. 🏚 *33,000.* 🚊 *from Budapest.* 🚌 *from Budapest.* 🛈 *Tourinform, Március 15 tér 17, (27) 31 61 60.* 🔲 *daily, behind Március 15 tér.* **www**.tourinformvac.hu

Vác has stood on the eastern bank of the Danube since the year 1000. Destroyed by war in the late 17th century, the town was rebuilt. Its centre, around Március 15 tér, dates

from the 18th century and was a thriving market place until 1951. The market itself survives, though it is now hidden behind the Town Hall, a Baroque masterpiece from 1680. The façade – with two Corinthian half-columns guarding the entrance – is adorned with an intricate wrought-iron balcony. Next door is the Sisters of Charity Chapel and Hospital, built in the 17th century and still a functioning hospital to this day (a more modern section was recently incorporated into the back of the hospital building, cleverly kept out of view from the square).

The pink Neo-Renaissance building opposite the hospital was for a short time the Bishop's Palace, then the Vác residence of Habsburg Empress Maria Theresa, who adored the town. Since 1802 the building has been the home of Hungary's Deaf and Dumb Society.

On the southern side of the square stands the **Dominican Church of Our Lady of Victory**, on which construction began in 1699. Due to the War of Independence, however, work on the interior decoration only began in 1755. As a result the façade is sober, while the interior is rich in Rococo artwork.

At the northernmost end of the old town, on Köztársaság út, stands the only triumphal arch in Hungary. This was built in 1764, ostensibly to honour Maria Theresa.

The Dominican Church in Vác with its rich Rococo ornamentation

Royal Palace of Gödöllő ❸

Crest above the
main entrance

Seemingly lifted directly from a fairytale, the Baroque Gödöllő Royal Palace is as enchanting now as it was the day it was completed in 1748. Designed by András Mayerhoffer, the palace was commissioned by the flamboyant Hungarian aristocrat Antal Grassalkovich I, a confidant of Empress Maria Theresa. Home to Hungarian rulers from Emperor Franz Joseph to Admiral Horthy, it is Franz Joseph's wife, the beautiful Sisi, who has left the most indelible mark on the palace.

★ Franz Joseph's Salon
The walls of the Emperor's suite are covered in the finest red silks. The wooden floor is the original, from the 18th century.

Bath and Orangerie

The Oratory
has a full-size mosaic portrait of Antal Grassalkovich I above the marble fireplace.

★ Chapel
The Chapel, consecrated in 1749, replaced the original Calvinist village church. It features two Rococo pulpits and a mosaic portrait of Antal Grassalkovich I.

Minor Coronation Hall
Originally the king's bedroom, an oversized and stunning depiction of Franz Joseph's coronation in 1867, commissioned by himself, is the centrepiece of this ground-floor room.

The Wardrobe of Franz Joseph I
contains replicas of his vast collection of uniforms, with which the Emperor was obsessed – he was rarely seen out of uniform.

STAR FEATURES

★ Chapel

★ Grand Hall

★ Franz Joseph's Salon

★ Queen Elizabeth's Salon

Main Façade
Used as an old people's home and to house Soviet troops after World War II, the palace was rebuilt and renovated in 1986–91.

★ Grand Hall
A vast ballroom, with marble and gilded stucco decoration on walls and ceiling, the Hall also has a hidden music room above the entrance.

VISITORS' CHECKLIST

Gödöllő 35 km (20 miles) northeast of Budapest. **Road Map** D3. **Tel** (28) 41 01 24. 🚌 🚋 ⏱ Apr–Oct: 10am–6pm daily; Nov–Mar: 10am–5pm daily. 📷 🎫 tours of palace and grounds available. ♿ 🏪 🚻 📧 check website for special events. **www**.kiralyikastely.hu

Grand Staircase
The elegant double staircase features stucco decoration and Rococo motifs. The balustrade is a simple, open design in painted stone.

Main entrance

In the Secret Room of Queen Elizabeth key negotiations led to Hungary's independence in 1867 *(see p42)*. Portraits of those involved line the walls.

Baroque Painted Room
This informal room, its walls covered with paintings, is today furnished with items from Queen Elizabeth's private waiting room at Gödöllő railway station.

The Queen Elizabeth Memorial Exhibition suite has been restored to its original violet, the Queen's favourite colour. On display are her most cherished paintings.

★ Queen Elizabeth's Salon
A symbolic portrait here depicts Elizabeth as a Hungarian Queen, dressed in traditional Hungarian costume and mending the coronation robe.

View of the Basilica across the Danube, Esztergom ▷

Szentendre ●

For any visitor, Szentendre is a delight. Its Baroque architecture, Orthodox churches, galleries, cobbled streets and riverside setting make it an idyllic place to visit. A horse-drawn carriage ride along the Danube at sunset will be an unforgettable experience.

Although known as the largest Serb settlement in Hungary – Serbs fled here from the Turks after the Battle of Kosovo Polje in 1389, and again after the Battle of Belgrade in 1690 – it was the Romans who founded the town in the 4th century. Many Serbs moved away in the 1920s and artists moved in, attracted by the town's air and light; it remains popular with artists today.

⊞ Fő Square
Fő tér

Fő tér is the bustling heart of Szentendre, which is packed with hawkers and street artists in summer. Its wrought-iron cross was raised in 1763 by survivors of the last major outbreak of bubonic plague.

On the Danube side of Fő tér is its tallest building, the **Blagovestenska Church**, built from 1752–4 to designs by András Mayerhoffer. Its elegantly curved balcony and tall, split-level belfry are models of late-Baroque simplicity. Inside, the choir, frescoes of Emperor Constantine and a large, colourful iconostasis depicting the Annunciation vie for the visitor's attention.

Next door is the pastel pink **Szentendre Gallery**, featuring the works of local artists. The building was once a terrace of six identical merchants' houses. It was converted into a gallery in 1987.

Opposite, in an early-19th-century Saxon-style house, is the **Kmetty Museum**, devoted to the life and works of the painter János Kmetty (1889–

1975), a pioneering Cubist who lived here for 45 years, from 1930 until his death.

🏛 Kmetty Museum
Fő tér 21. *Tel* *(26) 31 02 44.*
◯ 2–6pm Wed–Sun. 📷 🎫 ♿

🏛 Szentendre Gallery
Fő tér 2–5. *Tel* *(26) 31 02 44.*
◯ Oct–Apr: 2–6pm Wed–Sun; May–Sep: 10am–6pm Wed–Sun. 📷 ♿

🏛 Szamos Marzipan Museum
Dumtsa Jenő utca 12. *Tel* *(26) 31 05 45.* ◯ May–Sep: 9am–8pm; Oct–Apr: 9am–7pm. **www**.szamosmarcipan.hu
Since 1935, Szamos has been making marzipan and other sweet treats; today, the name is nothing short of legendary in the Hungarian confectionery world.

The museum in Szentendre opened in 2003. There is a shop and small café on the ground floor offering pastries, bonbons and cakes. These can be enjoyed immediately or be boxed up for later indulgence. Upstairs in the museum children of all ages will delight in the exhibition of a wide range of objects, inlcuding flowers, buildings

The Szamos Marzipan Museum, a homage to confectionery

and figurines – all meticulously and skilfully crafted from marzipan.

⊞ Templom Square
Templom tér

At the top of a small hill above Fő tér, this walled square, the centre of the town in the Middle Ages, stands on the site of the original Roman fort of Ulcisia.

The Catholic Church in the middle of the square was first built in Romanesque style in the 14th century and renovated in Baroque style in the 18th century. A few original features remain, including the sundial on the right-hand side.

Opposite the church is a charming building, home to the **Czóbel Museum**. Béla Czóbel, a painter famous for landscapes and nudes, lived in Szentendre from 1946 to his death in 1976.

🏛 Czóbel Museum
Templom tér 1. *Tel* *(26) 31 02 44.*
◯ mid-Mar–Sep: 9am–5pm Tue–Sun; Oct–mid-Mar: 1–5pm Wed–Sun. 📷 🎫 ♿

🔒 Belgrade Church and Museum of Serbian Orthodox Ecclesiastical Art
Szerb Ortodox Egyházművészeti Gyűjtemény, Könyvtár és Levéltár
Pátriárka utca 5. *Tel* *(26) 31 23 99.*
◯ May–Sep: 10am–6pm Tue–Sun; Oct–Dec, Mar–Apr: 10am–4pm Tue–Sun; Jan–Feb: 10am–4pm Fri–Sun.
📷 ♿

Built by Serbs (but often known as the Greek Church) the Belgrade Church is the Hungarian seat of the Serbian Orthodox Patriarch and so officially a cathedral. Built from 1756–64,

Monument and pretty coloured houses in Fő Square

For hotels and restaurants in this region see p265 and pp286–7

it is a sublime mix of Baroque and Rococo styles, its clock tower topped by a tall spire. Inside it contains icons of Orthodox saints by Vasili Ostoic and a red marble altar.

In the gardens, the Museum of Serbian Orthodox Ecclesiastical Art has some 2,000 icons, vestments, treasures and art objects, all brought here in the 19th century after the closure of their original host churches: testament to the demise of the Serb population of Hungary (see p140).

Icons of Orthodox saints in the Belgrade Church

🚻 Bogdányi Street
Bogdányi utca

Winding its way north from Fő tér, Bogdányi utca is a lively thoroughfare lined with historical buildings, and packed with many shops, stalls and portrait painters.

The **Imre Ámos/Margit Anna Museum** at No. 10 commemorates the life and work of painters Imre Ámos and Margit Anna, who married in 1936, and moved to Szentendre in 1937. Ámos, a Jew, was taken to a labour camp in Vojvodina in 1940, where he continued to paint. He was deported to Germany in 1944, where he died, probably in a concentration camp. His wife Margit lived until 1991. Her Cubist paintings are on the ground floor, while Ámos's work, including his accounts of life in a labour camp, is on the first floor.

A wine barrel sign in Bogdányi Street

A cross on the corner of Bogdányi utca and Lázár tér stands where the body of the legendary Serb ruler Prince Lázár once lay in a church. He was killed by a traitor at the Battle of Kosovo Polje in 1389. His body was taken back to Serbia in the 19th century, and the church was later destroyed in a fire. Preobrazenska Church, at the top of the street, built in 1741–6, is another fine Baroque Serbian Orthodox church. The annual Serb Folk Festival takes place here on 19 August.

🏛 Imre Ámos/Margit Anna Museum
Bogdányi utca 10. ◯ 10am–6pm Thu–Sun. 🎦 🖼 ♿

VISITORS' CHECKLIST

25 km (16 miles) north of Budapest. **Road Map** D3. 🏠 22,000. 🚋 Szentendre (HEV). 🚌 Dunakanyar Körút. 🚢 Dunakorzó (summer only). 🚍 Dunakanyar körút. 🛈 Tourinform, Dumtsa Jenő utca 22, (26) 31 79 65. www.szentendreprogram.hu

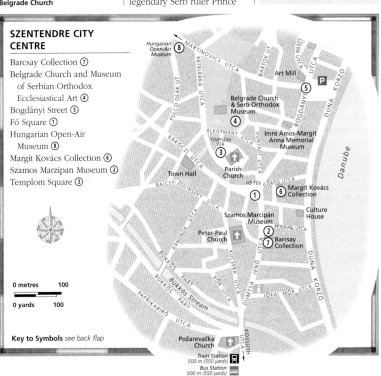

SZENTENDRE CITY CENTRE

Barcsay Collection ⑦
Belgrade Church and Museum of Serbian Orthodox Ecclesiastical Art ④
Bogdányi Street ⑤
Fő Square ①
Hungarian Open-Air Museum ⑧
Margit Kovács Collection ⑥
Szamos Marzipan Museum ②
Templom Square ③

Hungarian Open-Air Museum ⑧
MARTINOVICS UTCA
PATRIÁRKA UTCA
FULCO DEÁK UT
BARTÓK ÚT
SZERB UTCA
Art Mill
DUNA KORZÓ
BOGDÁNYI UTCA
P
⑤

Belgrade Church & Serb Orthodox Museum ④
ALKOTMÁNY UTCA
RÁKÓCZI UTCA
TEMPLOM TÉR
HUNYADI UTCA
Imre Amos-Margit Anna Memorial Museum
Danube

③
Parish Church
Town Hall
BAJCSY-ZSILINSZKY UTCA
FŐ TÉR
GÖRÖG UTCA
①
Margit Kovács Collection ⑥

Szamos Marcipán Museum
PÉTER-PÁL UTCA
Culture House

Peter-Paul Church
KANONOK UTCA
KUCSERA UTCA
DUMTSA JENŐ UTCA
②
⑦ Barcsay Collection
DUNA KORZÓ

0 metres 100
0 yards 100

BÜKKÖS PART
BÜKKÖS PART
BÜKKÖS Stream
PAPRIKABÍRÓ UTCA
KÖR UTCA
JÓKAI MÓR UTCA
KOSSUTH UTCA

Key to Symbols see back flap

Požarevačka Church
Train Station 500 m (550 yards) 🚆
Bus Station 500 m (550 yards) 🚌

🏛 Margit Kovács Ceramics Collection

Kovács Margit Kerámiagyűjtemény

Vastagh György utca 1. *Tel (26) 31 02 44.* ☐ *10am–6pm Mon–Sun.*
🖼 🛇

This 18th-century building (whose entrance is somewhat hidden at the back of a court-yard) was originally a salt storage facility, and became a vicarage for the Blago-vestenska Church a century later. Since 1973 it has been Szentendre's best gallery, devoted to the eclectic work of Margit Kovács (1902–77), a ceramic artist. Kovács attended Budapest's School of Applied Arts before learning the fundamentals in the pottery workshop of Herta Bücher in Vienna, from 1926–8. She developed her skills further in the State School for Applied Arts in Munich, before returning to Hungary where she produced most of her best-known works.

Nursing (1948) is an example of Kovács's obsession with the Madonna, a common theme in many of her early works, while the later *Bread Cutter* (1962) is a witty satire of the idealized Hun-garian peasant woman from a feminist perspective.

Margit Kovács Collection, Szentendre

🏛 Barcsay Collection

Barcsay Gyűjtemény

Dumtsa Jenő utca 10. *Tel (26) 31 02 44.* ☐ *mid-Mar–Sep: Tue–Sun 9am–5pm; Oct–mid-Mar: Wed–Sun 1–5pm* 🖼 🛇

This museum, located in a fine 19th-century Saxon house, is dedicated to Jenő Barcsay (1900–88), who settled in Szen-tendre in 1926 after studying art in Budapest and Paris, where he was influenced by the work of Cézanne. Widely regarded as the first Hungarian Constructivist, he strongly affected his contemporaries. Barcsay's finest works are on display here. Among the most representative are *Street at Szentendre* (1932), *Landscape at Szentendre* (1934) and *Female Portrait* (1936).

A thatched building in the Hungarian Open-Air Museum in Szentendre

🏛 Hungarian Open-Air Museum

Szabadtéri Néprajzi Múzeum

Sztaravodai út. *Tel (26) 50 25 00.* ☐ *Apr–Nov: 9am–5pm.* 🖼 🚗 🛇
www.skanzen.hu

Hungary's largest and best open-air village museum is 4 km (2 miles) from Szentendre; buses depart every 30 minutes (every hour at weekends) from the bus station on Dunakanyar Körút (stop No. 7). The museum, opened in 1967, is spread over 55 hectares (136 acres) and features a reconstructed village from each of Hungary's five historic regions.

Each of the five villages is complete and self-contained, comprising houses, churches, schools, mills, wine presses, forges and stables. Worth looking out for in particular are the three huge outdoor ovens in the village of the Great Plain (brought to the museum from the village of Kisbodak), the roadside crucifixes in the Central Transdanubian village, and the flint-stone walls of the Bakony region houses.

All of the buildings in the museum are open to the public, and some are working museums, with artisans demonstrating traditional skills from pottery to wine-making to visitors. At various times of the year special courses are organized for visitors who want to acquire traditional skills.

The Skanzen Nostalgia Train takes in the main sights of Skanzen. Visitors should allow plenty of time for a visit here.

HUNGARY'S SERBS

The development of the towns and cities of the Danube Bend, especially Szentendre *(see pp138–40)*, was marked by two major waves of Serb migrations to the region. The first, when around 10,000 Serbs fled north following a defeat by the Turks at Kosovo Polje in 1389, was followed by a larger migration in 1690 after another defeat at the hands of the Turks. This second time more than 30,000 Serbs fled north, with as many as 6,000 Serbs settling in Szentendre, founding churches and schools. In the 18th century, Empress Maria Theresa sent many of Hungary's Serbs to settle in the border lands of the Vojvodina, rewarding them with large parcels of land. Today, just 3,800 Serbs officially remain in Hungary.

Crucifix from the Serb Orthodox Museum in Szentendre

Visegrád ❼

40 km (25 miles) north of Budapest.
Road Map C3. 🏚 1,700. 🚌 from
Budapest. 🚃 from Budapest.
🚢 from Budapest, Esztergom; from
Szentendre (summer only).
www.visegrad.hu

Set on the narrowest stretch of the Danube, the village of Visegrád is a popular tourist destination that is dominated by its spectacular ruined citadel. Built in the 13th century by King Béla IV, this was once one of the finest royal palaces in Hungary. The massive outer walls are still intact, and offer the visitor superb views.

Halfway down the hill, in the Salamon Tower, is the **Mátyás Museum**, a collection of items excavated from the ruins of the **Royal Palace**. Built by Béla IV at the same time as the citadel, the palace was renovated two centuries later, in magnificent Renaissance style, by Mátyás Corvinus (see p37). It fell into dereliction in the 16th century after the Turkish invasion and was then buried in a mud slide. The ruins were not rediscovered until 1934, when excavations took place.

The Royal Palace itself is accessible via a 10-minute uphill walk along Fő utca. Now largely reconstructed and whitewashed, several rooms recreate life in the Renaissance Palace.

🏛 **Mátyás Museum**
Salamon-torony utca. **Tel** (26) 59
70 10. ⬤ May–Oct: 9am–5pm
Tue–Sun. 🖼
🏛 **Royal Palace**
Fő utca 23. **Tel** (26) 39 80 26.
⬤ 9am–5pm Tue–Sun. 🖼 🖼

Zebegény's Roman Catholic Church, built in Secessionist style

Zebegény ❽

30 km (19 miles) east of Vác.
Road Map C3. 🏚 1,200. 🚌 from
Budapest. 🚃 from Budapest.

Famous for fine views of the Danube Bend, the tiny village of Zebegény also boasts one of Hungary's few Catholic churches in Secession style. Designed by Károly Kós, Dénes Györgyi and Béla Jánszky and built from 1910–14, its plain façade has Neo-Romanesque traits. It is its sharply angled and tiered, Christmas-tree-like roof that sets the church apart, while the tall adjoining spire adds elegance. Inside, the colourful frescoes of St Constantine are the last major works by the master painter Kriesch Aladár Körösfői (1863–1920).

Behind the church is the **István Szőnyi Memorial Museum**. One of the most

Signpost in Duna-Ipoly National Park

prominent Hungarian Expressionist painters, Szőnyi lived here most of his life until his death in 1960. The museum displays personal artifacts, family photos and some of his works, incuding *A Bench in the Garden* (1943).

🏛 **István Szőnyi Memorial Museum**
Bartóky utca 7. **Tel** (27) 37 01 04.
⬤ Mar–Oct: 10am–6pm Tue–Sun;
Nov–Feb: 10am–4pm Tue–Sun. 🖼
🖼 Hungarian and German. 🖼

Nagybörzsöny & Duna-Ipoly National Park ❾

24 km (15 miles) north of Visegrád.
Road Map C2/3. 🚃 from Szob (to
Nagybörzsöny). **www**.dinpi.hu

Home to the fine 14th-century stone Romanesque Church of St Stephen, a working mid-19th-century water mill (open to the public) and a mining museum, Nagybörzsöny is best known as the gateway to the Duna-Ipoly National Park, one of the largest in the country. The Buda Hill caves and the Sas-hegy nature trail outside Budapest are also within its borders.

The park is home to more than 70 protected plants and more than half of Hungary's native bird species (including black and white-backed woodpeckers).

A narrow-gauge railway runs at weekends from Nagybörzsöny to Nagyírtás across the Börzsöny Hills, from where well-marked hiking trails fan out across the park. There is also a long trail from Nagybörzsöny itself, leading up to Nagy Hideg Hegy peak, which offers views across to Slovakia.

A second narrow-gauge railway, from Kismaros to Királyrét, opens up the southern part of the park. There are hiking trails from Királyrét across the hills, and on to Nógrád, where there is a spectacular ruined castle.

The spectacular ruins of the citadel, towering over Visegrád

Esztergom ⓾

St István, Hungary's first king, was baptized in Esztergom, and crowned here on Christmas Day in the year 1000. Almost completely destroyed by the Mongol invasion 250 years later, the town was gradually rebuilt during the 18th and 19th centuries. Esztergom today is still Hungary's most sacred city, the seat of the Archbishop of Hungary. Although it is dominated by the huge Basilica *(see pp144–5)*, Esztergom has much to offer besides its mighty cathedral, including the remains of a 10th-century castle, a picturesque Old Town, an eclectic Watertown, the fascinating Danube Museum and Hungary's finest collection of ecclesiastical art.

🔒 Esztergom Basilica
See pp144–5.

♣ Royal Palace and Castle Museum
Vár & Vármúzeum
Szent István tér 1. **Tel** (33) 41 59 86.
⬭ 10am–4pm Tue–Sun (to 6pm Apr–Oct). 🎫 🎫 compulsory.

Opposite Esztergom Basilica are the partly reconstructed remains of the Royal Palace, one of the oldest buildings in Hungary. The southern walls date back to the 10th century. From 1256 onwards it served as the palace of Esztergom's Archbishops, and improvement was continuous right up until the Turkish invasion, when it was sacked. Much of the palace remained, however, and is open today as the Castle Museum.

The only way to see the palace is on a guided tour, which takes in the study of King Mátyás' tutor, with ceiling frescoes based on Florentine Renaissance palaces,

Statue of Queen Elizabeth in Víziváros

and the 12th-century Royal Chapel, with an original rose window and 13th-century portraits of the apostles.

To the south and north are well-preserved remains of the ramparts and steps back into the town. The Esztergom Castle Festival takes place in the palace grounds in June and July.

🏮 Víziváros
Berényi utca

Víziváros (Watertown) is a district of mainly Baroque buildings, narrow streets, single-storey houses and tiny well-kept gardens. The area was developed during the regeneration of Esztergom after the withdrawal of the Turks in the early 18th century.

Víziváros Parish Church, consecrated by Jesuits in 1728, is a perfect example of the Baroque architecture of the time with its rounded façade and high nave. The twin spires were added much later, in the middle of the 19th century. The Baroque interior was unfortunately lost during World War II, and has yet to be replaced. The statue in front of the church was raised in 1740 by the people of Esztergom, grateful for having survived an outbreak of the plague. A bridge behind the church leads to Prímás Sziget, an island of gardens and parks in the Danube, from where another bridge crosses the river into Slovakia.

The Lord's Coffin of Garamszent-benedek, in the Christian Museum

🏛 Christian Museum
Keresztény Múzeum
Mindszenty tér 2. **Tel** (33) 41 38 80.
⬭ Mar–Nov: 10am–5pm Wed–Sun.
⬤ Dec–Feb. 🎫 🎫

The Roman Catholic Primate of All Hungary, János Simor, resided in this grand Neo-Renaissance palace after it was completed in 1882, and immediately opened the palace and its vast collection of paintings, including works by early Italian Renaissance artists Migazzi and Bertinelli, to the public. The building has been a dedicated museum since 1924, and its collection of church art, bolstered by many subsequent purchases, is now the finest in Hungary.

The splendid, wheeled Lord's Coffin of Garamszentbenedek (now in Slovakia), dating from 1480, is decorated with carved figures and is still used in Easter processions. It is thought not to contain any human remains: its purpose has always

View of Esztergom's huge basilica, rising high on Castle Hill

For hotels and restaurants in Esztergom see p265 and p286

been symbolic. The room devoted to altarpieces, some dating back to the 14th century, is stunning in its colour and historical import. Tamás Koloszvári's *Ascension* is considered the most significant medieval painting in Hungary.

Besides the picture gallery, there are equally stunning sculpture and icon galleries.

🏛 Bálint Balassa Museum
Balassa Bálint Múzeum

Mindszenty tér 5. **Tel** (33) 50 01 75. May–Oct: 11am–5pm Tue–Sun; Nov–Apr: open by appointment. Hungarian only.

Situated opposite the Víziváros Parish Church, the Bálint Balassa Museum is named after a Renaissance poet who died in 1594 while fighting the Turks. The museum's primary permanent exhibition focuses on life in Esztergom during the Middle Ages and the Turkish era, and includes some archaeological finds from the Royal Palace. The two-storey museum building itself, with its huge, tunnel-like entrance, dates from 1860, and was originally a boys' school.

The Danube Museum, devoted to life with the river

🏛 Danube Museum and Lower Esztergom
Duna Múzeum & Belváros

Kölcsey utca 2. **Tel** (33) 50 02 50. May–Sep: 9am–5pm Tue–Sun; Oct–Dec & Feb–Apr: 9am–4pm Tue–Sun. Jan.

The role of the Danube in the history and development of Esztergom is given due importance in this outstanding museum close to the city centre. The building itself is a gem. It was built in the 18th century in Baroque style and was a crumbling wreck until renovated in 1973, when the museum moved here from its previous home on the Danube. The museum houses all sorts of hydraulic equipment from the past century, as well as exhibits devoted to damming the Danube and navigation, water supply and purification. There is a collection of engineering tools, as well as a history of water management since Roman times. Children will enjoy the many hands-on displays, which enable them to get very wet indeed.

A five-minute walk south along Vörösmary utca leads to Széchenyi tér, centre of the Lower Town and surrounded on all sides by a mixture of Baroque and Neo-Classical houses, many of which are now cafés. Its focal point is the Town Hall, an immaculately preserved Rococo building from 1729.

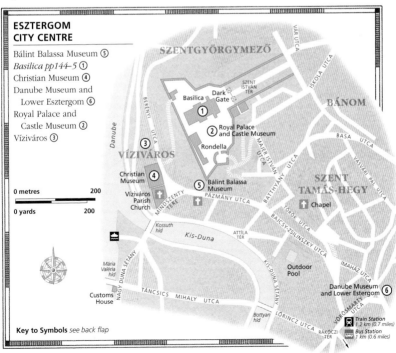

ESZTERGOM CITY CENTRE

0 metres 200
0 yards 200

Key to Symbols *see back flap*

Esztergom Basilica

Detail of the Dome of the Basilica

Rising high above the Danube, its bright blue cupola visible from afar, the cathedral at Esztergom has been a symbol of Hungary for a millennium, ever since St István was crowned here on Christmas Day 1000. Hungary's largest cathedral, the present structure, dating from the 19th century, was built over a 47-year period from 1822 to 1869. It replaced the much smaller 12th-century St Adalbert's Cathedral that was destroyed by the Turks as they retreated in the 18th century.

Basilica
Esztergom Basilica is distinguished by its outer simplicity and inner beauty. A grand but plain façade gives way to priceless treasures and superbly rich decoration.

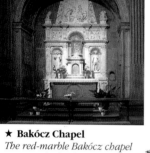

★ Bakócz Chapel
The red-marble Bakócz chapel opens to the basilica's nave. Built in Florentine Renaissance style, it is named after Cardinal Tamás Bakócz (c.1442–1521), who is laid to rest here.

Corinthian Columns – 22 in total – give the basilica's entrance an unmistakable Neo-Classical appearance.

Main entrance

Primate of All Hungary
In 1887 the Roman Catholic Primate, János Simor, entrusted his vast private Christian art collection to the cathedral. It formed the basis of the Esztergom Christian Museum (see p142).

North Tower is one of two identical basilica bell towers which rise to 71.5 m (235 ft), matching exactly the height of the main dome's interior. The unusual, octagonal form of their bases is thought to be unique in Hungary.

★ Dome/Cupola

A steep flight of steps leads up to the dome's viewing platform, from where there are superb views over Esztergom and the Danube Bend – and Štúrovo in Slovakia on the northern bank.

Pillars supporting the Dome

VISITORS' CHECKLIST

Szent István tér 1. **Road Map** C3.
Tel (33) 40 23 54. 🚌 🚐 🚤 ⚪
Cathedral *Mar–Oct:* 8am–6pm;
Nov–Dec: 8am–4pm daily;
Cupola & Bell Tower *Apr–Oct:*
9:30am–5pm daily; **Treasury**
Mar–Oct: 9am–4:30pm daily;
Nov–Dec: 11am–3:30pm Tue–Sun,
10am–3:30pm Sat & Sun. **Crypt**
Mar–Oct: 9am–4:30pm; *Nov–Dec:*
10am–2:30pm daily. 📷 🎫 ♿ 🚫
Treasury, Crypt. 🍴 📷 *Jun–Aug.*

★ Copy of Titian's *Assumption of the Virgin (1853–4)*

Behind the altar, this is the largest single-canvas painting in the world. The original (1516–18) hangs in Venice's Santa Maria Gloriosa dei Frari.

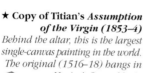

Tomb of Cardinal Mindszenty in the Crypt

Cardinal József Mindszenty was a pillar of resistance to both the Nazi and Communist regimes. He died in exile in 1975, and his body was laid to rest here in 1991.

Treasury

Hungary's most valuable collection of liturgical and royal art, dating back to the early Árpád dynasty, is kept here, as well as a shrine with St István's skull.

STAR SIGHTS

★ Bakócz Chapel

★ Copy of Titian's *Assumption*

★ Dome/Cupola

NORTHERN TRANSDANUBIA

For centuries, Northern Transdanubia was Hungary's golden triangle, the conduit in trade and commerce between the twin capitals of Vienna and Budapest; it was where the empire's greatest families built their mansions with profits made in the region's factories. Recently, tourism has surpassed industry as a main source of income, with Bük's thermal baths and Lake Fertő the main attractions.

Much of the western part of this region is classic frontier territory. The Őrség region, Kőszeg, Szentgotthárd and Sopron, Hungary's most westerly city, were for centuries bulwarks against invaders. Nowhere else in Hungary is it more apparent that Austria and Hungary were once parts of the same empire. Sopron, in fact, is closer to Vienna than to Budapest – its street signs are often in German and well-dressed Viennese throng its charming Old Town. Further south, in Szombathely, German as well as Hungarian can be heard, and at the popular Lake Fertő, Hungarians are outnumbered by visitors in summer. Yet this is proudly Hungary.

Close to Győr, a city of legends that is as far from Vienna as it is from Budapest, is the astonishing abbey of Pannonhalma. One of Hungary's most historic complexes, its Benedictine monks resisted all invasions and tests of their faith. The abbey at Zirc, further south, is no less important.

In recent times the west of the region has seen a determined search for oil. Although some oil has been found, many probes found little except hot water, indeed, the springs that serve the thermal resort of Bükfürdő were discovered this way.

The east of Transdanubia includes Székesfehérvár, where for 500 years Hungarian kings and queens were crowned, and Lake Velence, a quiet spot and a favourite with all nature-lovers. The real natural wonder of Northern Transdanubia, however, is the Bakony Forest, which offers some of the most spectacular driving routes in the country.

A verdant landscape in the rolling Northern Transdanubia hills

◁ **Detail of the portal on the main entrance to the Abbey, Ják**

Exploring Northern Transdanubia

The most varied region of Hungary, Northern Transdanubia is characterized by its gentle hills, green valleys, lush forests and beautiful imperial towns, including Székesfehérvár, one of the country's architectural gems. There is also the historic town of Kőszeg to see, the fortress-like Pannonhalma Monastery to explore, the thermal waters of Sárvár and Bük and Lake Fertő to relax in, as well as the vineyard around Pápa to visit.

SEE ALSO

- **Where to Stay** pp266–8
- **Where to Eat** pp287–9

The Trinity Column in Fő tér in Sopron, celebrating relief from the plague

Bratisla
Vienna
M15   15
MOSON-MAGYARÓVÁR
Jánossor
FERTŐRÁKOS Neusiedler
20   See
SOPRON 18
FERTŐ-HANSÁG
NATIONAL PARK   Répce
NAGYCENK 17   19   21   KAPUVÁR
FERTŐD   22   CSOR
84   23
GYŐR-MOS
84   86   Szar
Répcelak
BÜK 15
KŐSZEG 16
87   Rába
SZOMBATHELY   Márca
89   13   88   14
SÁRVÁR   Celldö
12 JÁK   V A S   84
86   Jánosháza
Vasvár   8
Körmend   74   SÜMEG
Szentgotthárd   Zalaszentgrót
ÓRSÉG REGION
Szalafő 11   76   Keszt
Őriszentpéter   Zalalövő   9 ZALAEGERSZEG
86
Keszthely
Bak
75   Z A L A
Lenti   74
Principális-cs.
Siófok
M70   7
Mura Letenye   M7   7   10
Zagreb   NAGYKANIZSA
61
Kaposvár

KEY

▬▬	Motorway
▬▬	Major road
—	Secondary road
⋯⋯	Minor road
┈┈	Main railway
──	Minor railway
▬▬	International border
▬▬	Regional border

For additional map symbols see back flap

GETTING AROUND

The M1 motorway between Budapest and Vienna provides quick access to Northern Transdanubia, and is ideal for exploring the places in this chapter, including Győr, Tata, Mosonmagyaróvár and Lake Fertő. High-speed trains run between Budapest and Vienna, many of which stop at Győr. Slower, local services serve other towns and cities in the region. From Győr, there are good roads – but poor rail and bus services – to the western cities of Zalaegerszeg and Szombathely.

Bas-relief on the Széchenyi Mansion in Nagycenk

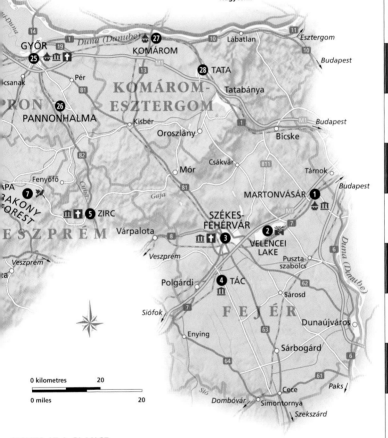

SIGHTS AT A GLANCE

Brunswick Mansion in Martonvásár, housing a small Beethoven Museum

charm, though all offer a variety of places to stay. Agárd is the most developed, and has an excellent thermal bath complex. Most non-Hungarian visitors to Velence head for the western shore. More than 30,000 birds spend the spring here, nesting in the marshes and reeds. Species to be spotted include spoonbills, herons and geese. Since 1958 the lake has been a protected bird reserve. The Tourinform office in Gárdony can put birdwatchers in touch with local tour groups and guides.

Martonvásár ❶

30 km (19 miles) southwest of Budapest. **Road Map** C3. ♞ *5,500.* ▣ *from Budapest.* ▥ *from Budapest.*

The village of Martonvásár has existed since medieval times, but its principal attraction is **Brunswick Mansion**. Towards the end of the 18th century, the entire village was bought by the German Brunswick family, and the original Baroque palace was built for Antal Brunswick. A century later, in 1875, it was totally rebuilt, this time in the Neo-Gothic style. While the house is closed to the public, the superb parklands can be enjoyed by visitors. The estate's church, built in 1775, is largely unaltered. Its interior is decorated with well-preserved frescoes.

Ludwig van Beethoven was a regular visitor to the original mansion and gave music lessons to the daughters. Some rooms adjoining the mansion now house a small **Beethoven Memorial Museum** (Beethoven Emlékmúzeum).

🏛 Brunswick Mansion
Brunszvik utca 2. ◯ *8am–dusk daily (park only).* ⭐ ⭐

🏛 Beethoven Memorial Museum
Brunszvik utca 2. **Tel** *(22) 56 95 00.* ◯ *May–Oct: 10am–noon, 2–6pm Tue–Sun; Nov–Apr: 10am–noon, 2–4pm Tue–Sun.* ⭐ ⭐

Lake Velence ❷

50 km (31 miles) southwest of Budapest. **Road Map** C4. ▣ *from Budapest to Velence or Gárdony.* ▥ *from Budapest to Velence or Gárdony.* ℹ *Tourinform, Szabadság út 16, Gárdony, (22) 57 00 77; Halász utca 37, Velence, (22) 50 70 30.*

Velence means "Venice" in Hungarian, although there the similarities end. A shallow body of water with no islands, Lake Velence is popular with day-trippers from Budapest. It is less crowded than Lake Balaton, attracting mainly anglers and swimmers, the latter enjoying the warm water (up to 26° C / 80° F in high summer). Three small beach resorts on the eastern shore, Velence, Gárdony and Agárd, more or less blend into each other. None has any great

Piano in the Beethoven Memorial Museum

Székesfehérvár ❸

See pp152–3.

Tác ❹

11 km (7 miles) south of Székesfehérvár. **Road Map** C4. ♞ *1,500.* ▥ *from Székesfehérvár.* ◈ *Ludi Romani Theatre Festival (last week of Aug).*

On a vast site a 10-minute walk outside the tiny village of Tác are the impressive remains of the Roman city of Herculia. Uncovered during excavation work in 1934–9, Herculia began life in the 1st century AD as a military base called Gorsium, growing in size and importance to become the capital of the province of Valeria (Lower Pannonia) by the 3rd century.

Set up as the **Gorsium Open-Air Museum** (Gorsium Szabadtéri Múzeum in Régészeti Park) since 1962, the site is well cared for though lacking in major attractions. While

The mooring jetties on Lake Velence, popular with visitors from Budapest

it is possible with the naked eye to make out the shapes of houses, the theatre and the forum, the guidebook available from the ticket office is a must to understand how it all worked. Digs continue and finds are common: the unearthed treasure (including pottery, coins, masonry and weaponry) is displayed in a small museum by the entrance.

In the last week of August, the Ludi Romani Theatre Festival stages Greek and Roman theatre here. Details are available from the Tourinform office in Székesfehérvár.

🏛 Gorsium Open-Air Museum

Fő utca 6, Tác. **Tel** (22) 36 22 43.
⬜ Apr–Oct: 10am–6pm daily; Nov–Mar: 10am–4pm daily. 🖼 ♿

Excavated Roman ruins, at the Gorsium Open-Air Museum in Tác

Zirc ❺

51 km (32 miles) northwest of Veszprém. **Road Map** B3. 🏘 7,500.
🚆 from Veszprém, Győr. 🚌 from Veszprém. ℹ️ Tourinform, József Attila utca 1, (88) 41 68 16.

The small town of Zirc, on the northern fringes of the Bakony Forest (see pp156–7) is dominated by its **Cistercian Abbey** (Római katolikus, cisztercita templom, Nagyboldogasszony). Standing on a hill above the town, at an altitude of 400 m (1,312 ft), the Abbey was founded as early as 1182, although the current complex (including the twin-spired Baroque

Façade of the Zirc Cistercian Abbey, home to the Reguly Antal Library

basilica) dates from 1750. The altar paintings and frescoes inside are the work of Franz Anton Maulbertsch. The most visited part of the abbey, however, is its Reguly Antal Library, complete with 80,000 volumes kept on lush, cherry-wood bookshelves. The abbey is also home to the Bakony Natural History Museum, with exhibitions on the flora and fauna of the Bakony hills and forest.

In the town of Zirc itself is an extensive Arboretum, with more than 60 kinds of trees and shrubs, including a 400-year-old oak tree. The Reguly Antal Museum, a small but interesting exhibition, is dedicated to the life of the early-20th-century pioneer in Finno-Ugric linguistics and explorer.

🏛 Zirc Cistercian Abbey

Rákóczi tér 1. **Tel** (88) 59 36 41.
⬜ 9am–5pm Tue–Sat, 11am–5pm Sun. 🖼 🖼

Pápa ❻

51 km (32 miles) northwest of Veszprém. **Road Map** B3. 🏘 34,000.
🚆 from Budapest, Tatabánya, Győr.
🚌 from Tatabánya, Veszprém. ℹ️ Tourinform, Kossuth Lajos utca 18, (89) 31 15 35. **www**.papa.hu

An important fortified town first mentioned in 1051, Pápa was held by the Turks from 1594–1683. It fell into decline after being razed by fire in 1685. In the 18th century it was rebuilt and found new purpose in 24 watermills driven by the Tapolca river. The mills served the corn, textile and paper industries of the region. Pápa's two most important sights stem from this boom period.

The **Esterházy Palace** (Esterházy Kastély), on Fő tér, was constructed from 1783–4 by József Grossmann for Count Ferenc. Baroque in style, it was badly damaged in World War II and neglected under the Communists. Today, however, it is completely renovated.

The giant **Great Church of St Stephen**, built in 1774–86 to designs by Jakab Fellner, dominates everything. After his death, József Grossmann completed the work. The statue above the gable and the frescoes inside feature St Stephen the Martyr.

🏛 Esterházy Palace

Fő tér 1. **Tel** (89) 31 35 84.
⬜ 10am–6pm Wed–Sun. 🖼 🖼
♿ **www**.vmmuzeum.hu

Statue of a lion outside the Esterházy Palace in Pápa

Street-by-Street: Székesfehérvár ❸

The cobbled, car-free streets of the old town in Székesfehérvár are packed with historically and religiously significant buildings. For 500 years this was the location of Hungary's coronation church; the sarcophagus of the country's first Christian king, St István, is still here today. As one of the last stands of the German army during World War II took place in these streets, it is little short of a miracle that the medieval and Baroque buildings surrounding Városház tér survive. Around them everything was destroyed – hence the bland feel of the rest of the city.

Town Hall
Székesfehérvár's 18th-century Town Hall was originally built as a palace for the Zichy family.

★ **St Anne's Chapel**
Dating from the 15th century, St Anne's Chapel is the only part of medieval Székesfehérvár to have survived the Turkish occupation.

★ **St István's Cathedral**
The entrance to the cathedral was remodelled in the 1770s by Franz Anton Hildebrandt. The statues above the door are of István, László and Imre.

Doll Museum

Budenz House

Carmelite Monastery
The magnificent altar (1768), featuring scenes from the life of the Virgin Mary, is the work of Viennese master Franz Anton Maulbertsch.

| 0 metres | 50 |
| 0 yards | 50 |

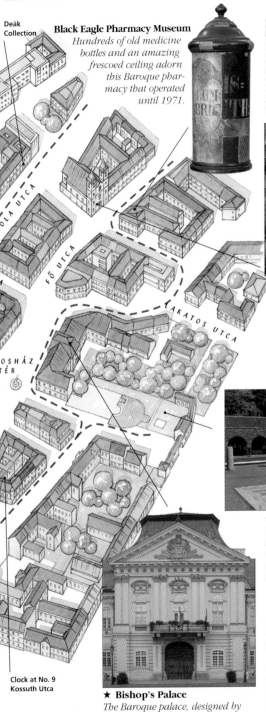

Black Eagle Pharmacy Museum
Hundreds of old medicine bottles and an amazing frescoed ceiling adorn this Baroque pharmacy that operated until 1971.

Deák Collection

OLA UTCA

FŐ UTCA

LAKATOS UTCA

OSHÁZ TÉR

Clock at No. 9 Kossuth Utca

★ Bishop's Palace
The Baroque palace, designed by Jakob Riedler, was built in 1801 using stone taken mainly from the ruins of the Royal Basilica.

VISITORS' CHECKLIST

60 km (37 miles) SW of Budapest. **Road Map** C4.
105,000. from Budapest. from Budapest. Piac tér. daily, Piac tér. Tourinform, Oskola utca 2–4, (22) 53 72 61. www.szekesfehervar.hu

Cistercian Church and Monastery
The Baroque 18th-century altar fresco in this church was painted by local artists under the direction of the German-born painter Caspar Franz Sambach.

Garden of Ruins
The vast size of the Royal Basilica and burial chapel that once stood here can be easily imagined by tracing the outline of the ruins.

KEY

– – – Suggested route

STAR FEATURES

★ Bishop's Palace

★ St Anne's Chapel

★ St István's Cathedral

Exploring Székesfehérvár

Around 897, Árpád *(see p35)* created a permanent settlement, and with it the first Hungarian town, on the Székesfehérvár plain. Prince Géza, his great-grandson, built a castle here in 972, and St István, Géza's son, erected a vast basilica. The walled city that grew up around it was the site of Hungary's Diet, or parliament, for 500 years, until the Turks occupied the city and the inhabitants fled in 1543. Székesfehérvár flourished in the 1800s and 1900s. In World War II much of the town was destroyed but the historic centre *(see pp152–3)* was spared.

Pot from St István Király Museum

🏛 St István Király Museum
Szent István Király Múzeum
Fő utca 6. *Tel (22) 31 55 83.*
◯ *May–Sep: 10am–4pm Tue–Sun; Mar, Apr, Oct–Dec: 10am–2pm Tue–Sun.* 🏷 📷 *German and Hungarian only.* **www.**szikm.hu

The friary of the Cistercian church *(see p153)* houses a collection of artifacts from the Fejér region. The earliest exhibits go back as far as the Neolithic Age, and there is also a significant collection of Roman treasure. The most recent finds include parts of the sarcophagus of St István, most of which is in the Garden of Ruins *(see p153)*. The friary itself was built at the same time as the church, and completed in 1751. It first housed Jesuit, then Franciscan, and finally Cistercian monks. The museum has temporary exhibitions at the Ceremonial Hall, Országzászló tér 3.

🏛 Black Eagle Pharmacy Museum
Fekete Sas Patikamúzeum
Fő utca 5. *Tel (22) 31 55 83.*
◯ *10am–6pm Tue–Sun.* ♿

The city's pharmacy moved into this elegant two-storey Baroque house in 1774. It remained open for business until as late as 1971, when it was bought by the State and renovated and reopened as a museum two years later. The museum has a collection of old medicine bottles and medical implements, but much more interesting are the colourful frescoes on the arched ceiling, and the gorgeously intricate original wooden fixtures and fittings dating from 1758.

🏛 Deák Collection
Városi Képtár Deák-gyűjtemény
Oskola utca 10. *Tel (22) 32 94 31.*
◯ *10am–6pm Tue–Sun.* 🏷 ♿

An overview of the history of modern Hungarian art, Dénes Deák's (1931–93) collection features early 20th-century artists Rippl-Rónai and Gulácsy, modern European-School artists Imre Ámos and Margit Anna and Tihamér Gyarmathy's contemporary abstract art. Sculpture and graphic art are also represented.

⛪ St István's Cathedral
Szent István Székesegyház
Arany János utca 9. *Tel (22) 31 51 14.* ◯ *Jun–Aug: 9:30am–5pm daily.*

Béla IV founded this church, later renovated in Baroque style, and parts of the original Hungarian coronation ceremony once took place here. After 1777 it became a cathedral and its prominent twin towers were added. The statues show István, László and Imre. The city's coat of arms sits above the main portal.

🏛 Budenz House and Ybl Collection
Budenz-ház & Ybl-gyűjtemény
Arany János utca 12. *Tel (22) 31 55 83.* ◯ *Apr–Oct: 10am–2pm Sat.* 🏷 ♿

Ervin Ybl, descendant of the architect Miklos Ybl *(see p89)*, bequeathed his collection of 18th-century furniture, family portraits and religious art to the city of Székesfehérvár on his death in 1965. Budenz House is named after József Budenz (1836–92), a pioneer in linguistics.

🏛 Székesfehérvár Doll Museum
Fehérvári Babaház
Megyeház utca 17. *Tel (22) 32 95 04.*
◯ *9am–5pm Tue–Sun.* 🏷

The Doll Museum, in the former county governor's offices, holds this large collection of mainly 18th-century dolls,

Exhibits from the Doll Museum, displaying fascinating detail

Interior of St Istváns Cathedral, with ceiling frescoes by Johannes Cymbal

dolls' houses, tin soldiers and castles and other toys, that have been assembled by Éva Moskovszky, a retired librarian of the Hungarian National Museum. The detail and opulence of these toys are astonishing – the dolls wear genuine pearl necklaces and the tiny homes, copies of homes built between 1800 and 1930, are immaculately furnished with real Herend porcelain (see p203). Even the clocks on the dolls' house walls are in full working order.

🔒 Carmelite Church
Karmelita templom

Petőfi utca. ⬜ by arrangement. ♿
Not fully completed until 1769, the church was designed by an anonymous architect. The Carmelites were so desperate for a place to worship that they began holding their services in the unfinished (but consecrated) church in 1732, a year after construction began, when the building was little more than a shell. The exterior is Baroque, with a single, modest tower. The real glory of the church, however, are the colourful, dramatic ceiling frescoes inside, most of which are the work of Franz Anton Maulbertsch, a native of Vienna who worked on a number of churches in the area around Lake Balaton. He also painted the altar and the crucifix in the oratory. The ceiling frescoes were damaged during a minor earthquake in 1800, and suffered further during the Napoleonic wars when the church was transformed into a hospital. They were restored during the 1950s. Outside the church, set into the southern wall, is a statue of Louis the Great, the work of Hungarian sculptor Ödön Moiret.

🎠 No. 9 Kossuth Street
Kossuth utca 9

Kossuth tér 9. ♿
The vivid and playful clock in the small pedestrian square behind No. 9 Kossuth utca chimes every hour on the hour, as small figures dressed as hussars stand guard. The clock is the focal point of a colourful Secessionist house that has become increasingly

Detail on the clock at No. 9 Kossuth Street

hemmed in by the less interesting buildings surrounding it. Once an art gallery, the house currently stands empty.

🏛 Open-Air Ethnographical Museum
Palotavárosi Skanzen

Rác utca 11. **Tel** (22) 37 90 78.
⬜ Mar–Oct: 10am–4pm Wed–Sun.
📷 🛇 ♿
Unlike other village museums in Hungary, which are usually located outside towns, Palotavárosi is set close to the city centre, in the suburbs of Székesfehérvár. Visitors entering the cobbled streets of the museum (which for centuries was the Rácváros, or Serb area of the city) find themselves in a lost world. At No. 11 Rác utca, a small museum tells the story of the area and of Székesfehérvár's

Serb community, of its traders and craftsmen, with exhibitions on shoemakers, leatherworkers and furriers. Also on Rác utca is the Ráctemplom, the single-nave Serb church, a Baroque 18th-century building with colourful, fully restored icons. Many of them had been hidden by soot for the best part of a century.

♣ Bory Castle
Bory Vár

Máriavölgy utca 54.
Tel (22) 30 55 70.
⬜ Mar–Nov: 9am–5pm daily. 📷
The most visited sight in Székesfehérvár is the whimsical Bory Castle, built over two decades by the sculptor and architect Jenő Bory (1879–1959). Construction first began in the mid-1920s, when Bory had a group of his students build him a small cottage and plant a vineyard. He then added various parts to it, the designs becoming gradually more colourful and daring, until, at the time of his death, the cottage had grown into a veritable fantasy land, part Roman forum, part Gothic castle, with touches of just about every other architectural style thrown in. Some of the castle's rooms exhibit Bory's sculptures, as well as paintings by his wife, Ilona Komócsin, also responsible for most of the exterior art.

The romantic Bory Castle, a blend of architectural styles

A Tour Around the Bakony 🐂

The Bakony refers to the volcanic mountain range that rises behind the northern shore of Lake Balaton, as well as to the dense forests that cover the hills and valleys of the region, stretching from the Balaton in the south as far as Pannonhalma Abbey in the north. Dotted with vineyards and old wine-press houses, it is one of the most scenic parts of Hungary. It was devastated during the Turkish withdrawal from Hungary in the 17th century, and resettled with Saxons from Germany in the 18th century. Many of the villages today have a distinctly Germanic feel.

Bakonykoppány ⑤
A centre of the Bakony wine-making industry, the area is famous for its full-bodied white wines. Visitors should look out for the wine-press houses, which are dotted amongst the vineyards.

Pápa ⑥
The Viennese artist Johann Ignaz Mildorfer is responsible for the beautiful ceiling fresco found at the Esterházy Palace Chapel. The town is also known for its rich, royal blue cloth, made here by the Kluge family since 1783, for seven generations until 1956.

Bakonyjákó ⑦
Set in a picture-postcard spot, this village was one of many in the Bakony that was popular with German settlers in the 18th century. Many of the houses are typically Saxon, set at a right angle to the main road.

Városlőd ⑧
At the meeting point of the Northern and Southern Bakony stand the ruins of the 11th-century Hölgykő Castle, destroyed by the Turks in the 16th century. Városlőd was repopulated by German settlers in the 18th century.

Ajka ⑨
Fine handmade glass, crystal and porcelain have been produced in Ajka since German settlers set up a factory here in 1878. Although the factory itself is not open to the public, there are two shops in the village selling wares made at the factory.

Úrkút ⑩
The route from Ajka to Herend, passing through Úrkút and the Szentgál Valley, is one of the most scenic in Hungary, offering up a wealth of gentle hills and wonderful views.

GYŐR
Csót
Béb
Pápa ⑥
Nagygyimót
Bakonyszü
Borsosgyőr
Ugod
Kéttornyúlak
Tapolcafő
Tapolca
Pápa-kovácsi
Ganna
Döbrönte
Iharkút
Némétbán
⑦
Farkasgyepű
Csehbánya
Magyarpolány
Bakonygyepes
8 E66
8 E66
Kislőd
⑧
Ajkarendek
KÖRMEND
Torna
⑨
⑩
Padragkút

Kőris-hegy ④

An easy hiking trail takes walkers from Bakonybél at the foot of the hill up to the summit of Kőris-hegy, at 704 m (2,309 ft) the highest of the Bakony hills. The path leads back down to Zirc on the other side.

Bakonybél ③

The gently sloping, grassy hills above the pretty village of Bakonybél are accessible via a number of well-marked hiking trails, and make superb spots for picnic lunches.

Zirc ②

Famous for its large Cistercian Abbey, Zirc is also home to the Bakony Natural History Museum.

TIPS FOR DRIVERS

Tour length: 130 km (81 miles) All the roads on the tour are in good condition, though the minor routes from Zirc to Pápa and from Ajka to Herend get very narrow and twisty in places.

Stopping-off points: Zirc, with its museum, Cistercian Abbey and Arboretum, is a good choice for a short stop, while Pápa offers a wealth of choices for lunch, for example the ornate Arany Griff Hotel (see p290).

Veszprém ①

Hungary's best preserved castle district rises above one of the country's most prosperous cities. With many fine restaurants, this is a good place to start and end the tour.

Herend ⑪

The hand-painted porcelain made here is famous the world over. Visitors may visit the museum and exhibitions, and also watch some of the 600 artists who work here in action.

Map labels:
GYŐR
Borzavár
Nagyesztergár
Tündérmajor
Zirc ②
Akli
Olaszfalu
Pénzesgyőr
Eplény
pső-Hajag 646
Lókút
Hárskút
Gyulafirátót
⑪ Herend
SZÉKESFEHÉRVÁR, BUDAPEST
Szentgál
Márkó
Kádárta
Séd
① Veszprém
73

0 km 5
0 miles 5

KEY

═══ Motorway

▬▬▬ Tour route

══ Major road

═ ═ Other road

┄┄ Main railway

☀ Viewpoint

△ Peak

Sümeg ❽

43 km (27 miles) north of Keszthely.
Road Map B4. 🏯 *7,000.*
🚉 *from Keszthely, Tapolca.*
🚌 *from Keszthely, Zalaegerszeg.*
ℹ️ *Tourinform, Kossuth Lajos utca 15*
(87) 55 02 76.

This pretty town has been inhabited since Roman times and is dominated by its castle, which sits atop the 270-m (885-ft) high Castle Hill. **Sümeg Castle** (Sümeg Vár), first built in the 13th century though almost completely reconstructed in the 16th, is one of the best preserved in Hungary. It houses an exhibition on the town's history, weapons, and coaches, as well as a hair-raisingly realistic torture chamber. During the summer there are lively re-enactments of historic battles, jousting contests and medieval dancing in the courtyard. Tourinform will have details of performances.

The town's main attraction, however, is the **Roman Catholic Church of the Ascension** (built 1756–7) on Bíró Márton utca. Though unspectacular from outside, inside it has a series of frescoes by Austrian Franz Anton Maulbertsch, a leading figure in late-Baroque art. The frescoes, perhaps his greatest work, were painted in 1757–8 and tell the story of the gospel, from the Annunciation below the organ gallery to the Ascension in the dome.

♣ **Sümeg Castle**
⭕ *May–Sep: 9am–6pm daily; Oct–Apr: 9am–4pm daily.* 📷

Decorative elements on the former synagogue in Zalaegerszeg

Zalaegerszeg ❾

37 km (23 miles) east of Keszthely.
Road Map A4. 🏯 *62,000.* 🚉 *from Budapest.* 🚌 *from Keszthely.*
ℹ️ *Tourinform, Széchenyi tér 4–6,*
(92) 31 61 60. 🎪 *Deák tér, daily.*
www.zalaegerszeg.hu

Zalaegerszeg, capital of the Zala region and Hungary's leading oil town, has two attractions that make a stop here worthwhile. The first is the **Göcseji Village Museum** (Göcseji Falumúzeum), the oldest such in Hungary, located on a tranquil backwater of the river Zala. Set up in 1968 it displays more than 40 buildings, brought here from 22 nearby villages. The museum also hosts a Finno-Ugric exhibition, with Finnish, Hanti and Manysi homes. The Nodding Jennies are part of Hungary's Oil Industry Museum.

Zalaegerszeg's city centre is brightened up by the former **synagogue**, today a concert and exhibition hall. It was designed by József Stern. Its bright and lively motifs betray its late Secession-era construction (1904), though the two domes add a little religious dignity.

🏛 **Göcseji Village Museum & Finno-Ugric Ethnographical Museum**
Falumúzeum utca. **Tel** *(92) 70 32 95.*
⭕ *Apr–Oct: 10am–4pm; Nov–Mar: 9am–5pm Tue–Sat.* 📷
Hungarian. ♿ **www**.zmmi.hu

Statue of Sándor Petőfi and a soldier, in Nagykanizsa

Nagykanizsa ❿

50 km (23 miles) south of Zalaegerszeg. **Road Map** A5. 🏯 *53,000.*
🚉 *from Budapest.* 🚌 *from Keszthely, Zalaegerszeg.* ℹ️ *Tourinform, Csengery utca 1–3, (93) 31 32 85.*

Originally a castle town, Nagykanizsa found wealth in the late 17th century first as a cattle-trading town, then in the late 19th century as a hub for food processing. The city centre around Szabadság tér was built over the site of the castle, used as a mosque by the Turks and destroyed by the Habsburgs in 1705. The fountain in the middle of the square marks the former castle entrance. The Baroque Catholic Church, on Zárda utca, was built in 1702–14 using remnants of the castle. The city's Neo-Classical synagogue, at Fő utca 6, built in 1807–10, is being restored. In the middle of Deák tér is a statue of the Hungarian poet Sándor Petőfi (1823–49).

Courtyard of Sümeg Castle, now site of re-enactments of medieval battles

For hotels and restaurants in this region see pp266–8 and pp287–9

Őriszentpéter, the largest of the villages in the Őrség region

Őrség Region ⓫

50 km (31 miles) west of Zalaeger-szeg. **Road Map** A4. 🚃 to Szentgotthárd from Körmend. 🚌 to Őriszentpéter from Szentgotthárd and Körmend. 🛈 Tourinform Őriszentpéter, Siska-szer 26A, (94) 54 80 34. **Szalafő Village Museum** ◻ Apr–Oct: 10am–6pm daily. 🖼

Since the 10th century and the first Magyar excursions into the region, the Őrség has been a frontier land, populated by hardy warriors who swore to defend Hungary's borders in exchange for a lifetime's tax exemption. Covered in lush forests, the gently sloping hills of the Őrség – today designated a National Park – were traditionally sprinkled with small hilltop settlements, never comprising more than ten houses. Some 18 of these settlements remain, almost all of which are beautifully preserved, many containing wooden houses with characteristic overhanging roofs, dating back to the 13th century. The settlements, called *szers*, all follow the same pattern: the houses are grouped around a courtyard, in the middle of which are stables.

The largest of the Őrség villages is **Őriszentpéter**, which in June hosts the Őrség Fair, a weekend of folk music, craft fairs and traditional dancing competitions. Őriszentpéter is, in fact, a collection of timber and thatched *szers* that came together to form one community. The village is rightly proud of its 13th-century Romanesque St Peter Church, at Templomszer 15. It is almost entirely original, containing fragments of 16th-century frescoes, which, given the number of fires that have plagued the village over time, is little short of miraculous.

Six km (4 miles) away, **Szalafő** is the second largest village in the region, consisting of six *szers*. The largest of these is today the **Szalafő Open-Air Ethnographical**

Museum (Őrségi Népi Műemlékegyüttes). Here, visitors can see an Őrség house as it would have looked in the early 19th century, complete with cooking utensils and other domestic items. Other settlements worth visiting are **Velemér**, which has a 14th-century church with fine frescoes, and **Hegyhátszentjakab**, where visitors can admire a splendid medieval church.

Nearby, **Lake Vadása** is popular with swimmers and anglers. On the northern borders of the Őrség are two towns of note: **Szentgotthárd** and **Körmend**. Both are good access points for the Őrség, and both have attractions of their own: Körmend is home to the Baroque **Batthány Mansion** built for the family in the 17th century. A small part of the building is open to visitors. At Szentgotthárd the ceiling frescoes of the Cistercian Monastery Church, painted in 1785 by Stephen Dorffmaister, are outstanding.

🏛 **Szalafő Open-Air Ethnographical Museum**
Pityerszer 12. **Tel** (30) 467 70 22.
◻ Apr–Oct: 10am–6pm daily. 🖼
🎦 Hungarian only. ♿

The grand façade of the 17th-century Batthány Mansion in Körmend

Holy Trinity monument, Fő tér, Sopron ▷

The impressive hilltop Benedictine abbey church in Ják

Ják ⑫

12 km (7 miles) south of Szom-bathely. **Road Map** A4. 🏠 *2,400.*
🚌 *from Szombathely.*

The Benedictine **St George's Abbey Church** (Jáki Szent György Bence's Apátsági Templom) is the best preserved and most impressive example of Romanesque architecture in Hungary. Built in 1214–56, this twin-towered masterpiece, influenced by late Norman architecture, sits imposingly on a hilltop above the village. The western façade is worthy of note, with its recessed doorway, a richly decorated portal featuring almost life-size carvings of Jesus and the apostles. This style, called the Porta Speciosa technique, was refined before becoming a model for Roman-esque churches all over Hungary. Inside the church are original 14th-century frescoes showing the church's founder, Jáki Nagy Márton, and his family. The church was fully restored in 1890 by Frigyes Schulek who also restored the Mátyás Church in Budapest (*see pp62–3*). The tiny St Jakab Chapel opposite was built in 1260 for the use of non-monastic villagers.

Detail on the portal of the Benedictine Abbey in Ják

🏠 **St George's Abbey Church**
Fő tér. **Tel** (94) 35 60 14.
🕐 *8am–6pm daily.* ♿

Szombathely ⑬

101 km (60 miles) southwest of Győr.
Road Map A3. 🏠 *115,000.* 🚆 *from Sopron, Győr.* 🚌 *from Zalaegerszeg.*
ℹ️ *Tourinform, Király utca 1/A, (94) 51 44 51.* 🎵 *Bartók Classical Music Festival (Jul); Savaria Carnival (Aug).*

Founded by the Romans in AD 43, and known as Savaria, Szombathely was an important trading and staging post on the "Amber Road" from the Baltic Sea to Italy. Every August the Savaria Carnival recreates those ancient days, and hundreds of volunteers don Roman costumes and engage in battles, dancing and music. The remains of the once-vast Roman Forum (Savaria was the capital of Roman Pannonia Superior) are among the city's leading sights, with mosaic floors and the public baths clearly visible. There is more Roman treasure on show at the Savaria Museum. Standing next to the ruins is the city's cathedral, Hungary's largest Baroque church, built in 1791–4. Its interior suffered great damage during World War II and is undergoing continuous restoration work. However, it is open to the public. Next to it is the Bishop's Palace, an attractive Rococo building whose Sala Terrena houses the Diocesan Museum, which has a fine collection of ecclesiastical art. Another room contains a series of frescoes by Stephen Dorfmeister based on life in ancient Savaria.

A short walk from the cathedral is Fő tér, today the main centre of the city and a shopper's paradise that is popular with mothers and children. There are further Roman ruins at the Iseum Ruin Garden on Batthány tér, featuring a temple to the goddess Isis, believed to be one of only three ever found in Europe. Next door is the Szombathely Gallery. In May, when more than 50 kinds of rhododendron are in full bloom, the Kámoni Arboretum north of the city centre is well worth a visit.

Szombathely Cathedral, Hungary's largest Baroque church

Sárvár ⑭

25 km (16 miles) east of Szom-bathely. **Road Map** A3. 🏠 *16,000.*
🚆 *from Szombathely.* 🚌 *from Szombathely.* ℹ️ *Tourinform, Várkerület 33, (95) 52 01 78).*

The Magyars built an earth castle (*Sárvár* translates quite literally as mud castle) here in the 10th century. Long before that it appears the Romans had some fortifications here, and even the Celts found this confluence of the Rába river a sound defensive position. The **Sárvár Castle** that now attracts visitors is far from the mud of yore, however, having been built in the 16th century. Its patrons were the Nádasdy family, who bought the town in 1534. Patriarch Tamás Nádasdy brought in Italian architects to create a genuine Renaissance masterpiece, which, with various additions, survives more or less intact to the present day.

Much of the castle is given over to the **Ferenc Nádasdy Museum**, the highlight of which are two series of frescoes: 17th-century works showing the Hungarians in battle with the Turks and scenes from the Old Testament painted by Stephen Dorffmaister in 1769. There are also exhibitions of the family's and town's histories, regional folk art and period furniture. The castle is reached via a long stone bridge over what was once a moat.

In 1961, during a search for oil *(see below)*, hot springs (44 °C/111 °F) were found in Sárvár, and the **Sárvár Spa and Wellness Centre** is now one of the largest bath complexes and, after its renovation and extension, the most modern in Hungary. It comprises indoor and outdoor pools, leisure and splash pools, a sauna and a treatment centre offering various therapies.

🏛 **Ferenc Nádasdy Museum**
Várkerület 1. **Tel** (95) 32 01 58.
⏰ 9am–5pm Tue–Sat.
♿ 🈯 Hungarian only.

⚓ **Sárvár Spa and Wellness Centre**
Vadkert utca 1. **Tel** (95) 52 36 00.
⏰ 8am–10pm daily. 🈯 ♿

One of the outdoor pools at the Bük Medicinal Baths

Bük ⓯

24km (15 miles) northeast of Szombathely. **Road Map** A3. 🚗 *3,100.* 🚆 *from Szombathely.* 🚌 *from Szombathely.* ℹ *Tourinform; Eötvös utca 11, (94) 55 84 19.*

Thermal springs were discovered at this village near the Austrian border in 1956 during a search for oil. Since then the **Bük Medicinal Baths** (Bükfürdő) have grown to become one of Hungary's largest, and most attractive medicinal bath complexes. There are indoor and outdoor pools of various sizes and temperatures, offering treatments for a variety of different disorders, and the grounds are well laid out with grassy areas, children's playgrounds, snack bars and restaurants. A fair-sized resort has also grown up around the pool complex, and the Birdland Golf and Country Club *(see pp300–3)*, a short walk from the thermal baths, is home to Hungary's finest golfing centre. It is the only 18-hole course in Hungary to have hosted a professional golf tournament.

⚓ **Bük Medicinal Baths**
Termál kőrút 2. **Tel** (94) 55 80 80.
⏰ *winter: 8:30am–6pm daily; summer: 8:30am–7pm daily.* 🈯 ♿

OIL AND WATER

Many of the largest thermal bath complexes in Hungary, such as those at Bük and Sárvár, have only been in existence since the latter part of the 20th century, when the thermal springs that serve them were found during oil searches. Desperate to fuel its industrialization, Hungary's Communist

Indoor thermal baths in Sárvár

government hoped that the discovery of the Nagylengyel oil field in the west of the country in 1951 would be the first of many oil strikes in the region. Vast sums of money were spent foraging for oil, though all that was found was what became known as "white gold": thermal water. Some small deposits of crude oil were eventually located, but although Hungary does produce oil (Zalaegerszeg is the centre of the industry, *see p158*) domestic production accounts for less than 10 per cent of consumption.

The Knights Hall in Sárvár Castle, with superb battle frescoes

Kőszeg ⑯

Nestled in lowland hills just minutes from the Austrian border, modern-day Kőszeg is a small, quiet town, whose citizens are proud of its past. It is probably the only town in the world where the bells toll at 11am – in honour of Captain Miklós Jurisics, who led the Hungarians during a 25-day Turkish siege of Kőszeg Fortress in August 1532. The memory of Jurisics dominates the city, with its main square, castle and one of its museums carrying his name. Spared during World War II, Kőszeg is the most attractive town in the region.

♣ Jurisics Castle
Jurisics-vár

Rájnis József utca 9. **Tel** (94) 36 01 13. ☐ 10am–5pm Tue–Sun. ☒ ✔ Hungarian only. ♿

It was here, in the carefully preserved Jurisics Castle, that Miklós Jurisics and 450 Hungarian soldiers held a 30,000-strong Turkish force at bay for 25 days in August 1532. The Hungarians eventually abandoned their stand, only to return the following spring to retake the castle with Austrian help.

A fire in 1777 destroyed part of the castle: the interior arcades were built after the blaze. The Castle Museum has displays on the town's history, including various depictions of the siege. It also has 18th- and 19th-century interiors and displays on the region's viticulture.

Crest above the gate to Jurisics Castle

Heroes' Gate, in Miklós Jurisics Square

☷ Miklós Jurisics Square
Jurisics Miklós tér

In the heart of Kőszeg's Old Town is this enclosed charming square, surrounded on all sides by churches, houses, museums and courtyards. The impressive entrance to the square, the Heroes' Gate, was erected to commemorate the 400th anniversary of the Turkish Siege. Though built in 1932 it recreates much older towers, and blends in impeccably with the surrounding – mainly Baroque – buildings. Of these, the Arcade House (Lábasház) next to the tower at No. 2 Jurisics tér, is a highlight, complete with its courtyard colonnades. The Jurisics Museum on the other side of the tower, housed in the late-Renaissance General's House (Tábornok), has a fine collection of memorabilia of the various guilds, artisans and tradesmen who inhabited the town. Next to the museum is the Town Hall, originally built in 1487, though the façade was remodelled in the Baroque style in the 18th century.

Today a pizzeria, the ornate Sgraffito House at No. 7 Jurisics tér dates from the 16th century. Sgraffito was an Italian method of creating lavish decorations by scratching through several layers of plaster. This is one of only few Sgraffito houses in Hungary, and while time has not been kind to the façade, the effect is just still visible.

At the northern end of the

square is the Baroque St Imre Church, completed in 1640 by Hungarian Lutherans who had been expelled from St James's Church (see below) by German Lutherans.

Medieval wall painting in the southern nave, Church of St James

⛪ Church of St James
Szent Jakab templom

Rájnis utca 2. **Tel** (94) 56 33 97. ☐ 10am–6pm daily. ☒ donation. ♿

Standing next to the more recent Church of St Imre, the Church of St James was completed in 1407, but much reconstructed in the 18th century. It remains clearly a Gothic building, however. The most important historic building in Kőszeg, the church has served Jesuit, Protestant and Roman Catholic congregations. The faded frescoes inside, by an unknown artist, depict the Magi, and are original, dating from 1403. Overpainted during the 17th century by the Lutherans, who disapproved of such ostentatious decoration, the frescoes were forgotten and only uncovered during interior restoration in the 1950s. The wooden statue of the Madonna is also an original from the Gothic era.

✡ Synagogue
Zsinagoga

Várkör 38. **Tel** Anikó Béres (20) 934 8730. ☐ 2–6pm Sat, or by appointment.

Completed in 1859, this well-sized and imposing red brick synagogue once served the considerable Jewish population in Kőszeg, which was entirely wiped out during the Holocaust. Closed for some time, the synagogue is

Window detail on the front façade, Kőszeg Synagogue

currently undergoing major restoration work, but parts of it can be visited on Saturday afternoons or by calling ahead to make an appointment. The synagogue's striking façade and Neo-Gothic towers can still be admired from the outside.

Golden Unicorn Pharmaceutical Museum
Arany Egyszarvú Patikamúzeum
Jurisics Miklós tér 11. *Tel (94) 36 03 37.* ◯ *Mar–Nov: 10am–5pm Tue–Sun.* 🅿 📷 ♿
Hungarians tend to be fascinated with old chemist

shops, but only rarely is one as deserving of interest as this particular example. As well as being set in a fine Baroque house on Jurisics tér, it contains a superb late 18th-century wooden apothecary counter, complete with old medicine bottles. It looks not unlike something from a film set. Upstairs the exhibition continues with a display showing how the medicines were cleaned, dried, stored and prepared. Most were remedies made from natural ingredients and plants grown in the pharmacy's own herb garden.

Jesus's Heart Church
Jézus Szíve templom
Fő tér. *Tel (94) 56 33 97.* ◯ *9am–6pm daily.* 🅿 ♿
This fantastical Neo-Gothic wedding-cake church is famous for its colourful stained-glass altar windows depicting Saints István, Imre and Elizabeth. Built in 1892–4 to designs by the Austrian

VISITORS' CHECKLIST

50km (31 miles) south of Sopron. **Road Map** A3. 🏠 12,000. 🚌 from Szombathely. 🚃 from Sopron. 🛈 Tourinform, Rájnis utca 7, (94) 56 31 20.

Otto Kott, its 60-m (196-ft) high tower is the tallest in the city. The interior is beautifully decorated, with delicately patterned marble columns.

Interior of Jesus's Heart Church

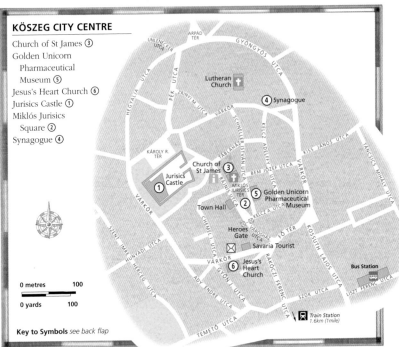

KŐSZEG CITY CENTRE

0 metres 100
0 yards 100

Key to Symbols see back flap

The façade of Széchenyi Mansion in Nagycenk

Nagycenk ⑰

15 km (9 miles) southeast of Sopron.
Road Map A3. 🏛 *1,900.*
🚉 from Sopron. 🚌 from Sopron.
🎭 *Nagycenk Art Days (Aug).*

There are probably more public squares, streets, boulevards and avenues named after Count István Széchenyi (1791–1860), often called "the greatest Hungarian", than any other public figure, including St István himself. A philanthropic industrialist, his family home was the **Széchenyi Mansion** at Nagycenk that is today a museum dedicated to his life and works. Stuffed with his personal effects, portraits, furniture and family history, the enormous Baroque mansion, built in the late 18th century for Széchenyi's grandfather, was all but destroyed in World War II, but was rebuilt as an exact replica of the original in the 1950s.

In 1815 the mansion was the first home in Hungary to benefit from gas lighting. Széchenyi made sure that the ordinary townsfolk of Nagycenk benefited from this technological wonder too, and they repaid his generosity by building him a mausoleum in the village cemetery. The Neo-Romanesque church, next to the cemetery, was designed by Miklós Ybl *(see p89).*

Nagycenk is also the starting point of the **Széchenyi Museum Railway**, a steam-powered train operation that runs along narrow-gauge tracks to Fertőbőz. In the locomotive museum at the terminus, steam engines, passenger coaches and freight and lumber wagons evoke the history of narrow-gauge railway lines.

🚋 **Széchenyi Mansion**
Kiscenki út 3. **Tel** (99) 36 00 23.
🕐 *Apr–Oct: 10am–6pm daily; Nov–Mar: 10am–5pm Tue–Sun.* 🎫 🅿 ♿

🏛 **Széchenyi Museum Railway**
Hársfasor. **Tel** (99) 51 72 44.
🕐 *Apr–Oct: Sat & Sun only.* 🎫

Sopron ⑱

See pp168–9.

Fertő-Hanság National Park ⑲

16 km (10 miles) east of Sopron.
Road Map A3. Rév-Kócsagvár, Sarród (Park Administration). **Tel** (99) 53 76 20. 🎫 ♿ 🚉 from Sopron, Győr. 🚌 from Zalaegerszeg.

Based mainly on Lake Fertő, which for 40 years was one of the most heavily guarded parts of the Iron Curtain, Fertő-Hanság National Park (Fertő-Hanság Nemzeti Park) is now a protected nature reserve. As one of Europe's most significant water habitats, it became part of UNESCO's list of World Heritage Sites in 2001. With the eastern Alps as its dramatic backdrop, the lake is shallow, in most places less than 1 m (3 ft) deep, and is famous for its vast expanses of tall reeds. The lake's main sources of water are rainfall and two small streams. In fact, the lake has completely dried up a number of times; the last in 1867–71. There are numerous rare plant species – the park is famous for its "gallery" of snowdrops – and more than 200 species of birds nest here, including the Hungarian ibis, spoonbill and little egret. Many parts of the park can only be visited with special permits or on organized guided tours. Visitors can find out about both visits and tours at the park's administration office in Sarród.

The lake is circumnavigated by one of Europe's best cycle paths, which takes in spectacular landscapes in both Hungary and Austria. Favourable, frequent winds also make the lake a popular place to sail, while the shallow waters are inviting to swimmers. The main resort on the Hungarian side is Fertőrákos, where there are sailing boat launches, grassy beaches for sunbathing and many attractive nature walks.

Fertőrákos ⑳

8 km (5 miles) north of Sopron.
Road Map A3. 🏛 *2,300.*
🚉 from Szombathely. 🚌 from Sopron. ℹ Tourinform, Fertőd, Joesph Hydn utca 2, (99) 53 71 40.
www.fertorakos.hu

The main resort on the coast of Lake Fertő, Fertőrákos is best known for its quarry, opened in 1628, which provided limestone for Vienna's St Stephen's Cathedral, among

Cave Theatre in the former limestone quarry at Fertőrákos

other buildings. The valuable Lajta rock was hewn here from the time of the Antonines, though quarrying ended shortly after World War II. What remains is a surreal series of man-made, uneven caverns, colonnades and porticoes.

In July the superb acoustics of the main cavern are put to perfect use as the setting for musical, dance and opera performances as part of the Sopron Festival Week. During the rest of the year the caves are open to the public as a **Quarry Museum** (Kőfejtő).

🏛 **Quarry Museum**
Fertőrákos Fő utca.
Tel (99) 35 50 26. ⬜ May–Sep: 8am–7pm daily; Feb, Nov, Dec: 8am–4pm daily; Oct, Mar, Apr: 8am–5pm daily. 📷 ✓

Fertőd ㉑

25 km (16 miles) east of Sopron.
Road Map A3. 🚌 3,400. 🚆 from Szombathely. 🚌 from Sopron.
ℹ Tourinform, Joseph Haydn utca 3, (99) 37 05 44. 🎵 Haydn Festival (Jun–Sep).

The small town of Fertőd was created in 1950 when two former estates belonging to the Esterházy family, called Süttör and Esterháza, were merged. It was for the Esterházy family (see box), the wealthiest family in the region, that the town's masterpiece, the **Esterházy Palace** (Esterházy Palota), was built. First constructed as a two-storey hunting lodge in 1720, the grand palace is the result of vast extensions by the architect Melchior Hefel in the 1770s. The Neo-Baroque French gardens were laid out at the same time, though these were much remodelled along English ideas of garden design at the beginning of the 20th century.

The wrought-iron entrance gate, with its Rococo stone vase separating columns, is the perfect front to the palace, at which the visitor arrives along a yew-tree-lined path. The palace was badly damaged during World War II, however, a restoration project is due to be completed by 2013 which will transform it

The bedroom of the prince in the Esterhazy Palace in Fertőd

into a Central European cultural centre. The main ballrooms and drawing rooms have already been restored to their glorious best – priceless French furniture, Venetian mirrors and Flemish tapestries abound.

Joseph Haydn's presence at the palace from 1766 to 1790 is celebrated by the annual Haydn Festival with concerts of the composer's work. The focus is on his chamber music, performed by outstanding musicians in the Grand Gallery and the gardens.

🎼 **Esterházy Palace**
Joseph Haydn utca 2. *Tel* (99) 53 76 40. ⬜ Nov–mid-Mar: 10am–4pm Fri–Sun; mid-Mar–Oct: 10am–6pm Tue–Sun. 📷 ✓ ♿

THE ESTERHÁZY FAMILY

For three centuries the Esterházy family was one of the richest and most powerful in Hungary. It flourished under the Habsburgs, whom family members served in a variety of political and military offices. The dynasty was founded by Count Nikolaus Esterházy (1583–1645) and his son, Prince Paul Esterházy, who sided with the Habsburgs during the Counter-Reformation (see pp40–41). The family originated in – and derived its name from – the settlement Esterháza in modern-day Slovakia. The Esterhazys moved to Eisenstadt, in Austria, in the 17th century, and set up home there. It was Paul Esterházy who decided to build the palace at Fertőd. After World War I, the family lost influence and was further weakened by internal feuds. Much Esterházy property is still bitterly fought over by various family branches.

Crest from the Esterházy Palace in Fertőd

Street-by-Street: Sopron Belváros ⑱

When visitors step through the Gate of
Loyalty into Belváros – the Inner Town –
they arrive in another world. Surrounded
entirely by the modern city that has
grown up around it, this historic part of
Sopron is compact and easy to explore
on foot. Belváros is centred around Fő
tér and includes just four other streets,
yet contains most of the city's main
sights. There is a wealth of Secessionist
architecture to see, as well as the Firewatch Tower, from where stunning views
of Sopron unfold. A genuine city within
a city, it is one of Hungary's treasures.

County Hall
*Vencil Hild designed this
elegant Classical build-
ing, constructed in
1829–34.*

Museum of Mining
*The museum, at Templom
utca 2, is housed in the
former town residence
of the Esterházy princes.*

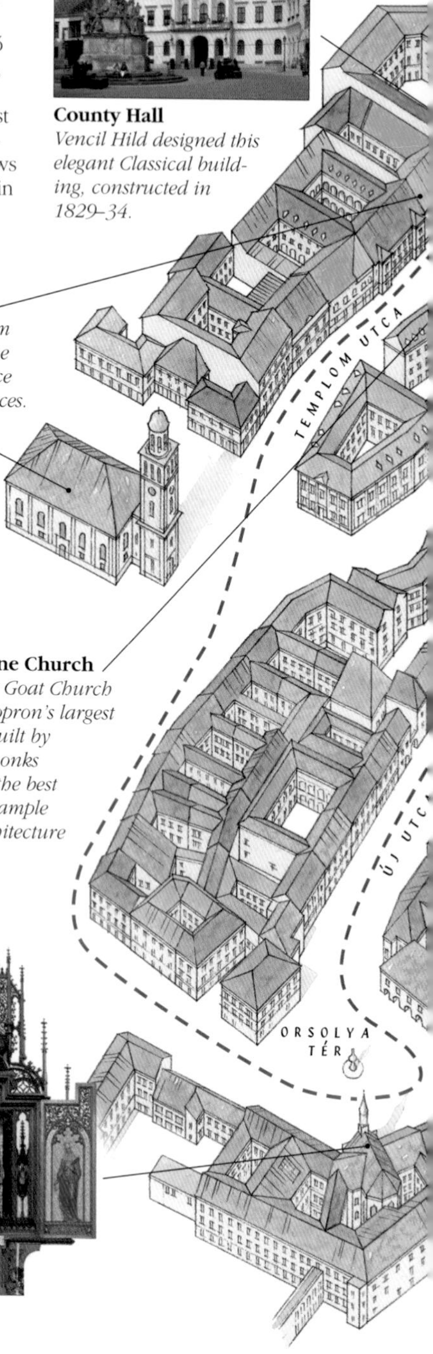

**The Lutheran
Church** (1782) was
made possible by
József II guaran-
teeing freedom
of worship to
his subjects.

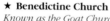

★ **Benedictine Church**
*Known as the Goat Church
(see p170), Sopron's largest
church was built by
Franciscan monks
in 1280. It is the best
remaining example
of Gothic architecture
in Hungary.*

Ursuline Church
*This former convent,
founded by Ursuline nuns
in 1747, is one of the most
impressive buildings in the
town. It holds an outstanding
collection of ecclesiastical art.*

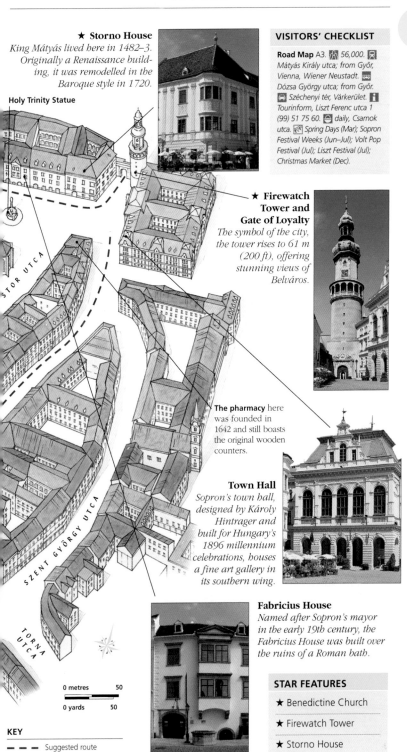

★ Storno House
King Mátyás lived here in 1482–3. Originally a Renaissance building, it was remodelled in the Baroque style in 1720.

Holy Trinity Statue

STOR UTCA

SZENT GYÖRGY UTCA

TORNA UTCA

VISITORS' CHECKLIST

Road Map A3. 56,000.
Mátyás Király utca; from Győr, Vienna, Wiener Neustadt.
Dózsa György utca; from Győr.
Széchenyi tér, Várkerület.
Tourinform, Liszt Ferenc utca 1 (99) 51 75 60. daily, Csarnok utca. Spring Days (Mar); Sopron Festival Weeks (Jun–Jul); Volt Pop Festival (Jul); Liszt Festival (Jul); Christmas Market (Dec).

★ Firewatch Tower and Gate of Loyalty
The symbol of the city, the tower rises to 61 m (200 ft), offering stunning views of Belváros.

The pharmacy here was founded in 1642 and still boasts the original wooden counters.

Town Hall
Sopron's town hall, designed by Károly Hintrager and built for Hungary's 1896 millennium celebrations, houses a fine art gallery in its southern wing.

Fabricius House
Named after Sopron's mayor in the early 19th century, the Fabricius House was built over the ruins of a Roman bath.

0 metres 50
0 yards 50

STAR FEATURES

★ Benedictine Church

★ Firewatch Tower

★ Storno House

KEY

– – – Suggested route

Exploring Sopron

A border town of the Pannonia province, Austrian number plates and German-language shop and street signs are much in evidence in Sopron today, and it is easy to forget that this is still Hungary. In 1921, the people of Sopron voted to stay in Hungary, rather than join Austria, and the Gate of Loyalty is dedicated to the result of that plebiscite. One of Hungary's oldest cultural centres, Sopron has remains of Roman edifices and city walls as well as grand medieval buildings, including both churches and a synagogue. Among other sights are a Pharmacy Museum and an outstanding art collection.

🏛 Collection of Roman Catholic Church Art
Római Katolikus Egyházművészeti Gyűjtemény
Orsolya tér 2. **Tel** (99) 31 22 21.
⬜ 10am–4pm Mon, Thu; 11am–4pm Sun. 📷 ♿

This fine collection of ecclesiastical art is owned and managed by Sopron's Catholic Convent, and housed in the Oratory of the Baroque former Ursula Monastery, built in 1861–4. Most items on display are from the Baroque period, complemented by an early 19th century collection. There are liturgical cups, crosses, christening bowls, historical altars and paintings. The finest painting, of St Dominic accepting the Rosary, was created by the Neapolitan Rococo master Martin Altamonte in 1710. In front of the building is the long-defunct Maria Fountain, transferred here from a nearby monastery in the 1930s.

Sculpture in the former Ursula Monastery

✡ Old Synagogue
Ó-Zsinagóga
Új utca 22. **Tel** (99) 31 13 27.
⬜ Apr–Oct: 10am–6pm Tue–Sun.

Thought to have been built around 1300, the medieval synagogue of Sopron is one of the oldest in Europe. In line with anti-Semitic legislation of the day, the local Jewish community had to build their prayer hall set back from the main buildings on the street, which is why it stands behind two Baroque houses. Abandoned in 1526 when the Jews were expelled from Sopron, many of its original features remain intact, however, including the recess in the east wall holding a replica Ark of the Covenant.

Across the road, the New Synagogue was built in 1370 for the private use of a Jewish banker. It too fell into disuse in 1526, and though its exterior is in reasonable repair, it is closed to the public.

The Old Synagogue, its prayer hall set back from the street

🔒 Benedictine Church
Kecske Templom
Templom utca 1, Fő tér. **Tel** (99) 523 768. ⬜ 9am–5pm daily. 📷 ♿

Built by Franciscans in 1280, this great Gothic church was handed to the Benedictines in 1787, when József II dissolved the Franciscan order. It has remnants of medieval frescoes inside and the simple, elegant Kapisztrán pulpit, unique in style. The church is known as Goat Church – a goatherd is said to have financed it from treasure found by his flock.

The Benedictine Church, originally belonging to the Franciscan order

🏛 Museum of Mining
Bányászati Múzeum
Templom u. **Tel** (99) 31 26 67.
⬜ 10am–4pm Tue–Sun. 📷

This engaging museum presents the history and science of mining in Hungary over a thousand years.

🏛 Fabricius House Archeological Museum
Régészet-kőtár
Fő tér 6. **Tel** (99) 31 13 27. ⬜ Apr–Sep: 10am–6pm Tue–Sun; Oct–Mar: 2–6pm Tue–Sun. 📷

The highlight of the museum is the *lapidarium*, with headstones, sarcophagi and altars from all eras of Sopron's history. Another display features Sopron and the Amber Road.

🏛 Storno House
Storno-gyűjtemény és Helytörténeti kiállítás
Fő tér 8. **Tel** (99) 31 13 27. ⬜ Apr–Sep: 10am–6pm Tue–Sun; Oct–Mar: 10am–2pm Tue–Sun. 📷 ♿

The Storno, a grand 15th-century medieval house and the one-time home of King Mátyás, displays a fine collection of art, antiques and period furniture.

Painting of *St Dominic*, above the main altar of the Holy Spirit Church

♛ Firewatch Tower
Tűztorony
Fő tér. ☐.*Apr–Oct 10am–6pm daily* 🖼

The symbol of the city, the Firewatch Tower was built on the remains of the Roman wall in the 13th century. Balcony and spire are Baroque; they were added after the building burned down in 1676. The Gate of Loyalty, at the foot of the tower, was added in 1928 to designs by Rezső Hikisch.

🏛 Pharmacy Museum
Patika Múzeum
Fő tér 2. **Tel** *(99) 31 13 27.* ☐ *Apr–Sep: 10am–6pm Tue–Sun; Oct–Mar: 2–6pm Tue–Sun.* 🖼 ♿

The former Angel Pharmacy (1601) opened as a pharmacy museum in 1966. It displays fascinating medical items, old manuals dating back to 1572 and beautiful Altwien china jars from Vienna.

♛ Széchenyi tér and Holy Spirit Church
Domonkos templom
Széchenyi tér.

Spacious and green, Széchenyi tér at the southern entrance to Belváros is surrounded by outstanding architecture on all sides. The Holy Spirit Church on its southeastern corner – easily missed if approaching from the railway station – was designed by Lorenz Eysenkölbl and built in 1719–25, with the spires added in 1775. A local artist, Stephan Schaller, painted the picture of St Dominic above the altar. The adjoining two-storey building is the Baroque Dominican Priory, built in 1750. Across the road stands the Széchenyi Palace, built in 1851 for Ferenc Széchényi. Today housing administrative offices and closed to the public, many of the first exhibits in Hungary's National Museum collection (*see pp98–9*) came from here. István Széchenyi is honoured with a huge bronze statue in the middle of the square. On the north side is the Ferenc Liszt Cultural Centre (*Müvelő-dési Ház*), built in 1872. Liszt performed here regularly, and it hosts cultural events today.

♛ Old City Walls
Várkerület.

Having survived many attacks, Sopron's city walls – built by the Romans and once encircling the entire Belváros – were dismantled by locals at the end of the 19th century in order to improve access to the city. The best place to view the remnants is from the Várkerület, opposite Árpád utca. As well as an 8-m (26-ft) thick portion of wall and part of the Great Round Bastion, the Roman parts of the city's defences are clearly visible.

🏛 Zettl–Langer Collection
Balfi utca 11. **Tel** *(99) 31 11 36.* ☐ *10am–noon daily.* 🖼 ♿

A century and a half ago, Gusztáv Zettl had to choose between his first love, art, or his father's business empire. He chose business, but never lost his love of art. Much of the money he made in business was invested in some of the finest art of the period. His collection, which encompasses works from all genres, periods and fashions, has been exhibited in the Zettl family home since 1955 (Zettl himself died in 1951). The house itself has artisan windows, frescoed ceilings, Biedermeier furniture and paintings by Rembrandt, Paolo Veronese and Anton Dorffmeister.

A room in the Zettl family home, housing the Zettl-Langer Collection

♛ Károly Lookout Tower
Károly-magaslati Kilátó
Lővérek. **Tel** *(99) 31 30 80.* ☐ *Summer: 9am–8pm daily.* 🖼

The 23-m (75-ft) high tower, built in 1876 atop the 398 m (1,306 ft) high Károly-magaslat, offers great panoramic views of the lush forests, Lake Fertő and the snow-covered Schneeberg range in the Wienerwald, west of Vienna. A small exhibition outlines the unique natural features of the Sopron Nature Conservation Area.

St Anne's Church in Kapuvár, built in the Neo-Baroque style

Kapuvár ㉒

47 km (29 miles) west of Győr.
Road Map B3. 🏠 11,000.
🚌 from Győr, Sopron.

This small town's name translates as "Gate Fortress", and that is exactly what it was: a fortress protecting the gate that controlled access to the border area. Built in 1270, the fortress was dismantled in 1884 to prevent it being used by Austrian forces. It was replaced with a Neo-Baroque mansion. This today is the office of the mayor and home to the **Rábaközi Museum**, which has an exhibition on the history of the town, a collection of regional folk art, as well as work by the sculptor Pál Pátzay, who was born in Kapuvár in 1896. Rising above the mansion is **St Anne's Church**, built at the same time as the museum, also to a Neo-Baroque design, and replacing a wooden chapel.

Regional costume in the Rábaköz Museum in Kapuvár

Csorna ㉓

30 km (19 miles) west of Győr.
Road Map B3. 🏠 11,000. 🚃 from Győr. 🚌 from Győr. 🎭 Folk Dance Festival (Jul).

Csorna is one of the oldest Christian towns in Hungary: a Premonstratensian Order settled here shortly after the Magyars, and in 1802 Csorna became one of the Hungarian centres for the Premonstratensians. The site of their monastery is now occupied by the magnificent 19th-century Neo-Renaissance Premonstratensian Csorna Palace. The palace contains an exhibition of local folk art. Here, visitors can find out about local wood carvings and so-called "spider embroidery", as well as the blue-dyers of Csorna and the potters of Dör. Together with the church order, the latter are two groups that contributed significantly to the town's wealth and growth in the 18th and early 19th centuries.

Next to the palace is the complementary Premonstratensian St Helen's Church, built in 1938 after the original 19th-century church on this site had burned down.

Moson-magyaróvár ㉔

37 km (23 miles) northwest of Győr. **Road Map** B3. 🏠 30,000.
🚃 from Győr. 🚌 from Győr.
🛈 Tourinform, Kápolna tér 16, (96) 20 63 04. 🎭 Voluta Water Carnival (Jun); Summer Festival (Aug).

The Romans built a fortress at Magyaróvár in the 3rd century AD. It was later extended by the Huns and then the Magyars, who constructed a large mud-brick fortress here. In 1271 Ottocar of Bohemia replaced this structure with the present stone **Magyaróvár Castle**. It has been extended and renovated many times since, and little of what remains is original apart from the two southern towers. Over the bridge from the castle (which is on an island) is Fő utca, on which stands at No. 19 the Gothic Cselley House (Cselley Ház). Inside is part of the Hanság Museum collection (the rest is at Szent István Király utca 1, further along Fő utca). Highlights include the Tibor Gyurkovich Collection, as well as a fine exhibition of Hungarian paintings, including works by Oszkár Glatz, Mihály Munkácsy and Gyula Rudnay. A short walk east on Szent Laszló tér is St Gotthard's Church. Its foundations were laid in 1668, although it was not completed until 1778, when the Baroque interiors were finished. The Habsburg prince Frederick and his wife Isabelle are buried in the crypt.

The town's long name, even by Hungarian standards, dates back to 1939, when the two separate towns

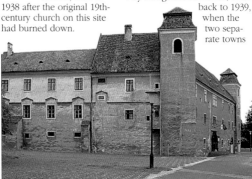

The Magyaróvár Castle in Mosonmagyaróvár, on the site of a Roman fort

Aerial view of the largely hidden Monostor Fortress in Komárom

of Moson and Magyaróvár became one and simply joined the two names together.

♣ Magyaróvár Castle
Vár utca 2. **Tel** (96) 56 66 37. 8am–4pm Mon–Fri. ⬛ ♿ to the grounds.

Győr ㉕

See pp174–5.

Pannonhalma Abbey ㉖

See pp176–7.

Komárom ㉗

Road Map B3. 38 km (24 miles) northeast of Győr. 🚷 20,000. 🚉 from Budapest, Győr. 🚌 from Győr. 🛈 Tourinform, Igmándi út 2, (34) 54 05 90.

A real border town, split in two by nature (the Danube) and politics (it straddles the Hungarian–Slovakian border), Komárom is the main crossing point between the two countries. Until 1920 this was one town, and on both sides of the river the two languages appear to be spoken interchangeably. The Hungarian part of the town is known for the colossal **Monostor Fortress** (Monostori Erőd), built by the Habsburgs 2 km (1 mile) up river from the city centre after the 1848–9 uprising. Covering approximately 4 hectares (10 acres) it is the largest fortress in the country, and one of the largest in Europe. Most of it is invisible from outside as it is buried underground. It was sparsely used by the Habsburgs before becoming the property of the Hungarian army, who used it as a training camp. After World War II, the Soviet army held political prisoners here. The story of the fortress is told clearly in the museum that now occupies much of the main bastion. There is also a bread museum, where visitors may taste the "ration bread" given to the soldiers who had to man the place in the 19th century. The fortress hosts cultural events and battle recreations throughout the summer.

♣ Monostor Fortress
Monostori Erőd, Dunapart 1. **Tel** (34) 54 05 82. Mid-Mar–mid-Oct: 9am–5pm Tue–Sun. ⬛ 🅿 groups only. **www**.fort-monostor.hu

Tata ㉘

60 km (37 miles) east of Győr. **Road Map** C3. 🚷 24,000. 🚉 from Budapest. 🚌 from Budapest. 🛈 Tourinform, Ady Endre utca 9, (34) 58 60 45.

Sitting on the banks of Lake Öreg, Tata is often referred to as the Hungarian Venice, mainly for the moated castle on the lake's north bank. Little except one tower and a wall remain of the 15th-century original: most of the current, nevertheless impressive building dates from 1893.

The lake was once surrounded by water mills, but only a few remain; the Cifra Mill next to the castle is the oldest, dating from 1587. Another mill a short distance north houses the German Minorities Museum, with interesting artifacts from the region's once numerous German population.

On the other side of the castle, on central Hősök tér, is the eclectic Esterházy Mansion, built in 1777. Used as a mental hospital for years, it has now been largely restored.

Across the square is the **Greco-Roman Statue Museum**, a former synagogue containing full-size replicas of classical statuary, from David to Zeus.

On the shore of Tata's second lake, Lake Cseske, stands the folly of a ruined church.

🏛 Greco-Roman Statue Museum
Hősök tere 7. **Tel** (34) 38 12 51. Apr–Oct 10am–6pm Tue–Sun; Nov–Mar by appointment only. ⬛ ♿

Replicas of famous statues in the Greco-Roman Statue Museum in Tata

Győr ㉔

Located exactly halfway between Budapest and Vienna, where the rivers Danube, Rába and Rábca meet, Győr has long been the place where empires met, and often clashed. Celts founded the city, and called it Arrabona, before giving way to the Romans. The Magyars saw the value of the town's position and created a bishopric here, while during the Turkish wars it became the home of the most impenetrable fortress in Hungary at the time. Full of monuments and buildings that tell of its eventful past, Győr is also a modern, vibrant city. Outstanding communications make it an excellent base for exploring the Győr–Moson–Sopron region.

♚ Bishop's Palace
Püspökvár
Káptalandomb 1. ◯ *Museum*
10am–4pm Tue–Sun.

The first castle on this imposing site was built during the reign of St István; nothing of it remains, however. The tower, known as the Runway Corridor, dates from the 14th (lower) and 18th century (upper part). The chapel was built from 1481–6, and unusually extends over two levels. The fortifications were largely added during the 16th century by the Italian architect Pietro Ferrabosco, to keep out the Turks. He completed his work in 1575, but by 1594 the Turks had taken the castle and the city. During the 18th century, Bishop Ferenc Zichy renovated the castle in the Baroque style. In 1984 further renovation was carried out. A museum in the treasury is dedicated to Hungarian priest Vilmos Apor, shot by Soviet soldiers in 1945 while trying to prevent rape and pillage.

The stunning 18th-century Baroque interior of Győr Cathedral

⛪ Győr Cathedral
Székesegyház
Káptalandomb. ◯ *8am–noon, 2–6pm daily.*

St István created the Győr Episcopate in the early 11th century, and the foundations of Győr Cathedral were laid then. Originally a three-aisled church with a raised sanctuary, it was destroyed by the Mongols in 1240, and rebuilt in Gothic style, with two imposing towers,

in 1257–67. The 15th-century Gothic Chapel houses the Holy Herm, the remains of St László, one of Hungary's most sacred relics. A fire destroyed the towers around 1580, and the cathedral was remodelled by the Italian architect Giovanni Rava in the 17th century. The Baroque interior dates from the time after the Turkish period, when the altarpieces and superb frescoes by Franz Anton Maulbertsch were added. The painting of the Virgin Mary above the Baroque altar is one of Hungary's most significant sites of pilgrimage. It allegedly wept blood in March 1697.

⛩ Ark of the Covenant
Frigyláda emlékmű
Gutenberg tér.

Built on the orders of Charles III in 1731, the Baroque Ark of the Covenant monument shows two angels holding the Ark in their hands. It was erected as an act of atonement for the violation of the Blessed Sacrament when Habsburg soldiers knocked the monstrance from the hands of the priest during the Corpus Christi procession in 1727. The soldiers were chasing a deserter and adulterer who had sought sanctuary in the procession.

🏛 Győr Diocesan Treasury and Library and Lapidary
Győri Egyházmegyei Kincstár, Könyvtár és Kőtár
Káptalandomb 26. **Tel** (96) 52 50 90. ◯ *Mar–Oct: 10am–4pm Tue–Sat.*

Hungary's finest collection of manuscripts is kept among this treasure trove of liturgical items. Alongside the Gothic chalices and Renaissance mitres is a codex from the 11th century, and the Korvina, an illuminated manuscript originating from the personal library of King Mátyás.

🏛 Margit Kovács Exhibition
Kovács Margit Állandó Kerámia Kiállítás
Apáca utca 1. **Tel** (96) 32 67 39. ◯ *10am–6pm Tue–Sun.*

A vast collection of ceramics is on display in a monumental 16th-century mansion that underwent renovations in

The Bishop's Palace, built to defend the town from Turkish invaders

For hotels and restaurants in this region see pp266–8 and pp287–9

1977. The exhibited works are by Margit Kovács (1902–77), a local-born ceramic artist who is Hungary's leading 20th-century abstract sculptor. The items on display range from vases to religious pieces, with personal items and a model of her workshop.

Ceramics on the stairs at the Margit Kovács Exhibition

🏛 Széchenyi Square

Széchenyi tér 4. ◯ **Imre Patkó Collection:** Apr–Sep: 10am–6pm Tue-Sun; Oct–Mar: 10am–4pm Tue–Sun. **Tel** (96) 31 05 88. 🖼 🔥

Once the city's market place, this cobbled square is ringed by splendid buildings. On the north side, in the so-called Iron Stump House, is the **Imre Patkó Collection** with ethnic pieces from Asia and Africa and 16th-century applied arts exhibits. The Baroque building next door houses the **Xantus János Museum**, the collection of the Petz family, which includes Hungary's first-ever postage stamps. The south side of the square is

dominated by the Baroque Ignatius Benedictine Church, built by the Jesuits in 1627. The beautiful Baroque pulpit was added in 1757. After the Jesuit order was dissolved in 1802, the Benedictines added the two towers. Next to the church stands a working **Pharmacy Museum** boasting a beautifully carved ceiling. The Maria Column outside was built in 1686 to celebrate Buda's recapture from the Turks.

The Maria Column, in the centre of Széchenyi Square

⛪ Carmelite Church & Monastery
Karmelita templom
Aradi vértanúk utca 2. 🔥

The Carmelites settled in Győr in 1697. Their church, a wonderful mixture of the Baroque and the Italianate, was built in 1721–5 to the plans of Athanasius Wittwer, a member of their order. The adjacent monastery was completed in 1732. Neapolitan master Martin Altomonte painted the main altarpiece featuring Sts István and Imre. In the church's chapel is a statue of the Virgin Mary made in Rome and blessed in the Vatican's Loreto Chapel before being brought here in 1717.

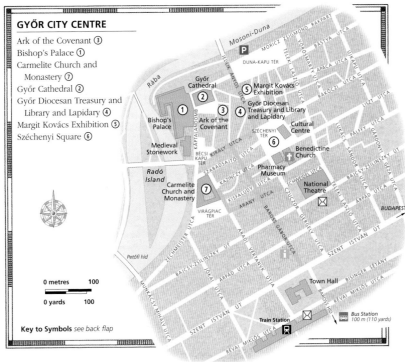

GYŐR CITY CENTRE

Ark of the Covenant ③
Bishop's Palace ①
Carmelite Church and Monastery ⑦
Győr Cathedral ②
Győr Diocesan Treasury and Library and Lapidary ④
Margit Kovács Exhibition ⑤
Széchenyi Square ⑥

Mosoni-Duna

Rába

Győr Cathedral ②

Margit Kovács Exhibition ⑤

Győr Diocesan Treasury and Library and Lapidary ④

Cultural Centre

Bishop's Palace ①

Ark of the Covenant ③

SZÉCHENYI TÉR

Benedictine Church ⑥

Medieval Stonework

BÉCSI KAPU TÉR

Pharmacy Museum

Radó Island

Carmelite Church and Monastery ⑦

National Theatre

VIRÁGPIAC TÉR

ARANY UTCA

BUDAPEST

Petőfi hid

Town Hall

0 metres 100
0 yards 100

Key to Symbols see back flap

Train Station

Bus Station
100 m (110 yards)

Pannonhalma Abbey ㉕

The story of Pannonhalma Abbey is as old as Hungary itself. A UNESCO World Heritage Site since 1996, there has been an abbey here since 1002, the same year St István brought Christianity to the Magyars. The original abbey burned down in 1137 and was replaced with a Romanesque construction that itself was superseded by the late-Romanesque basilica still in existence today. The basilica's main portal of receding arches is one of the most important surviving examples of a *Porta Speciosa* extant in Hungary.

Crest of the Pannonhalma Abbey

Basilica
The Basilica's stained-glass windows were added in 1860. One depicts St Martin of Tours, born at Szombathely in western Hungary.

★ Arboretum
The Arboretum on the eastern slope has been the site of hundreds of rare tree and shrub species since the 1840s. Over 80 of the species have grown wild in the Abbey's grounds.

★ Porta Speciosa
Though now hemmed in by extensions to the complex, the Porta Speciosa is an outstanding example of its kind – an ornamental portal held in red marble with rich wood carvings.

★ Library
The Neo-Classical library holds 330,000 volumes, including the Tihany Manuscript, the earliest written Hungarian.

Cloister
Late-Gothic vaulting in the cloister was added during renovation of the Abbey, carried out during the reign of King Mátyás, in 1486.

VISITORS' CHECKLIST

Vár 1, Pannonhalma, 20 km (12 miles) SE of Győr. **Road Map** B3. *Tel* (96) 57 01 91. 🚏 🚌 ⬜ **Abbey & Arboretum:** 22 Mar–Apr & Oct: 9am–4pm Tue–Sun; May–Sep: 9am–5pm daily (to 4pm May); Nov–21 Mar: 10am–3pm Tue–Sun. **Library: *Tel*** (96) 57 01 42. 📷 🅿️ ♿ 🚫 Abbey 🍴 🏪

The Benedictine Grammar School was founded in 1802 and is one of the finest in Hungary. The entrance exams are famously tough.

Main entrance

Our Lady Chapel
On the far side of the Abbey, behind the Basilica, Our Lady Chapel has three Baroque altars and a tiny organ. All the Abbey's monks are buried here.

Western Tower
Very much the Abbey's calling card, and its most recognizable feature, the Western Tower, added in 1832, can be seen from far away.

The Treasury is home to a rich collection of ecclesiastical art and historical artifacts.

STAR FEATURES

★ Arboretum

★ Library

★ Porta Speciosa

THE BENEDICTINE ORDER

The Order of St Benedict was founded by Benedict of Nursia, who set up the first monastery of the order at Monte Cassino, Italy, in 493. Benedict wanted the church to return to absolute devotion to the Pope. To this day Benedictines have no formal leadership structure and they are not, in fact, an official order, but rather a confederation.

Benedictine monks are known for living by their labour; Pannonhalma is no exception. The 40 monks who still live at the Abbey sell wine (vineyards surround the Abbey), Benedictine liqueur, honey, tea, lavender and CDs.

A wine produced by monks at Pannonhalma

SOUTHERN TRANSDANUBIA

*S*hallow and warm, the waters of Lake Balaton have attracted visitors for centuries, and today the long, narrow lake is surrounded by holiday resorts. South of Balaton, the region is sparsely populated, with Pécs the only city of any size. Great wines are made in this, the sunniest region of the country; the Villány-Siklós wine route offers a chance to sample some of them in superb surroundings.

Lake Balaton has something for everyone. From brash beach resorts such as Siófok on the south bank to the serene tranquillity of the Tihany Peninsula that juts into the lake from the north, it is not difficult to see why so many Hungarians choose to spend their holidays here. Motorized water sports are forbidden, so swimmers, anglers and sailors have the lake pretty much to themselves. Though the main Balaton season is limited to high summer (the only time hot, sunny weather can be guaranteed), the nearby cities of Keszthely, Tapolca and Veszprém are year-round destinations for visitors.

To the west of the lake is Kis-Balaton, a nature reserve of world renown; in autumn, bird-watchers flock here like the migrating birds they come to watch. There is more fauna, and flora, at the Duna-Dráva National Park, especially in the ancient Gemenc Forest, perhaps Hungary's lushest and most accessible nature reserve. To the south, human history takes centre-stage at the towns of Mohács and Szigetvár, both of which are known for the heroic battles that were fought and lost against the Turks here. In Pécs, the largest city in the region, the enormous former mosque is a permanent reminder that Sultans once held sway here.

Many of Hungary's best wines are made in Southern Transdanubia, both in the volcanic hills on the western shores of Balaton, and in the sun-kissed vineyards of the far south, in the Villány hills. Visitors will have ample opportunity to taste them all.

Vineyards near Badacsonytomaj with Mount Badacsony in the background, Lake Balaton

◁ The magnificent crypt of St Peter's Cathedral, Pécs

Exploring Southern Transdanubia

Outside the capital, Southern Transdanubia is
Hungary's most visited region. Most holidaymakers
are attracted by the vast Lake Balaton and the many
activities it offers. One of the nicest resorts to visit
here, and to enjoy the clean, warm waters of the lake,
is the elegant town of Keszthely. The region has great
topographical diversity, with the Gemenc forest, the
Villány hills and the Dráva river all having an impact.
The old town of Veszprém has narrow, cobbled streets
and the picturesque Vár Castle, while Pécs is home to
many fine galleries. Steeped in history, Southern
Transdanubia witnessed a crucial battle: the Ottoman
rout of the Habsburgs rulers at Mohács in 1526.

SEE ALSO

• *Where to Stay* pp268–72
• *Where to Eat* pp289–91

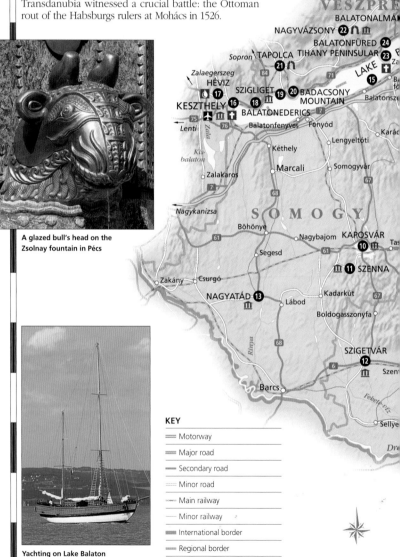

A glazed bull's head on the
Zsolnay fountain in Pécs

Yachting on Lake Balaton

KEY

═══ Motorway

═══ Major road

── Secondary road

┄┄┄ Minor road

╍╍╍ Main railway

─── Minor railway

━━━ International border

═══ Regional border

Interior of the Secession-style Town Hall, Kaposvár

SIGHTS AT A GLANCE

GETTING AROUND

The M7 (E71) motorway serves Lake Balaton, though it literally creaks under the pressure of traffic during the summer, especially in July and August and at the weekends, and jams can be long. There are also trains from Budapest-Keleti to the southern Balaton resorts, departing every 15 minutes or so in summer.

Pécs is served by route 6 from the capital, which is particularly pretty, as it follows the Danube for much of the way. Public transport connections in the far south of Transdanubia are poor, and a car is needed to explore the area around Pécs.

Bathing in the Thermal Lake in Héviz

Dunaföldvár ❶

69 km (43 miles) south of Budapest.
Road Map C4. 🏠 9,500.
🚋 from Paks. 🚌 from Budapest.
🛈 Tourinform, Rátkai kóz 2,
(75) 34 11 76.

With its elegant central square,
Béke tér, surrounded by well-
kept Baroque and Secession
buildings, especially the
spire-topped **Town Hall**,
Dunaföldvár is one of the
most attractive towns on the
southern stretch of the
Hungarian Danube.
Overlooking the town
is the Ruined Tower,
all that remains of a
fort which stood on
the site in the 16th
century. The tower,
on Rátkai utca,
affords superb views
of the city centre,
and of the
Danube. It is
reached by way
of the ornate
wooden castle
gate, a 19th-
century replica of the original.
In the same courtyard is the
Fafaragó Gallery, dedicated to
the town's wood carvers.

Town Hall clock tower in Dunaföldvár

Paks ❷

21 km (13 miles) south of Dunaföldvár. **Road Map** C4. 🏠 21,000.
🚋 from Dunaföldvár. 🚌 from
Budapest.

There would be little reason
to visit Paks were it not for
the town's strikingly modern
Catholic Church. Designed by
the controversial late
Hungarian architect Imre
Makovecz, it was completed
in 1988 and is constructed
entirely of wood. Resembling
the wooden churches of
the Romanian
Maramures region, it
has three spires,
which are topped
with a cross, a sun and
a crescent respectively.
The presence of the
crescent – a symbol of
Islam – caused much
furore when it was
unveiled.
The town, which
is the site of
Hungary's only
nuclear power
station, is also home to the
Paks Gallery (Paksi Képtár) of
contemporary art. Inside the
slightly worn but still
imposing Neo-Classical
building are four permanent
exhibitions dedicated to the
works of local experimental
and fine artists, dating from
1980 onwards.

🏛 **Paks Gallery**
Szent István tér 4.
Tel (75) 51 09 19.
🕙 10am–6pm Tue–Sun. ♿

Entrance arch to the Mohács Memorial Park

Mohács ❸

46 km (29 miles) east of Pécs.
Road Map C5. 🏠 20,000. 🚋 from
Villány. 🚌 from Budapest. 🚢 cross-
Danube car ferry. 🛈 Tourinform,
Széchenyi tér 1, (69) 50 55 15.
🛒 daily, Szabadság tér. 🎭 Busó
Carnival (Shrove Tue; Feb).

On 29 August 1526, in a field
7 km (4 miles) south of the
small town of Mohács, the
Turks comprehensively
defeated the Hungarians,
clearing the last obstacle on
their march to Buda (see box
opposite). To commemorate
the 400th anniversary of the
Battle of Mohács, a Byzantine
church was erected in the
main square, Széchenyi tér,
opposite the Gothic Town
Hall. The site of the battle
itself is marked by a memorial
to the soldiers who fell, both
in 1526 and in a lesser battle
in 1687. Their mass graves are
indicated by painted wooden
headstones. Five such graves
have been uncovered so far,
and work is ongoing in the
Memorial Park.
Mohács comes alive every
Shrove Tuesday when it is the
scene of the Busó Carnival
(Busójárás). Today, a colourful

The organically shaped Catholic Church in Paks with its three spires

event is held to mark the passing of winter. The ritual of dressing in rags and wearing startling masks was originally devised to scare off the Turks – but it clearly didn't work.

Duna–Dráva National Park ❹

Gemenc Excursion Centre, Bárányfok. **Road Map** C5.
Tel (74) 31 25 52. 🚂 narrow-gauge railway from Bárányfok to Pörböly (Jun–Oct: Sat & Sun).
🚌 to Bárányfok from Szekszárd.
🐴 Mar–Oct. **Horse riding** (20) 566 80 76. **Boat Tours** (summer).

This 500-sq-km (193-sq-mile) game reserve in the Gemenc Forest is Hungary's largest floodplain forest. A national park since 1996, it is covered with lakes and fens, and dotted with numerous islands. On many of these can be found old willow trees, high oaks and poplars, lilies-of-the-valley on the forest floor, and wildlife including egrets, bald eagles, herons, black storks and stags. Hunting is restricted to certain areas.

Most of the park is protected, and there are four ways of visiting: on a nature trail from the park's main entrance, near Bárányfok; with a guide from the Gemenc Excursion Centre at Bárányfok; by narrow-gauge railway from Bárányfok to Pörböly; and by organized boat trip. The nature trails vary in length from 2.5 km (1.5 miles) to 40 km (25 miles). There is also a cycle trail, and bikes can be hired from the Gemenc Excursion Centre.

One of the many wine cellars on Baross Gábor utca in Villány

Villány ❺

21 km (13 miles) southeast of Pécs.
Road Map C6. 🏠 2,800.
🚂 from Pécs. 🚌 from Budapest.
🍷 Wine Festival (first week of Oct in even years); European Wine Song Festival (Oct).

A village of wine cellars, Villány is the starting point of the 14-km (9-mile) Villány-Siklós (see p184) Wine Route, the first to be set up in Hungary in 1994. Wine has been made here since Roman times, and a small Wine Museum, housed in one of the village's traditional white-washed wine cellars, tells the story of local viticulture. Every two years the village hosts a Wine Festival, dedicated to promoting Villány wines,

including Kékoportó, Merlot, Blue Franc and Cabernet (red wines predominate around Villány, whites around Siklós). Visitors can sample local wines at the wine cellars on Bem József utca or Baross Gábor utca. Four of the town's vintners have been awarded the title of "Wine Maker of the Year": Gere, Tiffán, Bock and Malatinszky.

The village of Villánykövesd, 4 km (2.5 miles) northeast on the road to Pécs (and not strictly on the Wine Route), is even more spectacular than Villány as its many wine-cellar cottages are set on a split-level terrace. The village's Batthyány cellar, built by Italian artisans in 1754, hosts the opening of the annual European Wine Song Festival every October.

THE BATTLE OF MOHÁCS

The Battle of Mohács is one of the most important battles in Hungarian – and European – history. On 29 August 1526, the Turks, having just achieved victory in the Battle of Belgrade, faced one final obstacle before reaching Buda: the Magyar garrison at Mohács. The Turks, however, outnumbered the Magyars three to one, and after a day-long battle they achieved victory by nightfall, killing at least two-thirds of the estimated 25,000 Hungarian soldiers at arms. The young Hungarian King, Lajos II, was killed during the battle. The Turks captured Buda soon after, and ruled Hungary for more than 150 years. To this day the battle is remembered as one of the greatest Hungarian tragedies.

The death of King Lajos II in battle

An idyllic spot in the Duna–Dráva National Park

The impressive path to the drawbridge in Siklós Castle

Siklós ❻

15 km (9 miles) west of Villány.
Road Map C6. 👥 11,000. 🚉 from
Villány. 🚌 from Pécs. 🛈 Tourinform,
Felszabadulás utca 3, (72) 57 90 90.
🚇 daily, Dózsa György utca.

The star attraction in Siklós,
the southernmost town in
Hungary, close to the border
with Serbia, is **Siklós Castle**,
one of the best-preserved
medieval forts in the country.
The fort, which dates back to
1294, has enjoyed something
of a charmed life. Uniquely
among Hungarian fortresses,
it was spared by the Turks as
well as the Habsburgs (twice).
  The fort's entrance is via an
old drawbridge and through a
gate decorated elaborately with
the Batthyány family coat of
arms. From the immaculately
preserved ramparts spectacular
views of the vineyards of the
surrounding area can be had.
Inside the fortress is a Gothic
chapel, decorated with fading
but impressive frescoes from
the late 15th century.
  The **Castle Museum**, in the
fort's south wing, is equally
impressive, containing a
collection of medieval items
and an exhibition on the lives
of the various members of the
Batthyány family who stayed
here as late as the 1940s.
  Elsewhere in Siklós, the
restored 16th-century Malkocs
Bei Mosque, which is full of
memorabilia from the Turkish

occupation, and the colourful
18th-century icons of the Serb
Orthodox Church are also
worth seeing.

⚓ **Siklós Castle**
Vajda János tér 8. **Tel** (72) 57 94 27.
🕙 Nov–Apr: 9am–4pm daily; May–
Oct: 9am–6pm daily. **Museum**
🕙 Tue–Sun. 📷 ♿ 🚻

Harkány ❼

25 km (16 miles) southeast of Pécs.
Road Map C6. 👥 3,400. 🚉 from
Villány. 🚌 from Pécs. 🛈 Tourinform,
Kossuth utca 2a, (72) 47 96 24.
🚇 daily, Bajcsy-Zsilinszky utca.

According to local legend,
the Devil ploughed the land
around Harkány, and filled

the furrows with sulphuric
water. As it happens, such
sulphuric water – said to be
a cure for rheumatic and
gynaecological disorders –
is found nowhere else, and
the Devil's work has become
a boon for Harkány.
  The town's thermal bath
complex was opened in 1823,
and is today one of the most
visited in Hungary. As well as
large indoor and outdoor pools
(so large that they are never
crowded), there is a special
section for taking mud baths.
  Other waters can be drunk
to cure catarrh and stomach
complaints. Solaria and a
range of beauty treatments
are also available.

♨ **Harkány Spa and Open-Air
Baths**
Kossuth Lajos utca 7. **Tel** (72) 48
02 51. 🕙 9am–6pm daily. 📷 ♿

Pécs ❽

See pp186–7.

Dombóvár ❾

39 km (25 miles) north of Pécs. **Road
Map** C5. 👥 21,000. 🛈 Tourinform,
Szabadság utca 16, (74) 46 60 53.

Dombóvár and its surrounding area is one of the oldest
inhabited regions of Hungary.
The ruins of a 4th-century
Roman fortress were found
underneath nearby Alsóhetény
and the Celts were here before
that. Relics of even earlier

Exercises in the outdoor pool, Harkány Spa and Open-Air Baths

unknown settlers from the Bronze Age have also been found. These are on display at the **Dombóvár Region Historical Museum** (Dombóvári Helytörténeti Múzeum). The museum is also home to a possibly unique exhibition on the history of the artificial language, Esperanto.

Among Dombóvár's other attractions are the Baroque Catholic Church, dating from 1757 and once a private chapel for the use of the Esterházy family *(see p167)*.

A short drive north is the tiny village of Gölle, the birthplace of István Fekete (1900–70), one of Hungary's most popular 20th-century writers. Fekete is best known for his novel *Tüskevár*, a charming story of two boys from Budapest who spend their summers around Gölle and Lake Balaton. Fekete's childhood home in Gölle is now a small museum.

🏛 **Dombóvár Region Historical Museum**
Szabadság utca 16.
Tel (74) 46 57 15, (mobile) 36 20 286 79 59. ◯ 9am–4pm Mon–Fri, by appointment Sat–Sun.
🎧 Hungarian only. ♿

Bust of the Hungarian writer István Fekete, born near Dombóvár

Kaposvár ❿

43 km (27 miles) northwest of Pécs.
Road Map B5. 🏛 66,000. 🚆 *from Budapest, Pécs.* 🚌 *from Pécs.* 🛈
Tourinform, Fő utca 8, (82) 51 29 21.
www.tourinformkaposvar.hu

Boasting one of Hungary's largest pedestrian-only zones, Kaposvár is a superb city in which to stroll and enjoy an eclectic mix of architecture. The town is the birthplace of

Stained-glass window, Town Hall in Kaposvár

József Rippl-Rónai (1861–1927) and János Vaszary (1867–1939), two of Hungary's most important artists. It was also the birthplace of Imre Nagy (1896–1958), leader of the 1956 revolution *(see pp44–5)*.

The city's focal point is Kossuth tér. Most of the main sights are located around this street, including the **Vaszary Gallery**, which displays the paintings of János Vaszary, who was born in the building. There are more Vaszary works next door in a Neo-Classical building, the former Somogy County Museum (now renamed the **Rippl-Rónai Museum**), formerly the County Hall. The museum also

presents an exhibition of local artifacts, including folk art that predates the Magyar invasion.

Kaposvár's **Town Hall** was built in 1904 in classic Secessionist style, though its slender spire carries a hint of the late Baroque. It is not officially open to the public but it is usually possible to go in and admire the interior. The frescoes above the lobby are by local artist Géza Udvary and the fine stained-glass windows of the ceremonial hall are the work of the Miksa Róth workshop.

A short walk south is the **Rippl-Rónai Memorial Museum**, the elegant Roma cottage where a number of Rippl-Rónai's works and personal items are on show.

🏛 **Vaszary Gallery**
Fő út 12. *Tel* (82) 31 49 15.
◯ 10am–6pm daily. 🎧 Hungarian only. ♿

🏛 **Rippl-Rónai Museum**
Fő út 10. *Tel* (82) 31 40 11. ◯ Nov–Mar: 10am–3pm Tue–Sun; Apr–Oct: 10am–4pm Tue–Sun. 🎧 ♿

🏛 **József Rippl-Rónai Memorial Museum**
Róma-hegy. *Tel* (82) 42 21 44.
◯ Nov–Mar: 10am–4pm Tue–Sun; Apr–Oct: 10am–6pm Tue–Sun. 🎧 recorded tours (fee). ♿

JÓZSEF RIPPL-RÓNAI

József Rippl-Rónai (1861–1927) was one of the three most important artists of the Hungarian Secession Movement. Born in Kaposvár he mastered a pastel-like style, seen best in his celebrated work *Mlle Dutile* (1892, József Rippl-Rónai Memorial Museum, Kaposvár). He moved to France when the Art Nouveau movement was at its peak. His masterpiece, *Woman in White-Spotted Dress* (1899, National Gallery, Budapest, *see pp58–9*), was painted during this period. It is regarded as the first Secessionist work by a Hungarian artist. On a visit to Italy, Rippl-Rónai became fascinated by decorative mosaics. His later works, including *The Manor House at Körtvélyes* (1907, National Gallery), reflect a move to bolder strokes and colour.

Rippl-Rónai's *Woman in White-Spotted Dress*

Pécs ❽

Cosmopolitan Pécs, 2010's European Capital of Culture, calls itself "Hungary's Mediterranean city", and given that the sun shines here more for than 200 days a year, and that the city's streets have a very Turkish, even Oriental, feel to them, this is not as strange as it may seem. Pécs was founded by the Romans, who called the place Sopianae, in the 3rd century AD. It served as the capital of Valeria Province and was an early centre of Roman Christianity – as evidenced by the 4th-century tombs on Apáca utca. It was the Turks, however, 1,000 years later who left the deepest marks on the city's landscape. No other city centre in Hungary is quite so dominated by a former mosque as Pécs's Széchenyi tér *(see pp188–9)*, yet no other city seems quite so at ease with the fact.

unique metallic glaze. Also on display are items of furniture and paintings produced by the family.

Entrance to the Zsolnay Museum, in the historic centre of Pécs

🔒 St Peter's Cathedral & Bishops' Palace
Szent Péter Székesegyház & Püspöki palota
Dóm tér. **Tel** *(72) 51 30 30.*
☐ *Apr–Oct: 9am–5pm Mon–Sat, 1–5pm Sun.* 🅿 &

The historic centre of Pécs, Dóm tér, is dominated by St Peter's Cathedral, which was first built as a Neo-Romanesque church in 1009 when St István made Pécs a bishopric. The original church, burnt down in 1064, was replaced by a Baroque cathedral built over nearly 200 years. Badly damaged by the Mongols, it was almost entirely rebuilt as a Gothic church in the 15th century. The current edifice, with its four severe corner towers, dates from 1891, and is the work of Viennese architect Friedrich Schmidt. The interior is impressive, especially the Károly Lotz frescoes in the chapels and the

reliefs in the crypt by György Zala. A bronze statue of Janos Pannonius, a leading humanist, stands in front of the cathedral.

Opposite is the attractive deep red, 19th-century Neo-Renaissance Bishops' Palace. It has a statue of Ferenc (Franz) Liszt in a raincoat on the southern balcony. The palace is home to one of Hungary's largest libraries.

🏛 Zsolnay Museum
Zsolnay Múzeum
Káptalan utca 2.
Tel *(72) 32 48 22.* ☐ *May–Oct: 10am–6pm Tue–Sun; Nov–Apr: 10am–4pm Tue–Sun.* 🅿 🗎 &

Located in the oldest known house of Pécs, this museum showcases the most significant pieces of the Zsolnay Ceramic Factory. Zsolnay tiles graced the palaces of the Austro-Hungarian monarchy and were famous for their

🏛 Csontváry Museum
Csontváry Múzeum
Janus Pannonius utca 11. **Tel** *(72) 31 05 44.* ☐ *May–Oct: 10am–4pm Tue–Sun.*

Most of Tivadar Csontváry Kosztka's (1853–1919) master-pieces, including the startling *View of the Dead Sea from the Temple Square in Jerusalem*, have been on display in this Neo-Renaissance building since 1973. A tortured soul and former pharmacist, Csontváry Kosztka produced most of his work in 1903–9, after which he moved to Naples and went quietly mad.

🏛 Apáca Street and Early Christian Mausoleum
Apáca utca & Ókeresztény Mauzóleum
Apáca utca 14. **Tel** *(72) 22 47 55.* ☐ *Apr–Oct: 10am–6pm Tue–Sun; Nov–Mar: 10am–3:30pm Tue–Sun.* 🗎 🗎 Early Christian Mausoleum, Szent István tér 12. ☐ *10am–5:30pm Tue–Sun.* 🗎 🗎 **Visitor Centre** *(72) 22 47 55.* **www**.pecsorokseg.hu

Four graves at Apáca utca 14, all from c.390 AD, mark one of the earliest Christian burial sites in Europe. The bodies are buried under the chapel, and not in sarcophagi. The mausoleum, below an exca-vated chapel, is even older, c.275 AD. It is decorated with biblical frescoes. These and two further burial chambers at Pécs have UNESCO World Heritage status.

St Peter's Cathedral, with its distinctive corner towers

For hotels and restaurants in this region see pp268–72 and pp289–91

🏛 Archaeological Museum

Széchenyi tér 12. **Tel** (72) 31 27 19.
May–Oct: 10am–4pm Tue–Sat;
Nov–Apr: 10am–3pm Mon–Fri.

The Archaeological Museum features Goths, Huns, Tatars, Visigoths and other invaders, but perhaps the highlight is the story of Roman Sopianae, a popular posting for Roman officers. A valuable treasure, a bust of Marcus Aurelius, has a room to itself.

🇨 Gazi Kasim Pasha Mosque/ Inner City Parish Church
Gazi Kasim Pasha Dzámi/Belvárosi templom

Széchenyi tér. **Tel** (72) 32 19 76.
mid-Apr–mid-Oct: 10am–4pm Mon–Sat, 11:30am–4pm Sun; mid-Oct–mid-Apr: 10am–noon Mon–Sat, 11:30am–2pm Sun.

Built on the site of a Gothic Christian church in 1579 for Pasha Gazi Kasim, this mosque was the largest in Hungary, and remains its most important Turkish monument. Converted into a Christian church in the late 17th century, calligraphy at the entrance and a prayer niche are reminders of its origins.

🏛 Király Utca
Király utca.

Largely pedestrianized, Király utca is an architectural showcase. Secessionist façades can be seen at Nos. 5 (Palatinus Hotel; superb lobby), 8, 10, 19 and the National Theatre; the twin-towered St Pauline Church at No. 44 is Baroque.

✡ Synagogue
Zsinagóga

Kossuth tér. **Tel** (72) 31 58 81.
May–Oct: 10am–noon & 12:45–5pm Sun–Fri.

This grand Neo-Renaissance synagogue, built in the 1860s, shows the high standing the 5,000 practising Jews had in Pécs society until 1944, when the Arrow Cross government sent all of them to Auschwitz. Less than 500 survived. A memorial commemorates those who were killed. Services take place in the smaller prayer hall at the side.

Façade of Pécs Synagogue

VISITORS' CHECKLIST

Road Map C5. 🏙 156,000.
🚆 Indóház tér. 🚌 Zólyom utca.
🚏 Zólyom utca, Széchenyi tér.
ℹ Tourinform, Széchenyi tér 7.
(72) 51 12 32. 🎭 Spring Festival (last two weeks Mar); Pécs Cultural Heritage Festival (first week Sep). **www**.iranypecs.hu

🇨 Jakovali Hassan Mosque
Jakovali Hassan Dzámi

Rákóczi út. 2. **Tel** (72) 31 38 53.
Apr–Oct: 10am–6pm Wed–Sun.

Even though the 16th-century mosque was converted into a Catholic church in 1714, its 23-m (75-ft) high minaret is still intact (but closed). A museum since 1975, it documents the Turkish occupation of Pécs. Many of the exhibits were donated by the Turkish government as a semi-official apology in the early 1990s.

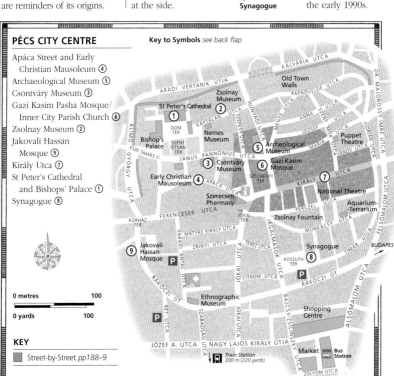

PÉCS CITY CENTRE

Apáca Street and Early Christian Mausoleum ④
Archaeological Museum ⑤
Csontváry Museum ③
Gazi Kasim Pasha Mosque/ Inner City Parish Church ⑥
Zsolnay Museum ②
Jakovali Hassan Mosque ⑨
Király Utca ⑦
St Peter's Cathedral and Bishops' Palace ①
Synagogue ⑧

Key to Symbols see back flap

0 metres 100
0 yards 100

KEY

Street-by-Street pp188–9

Street-by-Street: Around Széchenyi tér

Once the bustling medieval heart of Pécs, comprising a market place, meeting point and general forum, today Széchenyi tér is a far more serene and reflective place. Sloping gently from north to south, the square is dominated – as is much of Pécs – by the former mosque of Gazi Kasim Pasha, the largest surviving original Islamic construction in Hungary. It is now a Catholic church and a museum.

Archaeological Museum
This large collection traces the history of human settlement in Pécs from the Early Stone Age to the present day.

★ **Gazi Kasim Mosque**
Correctly known as the Inner City Parish Church of St Mary, this was for two centuries the city's primary mosque. Its dome stands 28 m (92 ft) high.

Zsolnay Museum
displays exquisite examples of Art Nouveau tiles.

Holy Trinity Monument
The column, restored by György Kiss in 1908, commemorates the victims of a plague outbreak in 1710.

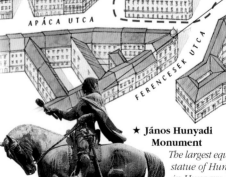

★ **János Hunyadi Monument**
The largest equestrian statue of Hunyadi in Hungary, it was erected by the local sculptor Pál Pátzay in 1956, the 500th anniversary of Hunyadi's death.

National Theatre
This impressive theatre was built in 1893–5, in a mix of styles. It hosts first-class opera and ballet performances.

★ Király Utca
Traffic-free Király utca is lined with shops and cafés, making it ideal for a stroll. Its buildings boast Secessionist (Palatinus Hotel) and Baroque (St Pauline Church) façades.

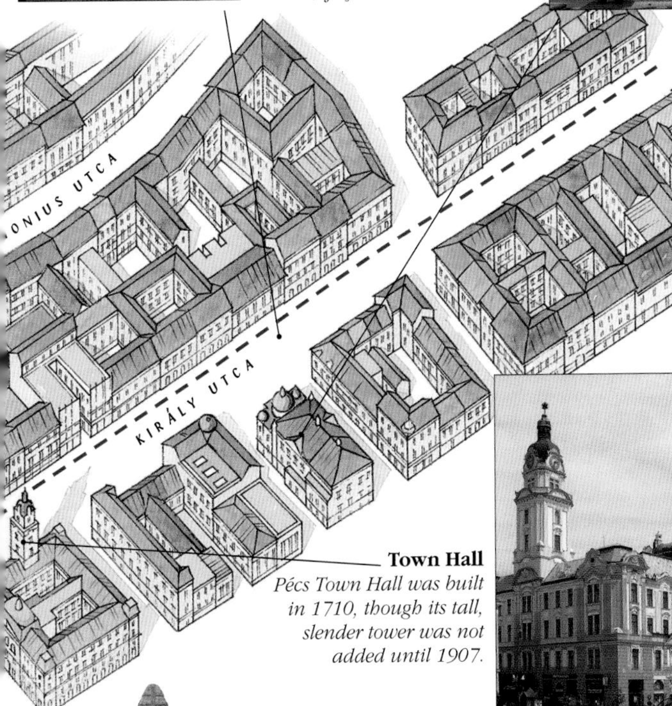

ONIUS UTCA

KIRÁLY UTCA

Town Hall
Pécs Town Hall was built in 1710, though its tall, slender tower was not added until 1907.

JÓKAI TÉR

| 0 metres | 20 |
| 0 yards | 20 |

KEY

– – – Suggested route

Zsolnay Fountain
This outstanding example of Secessionist design pays homage to Vilmos Zsolnay, who founded the Zsolnay tile factory nearby in 1853. It features the trademark Zsolnay blue glaze.

STAR FEATURES

★ Gazi Kasim Mosque

★ János Hunyadi Monument

★ Király Utca

A typical 19th-century house in the open-air folk museum in Szenna

Szenna ⓫

Road Map B5. 👥 *750.* 🚌 *from Kaposvár.*

The open-air **Szenna Ethnographic Museum** is unique in Hungary in that it has been established in a living village. Set around the village church, five thatched houses with wooden porches were brought here from surrounding villages in the 1970s. The houses date from the 1850s, and with their large kitchens are typical of post-revolutionary architecture in Hungary. All are decorated in the vernacular style. The whitewashed Calvinist church, erected in 1787 to a late-Baroque design is famous for its ceiling: the artist Tildy Zoltán painted it with 117 unique flowers, reflecting the rich flora of the Somogy region. Visitors can also admire the highly decorated wooden crown above the pulpit and the pews that are installed over two levels.

🏛 **Szenna Ethnographic Museum**
Rákóczi utca 2. **Tel** *(82) 48 42 23.*
⏰ *Apr–Oct: 10am–6pm daily; Nov–Mar: 10am–4pm daily.*
📷 ♿

Szigetvár ⓬

33 km (21 miles) west of Pécs. **Road Map** B5. 👥 *12,000.* 🚆 *from Pécs.* 🚌 *from Pécs.*

At the siege of Szigetvár, in 1566, Captain Miklós Zrínyi and a small band of soldiers held the town's fortress against a Turkish attacking force of over 100,000 for 22 days. Only when the beleaguered Hungarians were running desperately short of water did they leave the fortress, and even then they did not surrender, choosing instead to die heroic though futile deaths in close combat. Part of the fortress, restored in the 1960s, is the **Miklós Zrínyi Museum**, dedicated to the heroes of the siege. There is also a monument to the fallen in the town's central square, Zrínyi tér. The fortress courtyard also houses a former mosque, built by the Turks after their victory.

Another former mosque, also on Zrínyi tér, is today a Catholic church. It was converted in 1789, when the frescoes by István Dorffmaister were painted. In the house at Bástya utca 3, the so-called **Turkish House** (Török-Ház),

Exhibits in the former mosque inside the Szigetvár fortress

is a small exhibition of life in the town during the Turkish occupation. On the field where Zrínyi led his forces into battle (5 km/3 miles north of the town) stands the Turkish-Hungarian Friendship Park, set up in 1996 by both governments. There is a replica of Sultan Süleyman's tomb, and oversized statues of the Sultan and of Zrínyi.

🏛 **Miklós Zrínyi Museum**
Vár utca 19. **Tel** *(30) 947 72 87.*
⏰ *Apr–Oct: 9am–5pm Tue–Sun.* ♿

🏛 **Turkish House**
Bástya utca 3. **Tel** *(73) 51 43 00.*
⏰ *10am–4pm Tue–Sat.* 📷 ♿

Nagyatád ⓭

28 km (18 miles) north of Barcs.
Road Map B5. 👥 *13,000.* 🚌 *from Kaposvár.* ℹ️ *Tourinform, Széchenyi tér 1a, Nagyatád (82) 50 45 15.*

This city has a good thermal baths complex, with three covered and two large open-air pools as well as drinking cures, but Nagyatád is best known for its unique **Statue Park** featuring the works of a local wood carvers' collective. The park was set up in 1975, in an effort to preserve the wood-carving skills of the region. There are 64 monumental statues (some more than 7 m/ 23 ft high) in all, laid out in a spacious and attractive park to the south of the city centre. Considered living art, there are no restrictions on touching or even climbing the statues, making this a great place to introduce children to sculpture. Another 24 wooden statues can be found in the city's public squares and buildings.

The surrounding countryside offers superb hiking routes in the Forest Park (Parkerdő) and the Rower Lake (Csónakázótó) nearby.

A wooden wheel in the Statue Park in Nagyatád

🏛 **Nagyatád Statue Park**
Göröndi út. **Tel** *(82) 35 14 97.*
⏰ *daily.* 📷 *Hungarian only.* ♿

Hungary's Minorities

Some 90 per cent of Hungary's population are Magyars, but there are also significant minority groups of Serbs, Germans, Romanians and Jews. In all, 13 minority groups are recognized, although some (the Palóc, Armenians and Ruthenians, for example) number only a handful of people. The largest ethnic minority in Hungary is the Gypsies (Roma). The official figure is 400,000, yet many Gypsies see themselves as Hungarians, which means there could be as many as a million in the country. Until Hungary joined the EU in 2004, it had a less than fine record in its treatment of its ethnic minorities, especially of the Gypsies. Even since then, EU-funded programmes have been only marginally successful at integrating the Gypsy population.

The museum village of Hollókő, *while primarily a tourist attraction, showcases Palóc traditions and culture. Its inhabitants wear traditional costume.*

Few Roma still *live the romantic life of a traveller. Most are on the fringes of society, with an unemployment rate of almost 70 per cent.*

Szentendre was founded by Serbs *and although they no longer make up the majority population group here, many Serbs still celebrate Easter according to the Orthodox Julian calendar.*

People in Sopron *in 1920 voted to stay in Hungary rather than join Austria. Over the next few decades most ethnic Germans moved away, but since 1990 many have returned, which has given the city a very international feel.*

Fő tér
Hauptplatz

The popular image *of Gypsy musicians is a cigányzenekar, which is a Gypsy band. It is one of the few ways Gypsies can earn a living in Hungary.*

Budapest today is home *to one of Europe's most dynamic Jewish communities. Budapest's Synagogue is Europe's largest, and the city boasts many Jewish theatres, schools and kosher restaurants.*

Many Orthodox Romanians *are settled in and around the eastern town of Gyula. Although the two countries have had a strained relationship for centuries, more than 80,000 Romanians choose to live in Hungary.*

Marina in Siófok, departure point for pleasure cruises and water sports

Siófok ⑭

88 km (54 miles) southwest of
Budapest. **Road Map** C4.
23,000. from Budapest. from
Budapest. from Balatonfüred,
Tihany. Tourinform, Fő tér 11,
(84) 69 62 36. Siófok Summer
Evenings (Jun–Aug).
www.siofokportal.com

The largest and liveliest resort
on Lake Balaton's southern
coast, Siófok stretches along
the shore for 17 km (11 miles).
It is popular with weekenders
from Budapest, many of whom
have holiday homes in the
town. The main attraction is
the beach. It is split in two
parts – Aranypart (Golden
Shore) to the north and Ezüst-
part (Silver Shore) to the south
– by the Sió canal, which was
originally built by the Romans
in 276 AD. Like all of Lake
Balaton's resorts, however,
Siófok offers mainly grass
beaches. The resort's marina
is at the head of the canal,
from where pleasure cruisers
and ferries depart for the
Tihany Peninsula *(see p202)*.
The port is a good place to find
sailing boats for hire, and
to organize a variety of other
water sports *(see p299)*.
Visitors should note that
during the summer nights
Siófok comes alive with tens
of thousands of young people
looking for a good time in the
resort's innumerable bars,
discos and nightclubs, many
of which are in the open air.
If an early, quiet night is
required, one of the smaller
resorts along the coast would
be a far better option.

◁ **View across the glorious Lake Balaton**

Lake Balaton Tour ⑮

Lake Balaton is often referred to as Budapest-on-Sea,
and during the summer months it may seem as if half
the population of the capital has decamped here.
Lake Balaton, however, at 596 sq km (230 sq miles)
the largest lake in central Europe, is big enough to
cope, and even in the high season the visitor is never
far from a peaceful spot. Most of the southern side of
the lake is very shallow, with an average depth of just
3.5 m (11 ft) and the waters are fairly warm, making
this the most popular shore with bathers and families.

Kis-Balaton ⑪
The Kis-Balaton
Nature reserve at the
mouth of the Zala
river covers an area
of 40 sq km (15 sq
miles). It is inhabited
by many rare plants
and animals.

Balatonberény ⑩
One of the first genuine resorts on the
lake to become popular, Balatonberény
retains a late-19th-century charm, most
apparent in its delightful lakeside
cottages and rural houses.

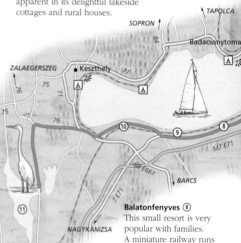

Balatonfenyves ⑧
This small resort is very
popular with families.
A miniature railway runs
to a nearby thermal bath.

Balatonmáriafürdő ⑨
This lively resort attracts
water sports enthusiasts
and those looking
for a good range of
bars and restaurants.

Zamárdi ①
A world away from noisy Siófok, Zamárdi is home to some fine thatched cottages, including this arcaded house on Fő utca, now the village's museum.

Balatonföldvár ②
Look out for the remains of the Iron Age fortifications *(földvár)* that gave this small town its name. The village's leafy promenade is generally considered the finest on the lake's south shore.

Kőröshegy ③
A short detour south of Balatonföldvár is Kőröshegy, where a well-preserved Gothic fortified church was built in 1460.

Balatonszemes ④
This quiet resort has a Postal and Carriage Museum. Its tree-lined streets are ideal for a stroll and nearby is an aquapark.

```
0 kilometres          10
0 miles          5
```

KEY

▬▬	Motorway
▬▬	Tour route
▭▭	Major road
▭▭▭	Other road
▭▭▭	Major railway
---	Ferry line
🔺	Camp site
🔷	Ferry port
✿	Viewpoint

Somogyvár ⑤
Somogyvár is well worth the detour south from Buzsák – the impressive ruins of the Benedictine monastery here date back to the 11th century.

Fonyód ⑦
Unremarkable as a resort, Fonyód sits at the foot of the largest hill on the southern shore, Várhegy (233 m/764 ft), which is an extinct volcano.

Buzsák ⑥
The Living Museum of Arts and Crafts at Buzsák is the best place around Balaton to learn about the traditions of the lake and its people. Fine cloth, pottery and costumes are still made here.

Keszthely ⑯

Keszthely is the oldest and largest of the towns that line the banks of Lake Balaton. Many of its elegant streets effortlessly preserve the small-town atmosphere of the 19th century, when the town was the sole property of the Festetics family, whose Baroque family seat, Festetics Palace *(see pp198–9)* is one of Hungary's finest stately homes. The town possesses one of the few genuinely sandy beaches on the lake, and it is also the cultural hub of Balaton, hosting the Balaton Festival every May. Since the conversion in 2006 of a nearby former Soviet airfield into Hévíz-Balaton Airport, Keszthely is fast becoming one of the most visited places in Hungary.

Town Hall (Városházá), one of the attractive buildings in Fő tér

🏰 Festetics Palace
See pp198–9.

🏰 Fő tér and Town Hall
Polgármesteri Hivatal
Fő tér.
At the heart of Keszthely is the attractive, bustling Fő tér, dominated on its northern side by the late-Baroque, pastel pink Town Hall. The Town Hall was built in 1790, although the façade was extensively remodelled in the 1850s. Built earlier, in 1770, the Baroque Trinity Column in the centre of the square looks at its best in early summer when it is surrounded by bedding flowers of every colour.

🏛 Franciscan Church
Magyarok Nagyasszonya templom
Fő tér 5. **Tel** (83) 31 42 71.
This grand building, towering over the southern side of the square, is the Franciscan Church and former monastery, built in the 14th century. The tall Neo-Gothic tower with a 10-m (33-ft) spire is, in fact,

an 18th-century addition. The crypt holds the tomb of György Festetics, the patriarch of the Festetics family and uncle of István Széchenyi. The church was originally built in Gothic style using stone taken from an

Stained-glass window in the Franciscan Church

old Roman settlement nearby. During restoration work in 1974, remains of 14th- and 15th-century frescoes were discovered. Lost during the Turkish occupation, when the church served as a fortress, these represent the largest collection of Gothic frescoes remaining in Hungary. The fine rose window above the eastern portal is also an original feature of the church.

🏛 Doll and Waxwork Museum
Történelmi Panoptikum
Kossuth Lajos utca 11. **Tel** (83) 31 88 55. ◯ May–Sep: 9am–7pm; Oct–Apr: 9am–6pm. 🈳
Three museums in one, the first contains a collection of 700 porcelain dolls. Each doll wears the traditional costume of one particular Hungarian village, and is handmade there. The dolls are complemented by a showcase of local village architecture, with more than 200 scale models of village buildings, including houses, stables and churches.
The second part of the museum is the waxworks, featuring 500 life-size figures of eminent Hungarians, from Árpád to Imre Nagy.
The third museum section is the astonishing 7-m- (23-ft-) long model of Hungary's Parliament that was made by Ilona Miskei from more than four million sea-snail shells.

🏛 Georgikon Farm Museum
Georgikon Majormúzeum
Bercsényi Miklós utca 65–7.
Tel (83) 31 15 63. ◯ Apr & Oct: 10am–5pm Mon–Fri; May–Sep: 10am–5pm Tue–Sun. 🈳 🅿 Hungarian and German only. ♿
Europe's first Academy of Agriculture was set up here by György Festetics, in 1797. It was made into a museum in 1972, and exhibitions focus on the history of Hungarian agriculture from Celtic times to the present day. There are separate displays on wine production in the Balaton area and domestic farming in Southern Transdanubia, as well as a selection of antique agricultural equipment, from bronze-age tools to steam ploughs, and an early motor tractor.

Wine bars in Kossuth Street, the widest street in the Old Town

🚇 Kossuth Street
Kossuth utca.

Keszthely's main thoroughfare
was built to allow the Festetics
family easy access from their
castle to the lake. Markedly
the widest street in the older
part of the town, it is lined
with some fine houses. The
oldest, at No 22, is the birthplace of the Hungarian-Jewish
pianist Karl Goldmark. With
its porticoes and covered
upper-level loggia, the house
is Mediterranean in feel. Just
behind, in a leafy courtyard,
is Keszthely's well-preserved
Neo-Renaissance synagogue.
Originally dating from 1780, it
was entirely rebuilt in 1851–2.

🏛 Balaton Museum
Balatoni Múzeum

Múzeum utca 2. **Tel** (83) 31 23 51.
◯ May–Oct: 10am–6pm Tue–Sun;
Nov–Apr: 9am–5pm Tue–Sat. 🎫 ♿

The mustard-yellow Neo-
Baroque Balaton Museum
building, erected in the 1920s
to a design by Dénes Györgyi,
is well worth seeing in its
own right. The exhibitions
inside are equally interesting
and include a fascinating look
at life around Lake Balaton in
pre-Roman times and displays
showing the development of
fishing on the lake. Children
will love the models of sailing
ships, steamers and paddle-
boats that once traversed the

lake. A more sombre display
explains the effects of pollu-
tion on life in the lake. Also
shown is Roman stoneware
from the region and an original milestone to Aquincum
(*see p110*), 43 miles away.

Excavated fishing equipment, on
display at the Balaton Museum

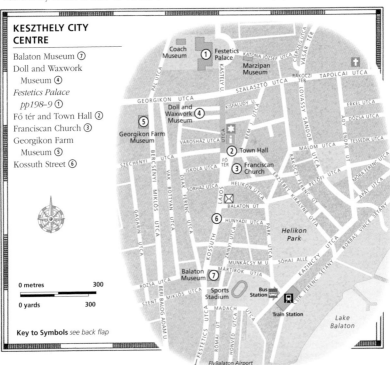

KESZTHELY CITY CENTRE

Coach Museum
Festetics Palace ①
Marzipan Museum
Doll and Waxwork Museum ④
Georgikon Farm Museum ⑤
Town Hall ②
Franciscan Church ③
⑥
Helikon Park
Balaton Museum ⑦
Sports Stadium
Bus Station
Train Station
Lake Balaton

0 metres 300
0 yards 300

Key to Symbols *see back flap*

FlyBalaton Airport
10km (6miles)

Festetics Palace and Helikon Palace Museum

Originally the home of the Festetics family, the stately, Neo-Baroque Festetics Palace is the *magnum opus* of little-known architect Viktor Rumpelmayer. Completed in 1754, it was requisitioned by the Soviet Union in 1944. Today the Palace houses the Helikon Palace Museum as well as a model railway and hunting exhibition. More than half of the Palace's 101 rooms are open to the public, and feature fine examples of exotic art, furniture, arms and other memorabilia from the Festetics family's many foreign expeditions. The Palace is famous for its 100,000-volume library and its magnificent English gardens, which cover over 42 hectares (104 acres) and are considered the finest in Hungary.

★ **Baroque Tower**
The Neo-Baroque façade is based on the French stately homes of the same era. The central tower's dome, however, evokes an earlier Baroque style.

Main Entrance

Weapons Display

★ **English Gardens**
English – not French – stately homes, were the inspiration for the Palace gardens. They were laid out by the English landscape artist Edward Miller.

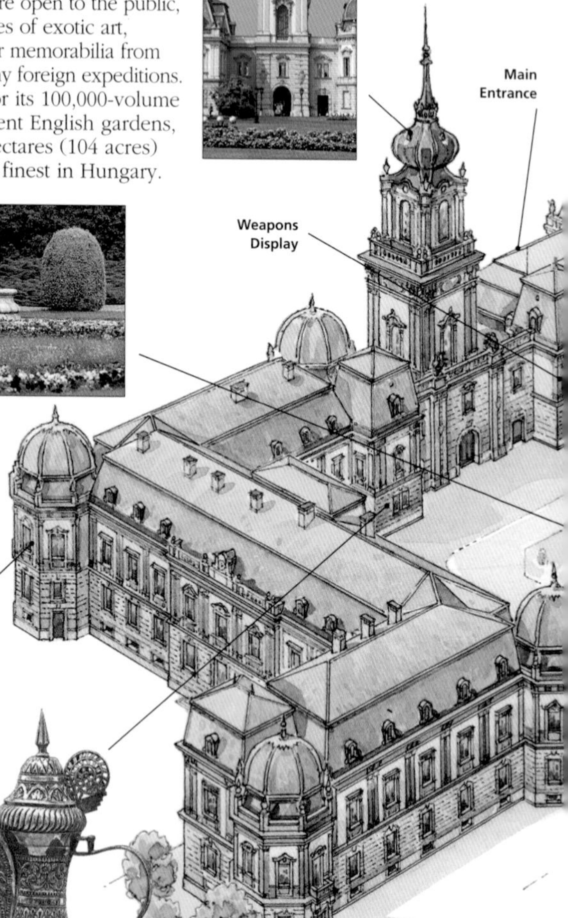

Rounded Eastern-style Tower of Southern Wing

The World of Islam
The Festetics family were great explorers, and filled the mansion with treasures brought back from their travels to North Africa and the Middle East. The collection has been complemented with loans from the Tareq Rajab Museum, Kuwait.

Carriage Museum
In the Palace's former stables, the Carriage Museum is home to a priceless collection of hunting and parade coaches and carriages from the 18th and early 19th centuries.

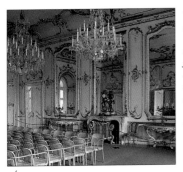

★ Mirror Room
Equipped with Venetian mirrors and English furniture, the Mirror Room, also known as the Main Hall, regularly hosts chamber music concerts and operettas.

VISITORS' CHECKLIST

Kastély utca 1, Keszthely.
Road Map B4. ***Tel*** *(83) 31 21 90.* *Tourinform, Kossuth utca 28; (83) 31 41 44.*
Sep–Jun: 10am–5pm Tue–Sun; Jul–Aug: 9am–6pm daily.
There is a fee payable for photography and use of video cameras.
www.keszthely.hu

Rooms are each decorated in a different colour scheme and fully furnished.

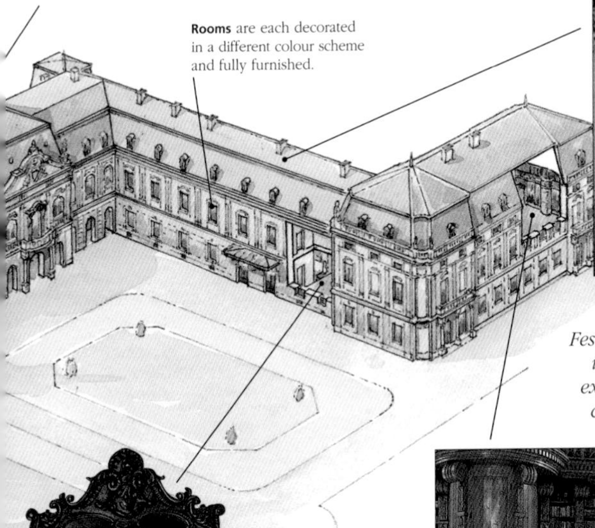

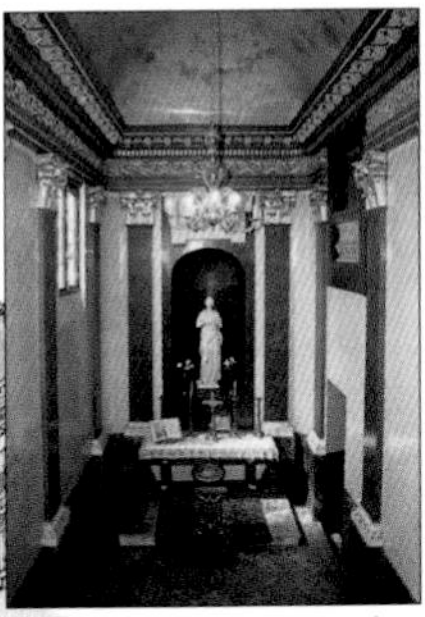

Chapel
The small, private Festetics Chapel was built in the 1880s, when the extent of the Palace was considerably enlarged.

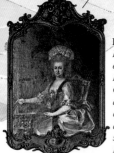

Portrait Gallery
Portraits of almost every member of the Festetics family, Croatian in origin, as well as of the cream of Hungarian and Viennese society, line the Palace's walls.

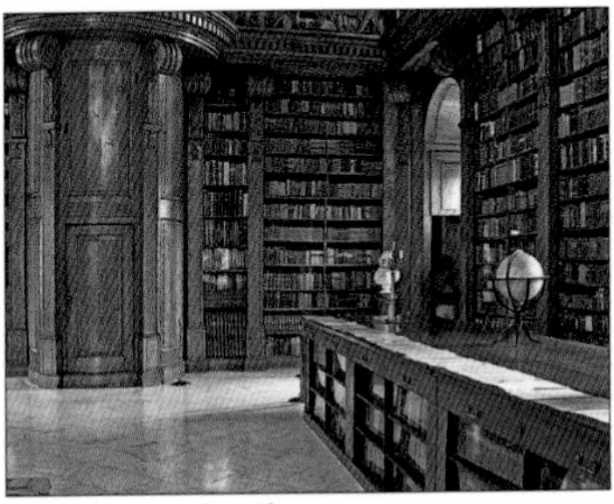

★ Library
The Rococo Helikon Library holds over 100,000 volumes on its oak shelves. Hungary's literary elite gathered here in the 19th century.

GYÖRGY FESTETICS

A polymath who combined a love of the land and the arts with the progressive ideals of the Enlightenment, György Festetics (1755–1819) was the grandson of Kristóf Festetics, who had been given the Helikon Estate in 1743 by the Habsburgs. György Festetics is best known for founding the Georgikon at Keszthely in 1798 *(see p196),* Europe's first agricultural college. A great explorer, Festetics travelled and hunted in Africa. Later, he became a generous patron of the arts and organized poetry and music festivals at the Palace.

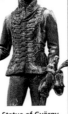

Statue of György Festetics

STAR FEATURES

- ★ Baroque Tower
- ★ English Gardens
- ★ Library
- ★ Mirror Room

The Central Pavilion, dominating the relaxing warm waters of the thermal lake in Hévíz

Hévíz ⑰

6 km (4 miles) north of Keszthely.
Road Map B4. 🏠 5,000. 🚌 from
Keszthely. 🔳 Tourinform, Rákóczi
utca 2, (83) 54 01 31.

With its vast Central Pavilion
in the middle of what is the
world's largest thermal
water lake, Hévíz is a
spectacular sight.
Covered with Indian
water lilies, which flow-
er in early September,
Lake Hévíz has been
used for bathing and
treatments since
1795. Up to 30 m
(98 ft) deep, the
lake has a surface
area of 47,500 sq
m (56,800 sq yd)
and a tempera-
ture of 36 °C
(96.8 °F) in sum-
mer. It is replenished by a
spring that produces 420 litres
(92 gallons) of water per second. Even in winter the water
temperature never drops below
28 °C (82.4 °F). The water is
slightly radioactive and recommended for the treatment of
rheumatism and arthritis. It also
tastes surprisingly good, and is
used to treat stomach disorders.
The radioactive mud from the
lake floor is also therapeutic.
   Although most patrons prefer
to bathe outside, even in winter,
there is a small indoor pool.
Hévíz also has the best range
of hotels in the area.

**Fountain in front
of the entrance to Hévíz
thermal baths**

🛁 **Lake Hévíz**
Dr Schulhof Vilmos sétány 1.
Tel (83) 50 17 00. ⏲ May–Oct:
8am–7pm daily; Nov–Apr:
9am–6pm daily. 📷 ⅃
www.spaheviz.hu

Balatonederics ⑱

14 km (9 miles) east of Keszthely.
Road Map B4. 🏠 1,200. 🚆 from
Tapolca, Keszthely. 🚌 from Tapolca,
Keszthely.

Balatonederics is one of the
oldest settlements on Lake
Balaton, its name first
mentioned as long ago as
1262. The Roman Catholic
church that stands in the
village centre was built
about the same time,
originally as a Roman-
esque structure. It
received its present
Neo-Gothic look
during renovation
work in 1870–71.
The Holy Trinity
monument in
front of the church
dates from 1871.
   An exclusive
resort without hotels, Balatonederics nevertheless welcomes
hundreds of thousands of day
trippers a year, all visiting its
**Africa Museum and Safari
Park** (Afrika Múzeum és
Állatkert). Founded in 1984
by a Hungarian big-game
hunter, Dr Nagy Endre, the
museum is home to Endre's
hunting trophies and ethnographical memorabilia that
he collected in Tanzania.
In the Safari Park, African
animals including buffalo,
zebra and camels – which
can be ridden – roam freely,
next to original Masai huts.

🦒 **Africa Museum and
Safari Park**
Kültelek 11. **Tel** (87) 46 61 05.
⏲ Apr–Oct: 9am–4pm daily (to
5:30pm Jul–Aug). 📷 ⅃ ⅃ ⅃
www.afrikamuzeum.hu

Szigliget ⑲

20 km (12 miles) east of Keszthely.
Road Map B4. 🏠 1,000. 🚆 from
Keszthely. 🚌 from Keszthely. 🚌
from Keszthely.

Underneath the ruins of the
13th-century **Szigetvár Island
Castle** (often referred to as

A camel at the Africa Museum and Safari Park in Balatonederics

Óvár, Old Castle), the village of Szigliget stands on a small peninsula that – as the castle's name suggests – was once an island. The last waters receded about the time the castle was destroyed, in 1702, after an explosion in the gunpowder store. Some of the towers, part of the living quarters and the stables remain. The ruins are a steep, 30-minute walk uphill from the village but the picturesque thatched cottages that line the route up and the stunning views from the top make the climb worthwhile.

The village itself is dominated by Esterházy Mansion, a Neo-Classical 19th-century building, now a hotel for the exclusive use of the Hungarian Writers' Union. The hotel's extensive gardens are open to the public. Szigliget also has a pleasantly quiet grass beach and an attractive harbour, always cheerful with its show of colourful sailing boats.

Badacsony Mountain ⑳

30 km (19 miles) east of Keszthely.
Road Map B4. 🚶 *2,400.*
🚉 *from Tapolca.* 🚌 *from Tapolca.*
🚌 *from Keszthely, Fonyód.*
🛈 *Tourinform, Badacsony, Park utca 6, (87) 43 10 46.*

Beginning at the railway station in lovely Badacsony village is a well-marked and fairly gentle trail, signposted in yellow, which winds its way up to the Kisfaludy Lookout Tower at the top of Badacsony Mountain (437 m/1,434 ft). An extinct volcano, this offers the best hiking in the Balaton area, with spectacular views from the top across the lake.

On the way up, almost hidden among the vineyards that cover the volcanic soil, are two superb former wine-press houses. The first, 3 km (2 miles) from Badacsony, is the Róza Szegedy House, named after the wife of the 18th-century poet Sándor Kisfaludy. The couple met on the mountain and the house contains a small display dedicated to Kisfaludy's poetry, as well as a wine cellar where

Badacsony Mountain, as seen from Szigliget Island Castle

the locally produced Grey Friar wine (Szürkebarát) can be sampled. The second wine-press house on the trail was once Kisfaludy's home, and today is also a wine cellar offering tastings. There are great views from its terrace. Passing Rose Rock, where the couple met, the trail continues to the top, from where longer, more strenuous hikes depart for two other hills, Gulács-hegy and Szent György-hegy.

Tapolca ㉑

26 km (16 miles) northeast of Keszthely. **Road Map** B4. 🚶 *18,000.*
🚉 *from Budapest, Keszthely.* 🚌 *from Budapest.* 🛈 *Tourinform, Fő tér 17, (87) 51 07 77.*

Encircled by 14 cone-shaped hills of basalt rock, Tapolca has one of the most spectacular settings of any town on Lake Balaton. Equally picturesque is the thermal pond in

the centre of the town, encircled by little squares and colourful 19th-century houses. Many have been converted into bars and restaurants, with terraces overlooking the lake.

An early 19th-century water mill in the middle of the mill pond is now the Hotel Gabriella. What most visitors really come to Tapolca for, however, is the **Cave Lake** (Tavas-barlang), a short walk from the town centre. The lake lies 18 m (59 ft) below the surface. It was discovered by accident when a well was being sunk in 1902, and is reached via a steep staircase. Part of 300-m (328-yd) cave system can be seen from dry land, though much more can be explored in a rented boat.

🛈 Tapolca Cave Lake
Kisfaludy utca 3.
Tel (87) 41 25 79.
🕐 *Jul–Aug: 9am–7pm daily; Sep–Jun: 10am–5pm daily; Nov–mid-Mar: Sat only.* ♿

Tapolca's unique attraction, the mysterious Cave Lake

Kinizsi Castle in Nagyvázsony, once a military fortress

Nagyvázsony ㉒

26 km (16 miles) southwest of Veszprém. **Road Map** B4. 🏰 *1,900.* 🚌 *from Balatonfüred.*

Set in a valley between the Balaton hills and Mount Kab, Nagyvázsony boasts **Kinizsi Castle**, a well-preserved 14th-century fortress. It was given to local warrior Pál Kinizsi in 1472 by King Mátyás in recognition of his outstanding military service. Kinizsi demilitarized it and turned it into a residence, which may be the reason why it survived.

From the top of the 29-m (95-ft) high keep a superb panorama of the surrounding countryside unfolds. In the dungeons is the **Pál Kinizsi Castle Museum** (Kinizsi Pál Vármúzeum), where a small waxwork display shows medieval torturers in action. Pál Kinizsi's sarcophagus lies in the chapel.

Opposite the castle stands St István Church, built for Kinizsi in 1470 but rebuilt in Baroque style in 1740. An **Ethnographic Museum** (Néprajzi Múzeum) with two cottages (a coppersmith's and a weaver's) remain as they were in the mid-1840s.

🏛 **Pál Kinizsi Castle Museum**
Vár utca 9. **Tel** (88) 26 40 11.
⏰ Jun–Aug: 9am–6pm daily; Sep–May: 10am–5pm daily. 🈺
🏛 **Ethnographic Museum**
Bercsényi utca 21. ⏰ May–Sep: 10am–6pm Tue–Sun. 🈺 ♿

Tihany Peninsula ㉓

15 km (9 miles) south of Veszprém. **Road Map** B4. 🚢 *to Balatonfüred.* 🚌 *from Balatonfüred to Tihany village.* 🚗 *car ferry from Szántód.* ℹ *Tourinform, Kossuth Lajos utca 20, Tihany, (87) 44 88 04.*

Declared Hungary's first conservation area in 1952, the Tihany Peninsula is an outcrop of volcanic rock extending for 5 km (3 miles) into Lake Balaton. The symbol of the peninsula, and visible from afar, is the Baroque Abbey Church, built in the 18th century on the site of an earlier church, which was consecrated in 1060 but destroyed in 1702. Beneath lies King András I, laid to rest here in 1055. Károly Lotz's superb frescoes of Faith, Hope and Charity adorn the church's ceiling.

The western half of Tihany is closed to motor traffic and accessible only on foot, along a number of well marked trails, most of which begin just outside Tihany village. The most intriguing route is the Lajos Lóczy Nature Trail, which takes visitors past the hermit caves overlooking Tihany village, and the peninsula's two inland lakes: Belső-tó (Inner Lake) and Külső-tó (Outer Lake). Belső-tó is a volcanic crater and an angler's dream, while Külső-tó is a bird sanctuary and nesting ground for tens of thousands of birds.

Tihany has good grass beaches, although the most popular, on the promenade at Tihany village, get very busy during high summer. The passenger port, Tihany-rév at the peninsula's southern tip, is the prettiest on the lake. Car ferries cross from here to Szántód on Lake Balaton's southern shore.

The High Altar in Tihany's ornate Baroque Abbey Church

A café near Lake Balaton in the elegant resort of Balatonfüred

Balatonfüred ㉔

23 km (14 miles) southeast of Veszprém. **Road Map** B4. 🚶 13,000. 🚆 from Budapest. 🚌 from Budapest. 🚢 from Siófok. 🛈 Tourinform, Petőfi utca 68, (87) 58 04 80. 🎭 Anna Ball (last Sat in Jul).

The site of the first medicinal retreat on Lake Balaton, Hungary's first sailing club and one of its oldest balls, Balatonfüred remains the grandest resort on the lake. Though its streets have a faded air, the villas, such as that of the romantic novelist Mór Jókai (1825–1904) still convey elegance; Jókai's home is today a museum dedicated to his works. Primarily a health spa,

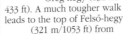

A sailing boat on Lake Balaton

patients flock to the town's hospital to drink its mineral-laced water. The "miracle" water is available to all from the colonnaded drinking fountain in Gyógy tér.

Gyógy tér is also where the grand annual Anna Ball is held at the Árkád Hotel in July. The first ball in 1825 was a showcase event for the granddaughter of a local businessman. Traditionally, the debutantes all wear exactly the same gown and the high point is the election of the belle of the ball.

Two great sandy beaches flank Balatonfüred's landing stage, from where the Lake Balaton ferry departs.

Balatonalmádi ㉕

13 km (8 miles) south of Veszprém. **Road Map** B4. 🚶 8,000. 🚆 from Budapest. 🚌 from Budapest. 🛈 Tourinform, Városház tér 4, (88) 59 40 80. 🎭 Balatonalmádi Days (last week in Jul).

The second largest resort on Balaton's northern shore, Balatonalmádi has welcomed bathers since the 1870s. It has a fine sandy beach, and is an excellent base for exploring the Balaton hinterland and hills on foot. From the railway station, a 6-km (4-mile) path (marked with blue crosses) leads up to the Wesselényi Viewing Tower at the top of Öreg-hegy (132 m/ 433 ft). A much tougher walk leads to the top of Felső-hegy (321 m/1053 ft) from the same starting

point. The Balatonalmádi Days feature a huge folk art fair, folk dancing, sports events and evening concerts.

Herend ㉖

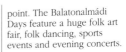

7 km (4 miles) northwest of Veszprém. **Road Map** B4. 🚶 3,400. 🚌 from Veszprém. **www**.herend.com

The small village of Herend is famous mainly for its porcelain manufactory that has been producing some of the finest porcelain in the world since 1826. The building itself is a masterpiece, and as such a listed building. A late-Classicist edifice built in 1840, it has an amazing entrance, topped with an egg-shaped dome guarded by two giant angels.

The **Herend Porcelain Art Museum** (Herendi Porcelánművészeti Múzeum Alapítvány), opened in 1964, has displays of the decorative Herend china and porcelain, from dinner plates to intricately painted figurines. There is also the opportunity to visit a workshop (porcelanium) to watch the production process. There are demonstrations by artists who meticulously hand-paint every detail. A vast factory shop sells some 12,000 porcelain items made here and painted in about 350 different patterns.

🏛 **Herend Porcelain Art Museum**
Kossuth Lajos utca 140. **Tel** (88) 52 31 97. ◻ Apr–Oct: 9:30am–6pm daily; Nov–Mar: 9:30am–5pm daily. 🖼 🚻 ♿

The astonishing entrance of the Herend Porcelain Art Museum

Veszprém ㉗

The site of the nation's first bishopric, and for centuries the seat of the Queen of Hungary's household, Veszprém is one of Hungary's great historical towns. It was all but razed by the Turks as they fled Hungary in the 17th century. Spread over five hills, the most picturesque part of the city is the Vár (Castle District, *see pp206–7*), but the lower city offers some fine Baroque architecture, great museums and quaint streets. The twin towers of St Michael's Cathedral, visible from afar, are a symbol of Veszprém and of the Balaton and Bakony regions. Visitors need to be fit to explore this city as many sights are at the top of long staircases or at the end of steep, cobbled streets.

Interior of St Michael's Cathedral, currently being restored

🔒 St Michael's Cathedral
Szent Mihály Érseki Székesegyház
Vár utca 20. **Tel** (88) 32 80 38.
◯ May–Oct: 10am–5pm.
◯ Nov–Feb.
There was a church here as early as 1001, when St István created a bishopric, but the cathedral's present look is early 20th century. Remains of earlier styles include the Gothic undercroft (underground store) and the crypt's vaulting, both from 1380. Following sensitive restoration of many older features, the cathedral has returned to its former glory, crowned by two tall towers dating from 1723.

🔒 Gizella Chapel
Gizella Kápolna
Vár utca 18. **Tel** (88) 42 60 88.
◯ May–Oct: 10am–5pm daily.
The tiny 13th-century Gothic Chapel commemorates the life of Gisella, wife of István and first Queen of Hungary. The chapel was lost and rediscovered only in the 1760s, during building work. Its faded Byzantine frescoes of the apostles on the walls are original.

🏛 Archbishop's Palace
Érseki Palota
Vár utca 16–18. **Tel** (88) 42 60 88.
◯ May–Oct: 10am–5pm Tue–Sun.
This Baroque mansion (1764) was designed by Fellner and has his trademark rounded four-columned loggia. It houses the Archbishop's archive and only a few rooms are open to the public with a fine collection of Baroque furniture and frescoes by Johann Cymbal.

🏛 Castle Gate and Museum
Várkapu és Múzeum
Vár utca. **Tel** (88) 40 45 48.
◯ Museum Apr–Sep: 9am–3pm daily.
Although it looks medieval, the gate is a faithful replica of the original castle gate, but it was built only in 1938 to commemorate the Hungarian dead of World War I. The gate's tower affords fine views of the city from the top.

🏛 Óváros tér & Town Hall
Városháza
Óváros tér.
Óváros tér sits directly below the Castle district. Veszprém's former market square, it is surrounded by some fine little houses, many of which are today cafés. The Pósa House at No. 3 was built for a local merchant, Endre Pósa, in 1783. Its showy decoration, especially the two cherubs below the roof, was to offset the linearity of the building. The contours of the Secession-era house next door are gentler. Opposite is the Neo-Classical Town Hall, built in 1896 as church offices, but renovated and converted in 1990. Behind the Town Hall, up a flight of stairs, is Lenke Kiss's fountain *Girl with a Jug*, affectionately known as "Zsuzsi" by locals.

A late-Secession-era stained-glass window in the Petőfi Theatre

🏛 Petőfi Theatre
Petőfi Színház
Óváry Ferenc utca 2. **Tel** (88) 42 42 35. ◯ 8am–10pm daily.
The late-Secession-era (1908) municipal theatre, set in well-kept gardens, is named after revolutionary playwright and poet Sándor Petőfi (*see p42*). The theatre was designed by István Medgyaszay, who studied in Vienna under Otto Wagner. It has intricate folk motifs on the façade, typical of later Secessionist buildings.

Façade of the Neo-Classical Town Hall, built in 1896

🏛 Laczkó Dezső Museum
Laczkó Dezső Múzeum

Erzsébet sétány 1. **Tel** *(88) 78 81 91.*
⏰ *Mar–Oct: 10am–6pm Tue–Sun;*
Nov–Feb: by appointment.

The Country Museum, designed by the local architect István Medgyaszay, was opened in 1922. Its collection consists of local artifacts, including folk costumes dating back to Celtic times. Most of the collection was donated by local Piarist monks, for whose leader, Laczkó Dezső, the museum was named. It also housed Hungary's first public library, still a leading research facility.

🏛 The Bakony Regional Folk House
Bakonyi Ház

Erzsébet sétány 3.
Tel *(88) 56 43 10.* ⏰ *May–Sep: 10am–6pm daily.*

Hungary's first ethnographic museum, the Bakony House (1935) was modelled on the 19th-century houses of Öcs, south of Veszprém. The house is built on high foundations and has a full-length covered terrace. A small staircase leads to a single door. Inside, items on show date back to 1700.

St István Viaduct, designed by the Hungarian architect Róbert Folly

🌉 St István Viaduct
Szent István völgyhíd

Szent István völgyhíd.
Stretching over the Fejes Valley, from Dózsa György utca to the St László Church, the St István Viaduct was built in 1938, a major engineering achievement at the time. Designed by a Hungarian, Róbert Folly, it rises 50 m (164 ft) above the River Séd at its highest point. It affords magnificent views of the castle, the Betekints Valley and the Bakony Mountains to the north.

A giraffe in Veszprém Zoo

VISITORS' CHECKLIST

44 km (27 miles) southwest of Székesfehérvár. **Road Map** B4.
🚌 60,000. 🚆 *Jutási út; from Budapest, Székesfehérvár.*
🚍 *Piac tér; from Budapest, Székesfehérvár.* 🚐 *Piac tér, Szabadság tér.* 🛈 *Tourinform, Óváros tér 2, (88) 40 45 48.*
www.veszpreminfo.hu
🎭 *Gizella Art Days (May).*

🐾 Veszprém Zoo
Kittenberger Kálmán Növény és Vadaspark

Kittenberger Kálmán utca 15–17.
Tel *(88) 56 61 40.* ⏰ *May–Sep: 9am–6pm daily; Mar & Nov: 9am–3:30pm Mon–Fri, 9am–4pm Sat & Sun; Apr: 9am–5pm daily; Dec–Feb: 9am–3pm daily.*
www.veszpzoo.hu

Hungary's best zoo, named after Africa explorer Kálmán Kittenberger (1881–1958), is spread over 13 hectares (32 acres) in the lovely Fejes Valley. It is home to 120 species, including Sumatran tigers and Kamchatka bears, though the zoo's best feature is its fine exotic birds.

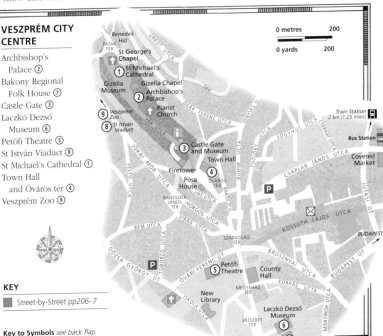

VESZPRÉM CITY CENTRE

Archbishop's Palace ②
Bakony Regional Folk House ⑦
Castle Gate ③
Laczkó Dezső Museum ⑥
Petőfi Theatre ⑤
St István Viaduct ⑧
St Michael's Cathedral ①
Town Hall and Óváros tér ④
Veszprém Zoo ⑨

0 metres 200
0 yards 200

KEY

⬛ Street-by-Street pp206–7

Key to Symbols see back flap

Benedek Hill
PATAK TÉR
ÚRKÚT UTCA
St George's Chapel
① St Michael's Cathedral
Gizella Museum
Gizella Chapel
② Archbishop's Palace
Piarist Church
DEÁK FERENC UTCA
⑨ Veszprém Zoo
⑧ St István Viaduct
VÁR UTCA
FENYVES UTCA
VÖGYIKÚT UTCA
CSERHÁT UTCA
Train Station 2 km (1.25 miles)
Bus Station
③ Castle Gate and Museum
Town Hall
Firetower
④ ÓVÁROS TÉR
Pósa House
JÓKAI MÓR UTCA
TESTO UTCA
THOLDY UTCA
BUHIM UTCA
BAKONY UTCA
CSAPLÁR JÁNOS UTCA
JUTÁSI UTCA
Covered Market
P
BÁNDORI JÁNOS TÉR
HORGOS UTCA
VAS UTCA
VIRÁG UTCA
BEM UTCA
☒
KOSSUTH LAJOS UTCA
SZABADSÁG TÉR
BUDAPEST
DÓZSA GYÖRGY ÚT
TOBORZÓ UTCA
P
ÓVÁRI FERENC ÚT
⑤ Petőfi Theatre
County Hall
MEGYEHÁZ TÉR
BRUSZNYAI UTCA
KORKÁZ UTCA
BUDAPEST ÚT
MÁRTÍROK UTCA
ISKOLA UTCA
New Library
ERZSÉBET TÉR
⑥ Laczkó Dezső Museum
⑦ Bakony Regional Folk House

Street-by-Street: Veszprém Vár

With the exception of Buda, Veszprém contains Hungary's best preserved and most accessible Castle District *(Vár)*. Built on an outcrop of dolomite rock it consists basically of one street, which is narrow in parts and delightful with its mixture of medieval and Baroque architecture. From here, the views over the modern city from the Szent István and Gizella Monument are stunning, and make the walk up worthwhile.

Gizella Chapel
Lost for hundreds of years, the 13th-century Gizella Chapel was rediscovered in 1760 during construction of the Archbishop's Palace.

PATAK TÉR

Szent István and Gizella Monument
Huge statues featuring Hungary's greatest king and his wife were raised in 1936, on the 900th anniversary of István's death.

★ **St Michael's Cathedral**
Standing on the site of an 11th-century church founded by King István, St Michael's Cathedral was extensively rebuilt in Neo-Romanesque style in 1908.

Dubniczay House
Built in 1751, the Dubniczay House incorporates part of the old castle wall.

Franciscan Church
After the original 18th-century church burned down in 1909, it was rebuilt to mirror the Neo-Romanesque façade of the Cathedral opposite.

Holy Trinity Statue
Commissioned by the then Bishop of Veszprém, Márton Padányi-Bíró, this statue was raised in 1750. The Bishop also commissioned the Bíró-Giczey House opposite.

STAR FEATURES

★ Archbishop's Palace

★ Castle Gate

★ St Michael's Cathedral

KEY

– – – Suggested route

★ **Archbishop's Palace**
Veszprém's finest building is an outstanding example of Baroque design, the work of Jakab Fellner, who also designed the dormitory for ecclesiastical staff next door. Seven of the mansion's rooms, including the frescoed dining room, are open to the public.

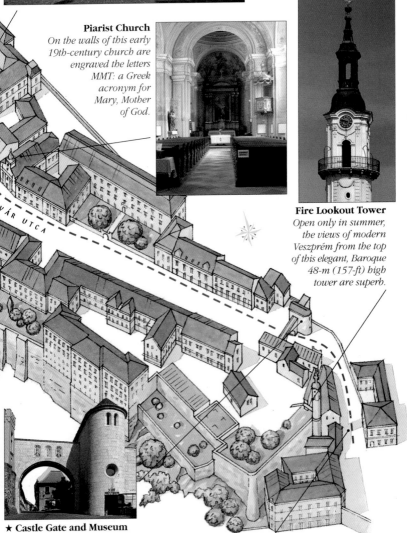

Piarist Church
On the walls of this early 19th-century church are engraved the letters MMT: a Greek acronym for Mary, Mother of God.

VÁR UTCA

Fire Lookout Tower
Open only in summer, the views of modern Veszprém from the top of this elegant, Baroque 48-m (157-ft) high tower are superb.

★ **Castle Gate and Museum**
Veszprém's Tourist Information Office occupies the ground floor of this 1930s replica of the original castle gate and tower.

| 0 metres | 30 |
| 0 yards | 30 |

Route down to Óváros tér.
Visitors should note that the Vár remains open to motor traffic, and beware of cars.

THE NORTHERN HIGHLANDS

A mong the gems hidden in the mountains and forests of the Northern Highlands are grand palaces and castles, mysterious caves and grottoes, healing baths and thermal springs. The Hungarian uplands are remote, lying beyond mountain passes and deep forests, and their plant- and wildlife are well protected in the national parks. This region also produces Hungary's best wine – Tokaji.

From Hollókő in the west to the Zemplén Hills on Hungary's eastern border with Ukraine, the Northern Highlands feel remote and other-worldly. Home to a number of peoples who are not of Magyar descent (the Palóc of Hollókő, for example), this is the least homogenous region of the country. Yet the people of the mountains are proudly Hungarian, and proud that at Eger Castle the most heroic rearguard action in the nation's history was fought and won – and the myth of Bull's Blood born.

The region has much for sports enthusiasts: skiing, hiking, caving and horse-riding are pursued in the resorts of the Mátra Mountains. Bathers and those seeking hydrotherapy can take the waters at Parádfürdő or at Miskolc-Tapolca, the most spectacular of all Hungary's thermal baths. Nature lovers will head for the Bükk National Park, where over 22,000 species of animal and plant live in a protected environment.

Tokaji is Hungary's finest wine: the golden wine of Aszú is made in the far east of the country, a place where Calvinism, not Catholicism, is the predominant religion. Many of the towns and villages east of the Tokaj hills are remote – to journey to gorgeous Baroque towns such as Sárospatak and Sátoraljaújhely really is to step off the beaten track.

This area is not short of good places to stay, however. Converted palaces such as the Sasvár Kastély in Parádfürdő, or the Palota in Lillafüred offer accommodation fit for royals.

Pedestrianized Széchenyi Street, leading to the Bishop's Palace and Lyceum, Eger

◁ Füzér Castle (1310) sits in splendour on a crag overlooking the sleepy village in the Zemplén Hills

Exploring The Northern Highlands

While the Mátra and Bükk Mountains, boasting Hungary's highest peaks, define the Northern Highlands, this is, in fact, the most geographically diverse region. Some of the country's most evocative sights are found here. Castles, such as the legendary fortress at Eger, bear witness to troubled times, while many thermal baths have drawn bathers since imperial times. This is also wine country, with Tokaj and Eger the foremost towns of international acclaim, and the home of the Palóc people, who fiercely guard their traditions.

The traditional Palóc settlement of Hollókő, preserved as a World Heritage Site

SEE ALSO

- **Where to Stay** pp272–3
- **Where to Eat** pp291–2

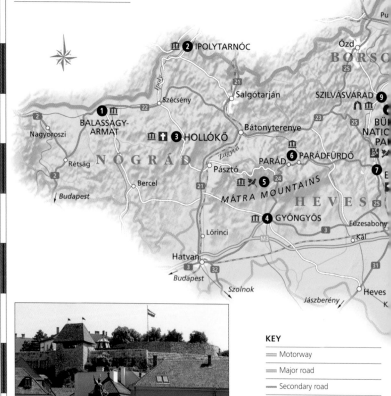

Eger, with Cannon Hill and the famous castle in the background

KEY

═══	Motorway
▬▬▬	Major road
━━━	Secondary road
⋯⋯	Minor road
▪━▪	Main railway
────	Minor railway
▬▬▬	International border
▬▬▬	Regional border

GETTING AROUND

The region is reasonably well-served by railway, although the geography may force visitors to travel back on themselves in order to reach a new destination by train. There are trains from Budapest to Gyöngyös, Eger and Miskolc, with regional onward services from there. To get the most out of a visit to the region, however, it is best to hire a car. Roads are good and allow much quicker access to some of the more remote sights.

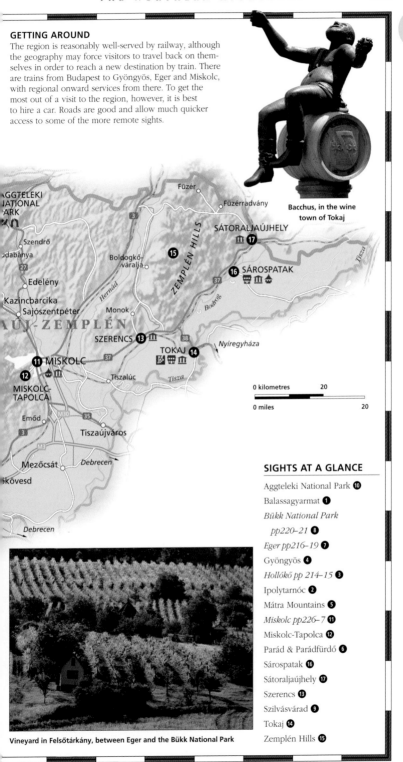

Bacchus, in the wine town of Tokaj

Vineyard in Felsőtárkány, between Eger and the Bükk National Park

SIGHTS AT A GLANCE

Aggteleki National Park **10**

Balassagyarmat **1**

Bükk National Park pp220–21 **8**

Eger pp216–19 **7**

Gyöngyös **4**

Hollókő pp 214–15 **3**

Ipolytarnóc **2**

Mátra Mountains **5**

Miskolc pp226–7 **11**

Miskolc-Tapolca **12**

Parád & Parádfürdő **6**

Sárospatak **16**

Sátoraljaújhely **17**

Szerencs **13**

Szilvásvárad **9**

Tokaj **14**

Zemplén Hills **15**

The Palóc Museum in Balassagyarmat, keeping up folk traditions

Balassagyarmat ❶

80 km (50 miles) north of Budapest.
Road Map D2. 🏘 18,000.
🚊 from Vác. 🚌 from Budapest.
ℹ Tourinform, Köztársaság tér 6,
(35) 50 06 40.

Capital of the Palóc region,
Balassagyarmat stands on the
southern bank of the Ipoly
river, which marks the border
between Hungary and Slovakia.
The origin of the Palóc people,
famous for retaining their own
cultural traditions, remains
something of a mystery. The
nearby village of Hollókő
(see pp214–15) is the best-
known and best-kept Palóc
settlement in Hungary.
  The townsfolk of Balassagyarmat no longer wear Palóc
costume, but many examples
of their colourful, elaborate
dress are on display at the
city's **Palóc Museum** (Palóc
Múzeum). Here, visitors can
also admire the rich artistic
skills of the Palóc in the handi-
crafts on show. There are
superb embroidery, intricate
wood carvings and colourful
ceramics as well as a mock-
up of a classroom and a
wedding. Unfortunately, there
is less on display than there
once was, because as much
as 90 per cent of the collection
was looted by the German
army during World War II.

🏛 **Palóc Museum**
Palóc liget 1.
Tel (35) 30 01 68.
⬜ 10am–4pm Tue–Sat.
⬤ Nov–Dec. 🎦 &

Ipolytarnóc ❷

43 km (27 miles) northeast of Balassagyarmat. **Road Map** D2. 🏘 550.
🚊 from Szécsény, Balassa-gyarmat.
🚌 from Szécsény.

Around 22 million years ago,
a volcanic eruption buried the
area around what is today the
village of Ipolytarnóc in hot
ash. Hundreds of animals
were caught at their drinking
place and their fossilized
remains can be seen today
as part of a Geological Study
Path that is unique in Europe.
It departs from the visitors'
centre of the **Ipolytarnóc
Fossils Nature Protected Area**
(Ipolytarnóci Ősmaradványok
Természetvédelmi Terület) on
the village's outskirts. Before
setting off, watch the short
film telling the story of the
eruption and explaining the
natural history of the area. A
guide is needed for the
Geological Study Tour but
the Biology and the Rock
Park Tours can be taken

Fossilized rhino footprints in Ipolytarnóc

unaccompanied. In the
visitors' centre, the teeth of
24 species of sharks, croc-
odiles and dolphins, fossilized
trees, the imprints of more
than 5,000 subtropical exotic
leaves and the footprints of
2,000 animals can be admired.

🌺 **Ipolytarnóc Fossils Nature
Protected Area**
Ipolytarnóc külterület. **Tel** (32)
45 41 13. ⬜ Apr–Oct: 9am–4pm
Tue–Sun; Nov–Mar: 9am–3pm Tue–
Sun. 🎦 🎦 &

Hollókő ❸

See pp214–15.

Gyöngyös ❹

77 km (48 miles) east of Budapest.
Road Map D3. 🏘 33,000. 🚊 from
Vámosgyörk. 🚌 from Budapest,
Eger. ℹ Fő tér 10, (37) 51 03 10.
🛒 daily (until noon), Köztársaság tér.

At the foot of the Mátra hills,
Gyöngyös is the home of
some of Hungary's best white
wines. Visitors can sample
many of these at the Mátra
House of Wines, a shop and
cellar that stocks over 200
locally produced vintages. It
is located on Fő tér, Gyöngyös's
elegant pedestrianized central
square. The centrepiece of
the square, however, is the
yellow Baroque **St Bertalan
Parish Church**, originally built
in 1301, then remodelled in
the 18th century. The high-
ceilinged – but plain – main
hall is the largest surviving
Gothic church building in
Hungary. Opposite the church
is the House of the Holy
Crown, so-called because the
Hungarian royal
crown was brought
here for safekeeping
early in the 19th
century. Today,
the **St Bertalan
Treasury Museum**
(Szent Bertalan
Templom Kincstára)
accommodates a
large treasury of
ecclesiastical art.
  Gyöngyös's only
other star sight is
the **Mátra Museum
and Microarium**

Interior of St Bartalan Church in Gyöngyös

(Mátra Múzeum és Mikroárium), housed in the former Orczy Mansion, close to the narrow-gauge railway station. The late-18th-century mansion is a mixture of Neo-Baroque and Neo-Classical styles.

Heves county is known for its sports, and the Mátra Museum's best exhibition is devoted to hunting, complete with various trophies. In the basement is the Microarium, a vast collection of tiny reptiles, insects and fish, including such exciting creatures as piranhas, giant scorpions, water lizards and poisonous frogs.

🏛 St Bertalan Treasury Museum
Szent Bertalan utca 3. *Tel (37)*
31 11 43. ◻ *10am–noon, 2pm–5pm Tue–Sun.* 🔲

🏛 Mátra Museum and Microarium
Kossuth Lajos utca 40. *Tel (37)*
50 55 30. ◻ *Mar–Oct: 9am–5pm Tue–Sun; Nov–Feb: 10am–4pm Tue–Sun.* 🔲 ♿

Mátra Mountains ❺

85 km (52 miles) northeast of Budapest. **Road Map** D3. 🔲 *from Mátrafüred.* 🚌 *from Mátrafüred.*
ℹ *Tourinform Gyöngyös, Fő tér 10, (37) 51 03 10.*

The most spectacular way to traverse the steep Mátra mountains is by narrow-gauge railway from Gyöngyös to **Mátrafüred**, the largest village in the region. In summer, Mátrafüred is pure heaven for lovers of challenging mountain hikes. There are trails of various lengths, all well

marked, but note that all contain at least one relatively difficult section. Mátrafüred is also great for mountain biking, and many pensions hire out good-quality bikes. Non-hikers can pass the time at the **Palóc Ethnographical Museum** (Palóc Néprajzi Magángyűjtemény és Baba-kiállítás), where a large and colourful collection of dolls shows the traditional costumes of the Palóc people.

About 8 km (5 miles) further into the mountains is the smaller resort of **Mátraháza**, with more hiking trails, and slightly further north is **Mátraszentistván**, Hungary's leading ski resort and also a base for summer hiking.

Kékestető, at 1,015 m (3,330 ft) the highest peak in Hungary, lies east of Mátraháza. It is served by bus or takes 45 minutes to hike up. The mountain is topped by a 90-m (295-ft) high TV tower, which offers spectacular views from the viewing platform at the top.

For more relaxing pursuits, there is good fishing at the picturesque **Lake Sástó** which, at an altitude of 500 m (1,640 ft), is one of the highest in Hungary. It is found between Mátrafüred and Mátraháza.

🏛 Palóc Ethnographical Museum
Pálosvörösmarti utca 2, Mátrafüred.
Tel (37) 32 01 37. ◻ *Apr–Oct: 9am–5pm Tue–Sun; Nov–Mar: 10am–4pm Tue–Sun.* 🔲 🖼
Hungarian only. ♿

Parád and Parádfürdő ❻

30 km (19 miles) north of Gyöngyös. **Road Map** E3. 🏚 *2,400.* 🔲 *from Budapest.* 🚌 *from Budapest.*

The waters at Parádfürdő have been taken as a cure for digestive disorders, and bathed in as a cure for gynaecological ailments since the 17th century. The real treasure of the twin villages, however, is the so-called Fancy Stable (Cifra Istálló). Commissioned by Count György Károlyi it was designed by Miklós Ybl (who also designed the Budapest Opera House *(see p89)*). Completed in 1880, much of the stable's elaborate decoration is of red marble. Few horses have finer homes, and the famous Lipizzaner horses are still bred here. The rest of the building is the **Parád Coach Museum** (Parádi Kocsimúzeum), which has a wide selection of elaborate horse-drawn coaches, some of which were once used by the Hungarian royal family. There are also interesting displays on carriage building, traditional Palóc music, dance, folk costumes and tools.

Footpath marker in the Mátra Mountains

🏛 Parád Coach Museum
Kossuth Lajos utca 217. *Tel (36)*
36 43 87. ◻ *Apr–Sep: 10am–5pm Tue–Sun; Oct–Mar: 10am–4pm Tue–Sun.* 🔲 🖼 ♿

A typical thatched Palóc cottage in the village of Parád

Street-by-Street: Hollókő ❸

House for overnight stays

Set in a narrow valley in the Cserhát hills, Hollókő is the only entire village in the world so far to have been placed on UNESCO's World Heritage List. The Palóc have lived here since the 13th century, when the castle on Szárhegy was built. They use colourful language and costume. Yet in Hollókő all is not what it appears: the 58 houses, churches and workshops protected by UNESCO are little more than a century old. Once entirely made of wood and thatch, the village has burned down many times, and was almost completely rebuilt in 1909 with brick walls and tiled roofs.

★ **Palóc Village Museum**
The colourful costumes and lifestyles of the Palóc people, with three generations living under one roof, are vividly represented at the museum.

★ **Hollókő Castle**
A short walk from the village centre are the ruins of a 13th-century fortress, destroyed during the Turkish retreat. It was partly rebuilt in the 1990s.

Ruins of the Castle

LOCAL DRESS

The Palóc are Slovak in origin, and their traditional dress, worn by many of the village's residents, is distinctly Slavic, with intricately embroidered motifs, often of bright flowers. Married women wear head-scarves; unmarried girls lace bonnets. Palóc men wear black hats with embroidered ribbons. The finest costumes can be seen on Sundays when locals dress up for the morning church service.

Women in traditional Palóc dress

Doll Museum
These wonderfully detailed china dolls are dressed in miniature versions of Palóc dress. The Doll Museum has more than 200 dolls in its collection.

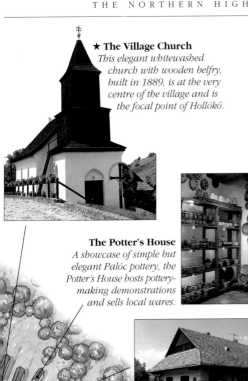

★ The Village Church
This elegant whitewashed church with wooden belfry, built in 1889, is at the very centre of the village and is the focal point of Hollókő.

The Potter's House
A showcase of simple but elegant Palóc pottery, the Potter's House hosts pottery-making demonstrations and sells local wares.

Village House
This 19th-century wooden house with a thatched roof is one of the few to have survived the many fires that ravaged the village over the centuries.

Post Museum
Two rooms in a small cottage display telegraph and communications equipment, as well as documents relating to the history of the postal service in Nógrád County.

Main entrance

KEY

– – – Suggested route

STAR FEATURES

★ Hollókő Castle

★ Palóc Village Museum

★ The Village Church

0 metres	50
0 yards	50

Eger ❼

Situated off the main road from Budapest to the east of Hungary, Eger is a sleepy, provincial town known today for its Bull's Blood wine *(see p219)* and for its university. The castle *(see pp218–19)* and the legend of the great siege of 1552 dominate but it is, in fact, the Church that has twice saved the city from doom. After destruction by the Mongols in 1241, it was rebuilt with money from the Minorite and Franciscan orders. And after the withdrawal of the Turks in 1687, the local bishopric revived the city by commissioning many of the Baroque masterpieces that remain today, including the cathedral, the Lyceum and the Bishop's Palace.

⛪ Eger Cathedral
Főszékesegyház – Szent János apostol és evangélista Szent Mihály főangyal
Pyrker tér 1. *Tel (36) 51 57 25.*
◯ 8:00am–7:30pm daily. ♿

Although its garish yellow colour and architectural mixture of Neo-Classical and Neo-Romanesque styles may not be to everyone's taste, there is no doubt that Eger Cathedral – the second largest church in Hungary – is the most astonishing sight in the city. It was built from 1831–7 to a design by the architect József Hild, who would later design the even larger and more stunning basilica at Esztergom *(see pp144–5)*. The cathedral at Eger is unique in Hungary, having a cupola – at 40 m (131 ft) – that is shorter than the two western towers, measuring 44 m (144 ft). At the other end of the building, three gargantuan statues loom over the colonnaded Neo-Classical façade. They represent Faith, Hope and Charity and were the work of the Italian sculptor Marco Casagrande.

Inside, the cupola is decorated with frescoes of the *Kingdom of Heaven* by Viennese artist Johann Kracker. The cathedral is also home to Hungary's largest organ; it is played every Sunday after morning mass, at 12:45pm.

🏛 Bishop's Palace
Római katolikus érseki palota
Széchenyi utca 1. *Tel (36) 51 75 89.*
◯ Apr–Oct: 9am–5pm Tue–Sat; Nov–Mar: 8am–4pm Mon–Fri. 📷

The second element of central Eger's ecclesiastical architectural triumvirate is the former Bishop's Palace on Széchenyi utca. Like the Lyceum it was built in Baroque style to the designs of Jakab Kellner, and completed in 1766. Inside, the palace houses the Ecclesiastical Collection of the Eger Bishopric, which includes the coronation cloak of Habsburg Empress Maria Theresa (r. 1740–80) and other priceless objects.

🏛 Lyceum
Líceum, Eszterházy Károly Főiskola
Eszterházy Károly tér 1. *Tel (36) 52 04 00.* ◯ Feb–mid-Oct: 9:30am–1:30pm Tue–Sun; mid-Oct–mid-Dec: 9:30am–1:30pm Sat–Sun. ● mid-Dec–Jan. 📷 ♿ ♿

The Lyceum was founded in 1765 by Bishop Károly Eszterházy as a Catholic university. Imperial authorities opposed the idea of a church university and relegated it to the rank of lyceum. The ceiling of the library boasts Johann Kracker's fresco depicting the meeting of the Council of Trent (1545–63). The library itself holds over 150,000 volumes, including the first book ever printed in Hungary, in 1473. In the 53-m (174-ft) tower is Hungary's leading centre of astronomy, with a collection of astronomical items and a 19th-century camera obscura.

Main façade of the Lyceum, built as a Catholic university

🏛 Kossuth Street
Kossuth Lajos utca.
Kossuth Lajos utca, a wide boulevard, has long been Eger's best address. For centuries it was where the richest and holiest men in the city lived. At No. 4 is the Vice-Provost's Palace, a pastel-shaded Rococo mansion with a façade of hewn stone dating from 1758, which today is closed to the public. On the same side of the street, at No. 14, is the Franciscan Church and Monastery, a single-nave church built in 1738 on the ruins of a former mosque. Opposite (at No. 9) is the Baroque County Hall, completed in 1758. It is famed for its two grand wrought-iron gates, crafted by the blacksmith Henrik Fazola (1730–79), who moved to Eger from

The sombre interior of Eger Cathedral, brightened by ceiling frescoes

Kossuth Street, Eger's smartest address, seen from the air

Würzburg to take the city's waters. He is also responsible for most of the ironwork that typifies many of the buildings on Kossuth Street, as well as the Hungarian National Gallery in Budapest (see pp58–9) and Festetics Castle in Keszthely (see pp198–9).

🏛 Minorite Church
Szent Antonius Minorita templom
Dobó István tér
Set against the background of the open spaces of Dobó István tér, the ornate exterior of the former Minorite Church is far more pleasing on the eye

than that of Eger Cathedral. The rounded, tiered façade and twin towers are the work of Bohemian architect Johann Ignaz Dientzenhofer, who completed the church in 1773. Dedicated to St Anthony of Padova, scenes of the saint's life feature in the ceiling frescoes painted by Márton Reindl. He is also depicted alongside the Virgin Mary on the altar, in a painting by the Austrian Johann Kracker.

Main façade of the former Minorite Church, built in the 18th century

VISITORS' CHECKLIST

Road Map E3. 🏠 56,000. 🚉 Vasút utca; from Budapest. 🚌 Pyrker János tér; from Budapest. 🚍 Dobó István tér 9. 🛈 Tourinform, Bajcsy-Zsilinszky utca 9; (36) 51 77 15. 🎪 Dobó István tér; daily.

🕌 Minaret
Minaret
Knézich Károly utca 4. **Tel** (36) 41 02 33. ◯ Apr–Oct: 10am–6pm daily. 🖼
The most northerly Ottoman relic in Europe, Eger's minaret is a classic of its genre. Sleek and perfectly symmetrical, the fourteen-sided sandstone tower rises on an incline to its needle-like point 40 m (131 ft) above the street. It is topped with a crescent moon and a cross. Closed for 150 years after the mosque next to it was demolished in 1841, the 17th-century minaret is now open to visitors, who are rewarded for climbing the 97 steps up to the balcony with fine views of the city.

♜ Castle
See pp218–19.

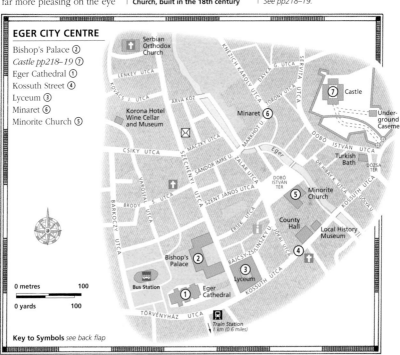

EGER CITY CENTRE

Bishop's Palace ②
Castle pp218–19 ⑦
Eger Cathedral ①
Kossuth Street ④
Lyceum ③
Minaret ⑥
Minorite Church ⑤

0 metres   100
0 yards   100

Key to Symbols *see back flap*

Eger Castle

One of the cannons on Cannon Hill

Entering Eger Castle through its tiny gate set into walls 3 m (10 ft) thick, with the walls of the upper fortress menacing in the background, it is not difficult to understand how its defenders held out for so long against the invading Turks. For it was here at Eger, in 1552, that the greatest rearguard action in Hungarian military history was carried out. The castle, defended by a garrison of just 2,000 soldiers ably assisted by the women of the town, held out against a Turkish force five times that size for six weeks. The Turks retreated, but took the castle 44 years later, only for much of it to be destroyed in 1702 by the Habsburgs.

★ Bishop's Palace
The names of all those who defended the castle in 1552 are engraved in a marble tablet in the main hall.

Ticket office

Waxworks in Fold Bastion
A great collection of lifelike figures, displayed over three levels of the bastion, recreates scenes from the siege.

Art Gallery
The Art Gallery hosts an unrivalled collection of Baroque Hungarian paintings and sculptures, including this bas-relief above the entrance.

Round Tower

Dobó Bastion
The bastions and walls were built or forti-fied from the mid-1500s under István Dobó, who led the defenders at the Siege of Eger.

★ Ruins of Romanesque Cathedral
The ruins of a 10th-century Baptistry in the inner court-yard feature the grave of Eger's first Bishop, Buldus.

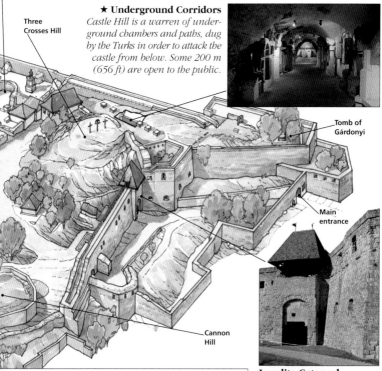

★ Underground Corridors
*Castle Hill is a warren of under-
ground chambers and paths, dug
by the Turks in order to attack the
castle from below. Some 200 m
(656 ft) are open to the public.*

Three
Crosses Hill

Tomb of
Gárdonyi

Main
entrance

Cannon
Hill

**Ippolito Gate and
Bornemissza Bastion**
*The castle gate is named
after an Italian cardinal,
Ippolito d'Este, who became
Archbishop of Esztergom.*

BULL'S BLOOD WINE

Bull's Blood of Eger is Hungary's most celebrated
wine. Comparable to Bordeaux wines, Bull's Blood
is robust and fruity, made of a mix of Cabernet
Sauvignon, Merlot and Cabernet Franc grapes.

During the Siege of Eger in 1552, copious
amounts of the wine were drunk by the soldiers
who defended the castle against the Turks, and
word was put about that their bravery was based
on the blood of bulls that had been added to
the wine. The stories were almost certainly false,
but they impressed the superstitious Turks, and
played a minor role in their defeat and retreat.

Egri Bikavér, Hungary's Bull's Blood wine

STAR FEATURES

★ Bishop's Palace

★ Ruins of Romanesque
Cathedral

★ Underground Corridors

Bükk National Park **8**

Wildlife in the Park

The Bükk Mountain region, most of which has been classified as a National Park since 1977, extends from Eger to Miskolc, along Hungary's northern border with Slovakia. An area of outstanding natural beauty, it is renowned for its more than 800 caves, steep cliffs and lush beech forests (*bükk* means beech). There is some skiing in winter at Felső-Borovnyák, but the main activities in the park are hiking, climbing and caving. Routes of all grades and lengths criss-cross the range, linking up the main towns of Miskolc, Eger, Lillafüred, Szilvásvárad and Újmassa.

Lipizzaners in Szilvásvárad Horse Museum
The famous white horses were first brought here from Lipica, in Slovenia, in the 16th century.

Fátyol Waterfall
Staggered limestone steps make this 17-m (56-ft) long waterfall one of the most attractive in Hungary. The steps enlarge a little every year as the water deposits more lime.

Romanesque **Bélapátfalva Abbey**, erected by Cistercian monks in the 1200s, is the best preserved in Hungary.

The **Szalajka Narrow-Gauge Railway** runs along the entire length of the Szalajka Valley in the summer.

Vineyards in Felsőtárkány
The leafy town of Felsőtárkány, surrounded by vineyards and parks, is one of the best entrance points for Bükk National Park.

Nagyvisnyó

2506

Szilvásvárad

956 m (

Szalajka

Istállós-kő
959 m (3,146 ft)

Istállós-kői Cave

Bélapátfalva

2506

Mónosbél

Pes-kő
865 m (2,838 ft)

*698 m
(2,290 ft)*

Stimecz-ház

Szarvaskő

ÓZD

*512 m
(1,680 ft)*

Felsőtárkány

25

Várhegy
669 m (2,195 ft)

Sík

2505

Eger

Felnémet

EGER

Climbing on Felső-Borovnyák
The steep, high cliffs of the Bükk offer outstanding rock-climbing challenges for even the most experienced climbers.

VISITORS' CHECKLIST

Between Eger and Miskolc; roads 25 and 2505 cut through the park. **Road Map** E2. 🚉 🚌 to Eger, Miskolc, Lillafüred, Szilvásvárad. 🏢 Tourinform Eger, Bajcsy-Zsilinszky út 9, Eger (36) 51 77 15; Tourinform Miskolc, Városház tér 13, Miskolc; (46) 35 04 25. **Anna Cave (Lillafüred)** (46) 33 41 30. ☐ Apr–mid-Nov: 10am–4pm. ● mid-Nov–Mar. 🪧 **Suba-Lyuk Cave** ☐ year-round. 🖥 **www**.bnpi.hu

Anna Cave
Six interconnected caves are accessible via a series of natural limestone staircases.

Bükk Mountains
The region is renowned for its impeccably clean air. The highest point in the Bükk Mountains is Istállós-kő, at 959 m (3,146 ft).

Suba-Lyuk Cave
Traces of Palaeolithic Man have been found in this cave, making it one of the oldest known dwellings in Europe.

KEY

═══	Main road
══	Other road
⚊	Narrow gauge railway
– –	Trail
❋	Viewpoint
△	Peak
⋔	Cave
🛷	Skiing runs
🚉	Railway terminus

0 kilometres 3

0 miles 3

Vineyards and small church near Tokaj ▷

The Fátyol Step-Waterfall in Szilvásvárad

Szilvásvárad **❾**

30 km (19 miles) north of Eger.
Road Map E2. 🏠 *2,000.* 🚆 *from Eger.* 🚌 *from Budapest, Eger.* 🎠 *Bükk Carriage Driving Trophy (last weekend in Aug).*

Szilvásvárad is a leading centre of Hungarian equestrianism, and white Lipizzaner horses – the same breed as those used at the famous Spanish Riding School in Vienna – are bred at the **Szilvásvárad Stud Farm** (Állami Ménesgazdaság Szilvásvárad). The farm is open for visitors who can also book riding and even carriage-driving courses here. At the end of every August an international carriage-driving race takes place here.

The village itself has more information on the famous horses in its fascinating **Lipizzaner Horse-Breeding Exhibition** (Lipicai Lótenyésztés Történeti Kiállítás). Also on display here are a number of coaches and a complete working smithy.

But there is more to Szilvásvárad than horses – it is also the gateway to the beautiful Szalajka Valley. A narrow-gauge steam railway runs the 5 km (3 miles) from the village to Szalajka-Fátyol-vizesés, site of the gentle but wide Fátyol Step-Waterfall, as well as the **Open-Air Forestry Museum** (Szabadtéri Erdészeti Múzeum). The exhibits of early people's tiny huts, furnaces and elementary hunting tools are fascinating. At the head of the

valley is the Istállóskő Cave, which burrows under Mount Istállóskő – at 959 m (3,146 ft) the highest peak in the Bükk Mountain Range. The cave is known to have provided giant shelter for prehistoric people as early as 7,000 years ago.

🐴 Szilvásvárad Stud Farm
Egri út 16. **Tel** (36) 56 44 00.
⏰ 8am–7pm Mon–Sun. 🅿️ ♿

🏛 Lipizzaner Horse-Breeding Exhibition
Park utca 8. **Tel** (36) 35 51 55.
⏰ 9am–noon, 1–5pm Tue–Sun.

🏛 Open-Air Forestry Museum
Szalajka-völgy. **Tel** (36) 35 55 05.
⏰ May–Sep: 8:30am–4:30pm daily; Oct–Apr: 8:30am–2pm daily. ♿

Aggtelek National Park **❿**
Aggteleki Nemzeti Park

Tengerszem oldal 1, Jósvafő.
Road Map E2. **Tel** (48) 50 60 00.
🚆 *from Miskolc.* 🚌 *from Budapest.*
ℹ️ *Baradla oldal 1, Aggtelek (048) 50 30 00.* **www**.anp.nemzetipark. gov.hu

First established in 1985, the Aggtelek National Park is one of Hungary's World Heritage Sites. It straddles the Slovak border, and officially also includes a vast area of the Slovak Karst National Park. Large parts of the park are covered with deciduous forest, with clearings scattered liberally throughout the area. These rocky outcrops provide a perfect habitat for rare plants and insects, including giant swallowtail butterflies, as well as 220 species of birds. Imperial eagles and woodpeckers are a common sight. There are marked nature trails, including a 7-km (4-mile) trail from Aggtelek to Jósvafő.

The park also has some 200 caves to explore, of which the longest system – both in the park and in Hungary – is the **Baradla Cave** (Baradla Barlang). At 25 km (16 miles), it extends into Slovakia. While archaeological evidence

Spectacular rock formations in the Baradla Cave in Aggtelek National Park

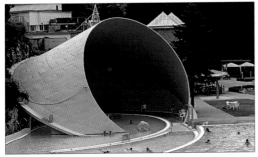

The Cave Baths in Miskolc-Tapolca, unique in Europe

suggests the cave was used by early humans thousands of years ago, all knowledge of it was lost, and its entrance was rediscovered only in 1569. The cave was fully mapped in 1839, and has been open to the public ever since. There are entrances in both Aggtelek and Jósvafő. Many caverns have been spectacularly lit. Parts of the cave are open to all-comers, but the best way to view it is on a tour. There are several to choose from, all beginning at the Aggtelek entrance; one tour of seven hours takes in a part of the cave known as Domica under Slovakian territory. Occasionally the cave, which boasts splendid acoustics, hosts classical music concerts.

♉ Baradla Cave
Baradla oldal 1, Aggtelek.
Tel *(48) 50 30 00.* ☐ *Apr–Sep: 8am–5pm daily; Oct–Mar: 8am–3pm daily; Oct: 8am–5pm Sat.* 🖼 🗹

Miskolc ⓫

See pp226–7.

Miskolc-Tapolca ⓬

Pazár sétány, Miskolc-Tapolca.
Road Map E2. ***Tel*** *(46) 56 00 30.* 🚌
from Búza tér, Miskolc. ☐ *May–Aug: 9am–7pm daily; Sep–Dec, Feb–Apr: 9am–6pm daily.* 🖼 ♿ 🍴 ☐ 🚻
www.barlangfurdo.hu

The cave baths of Miskolc-Tapolca, set amid the backdrop of the Bükk Hills, are the most spectacular in Hungary. A vast resort has grown around the caves, which, discovered in the 16th

century, have been attracting bathers ever since. Carved out over centuries, the caves contain water that is high in calcium and magnesium, and is particularly suited for treating joint and back problems. The water is a warm 30° C (86° F) all year round. The cave baths are surrounded by a large park with a rowing lake, and there is also a cave chapel nearby. While the 150-m (492-ft) long cave baths are the primary attraction, the resort town of Miskolc-Tapolca also offers a conventional thermal bath complex, complete with water slides, near-freezing cold plunge pools and children's pools.

Szerencs ⓭

32 km (20 miles) east of Miskolc.
Road Map F2. 🏠 *11,000.* 🚉 *from Miskolc, Budapest.* 🚌 *from Budapest.*

The little town of Szerencs is dominated by its historical links with the Rákóczi family, who owned the town and much of the surrounding

area for centuries. It was the Rákóczis who built **Szerencs Castle** at the beginning of the 16th century, today the most visited attraction in the town. Converted to domestic use after defeat against the Turks, the castle houses the **Zempléni Museum**, which tells the story of Rákóczi Zsigmond and the castle's military history, as well as boasting the largest postcard collection in the world (over 900,000). Exhibits also include period furniture, arms and the artistic works of goldsmiths.

Szerencs's main source of wealth and employment, however, is Europe's third-largest sugar factory, whose production lines and **Sugar Museum** are open to visitors by prior appointment. It provides fascinating details about the history and technology of sugar beet cultivation and sugar production, and displays some 800 sugar packages from around the world.

The Gothic Reformed Church on Kossuth tér dates from 1480, and hosted the Hungarian parliament in 1605. Three generations of the Rákóczi family are buried in the crypt. Szerencs also has an elaborate, though badly weathered, Baroque Greek Orthodox Church, built in 1799, on Ondi utca in the north of the town.

🏛 Zempléni Museum
Rákóczi-vár. ***Tel*** *(47) 36 28 42.*
☐ *10am–4pm Tue–Sun.* 🗹 ♿

🏛 Sugar Museum
Gyár utca 1. ***Tel*** *(47) 56 51 00,*
(mobile) 06 20 992 0843. ☐ *by appointment, 8:30–11:30am Tue–Fri.*
🗹 *8:30am, 10am, 11:30am Sat–Sun.*

Szerencs Castle, housing the Zempléni Museum

Miskolc ❶

Home of Hungary's largest university, Miskolc is the third largest city in the country. An industrial town first and foremost, much of the outskirts, and even parts of the city centre, are less than attractive, having been built in the aftermath of heavy bombing during World War II. Amid the concrete, however, a wealth of historical buildings can be explored, including Hungary's oldest theatre, wooden churches of every Christian denomination, fine public squares and a fascinating museum. Miskolc is also the site of Diósgyőr Castle, renovated and restored to its full medieval glory.

Façade of the National Theatre, the oldest in Hungary

National Theatre
Miskolci Nemzeti Színház
Déryné utca 1. **Tel** (46) 51 67 35.

Hungary's oldest theatre – the first stage to host Hungarian-language plays – stood here in 1823–43. A Neo-Classical replacement was opened in 1857, with a play by Mihály Vörösmarty, and despite much renovation over the years, it is that structure which mostly survives today. With its protruding three-arched loggia over the entrance it resembles Hungary's State Opera House in Budapest (*see pp88–9*). The tower, added in 1880, was originally used as a fire look-out point.

The restored Baroque interior has intricate statuary decorating the two rows of private boxes. The theatre is the main venue of the Miskolc Opera Festival, which takes place here every July and August, and features the work of the Hungarian composer Béla Bartók and others.

Theatre Museum
Színháztörténeti és Színészmúzeum
Déryné utca 3. **Tel** (30) 660 92 99.
9am–5pm Tue–Sun.

In this museum, visitors can discover the secrets behind the fire that destroyed the original Miskolc Theatre in 1843, as well as the fact that an earlier theatre in Kolozsvár (today the town of Cluj-Napoca in Romania) in fact has a previous claim to the title of first Hungarian theatre. There are also countless costumes, bill posters and theatrical memorabilia on display, as well as a photographic exhibition about the theatre's role in the city's development. A sketch shows the late 18th-century wooden theatre that once stood on the site.

Greek Orthodox Church and Museum
Görögkeleti, Ortodox templom; Magyar Ortodox Egyházi Múzeum
Deák Ferenc tér 7. **Tel** (46) 35 04 25.
Church May–Sep: 10am–6pm Tue–Sun; Oct–Apr: 10am–4pm Tue–Sun; **Museum** prior booking.

At 16 m (52 ft) in height, and boasting 88 images of the life of Jesus, the iconostasis in the Greek Orthodox Church is the most important sight in Miskolc. Dating from 1793, it was carved in the workshop of Miklós Jankovits of Eger; the pictures were painted by Anton Kuchelmeister. To its left is a painting of the *Black Mary of Kazan*, a gift from Empress Catherine II of Russia. The church itself was

Icon from the Greek Orthodox Church

completed in 1806, and was originally intended to be topped with a classic Orthodox onion dome, but local Protestant authorities forbade this. Next door in the **museum** is the richest Orthodox liturgical collection in Hungary, opened in a former school in 1988. Its permanent exhibition includes ceremonial robes, sepulchres and more than 200 icons.

Entrances to the many wine cellars on the slopes of Avas Hill

Avas Hill and Ottó Herman Museum
Avas hegy.
More than 800 limestone caves have been dug out here and used as wine cellars since the 16th century; some are open during the summer for tastings. The cellars line cobbled streets that wind their way up to the Look-Out Tower on Avas Hill, from where splendid views of the city are to be had.

At the foot of the hill is the **Ottó Herman Museum**, named after Ottó Herman (1835–1914), a local archaeologist. The museum is housed in a charming 19th-century house, with wooden, external balconies. It contains good collections of archaeological finds, stones and minerals, as well as displays on industrial history and coins. The fine art collection comprises masterworks by all famous Hungarian painters. The museum's library (on Görgey Artúr utca) holds more than 200,000 volumes and is renowned throughout the world for its collection of scientific works.

Ottó Herman Museum
Görgey Artúr utca 28. **Tel** (46) 56 01 70. 10am–4pm Tue–Sun.

🔒 Calvinist Church
Avasi református templom

Papszer utca 14. **Tel** *(46) 35 86 77.*
The Calvinist Church below
the Avas Hill, with its steep,
detached belfry, is the oldest
building in Miskolc. Originally
Romanesque in style, the
13th-century building was
destroyed by Turks in 1544. It
was rebuilt – with the tower –
in 1557. The clock on the
belfry is one of the symbols
of the city, and can be heard
chiming every 15 minutes.
The large and immaculately
kept cemetery that surrounds
the church is the resting place
of a number of local digni-
taries, including the poet
Mihály Tompa, author of the
romantic collection *Virágregék*
(Legends of Flowers).

♣ Diósgyőr Castle
Diósgyőri vár

Miskolc-Diósgyőr, Vár utca 24.
Tel *(46) 53 33 55.* ◯ *May–Sep:*
9am–6pm daily; Oct–Apr:
9am–5pm daily. 🎟 ✔ ♿
Diósgyőr's medieval castle is
located 8 km (5 miles) from
the centre of Miskolc. The
first castle here was probably
built in the 12th century, and

is thought to have been an
earthwork castle. It guarded
the route from Venice to
Cracow for a long time and
was destroyed during the
Mongol invasion of 1241–2.
The castle that stands here
today was built during the
reign of Béla IV who, after
the Mongols left the country,
decreed that a castle be built
"on every hilltop". The castle
was subsequently used as
a residence by several
monarchs, although it lost
its military status after the
withdrawal of the Turks in
1687, and fell into neglect.
Completely restored over
two decades from 1953 to

1971, the castle today hosts
an exhibition of its history
(in the northeastern tower),
alongside a display of medieval weaponry. Life-sized waxworks recreate the signing
of the Treaty of Turin in 1381,
while others, in the
outer battlements,
feature scenes
of everyday life in
medieval Diósgyőr.
Twice a year, in
May and August,
plays and a medie-
val fair are held in
the castle grounds,
with jousting, archery
and dance. It is also
one of the venues
for Miskolc Opera
Festival in summer.

Diósgyőr Castle, rebuilt in the 13th century

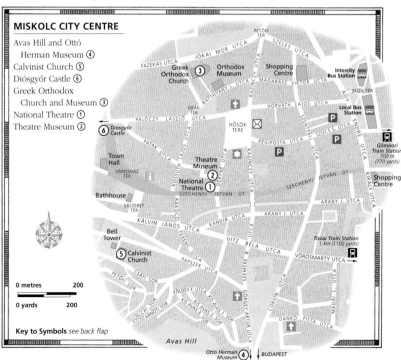

MISKOLC CITY CENTRE

Avas Hill and Ottó
  Herman Museum ④
Calvinist Church ⑤
Diósgyőr Castle ⑥
Greek Orthodox
  Church and Museum ③
National Theatre ①
Theatre Museum ②

0 metres   200
0 yards   200

Key to Symbols *see back flap*

Tokaj

40 km (25 miles) northwest of Nyíregyháza. **Road Map** F2. ⛰ 4,600. 🚆 from Miskolc. 🚌 from Debrecen, Budapest. ⓘ Tourinform, Serház utca 1, (47) 55 20 70 or (47) 35 22 59.

At the confluence of the rivers Bodrog and Tisza, rich, fertile soil facilitates the cultivation of Hungary's best grapevines. These produce the country's finest wines. Smooth and delicately sweet, Tokaji dessert wine is made exclusively in and around Tokaj. In 2002 UNESCO placed the region on its World Heritage List.

The best place to learn about Tokaji wine is in one of the many cellars. The most famous are the 16th-century **Rákóczi Cellars**. Here, visitors can taste Aszú, which is matured on the premises.

The wine industry dominates the town, but the **Tokaj Museum** (Tokaji Múzeum) is mainly devoted to revealing life on the Bodrog and Tisza rivers long before wine was made in these parts. There is also a large collection of ecclesiastical art on display.

🏛 **Tokaj Museum**
Bethlen Gábor út 7. **Tel** (47) 35 26 36. ⓘ Jun–Oct: 10am–4pm Tue–Sun; Nov–May: 10am–4pm Tue–Sat. 📷 🚫 ♿

🏛 **Rákóczi Cellars**
Kossuth Lajos tér 15. **Tel** (47) 35 20 09. ⓘ 10am–8pm daily. 📷 🚫 ♿

The Louis XI-style Lajos Kossuth Memorial Museum in Monok

Zemplén Hills

50 km (31 miles) north of Nyíregyháza. **Road Map** F2. 🚆 to Sátoraljaújhely. 🚌 to Sátoraljaújhely, Pálháza, Füzér. ⓘ Tourinform Sátoraljaújhely, Kossuth Lajos tér 5, (47) 32 14 58.

More than 2,000 km (1,243 miles) of marked hiking trails cover both the eastern and western flanks of the Zemplén range. Volcanic in origin, the highest of the hills is the 896-m (2,940-ft) high Nagy-Milic, which marks Hungary's border with Slovakia.

The village of **Pálháza**, 19 km (12 miles) north of Sátoraljaújhely, is a good base to explore the Zemplén. It is also the starting point of a narrow-gauge railway that runs up to **Rostalló**, from where the vast majority of the

Zemplén's hiking trails depart. Wildlife to look out for include snakes, birds of prey, woodpeckers, Ural owls, spoonbill ducks and a large number of butterflies, many of which, such as the twin-spotted fritillary, are thought to be unique to the Zemplén mountain range.

Further north, in the tiny village of **Füzér**, is the Füzér Village Museum, consisting of just one painted house, furnished as it would have been in the 1870s. High above the village on a crag sit the ruins of Füzér Castle (1310).

Monok, 10 km (6 miles) northwest of Szerencs, is the birthplace of the Hungarian lawyer and politician Lajos Kossuth, who was Regent of Hungary during the revolution of 1848–9. The **Lajos Kossuth Memorial Museum**, in the family's 18th-century home, exhibits portraits and memorabilia from flags to documents. The museum opened on 15 March 1948, the 100th anniversary of the revolution.

🏛 **Lajos Kossuth Memorial Museum**
Kossuth Lajos utca 18, Monok. **Tel** (47) 35 60 39. ⓘ Mar–Nov: 10am–5pm Tue–Sun. 📷 ♿

Sárospatak

70 km (43 miles) northeast of Miskolc. **Road Map** F2. ⛰ 15,000. 🚆 from Budapest, Miskolc. 🚌 from Debrecen, Miskolc. ⓘ Tourinform, Eötvös utca 6, (47) 31 53 16.

Try as it might to promote its other sights, it is the castle that is the first port of call for all visitors to the leafy, riverside town of Sárospatak. The reason is the inner keep, which bears an uncanny resemblance to the Palazzo Vecchio in Florence. It was the first part of the castle to be built, in the 1530s when the keeper of the Hungarian crown, Peter Perényi, was awarded the estate after the Battle of Mohács (see p183).

The castle was extended in the 17th century by Prince György I (Rákóczi), who added four wings, all built in extravagant Neo-Renaissance style.

TOKAJ'S GOLDEN WINE

Tokaji, also known as Aszú, is one of the world's great dessert wines. It was once thought to actually contain gold dust. Famous as far back as the time of Mátyás I, a chronicler wrote in 1458 that "the men of Tokaj are obtaining gold from their volcanic land. Even the vines bear golden fruit." A century later the Swiss philosopher Paracelsus tested the local grapes for traces of gold. He found none but concluded that "in the grapes of Tokaj the natural and the mineral combine." The secret of the wine's flavour and golden appearance is less exotic: the grapes for Aszú are harvested late (in early November), after they have begun to rot and a mould has formed. This "noble rot" naturally increases sugar content by up to 70 per cent.

Wine maturing in barrels in the Rákóczi Cellars, Tokaj

The Neo-Renaissance Castle in Sárospatak, home to the Rákóczi Museum

The balconies, loggias and entrances are all fabulously expressive. Much of this part of the castle is today given over to the **Rákóczi Museum**, which has exhibitions on the building of the castle and the history of the Rákóczi family, as well as Renaissance-era food and wine-making.

At the opposite end of the town centre is the Calvinist **Sárospatak Reformed College**, founded in 1531 but dating in its present form from 1806–22. There are guided tours of the library in the south wing, a masterpiece of Neo-Classical architecture that was designed by Mihály Pollack. Its enormous roof is supported by 16 marble columns. In the extensive gardens are statues of former pupils, including the Czech humanist Johann Amos Comenius.

The modernist shopping centre and apartment buildings in the centre of the city, the work of local architect Imre Makovecz, are also worth seeing. Built in 1972, the four-storey buildings form a series of interlinking white towers, all leaning slightly forwards and topped with steep brown roofs – a modern interpretation of Árpád tents.

🏛 **Rákóczi Museum**
Szent Erzsébet utca 19. **Tel** (47) 31 10 83. ◯ 10am–6pm Tue–Sun.
🖼 🎥 ♿

🏫 **Sárospatak Reformed College**
Rákóczi utca 1. **Tel** (47) 31 10 57. ◯ Library 9am–2:30pm Mon–Fri; Gardens 8am–4pm Mon–Sun.
🖼 🎥 ♿

Sátoraljaújhely 🔟

13 km (8 miles) northeast of Sárospatak. **Road Map** F2. 🏠 18,000. 🚉 from Miskolc. 🚌 from Sárospatak. 🛈 Tourinform, Kossuth Lajos tér 5, (47) 32 14 58.

At the foot of the Zemplén Hills, Sátoraljaújhely, the most northerly town in Hungary, is known for its atmospheric Baroque centre. Most of the town's sights are based on Kossuth Lajos tér, and of all the squares named for that revolutionary in Hungary, this is perhaps the most deserving. In 1830 Lajos allegedly made his first political speech from the balcony of the Baroque Town Hall (built in 1762–8) that stands at No 5. The building itself is a unique example of experimental architecture with its short, squat ground floor topped by an oversized upper level. An imposing

statue of Lajos Kossuth stands in the middle of the square that is named after him.

Just north of the town hall stands a Neo-Classical building that houses the **Ferenc Kazinczy Museum**, named after the language reformer Ferenc Kazinczy, a tireless campaigner for replacing German with Hungarian as the nation's official language and a reformer of the Hungarian language itself. The museum contains exhibits about Kazinczy's work, as well as regional history.

Kazinczy died in a cholera epidemic in 1831 and is buried in the elaborate **Kazinczy Mausoleum** (and memorial museum) at Széphalom, 3 km (2 miles) north of the town centre. Visited by tens of thousands of literary pilgrims each year, the Neo-Classical mausoleum was designed by Miklós Ybl (see p89) and built on the site of the Kazinczy mansion.

Near Kazinczy Ferenc utca, a derelict synagogue and its cemetery are sad reminders of the Jewish community that once lived here. Only a handful of the town's Jews survived the Holocaust.

🏛 **Ferenc Kazinczy Museum**
Dózsa György út 11. **Tel** (47) 32 23 51. ◯ 8am–6pm Mon–Sat, Sun by appointment only. 🖼 🎥 Hungarian only. ♿

🏛 **Kazinczy Mausoleum**
Kazinczy park, Széphalom. **Tel** (47) 32 23 51. ◯ 9am–5pm Tue–Sun.
🖼 🎥 ♿

Original furniture at the Ferenc Kazinczy Museum in Sátoraljaújhely

THE GREAT PLAIN

*I*f Budapest is Hungary's heart, then her soul is the Great Plain, where her character has been forged over the centuries, and preserved ever since in the work of the nation's writers, poets and musicians. Nomadic horsemen and their cattle, shepherds and their unique sheep, fields of ripening paprika and fish soup in huge kettles over open fires are evocative images that every visitor should see.

Mainly barren and dry, the Great Plain is a vast area, covering more than half of the country (about 56 per cent). Here, long, hot summers give way to bleak, freezing winters, with little in between. However, there is a wide variety of terrain on the Great Plain, as well as some outstanding cities and a diverse flora and fauna.

As recently as medieval times, the Great Plain was, in fact, not a steppe, but forested and lush, rich in agriculture and dotted with thousands of farmsteads that were set up by the Magyars as they populated these fertile lands on both banks of the Tisza. And this is where the legends begin: the Turks invaded Hungary, and almost two centuries of constant war, from 1526–1699, devastated the region. In many parts they chopped down the forests and burned vegetation and livestock. The population fled to the cities of Debrecen, Nyíregyháza, Szeged, Kecskemét and even Budapest for protection, food and livelihoods, and the term Puszta was coined to describe the emptiness left in the Ottoman wake.

A few hearty souls survived, and stayed on. The Csikós horsemen (see p235) thrived, as severe flooding in the 19th century allowed the grass to regrow, making the Plain prime grazing territory. Fortunes were made by cattle owners, and romantic poets wrote of the heroes and villains.

The Csikós survive, but today their traditions only entertain visitors. At the Hortobágy National Park and in other protected areas of the Plain, these historic grasslands are sheltered from the advances of industrial agriculture.

Cattle and herdsman in the Puszta, Hortobágy National Park

◁ Detail of the ornate façade of the Town Hall, at Kiskunfélegyháza

Exploring The Great Plain

Covering almost half the country, the Great
Plain defines Hungary, and the Hungarians,
more than any other region. It was here that
great battles were fought and that many of the
country's traditions were preserved during
foreign domination. Sparsely populated,
there are few cities and only a couple of large
towns, but there is much to see and do –
whether watching the stunning displays of the
Puszta horsemen or luxuriating in one of the
thermal spas, exploring Hortobágy National
Park or admiring Secessionist architecture in
Szeged and ambling around Debrecen.

The artificial Mediterranean beach at the
Hajdúszoboszló spa

The breathtaking "Puszta Fiver", at Bugac

GETTING AROUND

The Great Plain is not easily
accessible by public transport,
and to get the best out of this
region visitors are advised to
travel by car. The major cities
are, of course, well served by
train from Budapest, especially
Debrecen (the journey takes
around two hours). Debrecen
also makes an excellent base
for exploring much of the
northern part of the plain,
including Hortobágy National
Park and Tisza Lake.

KEY

▬▬▬	Motorway
▬ ▬	Motorway under construction
▬▬▬	Major road
▬ ▬	Major road under construction
▬▬▬	Secondary road
▭▭▭	Minor road
▬▪▬	Main railway
▬▬▬	Minor railway
▬▬▬	International border
▬▬▬	Regional border

Kisvárda

CSARODA **21**

4

Tokaj **38** **SZABOLCS** **41** *Tisza* **22** SZATMÁRCSEKE

SZATMÁR-BEREG Túristvándi

Tiszavasvári **36** Mátészalka

Miskolc **18** NYÍREGYHÁZA **49** *Szamos*

MÁRIAPÓCS **19** **20** NYÍRBÁTOR

M3 **35** Hajdúnánás **471**

Hajdúböszörmény

4

ZA **13** TISZAFÜRED **17** DEBRECEN

e HORTOBÁGY **33**

badszalók HORTOBÁGY **16** HAJDÚSZOBOSZLÓ **15**

GYKUN NATIONAL **48**

OLNOK PARK **HAJDÚ-BIHAR**

Püspökladány **47**

Kisújszállás Berettyóújfalu

E60 **42**

Túrkeve *Berettyó*

tú Szeghalom **47**

46 Gyomaendrőd

443

rvas **BÉKÉS**

44 Békés Sarkad

47 GYULA

Békéscsaba **10**

47

Orosháza

The dome in the New Synagogue in Szeged, a stunning Secessionist building

SIGHTS AT A GLANCE

Baja **1**
Csaroda **21**
Debrecen pp250–51 **15**
Gyula **10**
Hajdúszoboszló **16**
Hajós **2**
Hódmezővásárhely **9**
Hortobágy & Hortobágy
  National Park **17**
Jászberény **12**
Kalocsa **3**
Kecskemét pp236–9 **5**
Kiskunfélegyháza **6**
Kiskunsági National Park **4**
Máriapócs **19**
Nyírbátor **20**
Nyíregyháza pp254–5 **18**
Ópusztaszer National Historical
  Memorial Park **8**
Szatmárcseke **22**
Szeged pp242–3 **7**
Szolnok **11**
Tiszafüred **13**

Tour
Tisza Lake **14**

Puszta buffaloes, enjoying a mud bath at Hortobágy National Park

The Fish Soup Festival in Baja, a record-breaking soup-cooking contest

Baja ❶

100 km (62 miles) west of Szeged.
Road Map C5. 🏔 38,000. 🚇 from
Budapest. 🚌 from Budapest, Kalocsa.
🛈 Tourinform, Szentháromság tér 5,
(79) 42 07 92. 🛒 fish market Tue–
Sun. 🎭 Fish Soup Festival (Bajai
Halászléfőző Népünnepély, second
weekend in Jul).

This wealthy town, long
populated by a large Serb
minority, is dominated by its
large public square, Szentháromság tér, one side of which
opens onto the Danube.
Baroque 18th-century town
houses, one of which is now
the Town Hall, line the other
three sides. The square plays
host every July to the unique
Baja Fish Soup Festival, when
hundreds of cauldrons are set
up to cook the local fish stew,
consisting of freshwater fish
and a very hot paprika.
    The **Türr István Museum** just
north of the square contains a
lively collection of exhibits
celebrating the role of the
Danube in Baja's history. Just
opposite stands a magnificent
Baroque Franciscan church,
complete with a superb bell
tower, built in 1756.
    North of the city centre
is the late-19th-century Neo-
Classical Synagogue. Now
a public library, the Hebrew
script above the portico is one
of few clues to its past. On
Miklós utca stands the Serb
Orthodox Church, built at the
end of the 18th century and
housing probably Hungary's
finest Orthodox iconostasis.
Some 10 m (33 ft) tall, it
depicts countless saints.

The beaches on Petőfisziget,
the island in the middle of
the Danube, serve as Baja's
summer playground, offering
sailing, water-skiing, fishing
and other leisure activities.
The island is reached via a foot-
bridge from Szentháromság tér.

🏛 **Türr István Museum**
Deák Ferenc utca 1. **Tel** (79) 32 41
73. ◯ mid-Mar–mid-Dec: 10am–
4pm Wed–Sat. 🖼 📷 ♿

Hajós ❷

21 km (13 miles) southeast of Kalocsa.
Road Map D5. 🏔 3,600. 🚌 from
Kalocsa. 🛒 craft market during the
St Orbán Wine Festival. 🎭 St Orbán
Wine Festival (last weekend in May).

In the small village of Hajós,
1,200 tiny 18th-century houses,
almost identical in size and
design, sit above 1,200 identical wine cellars dug into
the soft clay below. Built by
Swabians, a Germanic people
who settled here in the Middle
Ages in order to make use of

the fertile soil, almost all the
houses remain occupied
today. However, many are
used only as summer or holiday homes. Others offer wine
tasting and accommodation.
    The St Orbán Wine Festival
in May, celebrated to honour
the guardian saint of grape
growers and wine-makers, is
the village's annual highlight.
As many as 20,000 visitors
attend the wine tastings,
horse shows, craft markets
and folk dancing displays.

Kalocsa ❸

120 km (74 miles) south of Budapest.
Road Map C5. 🏔 19,000. 🚇 from
Kiskőrös. 🚌 from Budapest, Kiskőrös.
🚢 Danube cruisers. ◯ daily.
🎭 Kalocsa Paprika Days (last
weekend in Sep).

A popular stop for Danube
cruise ships, Kalocsa is at the
centre of Hungary's paprika-
growing region. There is a
paprika harvest festival here
every September and what is
perhaps the world's only
Paprika Museum (Fűszer-
paprika Múzeum). On display
are jars of the spice, in an
astonishing number of
different varieties.
    One of the most important
buildings in Kalocsa is the
cathedral, a twin-towered
Baroque construction from
1772, restored slightly after a
small fire in 1816. Ferenc
(Franz) Liszt adored the
cathedral's organ and often
played here. The town owes
its existence to St István, who
created an archbishopric here
in 1006. The Archbishop's
Palace (built in 1776 on the

The many small houses with wine cellars, in Hajós

site of a medieval castle) today houses an amazing collection of 100,000 manuscripts, codices and books, the earliest dating from 1040.

At the **House of Folk Arts** (Népművészeti Tájház), the local craft society displays and sells its colourful wares in a traditional Puszta cottage.

🏛 Paprika Museum
Szent István király út 6. **Tel** (78) 46 18 19. ⬜ Apr–Oct: 9am–5pm Tue–Sun. 🈲 🎫 Hungarian only. ♿

🏛 House of Folk Arts
Tompa Mihály utca 5–7. **Tel** (78) 46 15 60. ⬜ Mar–Nov: 10am–5pm Tue–Sun. 🈲 🎫 Hungarian only. ♿

Early machinery at the Paprika Museum in Kalocsa

Kiskunság National Park ④
Kiskunsági Nemzeti Park

25 km (16 miles) west of Kecskemét. **Road Map** D4. National Park Headquarters, House of Nature, Liszt Ferenc utca 19, Kecskemét, (76) 48 226 11. ⬜ 10am–4pm Tue–Sat. 🚂 from Kiskunfélegyháza to Bugac-felső; from Kecskemét to Izsák for Lake Kolon. 🚌 from Kiskunfélegyháza to Bugac park entrance; from Kecskemét to Fülöpháza. 🛈 Tourinform Kecskemét, Kossuth tér 1, Kecskemét, (76) 48 10 65. 🈲 ♿ 🚻 🅿 🏧 www.knp.hu

Kiskunság is Hungary's second largest national park after Hortobágy (see p252) . Spread over 759 sq km (293 sq miles), the park is divided into a number of unique natural habitats, which are not all interlinked. A visit to the park's administration office, in the Kecskemét (see pp236–9) House of Nature enables

visitors to get their bearings. A popular way into the park is via Nagybugac. This village is a worthy attraction in itself, with its fascinating horse-riding displays. The **Bugac Stud Farm** (Bugaci Ménes) just outside the village puts on daily shows. These may, however, be cancelled if there are too few spectators; it is best to book an organized tour (www.bugacpuszta.hu). Not to be missed are the performances of the legendary Puszta Fiver, where one man – usually with a moustache as long as his whip – rides five horses simultaneously (see box below). Visitors can ride one of the many thoroughbreds at the stables themselves, and join a day-long horseback-tour of the surrounding area.

Nagybugac's tiny **Herdsmen's Museum** (Bugaci Pásztormúzeum) exhibits a small collection of folk art, costumes and tools but most visitors to Nagybugac are merely passing through on their way to the park. The village is the gateway to the largest area of the park, the Bugac – a vast 100-sq-km (39-sq-mile) expanse of grassland, marshes, freshwater lakes and reeds. A number of well-marked nature trails start at the park entrance.

Bird-watchers should head for Lake Kolon, northwest of the Bugac and accessible via the village of Izsák, where

One of many bird-watching towers in Kiskunság National Park

great bustards, herons and spoonbills can be seen. The unparalleled flora and fauna in the reeds and marshes around the lake include rare species of orchid, as well as otters, weasels, water snakes, turtles and lizards.

The Fülöpháza with its shifting sand dunes is a unique environment in the park and is the habitat of hoopoes, golden orioles and bee-eaters. Trails around the dunes begin at the village of Fülöpháza, 30 km (19 miles) west of Kecskemét.

🅾 Bugac Stud Farm
Nagybugac Ménes. **Tel** (76) 57 50 28. ⬜ daily. 🈲 ♿ for horse shows it is advisable to book in advance with Herdsmen's Museum.

🏛 Herdsmen's Museum
Nagybugac, **Tel** (76) 57 51 12. ⬜ May–Nov 10am–5pm daily. 🈲

CZIKÓS' HORSE SHOWS
The equine skill of the Hungarian cowboys, or Csikós, goes back as far as the first Magyar migrations and was originally military in nature. The Hungarian mounted soldier typically carried light weapons and rode light horses without a saddle. Today's Csikós' shows contain much pseudo-military posturing, usually beginning with a horse parade and salute, followed by displays of equestrian skill, control and dressage. What is unusual is the way the Csikós can make their horses walk at almost a crawl: a legacy of fighting battles in the open plains. The highlight of these horse shows is the Puszta Fiver (pusztaötös): one man riding five horses simultaneously. The Fiver's origins are unknown – perhaps the rider was bringing back the horses of his dead comrades after a battle.

A horseman practising for the impressive Puszta Fiver

Kecskemét ❺

Logo of the Zwack Distillery

The town of Kecskemét dates back to 1368, though little of that era remains today. Kecskemét benefited from self-government during Turkish rule, and the Habsburgs encouraged the development of agriculture in the region, often termed the "Garden of Hungary". One local product is the plum, which is the source of a delicious brandy. An earthquake in June 1911 shook the city, but the outstanding Baroque and Secessionist city centre was mercifully spared. Home to some great museums, Kecskemét is a superb place to explore.

🏰 Piarist Church & School
Piarista Templom & Rendház
Jókai tér. **Tel** (76) 48 59 12. ◯ **Church** by appointment.

The Piarists are a relatively progressive, scientific Catholic order founded in Rome in 1597 by St Joseph Calasanctius. They arrived in Kecskemét in 1715 and founded the school on Jókai tér that operates to this day. (The present, bland school building, however, was built in the late 1940s.) The Baroque church opposite was erected between 1729 and 1765, to designs by Andreas Mayerhoffer. St Joseph Calasanctius is represented by one of four statues on the front of the building, alongside the Virgin Mary and Sts István and László.

🏛 Ornamental Palace
Cifra Palota
Rákóczi út 1. **Tel** (76) 48 07 76. ◯ 10am–5pm Tue–Sun. 🖼 &

This Secessionist masterpiece, completed in 1902, is the work of architect Géza Markus. The green and orange tiled roof is outstanding. An art gallery since World War II, the palace holds over 10,000 works, and exhibitions on the Secessionist architects Tóth and Glücks.

🏛 Hungarian Photography Museum
Magyar Fotográfiai Múzeum
Katona József tér 12. **Tel** (76) 48 32 21. ◯ 10am–5pm Wed–Sun (to 4pm Nov–Mar). 🖼 & www. fotomuzeum.hu

This outstanding museum, housed in a splendid 18th-century mansion, formerly the horse-changing station of the Pest–Szeged mail coach route and a synagogue, displays the work of every great Hungarian photographer, including André Kertész and László Moholy-Nagy. There are regular exhibitions by international artists, and the attached photography bookshop is one of the best.

🏛 József Katona Theatre & Holy Trinity Monument
Katona József tér 5. Tel (76) 48 32 83. ◯ for performances only. & Ⓧ

This Neo-Baroque theatre was the creation of Austrian architects Ferdinand Fellner and Hermann Helmer. Completed in 1896 it was named after Kecskemét's playwright son József Katona. It is as impressive inside as out; the ceiling in particular is worth attending a performance for. The Holy Trinity Monument in front of the theatre was erected to offer thanks after the passing of the most recent outbreak of plague, in 1742.

🏰 Great Catholic Church
Nagytemplom
Kossuth tér 2. **Tel** (76) 48 75 01. ◯ 9am–noon, 2–4pm Mon–Fri (to 5pm Thu); spire and viewing platform summer only. 🖼 &

The Great Catholic Church was built in 1772–96. Its spire rises to 73 m (240 ft), affording superb views. The Baroque exterior features statues and reliefs of figures from Hungarian history. Inside, grand steps lead up to the pulpit.

Room in the Museum of Medicinal and Pharmaceutical History

🏛 Museum of Medicinal and Pharmaceutical History
Orvos és Gyógyszerészettörténeti Kiállítás
Kölcsey utca 3. **Tel** (76) 32 99 64. ◯ May–Oct: 10am–2pm Tue–Sun. 🖼 &

Although this museum has a small collection, consisting mainly of some colourful medicine bottles, old surgical instruments and various reference works, it is housed inside a superb building, itself once a pharmacy, and seeing that alone is well worth the small entrance fee.

🏛 Museum of Hungarian Naïve Art
Magyar Naiv Művészek Múzeuma
Gáspár András utca 11. **Tel** (76) 32 47 67. ◯ Mar–Oct: 10am–5pm Wed–Sun. ◯ Nov–Feb. 🖼 🗷

This charming museum is devoted to contemporary and earlier local Naïve artists who produced some stunning work. Unique in Hungary, the museum provides a thorough survey of the genre: there are more than 2,500 exhibits on display, with the collection of small animal sculptures a special highlight.

The Secessionist Ornamental Palace

For hotels and restaurants in the Great Plain see pp273–5 and pp292–3

Display of mechanical toys in the Toy Museum and Workshop

were considered state of the art in the 1950s. There are also interactive toy workshops for children during the summer.

🏛 Zwack Fruit Brandy Distillery and Exhibition

Matkói utca 2. **Tel** (76) 48 77 11. ◯ 10am–6pm Mon–Fri, by appointment only. 🎫 📷 compulsory. The Hungarian market leader in plum brandy, the factory of the Zwack Unicum Company offers a fascinating insight into the world of alcohol distillation. Visitors can see how the brandy is made – before tasting it – as well as learning about the life of the Zwack family. The plant is open only for groups; Tourinform will provide information on where and when to join one.

🏛 Museum of Applied Folk Art
Népi Iparművészeti Múzeum

Serfőző utca 19. **Tel** (76) 32 72 03. ◯ Mar–Oct: 10am–5pm Tue–Sat; Nov–Feb: 10am–4pm Tue–Sat. ◉ 20 Dec–3 Jan. 🎫 📷 Hungarian only. ♿ This vast and enchanting building and garden was formerly a brewery for nearly 200

🏛 Szórakaténusz Toy Museum and Workshop
Szórakaténusz Játékmúzeum és Műhely

Gáspár András utca 11. **Tel** (76) 48 14 69. ◯ Mar–Oct: 10am–12:30pm, 1–5pm Tue–Sat; Nov–Feb: 10am–4pm Tue–Sat. 🎫 📷
Next to the Museum of Hungarian Naïve Art is this children's paradise, housed in a specially built wooden building. There are displays of Hungarian toys from the 18th century to the present, with dolls and wooden toys taking pride of place. Older children will enjoy the often clumsy mechanical toys that

VISITORS' CHECKLIST

Road Map D4. 🚏 105,000. 🚉 Kodály Zoltán tér; at least 20 daily from Budapest. 🚌 Kodály Zoltán tér; several daily from Budapest. 🚃 Narrow Gauge, Széchenyi tér. 🛈 Tourinform, Kossuth tér 1 (76) 48 10 65. 🎪 daily. 🎭 Zoltan Kodály Classical Music Festival (Jul–Aug); Hirös Hét Festival (Aug); World Pairs Driving Championship (Aug). **www**.kecskemet.hu

years. Opened to the public in 1984 as the Museum of Popular Folk Art, the permanent collection expanded rapidly and now covers woodcarving, pottery, embroidery and weaving. There are workshops on site where visitors can watch and then try embroidering a waistcoat or tablecloth themselves, before tasting local specialities fresh from the traditional ovens. Note, though, that the workshops and kitchen are open only on selected days in the summer.

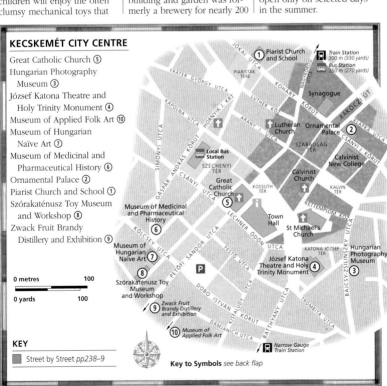

KECSKEMÉT CITY CENTRE

Great Catholic Church ⑤
Hungarian Photography Museum ③
József Katona Theatre and Holy Trinity Monument ④
Museum of Applied Folk Art ⑩
Museum of Hungarian Naïve Art ⑦
Museum of Medicinal and Pharmaceutical History ⑥
Ornamental Palace ②
Piarist Church and School ①
Szórakaténusz Toy Museum and Workshop ⑧
Zwack Fruit Brandy Distillery and Exhibition ⑨

0 metres   100
0 yards   100

KEY

▨ Street by Street pp238–9

Key to Symbols see back flap

Street-by-Street: Around Kossuth tér

At the heart of Kecskemét there are edifices of different eras, designs, religions and cultures. Few public squares in Europe are surrounded by all of these: Roman Catholic, Franciscan, Calvinist and Jewish places of worship; fewer still are those with Art Nouveau masterpieces on all sides. Even the modern Aranyhomok Hotel – which would be little more than a dreary box in most city squares – adds something to the eclectic Kecskemét mix. Large enough to take the summer visitor crowds with ease, the twin Kossuth and Szabadság squares bustle with life from morning until late.

Lutheran Church
Now hemmed in on three sides by surrounding buildings, this church was designed by Miklós Ybl (see p89), but built to a simplified plan in 1862–3. Inside stands a Romantic altar by József Gaál.

Mátyás Pharmacy

Great Catholic Church
Kecskemét's pride, the Neo-Baroque tower – topped with a small golden dome – can be climbed for superb views of the city.

Aranyhomok Hotel

ARANY J. UTCA

KÁPOLNA UTCA

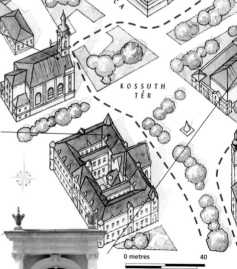

KOSSUTH TÉR

★ **Town Hall**
Bold in pink and yellow, this masterpiece was erected in 1891, when the Secessionist movement was in full swing.

| 0 metres | 40 |
| 0 yards | 40 |

Calvinist Church
The Turks allowed this stone church to be built in 1684, after a Catholic mob had burned down a wooden church during the Counter-Reformation in 1678.

KEY

– – – Suggested route

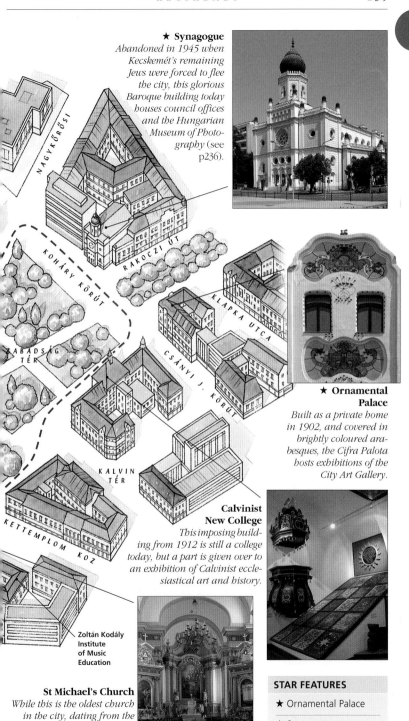

★ **Synagogue**
Abandoned in 1945 when Kecskemét's remaining Jews were forced to flee the city, this glorious Baroque building today houses council offices and the Hungarian Museum of Photography (see p236).

NAGYKŐRŐSI

KOHÁRY KÖRÚT

RÁKÓCZI ÚT

KLAPKA UTCA

ZABADSÁG TÉR

CSÁNYI J. KÖRÚT

★ **Ornamental Palace**
Built as a private home in 1902, and covered in brightly coloured arabesques, the Cifra Palota hosts exhibitions of the City Art Gallery.

KÁLVIN TÉR

Calvinist New College
This imposing building from 1912 is still a college today, but a part is given over to an exhibition of Calvinist ecclesiastical art and history.

KETTEMPLOM KÖZ

Zoltán Kodály
Institute
of Music
Education

St Michael's Church
While this is the oldest church in the city, dating from the 14th century, the Baroque tower and interior frescoes date from the 1790s.

STAR FEATURES

★ Ornamental Palace

★ Synagogue

★ Town Hall

Decorative detail of the Town Hall roof in Kiskunfélegyháza

Kiskunfélegyháza ❻

28 km (18 miles) south of Kecskemét. **Road Map** D4. 🏛 *33,000.* 🚆 *from Kecskemét, Budapest.* 🚌 *from Kecskemét, Budapest.*

Kiskunfélegyháza has a Roman Catholic church and a regional museum, but the Secessionist **Town Hall** is really the only sight worth seeing in this southern town. It is truly outstanding. Completed in 1912 it is something of a high-water mark for Secessionist architecture. Designed by József Vass and Nándor Morbitzer, its façade is a riot of colour, floral patterns and interwoven motifs. Many of the patterns are, in fact, copied from the folk art of the Kiskun region: they can also be seen on traditional lace tablecloths. The roof is covered entirely in tiles made at the Zsolnay factory in Pécs (*see pp186–9*). On a gable, the city crest can be seen, surrounded by tulip motifs.

Although the Town Hall is an official building and still used for administrative purposes today, nobody seems to mind visitors wandering in every day to admire the main hall, which is as richly decorated as the exterior.

🏛 **Town Hall**
Kossuth Lajos utca 1. **Tel** (76) 46 12 55. ◻ 7:30am–4pm Mon–Fri. ♿

Szeged ❼

See pp242–3.

Ópusztaszer National Historical Memorial Park ❽
Ópusztaszeri Nemzeti Történeti Emlékpark

31 km (19 miles) north of Szeged. **Road Map** E5. 🚆 *to Kistelek, then coach.* 🚌 *from Kistelek, local bus from Ópusztaszer.* 🛈 *Tourinform, Szoborkert 68, Ópusztaszer, (62) 27 51 33.* ◻ *Apr–Jun: 10am–6pm daily; Jul–Oct: 10am–6pm Tue–Sun; Nov–Mar: 10am–4pm Tue–Sun.* 🎫♿🖥
🖥 www.opusztaszer.hu

According to legend it was on this site in 896 that the Magyar clan chiefs made their blood pact and chose Árpád as their single leader. The enormous Neo-Classical **Árpád Memorial**, erected in 1896 for Hungary's Millennium Celebrations (*see p104*), commemorates the event. Before that, a monastery stood here, from perhaps the 12th century (its ruins can still be seen), and it may have been a pagan burial ground earlier still. In 1945 this historic site was chosen by the Communists to announce their agricultural collectivization policy.

North of the memorial stands a well-presented **Ethnographic Museum** which comprises some 19th-century houses, windmills, farmhouses and workshops from the surrounding area. In summer the workshops demonstrate various folk crafts, and much of what is produced is sold. To the left of the museum stand tents known as yurts.

The **Feszty Panorama**, an astonishingly detailed depiction of the Magyar migration onto the Great Plain can be seen here. The 120-m (394-ft) long painting was created by 24 artists in 1892–4. Badly damaged in World War II, the Panorama has been restored and is on public view.

Hódmezővásárhely ❾

22 km (14 miles) northeast of Szeged. **Road Map** E5. 🏛 *50,000.* 🚆 *from Szeged.* 🚌 *from Szeged.* 🛈 *Andrassy út, Kossuth tér.* 🛈 *Tourinform, Szőnyi utca 1, (62) 24 93 50.* 🎫 *Agricultural Festival (20–23 Apr); St István's Day (20 Aug).*

One of the oldest settlements in Hungary, the small city of Hódmezővásárhely is famous

The Neo-Classical Árpád Memorial at the Ópusztaszer Memorial Park

Gyula Castle, almost intact after many years of Turkish rule

for its Agricultural Festival. Much of the event is based on Kossuth tér, a large public square that was pedestrianized some years ago. Here stands the large Secessionist **Town Hall** whose tower can be climbed. The building next door (formerly a school) now houses the **Alföld Gallery**, which exhibits the work of Great Plain artists, for example József Koszta, Gyula Rudnay and Vilmos Aba-Novák.

The enormous New Calvinist Church in the city is impressive but a fair walk east along Andrássy utca. Opposite here is a superb Secessionist synagogue (1903), with an exhibition dedicated to those killed in the Holocaust. It often hosts official commemorative events on Holocaust Day.

Gyula ❿

15 km (9 miles) east of Békéscaba. **Road Map** F4. 🏠 34,000. 🚍 from Békéscaba, Budapest. 🚌 from Békéscaba. 🛈 Tourinform, Kossuth Lajos utca 7, (66) 56 16 80. 🎭 Gyula Castle Open-Air Theatre Festival (Jul, Aug).

At one time Scythians, Huns and Avars all passed through the area around the present town of Gyula, but a settlement called Gyulamonostora was first mentioned in 1313. The impressive **castle**, which miraculously survives almost intact, was built in the late 15th century. Taken by the Turks in 1566, it stayed under their control for 130 years.

The castle is the city's leading sight, and it dominates the sprawling park that makes central Gyula so pleasant a place. Visitors can clamber over its walls and climb the look-out tower, or in summer

enjoy a concert in the courtyard. Also in the park is the 18th-century **Almásy Mansion** which has one of Hungary's best thermal bath complexes.

Another attraction is the charming **Százéves**, Hungary's second oldest café, which opened in 1840. Ferenc Erkel, who composed grand operas and the Hungarian national anthem, was born in the house at Apor Vilmos tér 7. It now has a small museum dedicated to his life and work.

Szolnok ⓫

100 km (59 miles) east of Budapest. **Road Map** E4. 🏠 76,000. 🚍 🚌 🛈 Tourinform, Ságvári Endre körút 4, (56) 42 07 04.

Located where the river Zagyva flows into the Tisza, Szolnok has long been the last obstacle

for invaders on the road to Budapest. The city's substantial **castle** was built by St István in 1075 but sacked first by the Mongols, then by the Turks so that nothing remains of it today.

The most important historical monument in the city now, a short walk west of the centre, is the Baroque **Franciscan Church**, built in 1727–54. On the way is the former synagogue at Templom utca 2, a Secessionist building, restored in the 1950s. Also worth a visit is the **János Damjanich Museum**, north of the centre. Named after the general who led the Hungarians to victory over the Habsburgs in the Battle of Szolnok in 1849, it exhibits folk art, archaeological items, as well as work by the Szolnok Artists Colony.

The Baroque Franciscan Church, the oldest building in Szolnok

HUNGARIAN CALVINISM

Calvinism flourished in eastern Hungary and in Transylvania from the second half of the 16th century to around 1700. Preaching to a public that considered Catholicism the religion of the Habsburgs, and therefore foreign, a great number of reformers were active in Hungary before the Reformation movements of Martin Luther and John Calvin. The Turks actively encouraged the Reformation as a bulwark against Catholicism, and the Hungarian Reformed Church quickly became the largest in Central Europe. Calvinism rejected consubstantiation, and had a theocratic view of the state, popular with Hungarians under Turkish rule. When the Turks were finally expelled in 1699, the Habsburgs confiscated Calvinist property. This Counter-Reformation bred resentment, and was a major factor in the creation in the 18th century of a national independence movement, both in eastern Hungary and in Transylvania.

The Calvinist College in Debrecen, founded in 1538

Szeged ⑦

The fourth largest city in the country, Szeged straddles the River Tisza less than 20 km (12 miles) from the point where Hungary, Serbia and Romania meet. Almost completely destroyed by spring floods in 1879, Szeged was entirely remodelled before being rebuilt, and its wide avenues, numerous public squares and vast array of architectural styles, from the Neo-Romanesque cathedral to the Secessionist Reök Palace, are testimony to enlightened town planning. Famous for its free-thinking university, which was at the vanguard of the 1956 uprising, the city is today the most important on the southern Great Plain, and a centre of the salami and paprika trade.

The brown-brick twin-towered Neo-Romanesque Votive Church

🔒 Votive Church
Szegedi Dóm
Dóm tér. *Tel* (62) 42 01 57. ☐
8am–5pm Mon–Wed & Fri–Sat,
noon–5pm Tue, 1–5pm Sun. 📷 &
Neo-Romanesque in design, the Votive Church was constructed over a 17-year period from 1913–30. Everything about it is grand in scale. Designed by Frigyes Schulek, it is dominated by two towers that reach just short of 100 m (328 ft). The eastern tower can be climbed in summer. Above the 10-m (33-ft) tall entrance is an enormous Madonna with Child, while inside the church several frescoes by Schulek can be found, as well as the third largest organ in Europe.

🚇 Demetrius Tower & Dóm tér
Dóm tér. &
The oldest structure in Szeged is the 12th- and 13th-century Demetrius Tower (*Dömötör-torony*) in Dóm tér. Part of a once much larger church, and the traditional centre of town, the tower was only rediscovered in 1925 when a damaged

former Baroque cathedral was cleared to make way for the Votive Church. It was fully restored and converted into a baptistry by Béla Rerrich.

On the south side of the square, a pantheon celebrates famous Hungarians. The Ecclesiastical Museum and Treasury on the square's western side, in a wing of the Bishop's Palace, holds a good collection of Roman Catholic memorabilia. Behind Dóm tér is Aradi Vértanuk tere, with a monument to the Martyrs of Arad, and the Gate of Heroes (1937) honouring Admiral Horthy who launched his White Terror (*see p43*) from Szeged in 1919.

🔒 Serb Orthodox Church
Görögkeleti Szerb Templom
Révai utca. *Tel* (62) 42 42 46.
This single-towered church, founded by Serb immigrants in the 18th century, was remodelled in the Neo-Classical style in 1830. Its beautiful original iconostasis by Jovan Popovic contains 80 icons engraved in pear wood.

The superbly intricate iconostasis of the Serb Orthodox Church

🚇 Reök Palace
Reök palota
Tisza Lajos körút 56.
Built for István Reök, a wealthy local merchant, in 1907, this Secessionist masterpiece is comparable to Kiskun-félegyháza's town hall (*see p241*). Designed by Ede Magyar Oszadszki, it looks like a giant cake topped with striped marzipan. The rotund balcony on the corner, as well as the intricate ironwork – including the blue flowers that surround the building like a cummerbund – are the work of Fekete Pál, working to designs by Magyar Oszadszki. Today the building is used by a Hungarian bank.

Secessionist elements on the façade of Reök Palace

🚇 Széchenyi tér & Town Hall
Városháza
Széchenyi tér. &
The pond in this large square commemorates the devastating flood. In front of it stands a statue of Count Széchenyi (*see p42*). The balcony and colourful ceramic tiles of the Neo-Baroque Town Hall, built in 1883 by Ödön Lechner, pre-empt the Secession (which Lechner founded). A "Bridge of Sighs" replica links the Town Hall to the building next door. The Neo-Classical house (1844) at No 9 and Hotel Tisza (1866) (*see p277*) survived the flood.

🏛 Ferenc Móra Museum
Közművelődési Palota
Roosevelt tér 1–3. *Tel* (62) 54 90 40.
☐ Jun–Aug: 11am–6pm daily; Sep–May: 10am–5pm Tue–Sun. 📷 📷
Looking very much like a Neo-Classical mansion built for a wealthy merchant, the Palace of Popular Culture

For hotels and restaurants in the Great Plain see pp273–5 and pp292–3

(Közművelődési Palota) has in fact been a museum since its completion in 1899. There are excellent exhibitions on archaeology, ethnography and the history of the Csongrád region. One of the highlights is the enormous painting by Pál Vágó showing Szeged after the flood of 1879. The art gallery displays works by Hungarian master József Rippl-Rónai, though the main attraction is Mihály Munkácsy's *Hungarian Conquest*.

🏛 Castle Museum
Vármúzeum – Kőtár

Stefánia sétány 2. **Tel** (62) 54 90 40.
◻ 10am–5pm Tue–Sun.
The castle was built when Béla IV fortified Szeged in 1247 and extended by János in 1547. The scene of one of the Turks' last stands in Hungary, in 1688, it was all but destroyed in the floods of 1879. All that remains today is a tiny part of a bastion. The small museum tells the castle's history (open only in midsummer).

Detail on main entrance to the Castle Museum

🎭 National Theatre
Nemzeti Színház

Déak Ferenc utca 12.
Tel (62) 47 92 79.
Opened in 1883, the theatre burned down two years later. It was restored to its original Neo-Baroque design by the Austrian architects Fellner and Helmer. The lush interior, with three levels of boxes and an intricately decorated ceiling, can be seen during performances of the philharmonic orchestra, opera or ballet.

✡ Jewish Quarter
Zsidó Negyed

South of Nagy Jenő utca. **New Synagogue** Gutenberg utca 13. ◻ Apr–Sep: 10am–noon, 1–5pm Mon–Fri & Sun; Oct–Mar: 9am–2pm Mon–Fri & Sun.
The enormous **New Synagogue** was built in 1900–3 in Secessionist style, with a grand 48 m (157 ft) dome. Its marble tabernacle is covered with gold leaf, while the dome, representing the night sky, is topped by deep blue glass and dotted with stars. At Hajnóczy

VISITORS' CHECKLIST

Road Map E5. 🏠 97,000.
🚌 *Indóház tér, from Budapest.*
🚍 *Márs tér, from Kiskunfélegy-háza.* 🚌 *Roosevelt tér.* 🛈 *Tourinform, Dugonics tér 2 (62) 48 86 90.* 🛒 *daily, Mars tér.*
🎭 *Szeged Open Air Theatre Festival (mid-Jul–Aug).*
http://tip.szegedvaros.hu

New Synagogue, built and decorated in Secessionist style

utca 12, the **Old Synagogue** has a high-water mark on its outer wall showing the level of the floods in 1879.

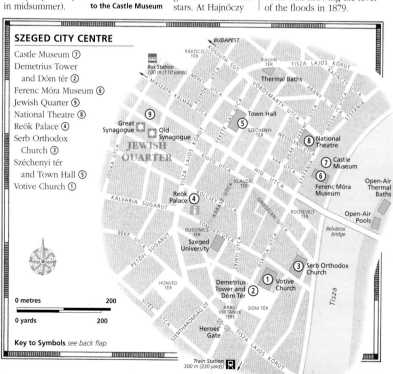

SZEGED CITY CENTRE

Castle Museum ⑦
Demetrius Tower and Dóm tér ②
Ferenc Móra Museum ⑥
Jewish Quarter ⑨
National Theatre ⑧
Reők Palace ④
Serb Orthodox Church ③
Széchenyi tér and Town Hall ⑤
Votive Church ①

0 metres 200
0 yards 200

Key to Symbols *see back flap*

Train Station 🚂
300 m (330 yards)

The Great Plain (Puszta), Hortobágy National Park ▷

Jászberény ⑫

50 km (31 miles) east of Budapest.
Road Map D3. ⚔ *29,000.*
🚃 *from Szolnok, Budapest.* 🚌 *from
Kecskemét.* 🚏 *Tourinform, Lehel vezér tér
33; (57) 40 64 39.* 🎭 *Csángó Folklore Festival (first week in Aug).*

Jászberény is named for the
Jász: an allegedly Iranian
people who settled in the
area around 1200. A number
of other towns and villages in
the region bear the Jász-
prefix, yet there is nothing to
set apart the Jász today. Their
Persian language has long
been assimilated, and their
heritage is preserved only in
the **Jász Museum**, the main
sight in Jászberény. Here
visitors will find the legendary
Lehel Horn *(see box)*, as well
as background on the life of
the Jász people. There is a
poignant exhibit commem-
orating Jász children, some as
young as 14, who fought and
defeated the Habsburgs in the
Battle of Tápióbicske in 1849.
   In August, the town plays
host to the Csángó Folklore
Festival, a celebration of the
traditions of the Csángós, a
Hungarian-speaking people
who fled eastern Hungary for
Moldavia during the Mongol
invasion. As many as 70,000
Csángós still live in Moldavia
(eastern Romania) today.

🏛 **Jász Museum**
Táncsics Mihály utca 5. **Tel** (57) 50
26 10. ☐ Apr–Oct: 9am–5pm Tue–
Sun; Nov–Mar: 9am–4pm Tue–Fri,
9am–1pm Sat–Sun. 🎫 ♿

Costumes of the Jász people, at the
Jász Museum in Jászberény

Fidibus Ship Hotel in Tiszafüred, organizing occasional boat trips

Tiszafüred ⑬

63 km (39 miles) west of Debrecen.
Road Map E3. ⚔ *15,000.* 🚃 *from
Debrecen.* 🚌 *from Debrecen, Budapest.* 🚏 *Tourinform, Fürdő utca 21;
(59) 51 11 23.*

The largest resort of Lake Tisza
(see pp248–9) is a bustling
town and probably the best
place for a long stay on the
Tisza. Though there are no
luxury hotels, there are plenty
of good, well-priced pensions
and many good traditional
restaurants. The only real sight
in the town is the **Pál Kiss
Museum**, based in a Neo-
Classical villa in the city centre. One of Hungary's oldest
regional museums, founded
in 1877, its displays include
wooden panels, painted furniture and pottery, as well as an
excellent archaeology exhibition, with Roman coins and
mosaics. The museum is
named after Pál Kiss, one of
the generals of the revolution
of 1848–9. It also showcases
leather goods made at the
Leather Production House,
on Ady Endre utca.
   A short walk from the city
centre, the Fidibus Ship Hotel
organizes occasional boat trips
out on the lake. Details can
be obtained on board ship.

🏛 **Pál Kiss Museum**
Tariczky sétány 6. **Tel** (59) 35 21 06.
☐ 9am–noon, 1–5pm Tue–Sat. 🎫
Hungarian only. ♿

THE LEHEL HORN

Legend has it that in AD 955, the Hungarians – who spent
much of the period pillaging throughout central Europe –
came up against fierce resistance at Augsburg in Germany.
Two Hungarian warriors, Lehel and Bulcsú, were captured
and brought before the German commander, who intended
to reward their bravery by allowing them to choose the
manner of their death. Lehel asked the Germans to bring
him his horn, to help him meditate upon his answer. Once
he had the horn in his hands he struck the German commander with it, killing him instantly. Lehel and Bulcsú were
brutally executed soon after, but having dispatched the
enemy first meant that he would have to serve Lehel in the
afterlife. The horn – miraculously – made its way back to
Jászberény. Sadly for
romantics and lovers of
legends, the horn on
display at the Jász
Museum dates from the
10th or 11th century,
and is of Byzantine origin.

The Lehel horn, one of Hungary's
most important treasures

For hotels and restaurants in this region see pp273–5 and pp292–3

The Horsemen of the Great Plain

Since AD 900, when Magyar horsemen struck fear into the hearts of all who crossed their paths as they rode through the Carpathians into western Europe, Hungarians have been renowned for their excellence in horsemanship. For more than 1,000 years, Hungarian military and economic power relied in many respects on the skill of its horsemen, and on the sturdiness of the short-necked horses they rode; since much of the country's history took place on horseback. While the romantic nomads of yore have long since disappeared, the Hungarian traditions of horsemanship are preserved in the many equestrian centres on the Great Plain, which offers an ideal climate for riding tours and hunting. Horsemen put on shows with great feats of horsemanship (such as the Puszta Five, see p235), and the enterprise of breeding thoroughbreds has enjoyed a renaissance.

The *patrac* is a unique saddle *without girth to tie it around the horse, used only on ceremonial occasions: Puszta horseman ordinarily eschew saddles.*

The classic view of the Puszta: *man, horse and an improvised well. It is not without reason that this part of Hungary is considered a land only for the hardy.*

Horsemen performing in a modern Puszta show *are strictly for the benefit of visitors, yet these shows allow the Puszta horsemen, known as Csikós, to preserve and demonstrate their prowess in – and out – of the saddle.*

Bogrács, the traditional method of Puszta cooking, *involves a large beef or pork stew being cooked very slowly in a kettle over an open fire.*

The horses of the Puszta *are mainly of the Hortobágy Nonius breed, known for their discipline. They are increasingly popular – especially in the US where they are trained as dressage and equestrian competition horses.*

The Horse Lay *was a necessary method of protection as the terrain offered little cover for the advancing cavalry. The Puszta horsemen trained their horses to lie down and to "crawl" in the grass.*

A Tour Around Lake Tisza ⓯

Although it is today considered one of the natural wonders of Hungary, Lake Tisza is, in fact, an artificial lake, created in the early 1970s when the River Tisza was dammed for the irrigation of the Great Plain. Covering 127 sq km (49 sq miles), it is second in size only to Lake Balaton, and is increasingly challenging its more famous neighbour as a popular summer holiday destination. Most of the northern part of the lake is a protected nature reserve, much loved by bird-watchers, and accessible only with a guide.

Négyes ⑧
Peregrine falcons are just one of many bird species which enjoy the micro-climate generated by the lake waters. Of the 380 species found in Hungary, up to 200 can be seen at the Lake Tisza Nature Reserve.

FÜZESABONY, EGER

Újlőrincfalva

Poroszló ⑦
Rowing boats are available for hire to those who wish to explore the lake, and there is a popular nature trail that snakes its way around this village and the surrounding countryside.

Sarud ⑥
Sarud is a superb little village, famous for its many attractive 18th- and 19th-century thatched cottages, and it also boasts a great shallow beach that is perfect for children.

Tiszanána

Borbély

HEVES   Hatházpuszta   Dinnyéshát

Tisza

Bánoms

Szalókirét

Pusztataskony

TISZABURA

KUNHEGYES

Kisköre ⑤
This delightful family-oriented resort is home to Lake Tisza's best beaches, which even in high summer rarely get crowded.

● Dózsatelep

● Borsodivánka ⑧

Tiszavalk

Pusztaráboly ●

Tisza

Δ 33

①

②

34

33

DEBRECEN

Puszta
domaháza

KUNMADARAS

Tisza

Tiszaszőlős ●

TIPS FOR DRIVERS

Tour length: *71 km (44 miles)*
Stopping-off points:
*Outside Tiszafüred the best places
to eat are the small pensions
and restaurants of Abádszalók,
while Kisköre has a good choice
of pensions offering fine local
food. Though not part of this
tour, note that the area of the
lake north of motorway 33 is
part of Hortobágy National Park
and accessible only with a guide.*

Tiszafüred ①
The main resort on the lake, Tiszafüred has
many grass beaches, boat launches and a
couple of good museums *(see p246)*. It is
also a major bird-watching centre.

Tiszaderzs ③
A quiet town set
slightly back from
the shores of the
lake, Tiszaderzs
has two fine church-
es, both on Fő utca: a
Romanesque church,
originally from the 13th
century but rebuilt in the
1600s, and a fine 18th-century
Baroque Reformed Church.

Patkós Csárda ②
A traditional Puszta restaurant just
outside Tiszafüred on motorway 33,
the Patkós (Horse Shoe) is a popular
stopping-off point for motorists. The
inn serves huge portions of local dishes,
including a wide range of game.

0 kilometres	3
0 miles	3

KEY

━━ Tour route

═══ Major road

═══ Other road

╍╍╍ Major railway

Δ Camping

Abádszalók ④
The large water park at Abádszalók is one of the most
popular attractions around the lake. The resort itself is
an excellent base from where to try water sports.

Debrecen ❶

This charming town of 200,000 people barely counts as a metropolis, yet it is Hungary's second largest town. Famous for its Calvinist Reformed College (1583) and Calvinist Church (1821), there has been a settlement here since Roman times, and Debrecen has always been an important market town. During the revolution of 1848 it served as Hungary's capital and its parliament met here. Today celebrated for its grand bath complex and excellent university, Debrecen is one of the most pleasant towns in Hungary. Almost all its sights are situated around a pedestrian-only public square, while its thermal baths are in a lovely wooded spot just north of the centre.

Interior of the Small Reformed Church, bastion of Protestantism

🏛 Piac Street and Town Hall
Piac utca; Városháza

Piac utca. 🚌 ♿
Piac utca translates as Market Street, and derives from the important cattle markets held here in the 16th and 17th centuries. Debrecen's main street, it leads from the rather bleak area around the railway station to its central square, Kalvin tér. The northern part is pedestrianized (except for trams) and is the site of craft markets every weekend in summer. On summer evenings, too, there are plenty of outdoor cafés and terraces, all popular with visitors and locals for people-watching. The square is also used to host concerts and festivals, including the Flower Carnival in August. The Neo-Classical building on the corner of Piac utca and Kossuth utca is Debrecen **Town Hall**, built in 1842–3 to a design by local architect Ferenc Povolny.

🏛 Great Reformed Church
Református Nagytemplom

Piac utca 4–6. **Tel** (52) 41 26 94.
🕐 Jun–Aug: 9am–6pm Mon–Fri, 9am–1pm Sat, noon–4pm Sun; Sep–May: 9am–4pm Mon–Fri, 9am–1pm Sat, noon–4pm Sun. ● during church services. 🎫 ♿
Debrecen's defining landmark towers above much of the city. Originally called St Andrew's Church and dating from 1291, it was destroyed by fire in 1802. The present church was built in 1819–23, to designs by Mihály Péchy. Its enormous organ was added in 1838. Hungary's parliament met at this quietly dignified church from 1848–9, and inside, the chair from

which Lajos Kossuth declared Hungary's independence has been preserved for posterity. From the western tower there are great views of the city.

The Great Reformed Church and fountain at Kossuth Square

🏛 Aranybika Hotel
Piac utca 11–15. **Tel** (52) 50 86 00.
♿ www.hotelaranybika.com
An inn belonging to a certain János Bika, known as *Arany Bika* (Golden Bull), has stood on this spot since the 16th century, and the current hotel is still named after him. A Secessionist masterpiece, it was built to the design of Alfréd Hajós, Hungary's first Olympic champion, and opened in 1915. Its exquisite details range from the colonnades of the grand entrance to the stunning balconies above the entire façade. Inside there is a swimming pool (open to the public) as well as a casino, night club and restaurant. The rooms, however, do not live up to the exterior. The terrace restaurant on the ground floor is popular in summer.

⛪ Small Reformed Church
Református templom

Révész tér 2. **Tel** (52) 34 28 72.
🕐 Jun–Oct: 10am–5pm Mon–Sat; Nov–May: by appointment. ♿
The tower of this charming church was originally topped by an Orthodox-style onion dome, but high winds blew the dome off in 1907, and a replacement suffered a similar fate a few years later. The tower was then finished with crenellations and took on the rather truncated look it has today, earning it its nickname of "stumpy church". A bastion of Protestantism, it was here in 1860 that Péter Balogh, Bishop of Debrecen, declared the Hungarian Protestant churches to be independent of the Habsburg Emperors.

⛪ St Anna's Church
Római katolikus templom Szent Anna

Szent Anna utca 15. **Tel** (52) 53 66 52. ♿ 🚫
Debrecen's largest Catholic Church was built in 1726–46 to appease the Habsburg emperor, who would not have one of his Royal Free Towns without a Catholic church. Quite who worshipped here is not known – when asked by the emperor in 1748, Bishop Csáky, the founder

Detail from the exterior of St Anna's Church

For hotels and restaurants in the Great Plain see pp273–5 and pp292–3 of the church, had converted none of the Calvinists. The key sight inside the church is its altarpiece, depicting St Anna teaching Mary. The work of an Austrian painter, Karl Rahl, it was added during reconstruction of the church in the 19th century.

🏛 Calvinist Reformed College
Református kollégium

Kálvin tér 16. **Tel** (52) 41 47 44.
◯ 10am–4pm Mon–Sat, 10am–1pm Sun. ◪ for museum. ♿

The college was founded by Dominican monks, anxious to create a seat of learning in the area, in 1538. Teachers were trained here (in Latin) before being sent to one of 140 free schools the college operated in the region. Rebuilt in 1675 and in 1816, the present building was designed by Mihály Péchy, who was also commissioned to design the Great Reformed Church. There is a small but interesting museum telling the story of the church and the school. The Oratory, where Hungary's provisional parliament met in 1944, while Budapest was still under siege, can also be visited.

🏛 Déri Museum and Square
Déri Muzeum

Déri tér 1. **Tel** (52) 32 22 07.
◯ Apr–Oct: 10am–6pm Tue–Sun; Nov–Mar: 10am–4pm Tue–Sun. ◪ ♿ www.derimuz.hu

Built in 1926–8 to house local industrialist Frigyes Déri's art collection, this excellent museum has a rich collection of antiquities from Egypt and Ancient Greece. There are also displays on Debrecen's history, ethnography and art – including the *Jesus Trilogy* by Mihály Munkácsy and *Four Spheres* by sculptor Ferenc Medgyessy. In the restful **square** in front of the museum, landscaped in the 1990s, are three fine statues by Medgyessy.

The grand main entrance to the Neo-Baroque Déri Museum

♨ Thermal Baths
Debreceni Gyógyfürdő; Aquaticum

Nagyerdei 1. **Tel** (52) 51 41 00.
◯ **Thermal Baths** 7am–8pm daily. **Aquaticum** 11am–9pm Mon–Thu, 10am–9pm Fri–Sun. ◪ ♿ www.aquaticum.hu

Debrecen's famous, extensive thermal bath complex comprises several large outdoor pools and baths, one indoor pool and a vast water-therapy treatment centre. The baths also have the added attraction of Aquaticum: a modern, indoor thermal baths catering to a younger generation and families, with water slides, children's pools and Thai massage.

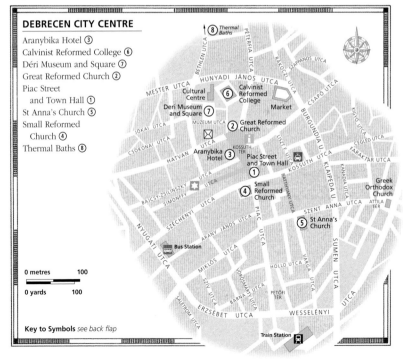

DEBRECEN CITY CENTRE

Aranybika Hotel ③
Calvinist Reformed College ⑥
Déri Museum and Square ⑦
Great Reformed Church ②
Piac Street and Town Hall ①
St Anna's Church ⑤
Small Reformed Church ④
Thermal Baths ⑧

0 metres 100
0 yards 100

Key to Symbols see back flap

The Mediterranean beach at the spa complex in Hajdúszoboszló

Hajdúszoboszló **⑯**

20 km (12 miles) west of Debrecen.
Road Map F3. 🚶 24,000. 🚆 from
Debrecen, Budapest. 🚌 from
Debrecen, Budapest. 🛈 Tourinform,
Szent István park 1–3; (52) 55 89 28.
www.hajduszoboszlo.hu

The most popular spa resort
on the Great Plain and the
largest thermal bath complex
in Hungary, the waters here
have been attracting visitors
since the 1920s. The extensive
Hajdúszoboszló Medicinal Spa
(Hajdúszoboszló Gyógyfürdő)
has been modernized, with
giant water slides, wave
pools, an artificial Mediterranean beach (complete with
imported palm trees) and children's play areas complement-
ing the traditional spa waters.
The latter are brown, very
salty and contain iodine and
bromine. Sufferers of rheumatism swear by their curative
effect, and they are also said
to help cure gynaecological
disorders. Non water-related
activities include restaurants,
cafés and the István Bocskai
Museum, which has an exhibition of the town's history,
including the story of how
the waters were discovered
during the search for oil
(see p163).

🔵 **Hajdúszoboszló**
Medicinal Spa
Szent István Park 1–3. **Tel** (52) 55 85
58. ◯ **thermal baths** 7am–7pm
daily; **Aqua Park** 10am–8pm Mon–
Thu, 10am–9pm Fri & Sun, 10am–
midnight Sat. 📷 🚻

Hortobágy & Hortobágy National Park **⑰**

Hortobágyi Nemzeti Park

Road Map F3. National Park (52)
58 91 70. 🚌 🛈 Tourinform, Pásztormúzeum, Petőfi tér 1, Hortobágy,
(052) 58 93 21. ◯ **National Park**
8am–4pm daily. 📷 🚻 📷 🚻 💻
📷 **www**.hnp.hu

This enormous national park
was the first to be cre-
ated in Hungary, in
1973, and remains
the largest, stret-
ching over 820 sq
km (317 sq miles)
from Lake Tisza to
Debrecen. It was
added to UNESCO's
World Heritage List
in 1999. The vast
plain, known locally
as the Puszta (mean-
ing emptiness), is
the nesting site of as
many as 152 species
of bird, including
great bustards, herons, storks
and spoonbills, while up to
342 different bird species
have been spotted here in
migration, including tens
of thousands of screeching
cranes, which can be seen in
late September.

A stork in the Hortobágy National Park

Cattle, horses, buffalo, the
Hungarian *racka* (a long-
haired sheep) and *parlagi* (a
goat) continue to be herded
by semi-nomadic farmers
here, as they have for almost
a thousand years.

The **Hortobágy Máta Stud
Farm** riding centre located
inside the park is an 18th-
century stud and Hungary's

best. It organizes Csikós
riding performances (see
p235), as well as riding
lessons for visitors throughout summer.

While much of Hortobágy
National Park is open to
visitors all year round, some
parts have limited access. The
park's administration and
visitors' centre is in the tiny
but charming village of
Hortobágy itself.

The village has three small
hotels and the 17th-century
Hortobágy Csárda restaurant,
which serves Hungary's
national dish, goulash (gulyásleves), which originated in
the Puszta. There is also a
small **Shepherds' Museum**
(Pásztormúzeum) with
fascinating facts
about the life of the
Puszta shepherd.
The unique Nine-
Arch Bridge (Kilen-
clyukú híd), built in
1827–33 to designs
by Ferenc Povolny,
crosses the river
Hortobágy and once
formed part of the main road
from Budapest to Debrecen.

🔵 **Hortobágy Máta**
Stud Farm
Czinege J. Utca 1, Hortobágy.
Tel (52) 58 93 69. ◯ 8am–8pm
daily. 📷 🚻 riding lessons.
🏛 **Shepherds' Museum**
Petőfi tér 1, Hortobágy. **Tel** (30) 565
7473. ◯ 15–31 Mar & Nov: 10am–
2pm daily; Apr & Oct: 10am–4pm
daily; May–Sep: 9am–5pm daily (to
6pm Jul–Aug). ◯ Dec–14 Mar. 📷

Nyíregyháza **⑱**

See pp254–5.

The 19th-century Nine-Arch Bridge in Hortobágy

The miraculous icon of the Virgin Mary in the Greek Catholic Church in Máriapócs

Máriapócs **19**

31 km (19 miles) from Nyíregyháza. **Road Map** F3. *2,300. from Nyíregyháza. from Nyíregyháza, Nyírbátor. 15 Aug (Assumption Day).*

In 1696 an icon of the Virgin Mary in the twin-domed **Greek Catholic Church** in Máriapócs was seen weeping. The icon was immediately taken to Vienna (to St Stephen's Cathedral) and replaced with a replica. When the replica wept again in 1715 and in 1905, the fate of Máriapócs as a place of pilgrimage was sealed. Today, as many as one million Catholics make the trip every year, many on or around Assumption Day (15 August), when the village is literally besieged by the faithful.

🏛 Greek Catholic Church
Kossuth tér 25.
***Tel** (42) 38 51 42.*
7:30am–7pm. ♿

Nyírbátor **20**

36 km (22 miles) from Nyíregyháza. **Road Map** G3. *14,000. from Nyíregyháza, Debrecen. from Nyíregyháza, Debrecen.*

This small town is inextricably linked to the notoriously bloody Báthory family, who owned it in the Middle Ages. Besides bloodlust and murder, however, the Báthorys left two magnificent churches to Nyírbátor's citizens. One of these, a **Roman Catholic** church, was built around 1480. Partially destroyed during raids by Vlachs (Romanians) in 1587, it was left to rot until 1720, when it was restored in the Baroque style by the Minorite Order.

The **István Báthory Museum** next door holds a number of artifacts from around the region, including a vast section on Count István Báthory, Prince of Transylvania, from 1488–1511 and the Báthory family.

The other historic church of the town is the **Calvinist Church** on Egyház utca, a late-Gothic building built by István Báthory. This church, built as the Báthory Mausoleum, is a masterpiece of medieval architecture. The nave consists of one single large hall, with a small tower in its southwestern corner and the two-storey sacristy at the northeastern side. Two István Báthorys rest here: the Lord Chief Justice of Hungary and author of psalms in a stone tomb and next to him, under red marble, the earlier Count István Báthory.

🏛 István Báthory Museum
Károlyi Mihály utca 15. ***Tel** (42) 51 02 18.* Apr–Sep: 9am–5pm Tue–Sun; Oct–Mar: 10am–4pm Tue–Fri. Hungarian only. ♿

Csaroda **21**

15 km (9 miles) east of Vásárosnamény. **Road Map** G2. *700. from Vásárosnamény, Tákos, Fehérgyarmat.*

Standing on a hill surrounded by Csaroda Creek, the Calvinist Church at Csaroda was built in late-Romanesque style in the 13th century. In 1640, its walls were whitewashed and decorated with flowers.

Restoration of the church revealed the original medieval frescoes depicting Saints Peter and Paul among others.

Szatmárcseke **22**

27 km (17 miles) southeast of Vásárosnamény. **Road Map** G2. *1,600. from Vásárosnamény, Fehérgyarmat.*

At Szatmárcseke, the Protestant cemetery is a unique sight worth visiting. Almost all the grave markers are 2-m (6.5-ft) high boats, preserving, it is thought, the ancient Finno-Ugric custom of burying the dead in boats. The tomb of poet Ferenc Kölcsey (1790–1838) is on a hill in the centre of the cemetery, surrounded by white Neo-Classical columns. The poet lived in the village in the early 19th century and wrote many of his famous poems here, including the words of the Hungarian National Anthem, written in 1823. An exhibition in the Cultural Centre commemorates the time Kölcsey spent in Szatmárcseke.

Some 10 km (6 miles) south, on the banks of the river Túr, is the tiny village of Túristvándi, known for its 18th-century wooden water mill. Although it is no longer used as a mill, visitors may see the wheels and the millstones at work.

Fresco from the Calvinist Church in Csaroda

Boat-shaped grave markers in the cemetery in Szatmárcseke

Nyíregyháza ⑱

A vibrant university town, Nyíregyháza is a charming place and its trio of churches and synagogue make it a great destination for lovers of ecclesiastical architecture. Centred on a large, leafy and bustling pedestrianized square, the city is particularly vibrant during term time, as its university is one of Hungary's largest. Only a short way north of Nyíregyháza is the spa resort of Sóstófürdő, home to one of the country's best village museums.

🏛 Kossuth Square and Town Hall
Városháza
Kossuth tér 1. **Tel** Town Hall (42) 52 45 01. ♿

The heart of Nyíregyháza is a very pleasant public square. It was completely rejuvenated by much redevelopment at the end of the 1990s and is now pedestrianized. There are statues and play areas, terraces and cafés, and even an old tramcar for children to climb aboard. Surrounded on three sides by colourful buildings, the most impressive of these is the very yellow, Neo-Classical **Town Hall**, dating from 1841 and originally designed by Alpár Ignác. The low balcony that is its outstanding feature today was added 30 years later, in 1871, during a facelift carried out by the architect Károly Benkó. On the other side of the square is the forget-me-not blue, early-Secessionist Corona Hotel, designed by Ignác and opened in 1895. The building does, however, look far better from the outside than from within.

View of the main altar and transept in the Great Catholic Church

🛕 Great Catholic Church
Római katolikus templom
Kossuth tér 4. **Tel** (42) 40 96 91. ⏰ 6am–7pm daily (to 6pm Oct–Apr). 🔵 during services. ♿

This red-brick Catholic church was built in 1902–4. Designed by local architect Virgil Nagy, its twin bell towers reflect the steep wooden bell towers common on older churches in the northern part of the Great Plain. The plain interior of the church is lit by the stained-glass windows.

The most beautiful part, however, is the impressive transept, with the figures of the four Evangelists in the bays of the arches.

🛕 Lutheran Church
Evangélikus templom
Luther utca 1. **Tel** (42) 50 87 70. ⏰ 9am–5pm Mon–Fri. 🖼 donation. Key at vicarage next door if locked.

The largest church in the city, on its highest point, is the Lutheran Church, reflecting the importance of the Reformation in this part of Hungary (see p40). Designed by the Italian Giuseppe Aprilis, it was built in the Neo-Baroque style in 1784–6. The church entrance has four Neo-Classical marble columns. Inside, the walls are adorned with paintings and the main altar, from the Greek Catholic Church in Máriapócs (see p253), is richly carved.

🏛 András Jósa Museum
Jósa András Múzeum
Benczúr tér 21. **Tel** (42) 31 57 22. ⏰ Apr–Oct: 9am–5pm Tue–Sun; Nov–Mar: 8am–4pm Tue–Sun. 🖼 🎭 Hungarian only.

Local painter Gyula Benczúr and writer Gyula Krúdy star at this fascinating museum, named after András Jósa, a wealthy local scientist who owned the building. Born in Nyíregyháza in 1844, Benczúr spent little of his life here, although the museum honours him with a permanent exhibition devoted to his life and work (note that most of his paintings are in Budapest's National Gallery, see pp58–9). Krúdy, famous the world over for his novel *The Adventures of Sinbad* (1918), was a chronicler of Budapest. The museum displays all his first editions, newspaper articles and other memorabilia.

🛕 Greek Catholic Church & Bishop's Palace
Görög Katolikus templom és Egyházművészeti Gyűjtemény
Bethlen Gábor utca 5. **Tel** (42) 41 59 01. ⏰ 8am–4pm Mon–Fri (get key from Sacristy next door). 🖼 museum.

This eclectic Greek Catholic Church was designed and built by Vojtovits and Baczó, and completed in 1897. Combining Byzantine and Baroque, it was hit by a Soviet bomb at the end of

Kossuth Square, and the yellow Neo-Classical Town Hall

The plain façade of the Synagogue, in early Minimalist style

World War II, and had to be
extensively rebuilt. Miraculously, the highly ornamented
iconostasis featuring St Nicholas
survived intact. The nearby
Bishop's Palace holds a priceless collection of Greek
Catholic religious artifacts.

✿ Synagogue
Zsinagóga

Mártírok tere 6. **Tel** (42) 41 79 39.
 by appointment only.
Nyíregyháza's synagogue is
a beautifully simple building
whose outside walls are devoid
of any real decoration. Built
in 1924–32 to the plans of
Lipót Baumhorn, its straight
lines and unfussy façade bear

witness to the birth of Mini-
malism. The murals on the
walls inside depicting the
night sky and biblical scenes
were painted by Pál Szalay, a
local artist and teacher. On an
outside wall a long plaque
commemorates the Nyíregyháza
Jews killed in the Holocaust.

Environs

Opened in 1979 the **Open-Air
Village Museum** at Sóstófürdő,
a spa town 7 km (4 miles) north
of Nyíregyháza, is famous for
its beautiful rural architecture.
More than 50 buildings (houses,
a school, a shop, a pub, a fire
station) represent the regional
styles. In summer, a wide range

of activities are organized: craft
fairs, dancing and concerts.
The **Aquanus Spa Resort** and
the **Sóstó Zoo** here are also
worth a visit.

Inside a house at the Open-Air
Village Museum at Sóstófürdő

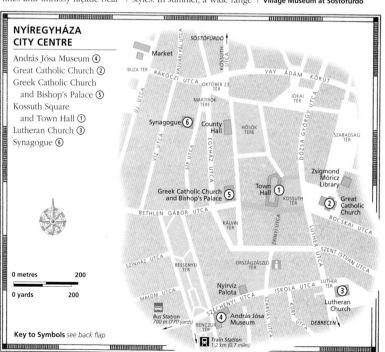

NYÍREGYHÁZA
CITY CENTRE

András Jósa Museum ④
Great Catholic Church ②
Greek Catholic Church
  and Bishop's Palace ⑤
Kossuth Square
  and Town Hall ①
Lutheran Church ③
Synagogue ⑥

0 metres   200
0 yards   200

Key to Symbols see back flap

TRAVELLERS' NEEDS

WHERE TO STAY

Hungary offers accommodation to cater for all tastes and pockets, from the smallest, family-run pension to the largest and most luxurious five-star hotels, with all the international chains represented. Many hotels have their own spa centres, providing on-site beauty, hydrotherapy and massage treatments for guests. In addition there are hundreds of campsites and youth hostels throughout the country with facilities for the budget-conscious. Choice is, of course, greatest in the capital, Budapest, which also has a range of luxury self-contained apartments, often far more competitively priced than luxury hotels. Outside the capital there is less choice, although most towns have one or two large, imperial-era hotels and a number of pensions. The exception is Lake Balaton, where the popular resorts boast hotels to rival Budapest.

Doorman at Hotel Gellért, Budapest

CHOOSING A HOTEL

Staying at one of Hungary's best hotels *(szálló, szálloda)* is expensive, but few places in Europe offer better pamper value than the Gellért *(see p261)* or Four Seasons in Budapest *(see p261)*, or the Civis Aranybika in Debrecen *(see p274)*. There are, however, also less expensive options providing good accommodation. Most hotels have official star-ratings, but note that Hungary's stars equate to one star less in western Europe.

Most of the larger and better hotels – especially the five-star ones in the capital – are mainly occupied by business travellers during the week. Fortunately, rates and prices fall at the weekend, and most of these hotels offer excellent weekend packages mainly in the low season.

Booking a room in advance is highly recommended, and is essential in Budapest and at Lake Balaton throughout the high season (Jun–Aug). For the Formula 1 weekend *(see p31)*, hotels in and around Budapest sell out months, sometimes years, in advance. Prices often triple for the duration of the event.

HOW TO BOOK

Hotels can be booked direct, through travel agents, via a central booking agency such as **Hotels Online Hungary** or **Hotel Guide Hungary Reservation System** *(see Directory)*. It is also possible to obtain savings on advertised rates from an internet-based room discounter such as **Hotels.hu** (partner of the National Tourist Office). Usually, the top hotels tend to offer their lowest prices on their own websites, however.

HOTEL CHAINS

There are several hotel chains in Hungary, with some operating different international brands. The chains offer good deals for longer stays. In the high season, their central reservations system may be able to find an available room when no one else can.

The **Accor Pannonia** (Ibis, Etap Mercure, Sofitel and Novotel); **Danubius** (Best Western, Hilton, Radisson SAS and Danubius); and **Hunguest** all operate several hotels in and around Budapest and elsewhere throughout the country.

Main entrance to the Danubius Grand Hotel *(see p264)*, Margaret Island

PRICES AND PAYMENT

Most hotels offer greatly reduced rates for booking in advance, or for staying at the weekend or in low season, often reducing the price by 5,000–20,000 forints.

Entrance to the art'otel Hotel *(see p264)*, in Budapest

◁ **Chess players in the famous Széchenyi Baths, in Budapest**

A room in the Cotton House Hotel *(see p261)* in Budapest

Almost all the hotels and pensions listed in the Where to Stay section accept major credit cards (Visa and Master-Card), but American Express and Diners Club are not usually accepted outside of Budapest. Most hotels will also change foreign currency, although mostly at less than favourable exchange rates.

TIPPING

Tipping in Hungary is a matter of personal discretion but not common practice in hotels, even in the larger ones. Tasks performed for guests by staff are considered part of the service. However, it is usual to tip the waiting staff in hotel restaurants: the standard tip is 10 per cent.

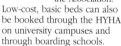

Sign for Leo Panzio pension *(see p262)* in Central Pest

CAMPING

Camping is popular in Hungary, and there are more than 200 well-equipped campsites *(kemping)* all over the country, from large, local authority-run sites to smaller sites, often in someone's garden (especially around Lake Balaton in high season). Campsites do not usually hire out tents, though some have small and basic bungalows for rent. **www. hotels.hu**, partner of the Hungarian National Tourist Office, has full details of the country's campsites, with information on what services they provide. Note that camping is only permitted in designated areas.

YOUTH HOSTELS

Most of Hungary's over 100 registered youth hostels *(ifjúsági szálló)* are affiliated to the **Hungarian Youth Hostel Association** (HYHA), itself a member of the Hostelling International Federation (HI). All the hostels display the HI symbol, a guarantee of cleanliness and good service. Beds can be booked online through **Hostelling International** or direct through the HYHA website.

A dorm bed in an HYHA-affiliated hostel costs around 3,000 forints outside the capital, and slightly more in Budapest itself. Most hostels offer small discounts for members of the Association.

Low-cost, basic beds can also be booked through the HYHA on university campuses and through boarding schools.

PENSIONS

Hungary's network of pensions *(panzió)* is large and legendary. These family-run establishments offer bed and breakfast (and often an evening meal) at low prices. Many are, in fact, large houses in the suburbs, often with gardens – a good choice for families travelling on a fixed budget.

Another low-cost option is private accommodation. This can be booked on the Hungarian Tourist Office's website *(see p305)*, which has extensive listings of private individuals and organizations who will arrange the rental of private homes and cottages for visitors' exclusive use.

SELF-CATERING APARTMENTS

Hungary, and Budapest especially, now have a massive range of self-catering apartments. Many are located in the city centre, and are a little short of luxurious, with maid service included in the price. For families and groups these apartments are often the best way to stay in the capital at a reasonable cost.

Less luxurious apartments for rent away from the city centre where prices are low can be a budget alternative.

DIRECTORY

CENTRAL BOOKING

Hotel Guide Hungary Reservation System
Tel (1) 453 31 01.
www.hotels.hu

Hotels Online Hungary
www.hotelonlinehungary.com

HOTEL CHAINS

Accor Pannonia
Tel (1) 457 87 00.
www.accor-pannonia.hu

Danubius Hotels
Tel (1) 888 82 00.
www.danubiushotels.com

Hunguest Hotels
Tel (1) 481 91 00.
www.hunguesthotels.hu

CAMPING, YOUTH HOSTELS, PENSIONS AND PRIVATE ACCOMMODATION

Hostelling International
www.hostels.hu

Hungarian Youth Hostelling Association
Tel (1) 411 23 90.
www.youthhostels.hu

IBUSZ Private Accommodation Service
Tel (1) 485 27 67.

Choosing a Hotel

The hotels in this guide have been selected across a wide price range for their good value, exceptional location, comfort or style. The chart lists hotels by region, starting with the capital, Budapest. Map references refer to the Street Finder of Budapest and the Road Map (see pp118–23 and inside back cover).

PRICE CATEGORIES
For a standard double room with bathroom per night, including breakfast, tax and service charges:

(HUF) Under 15,000 HUF
(HUF)(HUF) 15,000–25,000 HUF
(HUF)(HUF)(HUF) 25,000–35,000 HUF
(HUF)(HUF)(HUF)(HUF) 35,000–50,000 HUF
(HUF)(HUF)(HUF)(HUF)(HUF) Over 50,000 HUF

BUDAPEST

CASTLE DISTRICT Burg

Szentháromság tér 7, 1014 **Tel** (1) 212 02 69 **Fax** (1) 212 39 70 **Rooms** 26   Map 1 B4

Virtually opposite the Mátyás Church in the heart of the Castle District, location is everything at the Burg. The rooms are a little spartan but nevertheless comfortable, though the bathrooms (all en suite) are on the small side. There is no extra charge for a room overlooking the church, so ask for one when booking. **www.burghotelbudapest.com**

CASTLE DISTRICT Carlton Hotel Budapest

Apor Péter utca 3, 1011 **Tel** (1) 224 09 99 **Rooms** 95   Map 1 C5

Despite the rather bleak exterior, this is a very comfortable hotel situated beneath the Royal Palace, just off Fő utca and close to Clark Ádám tér (see p57), handy for the Chain Bridge and Pest. It has good-sized, if basic, single, double and triple rooms, all with large, bright bathrooms. A hearty buffet breakfast is available. **www.carltonhotel.hu**

CASTLE DISTRICT Buda Castle Hotel

Úri utca 39, 1014 **Tel** 36 70 321 7926 **Rooms** 25   Map 1 A4

Situated in the heart of Budapest's Castle District, this "fashion hotel" has stylish rooms and an elegant, cool courtyard in which to relax after a day's serious sightseeing. Breakfast is served in the orangery, plus there is a historic cellar used for special events. **www.ohb.hu/gudacastle**

CASTLE DISTRICT Hilton

Hess Andrástér 1–3, 1014 **Tel** (1) 889 66 00 **Rooms** 322   Map 1 B4

The Hilton, one of the most luxurious hotels in Budapest, is located in a building incorporating parts of a Gothic church and Jesuit monastery. In the heart of the Castle District, with magnificent views over the Danube and the Pest cityscape, the high prices here are more than justified. **www.budapest.hilton.com**

GELLÉRT HILL AND TABÁN Citadella

Citadella sétány, 1118 **Tel** (1) 466 57 94 **Rooms** 14   Map 3 C2

This hostel-style hotel occupies the casements of the Citadel. It offers relatively inexpensive, neat and clean double and multiple-occupancy rooms. A popular wine bar, restaurant and nightclub are located in the Citadella complex. No credit cards. **www.citadella.hu**

GELLÉRT HILL AND TABÁN Best Western Orion

Döbrentei utca 13, 1013 **Tel** (1) 356 85 83 **Fax** (1) 375 54 18 **Rooms** 30   Map 3 C1

In a secluded spot, this pleasant hotel offers clean but plainly decorated rooms, all with bathrooms, controlled air conditioning and colour televisions. A small restaurant serves a good range of inexpensive Hungarian and international cuisine. **www.bestwestern.com**

GELLÉRT HILL AND TABÁN Danubius Hotel Flamenco

Tas vezér utca 7, 1113 **Tel** (1) 889 56 00 **Rooms** 355   Map 3 B4

Architecturally unattractive, this good-value hotel is close to Buda's main sights. Built during the 1960s, the interior is decorated in a Spanish theme. The Solero restaurant and La Bodega wine bar offer Spanish specialities. Rooms are large, well furnished and comfortable. Popular with business travellers. **www.danubiusgroup.com/flamenco**

GELLÉRT HILL AND TABÁN Gold Hotel Buda

Hegyalja út 14, 1016 **Tel** (1) 209 47 75 **Rooms** 30   Map 2 D3

A grand house in the Buda hills, it offers enormous rooms, most with terrific garden views, and luxurious bathrooms. There is a classy restaurant on site, and the buffet breakfast is hearty. Families should go for the good-value apartments; romantics for the Tower rooms. **www.goldhotel.hu**

GELLÉRT HILL AND TABÁN Hotel Castle Garden

Lovas út 41, 1012 **Tel** 36 70 321 7926 **Fax** (1) 700 21 77 **Rooms** 38   Map 1 A5

Overlooking the peaceful, green Tabán parkland, this four-star hotel looks grimly functional from the outside, but the combination of its great location, thoughtful interior design and a classy restaurant make it a good choice. There is a wellness centre with a whirlpool and sauna. **www.ohb.hu/castlegarden**

Key to Symbols see back cover flap

GELLÉRT HILL AND TABÁN Danubius Hotel Gellért

Szent Gellért tér 1, 1111 **Tel** *(1) 889 55 00* **Rooms** *233* **Map** *4 D3*

This legendary spa hotel *(see pp70–71)* has both indoor and outdoor pools that provide an attractive environment in which to relax. Treatments such as massage are also available. Other facilities include two restaurants, a bar, a café, a nightclub and banqueting halls. The rooms have probably seen grander days. **www.danubiusgroup.com/gellert**

AROUND PARLIAMENT City Hotel Ring

Szent István körút 22, 1137 **Tel** *(1) 340 54 50* **Rooms** *39* **Map** *2 D3*

This hotel is within easy reach of Parliament *(see pp80–81)*. All rooms are clean and decorated in neutral shades. It has few facilities and services, and this is reflected in its very reasonable prices. Although there is no restaurant, there are many places to eat nearby. However, the hotel does have a cheerful breakfast room. **www.taverna.hu**

AROUND PARLIAMENT Andrássy Hotel

Andrássy út 111, 1063 **Tel** *(1) 462 21 00* **Rooms** *69* **Map** *2 E4*

Elegance and charm meet in the five-star boutique Andrássy Hotel, built in Bauhaus style and located on one of the most prestigious streets in Budapest. Luxury shops, cafés and historical monuments are minutes away, while the hotel itself provides beautiful Mediterranean-style rooms. The hotel's restaurant is excellent. **www.andrassyhotel.com**

AROUND PARLIAMENT K + K Opera

Révay utca 24, 1065 **Tel** *(1) 269 02 22* **Rooms** *205* **Map** *2 E5*

Belonging to the K + K Group, this hotel is situated close to the State Opera House. Behind a splendid façade it offers guests comfortable accommodation in modern, clean and incredibly spacious rooms. The hotel also features a café, a pub, a bar and secure car parking facilities. A full buffet breakfast is included. **www.kkhotels.com**

AROUND PARLIAMENT Radisson Blu Béke

Teréz körút 43, 1067 **Tel** *(1) 889 39 00* **Fax** *(1) 889 39 15* **Rooms** *247* **Map** *2 E3*

This fine old hotel, close to Nyugati pu metro station, has a beautiful mosaic on its façade. It is equipped with high-speed Internet access, air conditioning and satellite TV. The restaurants serve European and local delicacies, while the Zsolnay Café serves tea and coffee in stunning Zsolnay porcelain. **www.radissonblu.com/hotel-budapest**

AROUND PARLIAMENT Sofitel Atrium Budapest

Roosevelt tér 2, 1051 **Tel** *(1) 266 12 34* **Rooms** *349* **Map** *1 C5*

Located close to the Danube, most of the Atrium's rooms have terrific views of the Castle District and the Pest skyline. There are stylish restaurants, serving international and Hungarian cuisine, terrace cafés and a cocktail bar. Souvenir boutiques and the Las Vegas Casino are on the ground floor. **www.sofitel.com**

AROUND PARLIAMENT Hilton Budapest WestEnd

Váci út 1–3 (inside WestEnd City Center), 1069 **Tel** *(1) 288 55 00* **Rooms** *230* **Map** *2 E2*

The second Hilton to open in Budapest is situated next to the hubbub of the WestEnd shopping centre. Despite its location, the hotel is an oasis of calm (especially the surprisingly charming rooftop garden) with the usual Hilton mix of modernity, efficiency, class and outstanding service. **www.hilton.co.uk/budapestwestend**

AROUND PARLIAMENT Four Seasons Gresham Palace

Roosevelt tér 5–6, 1051 **Tel** *(1) 268 60 00* **Rooms** *179* **Map** *1 C5*

It is difficult to believe that this building was derelict from 1948 to 1990. The Gresham Palace has now been thankfully restored, housing one of the best hotels in central Europe. The lobby is a tourist attraction in itself, the restaurants among the city's finest, and the staff simply excellent. **www.fourseasons.com**

CENTRAL PEST Mercure Budapest Metropol

Rákóczi út 58, 1074 **Tel** *(1) 462 81 00* **Rooms** *130* **Map** *4 E1*

Located in the city centre, close to all amenities and transport links, the Mercure Budapest is housed in a 19th-century building. It offers every modern convenience, including sound-proofing – needed in this location – and Internet connections in all rooms. Popular with business travellers. **www.mercure-metropol.hu**

CENTRAL PEST City Hotel Pilvax

Pilvax köz 72, 1052 **Tel** *(1) 266 76 60* **Rooms** *32* **Map** *4 E1*

This is a comfortable hotel which is let down only by a lack of baths (rooms have showers only). Other than that it is elegant, service is excellent and the breakfast is very good. Good location for shops and sights; there's a good restaurant, the historic Pilvax, famed for its inventive Hungarian cuisine.

CENTRAL PEST City Hotel Mátyás

Március 15 tér 8, 1056 **Tel** *(1) 338 47 11* **Rooms** *85* **Map** *4 D1*

This small, neat pension offers basic rooms, all with showers (but no baths), at affordable prices. There is no bar or restaurant, but a very good buffet breakfast is available. The City Panzió Mátyás is in a good location and many of Budapest's attractions are within walking distance or are easily reached on public transport.

CENTRAL PEST Cotton House

Jókai utca 26, 1066 **Tel** *(1) 354 26 00* **Rooms** *18* **Map** *2 E3*

Upstairs at the Cotton Club bar is the Cotton House, a sublime hotel offering some of the best decorated rooms in Hungary. Luxurious and classy, this is a great choice for couples or music fans. All the rooms are named – and decorated – in honour of a star of the stage or silver screen. Good value. **www.cottonhouse.hu**

CENTRAL PEST King's Hotel Kosher

Nagydiófa utca 25–27, 1072 **Tel** *(1) 352 76 75* **Rooms** *79*

Map *2 F5*

Right in the heart of the Jewish Quarter *(see p100)*, this hotel is housed within a wonderfully restored 19th-century building. The rooms are modern and plain, but many have small balconies overlooking the quiet street outside. The hotel's restaurant offers tasty kosher meals in the restaurant Salamon, near the hotel. **www.kosherhotel.hu**

CENTRAL PEST Leo Panzió

Kossuth Lajos utca 2/a, 1053 **Tel** *(1) 266 90 41* **Rooms** *14*

Map *4 E1*

Situated in the very heart of Budapest, this is a superb little pension that offers good accommodation at a more than reasonable price. Rooms have private bathrooms (with showers and WC), air conditioning and TVs. Some have great views of the lively streets below. A good buffet breakfast is included in the price. **www.leopanzio.hu**

CENTRAL PEST Mercure Budapest City Center

Váci utca 20, 1052 **Tel** *(1) 485 31 00* **Rooms** *230*

Map *2 E2*

Situated on Váci utca, the hotel offers all the facilities associated with four-star hotels. The elegant rooms create oases of peace amid the noise and bustle of this busy commercial district. Suites come with Jacuzzis and saunas. The café on the ground floor is famous for its delicious pastries. **www.mercure.com**

CENTRAL PEST Mercure Budapest Korona

Kecskeméti utca 14, 1053 **Tel** *(1) 486 88 00* **Rooms** *424*

Map *4 E2*

Big, modern and classy, the Mercure Korona is situated in a small street off Kálvin tér, close to cafés and restaurants. The hotel has a wide range of amenities, including its own swimming pool, gymnasium, sauna and solarium. Although the hotel offers good value for money, breakfast is not included in the price. **www.mercure-korona.hu**

CENTRAL PEST Astoria

Kossuth Lajos utca 19–21, 1053 **Tel** *(1) 889 6000* **Rooms** *130*

Map *4 E1*

This old hotel, designed in the Secessionist style, but with a Neo-Baroque breakfast room, has been refurbished to recreate its original interior. Even for visitors not staying at the hotel, it is worth visiting the café to see the beautiful interior. Those staying at the hotel will find the bedrooms luxurious. **www.danubiusgroup.com/astoria**

CENTRAL PEST Le Meridien Budapest

Erzsébet tér 9–10, 1050 **Tel** *(1) 429 55 00* **Rooms** *218*

Map *2 D5*

Housed in the centrally located and tastefully renovated Adria Palace, Le Meridien is an elegantly furnished hotel, where attention to detail is paramount. Even standard rooms are among the largest hotel rooms in the city. The fitness centre is one of Budapest's best, complete with a plunge-pool and Jacuzzi. **www.budapest.lemeridien.com**

CENTRAL PEST M Gallery Hotel

József körút 4, 1088 **Tel** *(1) 477 20 00* **Rooms** *76*

Map *4 F2*

Built at the end of 19th century, this wonderful, vaguely Art Deco-style hotel features a magnificent grand staircase. Its other attractions are its brightly coloured façade, as well as the Secession-style restaurant, which offers good food. The rooms are comfortable, and those facing the courtyard are particularly pleasant. **www.mgallery.com**

CENTRAL PEST Marriott

Apáczai Csere János utca 4, 1052 **Tel** *(1) 486 50 00* **Rooms** *362*

Map *4 D1*

The Marriott's excellent facilities include banqueting rooms, three restaurants, a business centre, a sauna, pool and a fitness centre. The rooms are of a high standard and the staff provide an exemplary level of service. It was here, in 1991, that the decision was taken to dissolve the Warsaw Pact and Comecon *(see p45)*. **www.marriott.com**

CENTRAL PEST Corinthia Grand Hotel Royal

Erzsébet krt. 43–49, 1073 **Tel** *(1) 479 40 00* **Rooms** *414*

Map *2 F5*

Behind its distinguished façade, what was once the Grand Hotel Royal has been transformed into the modern and elegant Corinthia Grand Hotel Royal. The lobby is lovely, setting a luxurious scene even before guests reach their rooms, which are equally excellent. All are furnished in mahogany. **www.corinthiahotels.com**

CENTRAL PEST InterContinental

Apáczai Csere János utca 12–14, 1052 **Tel** *(1) 327 63 33* **Rooms** *398*

Map *4 D1*

This luxury hotel, situated close to Pest's riverside promenade, offers a magnificent view across the Danube to the Castle District. Rooms are classy, with wonderful bathrooms. The hotel's facilities include a cocktail bar and a buffet restaurant. **www.budapest.intercontinental.com**

CENTRAL PEST Kempinski Corvinus

Erzsébet tér 7–8, 1051 **Tel** *(01) 429 37 77* **Rooms** *369*

Map *2 D5*

This exclusive hotel – all glass and class – often welcomes heads of state and other notable personalities among its guests. The large and luxuriously furnished rooms are relaxing, and a perfect mix of luxury with modernity. The hotel has excellent fitness facilities, a pool, two good restaurants, bars and a pub. **www.kempinski-budapest.com**

CENTRAL PEST Buddha-Bar Hotel Budapest Klotild Palace

Vaci utca 34, 1052 **Tel** *(1) 799 73 00* **Fax** *(1) 799 73 01* **Rooms** *102*

Map *4 D1*

Created in one of the two Klotild Palace buildings, which flank the road leading to Elizabeth Bridge, the Buddha-Bar Hotel brings a taste of the Orient to town. Rooms are luxurious, fully equipped and the location is unbeatable. **www.buddhabarhotelbudapest.com**

Key to Price Guide *see p260* **Key to Symbols** *see back cover flap*

FURTHER AFIELD Boat Hotel Fortuna
11 ▤ P   (€)

Újlipótváros, Szent István park, Alsó rakpart, 1137 **Tel** *(1) 288 81 00* **Rooms** *49*   **Map** *2 D2*

If you're looking for something a little out of the ordinary try this boat hotel on the Danube, moored next to Margaret Bridge on the Pest side of the river. Some rooms are surprisingly large, though some are really minute. There's a bar and restaurant on board too, and a super lounge with classy leather sofas. **www.fortunahajo.hu**

FURTHER AFIELD Budai
11 ⫞ 🅼 P 🏾

Buda Hills, Rácz Aladár utca 45–47, 1121 **Tel** *(1) 249 21 86* **Rooms** *23*

Small but charming pension, well hidden from the city's bustle in the Buda Hills. Some of the rooms have great views, and some have balconies – ask for one when you book. Most attractive are the loft rooms, complete with wooden beams and sloping ceilings. Tram number 59 (from Moskva tér) stops outside. **www.hotelbudai.hu**

FURTHER AFIELD Ibis Budapest Aero
11 ⫞ ▤ P 🏾   (€)

Ferihegy, Ferde utca 1–3, 1091 **Tel** *(1) 347 97 00* **Rooms** *139*

Situated close to Ferihegy airport, this hotel is particularly convenient for a short stay in Budapest. The rooms and suites are cosy, tastefully decorated and all have balconies. There are also some especially adapted for the use of disabled guests. Good buffet breakfast. **www.ibis-aero.hu**

FURTHER AFIELD Ibis Budapest Heroes Square
11 ⫞ 🅼 ▤ P 🏾   (€)

Városliget, Dózsa György út 106, 1068 **Tel** *(1) 269 53 00* **Rooms** *139*   **Map** *2 F1*

Situated on the edge of the Heroes' Square and close to the Museum of Fine Arts, this bright, modern hotel features pleasant rooms which offer terrific value for money. Its facilities include a sauna, a solarium, Wi-Fi Internet connections and a rent-a-bike scheme. The buffet breakfast (included in the price) is excellent. **www.ibishotels.com**

FURTHER AFIELD Mohácsi Panzió
⫞ ▤ P   (€)

Buda Hills, Bimbó út 25a, 1022 **Tel** *(1) 326 77 41* **Fax** *(1) 326 77 84* **Rooms** *10*   **Map** *1 A2*

This small, pleasant and inexpensive pension is located just off Margit körút, in the Rózsadomb area of the Buda Hills. It offers clean rooms with either a shower or a bath, and all rooms have a television. Rooms on the upper floor boast marvellous views of Budapest. Underground parking is available at an extra cost. **www.hotelmohacsipanzio.hu**

FURTHER AFIELD Panda
11 ⫞ P   (€)

Buda Hills, Pasaréti út 133, 1026 **Tel** *(1) 394 19 35* **Rooms** *28*

This small hotel in the somewhat unusual shape of a step pyramid is situated in Pasarét, a quiet and exclusive residential district of Buda. Rooms are a little box-like but the hotel in general offers a family atmosphere, as well as a substantial, tasty breakfast. Bus number 5 provides quick transport into the centre. **www.budapesthotelpanda.hu**

FURTHER AFIELD Papillon
11 ⫞ ▤ P 🏾   (€)

Víziváros, Rózsahegy utca 3/B, 1024 **Tel** *(1) 212 47 50* **Rooms** *20*   **Map** *1 B3*

Small, garishly decorated in pinks and purples but charming all the same, the Papillon is an unpretentious place that makes all guests feel very welcome. Rooms are small but acceptable, pets are allowed, and there's a garden with a paddling pool for children. A continental breakfast is included in the price. **www.hotelpapillon.hu**

FURTHER AFIELD Vadvirág Panzió
⫞ P   (€)

Buda Hills, Nagybányai út 18, 1025 **Tel** *(1) 275 02 00* **Fax** *(1) 394 42 92* **Rooms** *16*

This superb, family-owned and operated pension, located in a quiet and green district of the Buda Hills (*see p111*), has a homely atmosphere. Its facilities include comfortable rooms with balconies, restaurant, terrace and sauna. To get there, take bus number 11 from Batthany tér to the end of the line. **www.hotelvadviragpanzio.hu**

FURTHER AFIELD Benczúr
11 ⫞ 🅼 ▤ P 🏾   (€)(€)

Benczúr utca 35, 1068 **Tel** *(1) 479 56 50* **Rooms** *153*

Situated in a quiet street close to Városliget, this hotel offers small but cosy rooms. In addition, there is a good restaurant, as well as a terrace and a garden. Guests are also able to make use of the services of an in-house dentist. Prices are sometimes reduced during the low season, so it is always worth making enquiries. **www.hotelbenczur.hu**

FURTHER AFIELD Danubius Hotel Budapest
11 🎵 💻 ⫞ 🅼 ▤ P   (€)(€)

Buda Hills, Szilágyi Erzsébet fasor 47, 1026 **Tel** *(1) 889 42 00* **Rooms** *289*

This establishment, built in the late 1960s, was the pride of the local hotel industry for many years. Its unique cylindrical shape makes it a landmark even today. The magnificent views from the roof terrace are unrivalled. The facilities include a restaurant with live music and a café. **www.danubiusgroup.com/budapest**

FURTHER AFIELD Golden Park
11 🅼 ▤ P 🏾   (€)(€)

Baross tér 10, 1087 **Tel** *(1) 477 47 77* **Rooms** *170*

The Golden Park Hotel is located in the heart of the business centre of Budapest, and has good public transport links to Budapest's major sights. It serves a plentiful buffet-style breakfast and offers comfortable accommodation for individuals and group travellers alike. **www.goldenparkhotel.hu**

FURTHER AFIELD Molnár Panzió
11 ⫞ 🅼 ▤ P 🏾   (€)(€)

Buda Hills, Fodor utca 143, 1124 **Tel** *(1) 395 18 73* **Rooms** *23*

This mid-range pension is situated in a residential district on the slopes of the Buda Hills. Its green surroundings add to the homely atmosphere and offer guests complete tranquillity. Family rooms are available. The amenities include a bar, fitness facilities, secure parking and a restaurant with a bright, sunny terrace. **www.hotel-molnar.hu**

FURTHER AFIELD Normafa

Buda Hills, Eötvös út 52–54, 1121 **Tel** *(1) 395 65 05* **Rooms** *70*

Guests have the option of indulging in perfect relaxation at the Normafa, or exploring the beautiful scenery on foot. All rooms have terraces, and there is also a large swimming pool, a sauna, a restaurant, a café and a bar. Rooms are not the largest in the world, but represent terrific value for money. **www.normafahotel.hu**

FURTHER AFIELD Novotel Budapest Congress

Krisztinaváros, Alkotás utca 63–67, 1123 **Tel** *(1) 372 54 00* **Rooms** *391*   **Map** *3 A2*

Conveniently situated in the immediate vicinity of the Congress Centre, the Novotel Budapest Congress offers pleasant and modern rooms. The facilities include a swimming pool, a sauna, a bowling alley and a cocktail bar. The hotel also has a large car park. **www.novotel-bud-congress.hu**

FURTHER AFIELD Radio Inn

Istvánmezo, Benczúr utca 19, 1068 **Tel** *(1) 342 83 47* **Rooms** *31*

This pension-style hotel is the official guesthouse of Hungarian National Radio and entertains many visiting personalities. The Radio Inn offers spacious suites with well-equipped kitchens. Although the facilities are fairly basic, it is ideal for families as it is situated in the peaceful embassy quarter and there is a garden. **www.radioinn.hu**

FURTHER AFIELD Ramada Plaza Budapest

Rózsadomb, Árpád fejedelem útja 94, 1036 **Tel** *(1) 436 41 59* **Rooms** *312*

This hotel offers guests everything to pamper themselves or improve their health. Facilities include hot- and warm-water spas, a Jacuzzi and massage treatments. The hotel also has a resident doctor and staff dedicated exclusively to the needs of disabled guests. Some rooms have beautiful views of the Danube. **www.ramadaplazabudapest.com**

FURTHER AFIELD Sissi

Ferencváros, Angyal utca 33, 1094 **Tel** *(1) 215 00 82* **Rooms** *42*   **Map** *4 F3*

Sissi was the affectionate name by which Hungarians and Austrians referred to Empress Elizabeth, wife of Emperor Franz Joseph. Many hotels have been named in her honour, although she certainly did not stay here. The rooms are luxurious and most have balconies. Breakfast is included, and there's a nice garden and terrace. **www.hotelsissi.hu**

FURTHER AFIELD Victoria

Viziváros, Bem rakpart 11, 1011 **Tel** *(1) 457 80 80* **Rooms** *30*   **Map** *1 B3*

Situated on the western bank of the Danube, the Victoria is within easy reach of Buda's main tourist sights. This hotel provides big, comfortable rooms, many with views of the Chain Bridge, the Elizabeth Bridge and Pest. There is no restaurant, so breakfast is served in the bar. Facilities include a sauna and an in-house doctor. **www.victoria.hu**

FURTHER AFIELD art'otel

Viziváros, Bem rkp. 16–19, 1011 **Tel** *(1) 487 94 87* **Rooms** *164*   **Map** *1 B3*

Everything at the art'otel – from the artwork decorating the rooms to the design of the carpets and chinaware – is the work of Donald Sultan. The rooms are large with high ceilings, and each one is individually decorated and furnished in the best taste. There's also a trendy restaurant and bar, and breakfast is included. **www.artotel.de**

FURTHER AFIELD Best Western Hotel Hungaria

Erszebetváros, Rákóczi út 90, 1074 **Tel** *(1) 889 44 00* **Rooms** *499*   **Map** *4 F1*

Reputedly the largest hotel in the country, the Hungaria offers comfortable rooms and the location is superb. Rooms are air-conditioned and have satellite TV and Internet access. The hotel also has an excellent wellness centre. **www.danubiushotels.com/bwhungaria**

FURTHER AFIELD Danubius Grand Hotel Margitsziget

Margaret Island, Margitsziget, 1138 **Tel** *(1) 889 47 00* **Rooms** *164*   **Map** *1 C1*

This hotel on Margaret Island is linked by a tunnel to the Danubius Health Spa Resort, whose spa facilities guests at the Grand can use. There are shaded terrace cafés and restaurants, and numerous possibilities for taking relaxing walks around the tranquil island. A pool and bike hire are also available. **www.danubiusgroup.com/grandhotel**

FURTHER AFIELD Danubius Health Spa Resort Helia

Rózsadomb, Kárpát utca 62–64, 1133 **Tel** *(1) 889 58 00* **Rooms** *262*   **Map** *2 D1*

This is a light and airy hotel located on the bank of the Danube, opposite Margaret Island. The most modern spa hotel in Budapest, the Helia offers a full range of health and beauty facilities, as well as the services of a qualified medical practitioner. **www.danubiusgroup.com/helia**

FURTHER AFIELD Danubius Health Spa Resort Margitsziget

Margaret Island, Margitsziget, 1138 **Tel** *(1) 889 47 00* **Rooms** *267*   **Map** *1 C1*

The renamed spa resort Margitsziget, one of Europe's leading health centres, sits on top of a natural spa that brings water to the surface at 70° C (158° F). The rooms offer a great deal of comfort and luxury. There are good restaurants on site. **www.danubiushotels.com/margitsziget**

FURTHER AFIELD Platánus

Népliget, Könyves Kálmán körút 44, 1087 **Tel** *(1) 333 65 05* **Rooms** *128*

A comfortable, inexpensive hotel situated on the edge of the People's Park and close to the Népliget metro station. From the outside it looks like a suburban block of flats, but the hotel has clean, functional rooms. Other facilities available include a sauna, a solarium and an in-house doctor. Breakfast is included. **www.hunguesthotels.hu**

Key to Price Guide *see p260* **Key to Symbols** *see back cover flap*

FURTHER AFIELD Rubin Hotel & Business Center

Kelenföld, Dayka Gábor utca 3, 1118 **Tel** *(1) 505 36 00* **Rooms** *90*

This modern hotel offers various relaxation and sporting facilities, including sauna, swimming pool, squash courts and bowling alley. It is in a quiet location close to the M1 and M7 motorways. The accommodation available includes some suites with kitchenettes and some larger maisonettes for families. **www.hotelrubin.com**

AROUND BUDAPEST

ESZTERGOM Alabardos

Bajcsy-Zsilinszky út 49, 2500 **Tel** *(33) 312 640* **Rooms** *23* **Map** *C3*

A great little bed-and-breakfast at the foot of Castle Hill, every room is individually furnished, in an eclectic style. Some are far larger than others – the attic rooms are the best – and the prices vary accordingly. All rooms are clean, bright and air-conditioned, and have at least an en suite shower and toilet. No credit cards. **www.alabardospanzio.hu**

ESZTERGOM Pension Ria

Batthyány utca 11–13, 2500 **Tel** *(33) 313 115* **Rooms** *15* **Map** *C3*

An immaculately run little pension housed in a bright green building close to central Esztergom. Besides the rooms – which vary in size but all of which are excellently furnished – there is a small fitness centre, complete with sauna, and an internet room. This is one of the best value-for-money places in town. **www.riapanzio.com**

ESZTERGOM Szent Anna Panzió

Erzsébet Királyné útja 2, 2500 **Tel** *(33) 404 050* **Fax** *(33) 437 029* **Rooms** *5* **Map** *C3*

Once a water mill this superb property has been converted into the most delightful pension in town. The rooms are simple but big enough to sleep a family of four or larger groups. A delicious Hungarian breakfast is included in the price. The owners will meet you at the railway station for a small extra charge.

ESZTERGOM Esztergom

Prímás-sziget, Helischer J. utca, 2500 **Tel** *(33) 412 555* **Rooms** *36* **Map** *C3*

Close to the basilica this is a well-located and reasonably priced three-star hotel. The rooms may all have seen better days but they are large and well furnished – albeit in ubiquitous beige. Common areas reek somewhat of the 1960s but are well-kept and spacious. Staff are happy to help in many languages. **www.hotel-esztergom.hu**

GÖDÖLLŐ Galéria

Szabadság tér 8, 2100 **Tel/Fax** *(28) 418 691* **Rooms** *7* **Map** *D3*

A cracking central location on the town's main square and friendly owners make this a good choice. While the rooms are not exactly luxurious, they do have en suite bathrooms (showers only, no baths) and a good breakfast is included in the more than reasonable price. There is also a good on-site restaurant.

GÖDÖLLŐ Sunshine

Szabadság út 199, 2100 **Tel** *(28) 420 602* **Fax** *(28) 417 346* **Rooms** *23* **Map** *D3*

Set around a courtyard in a secluded location close to the centre of town, this hotel has a whitewashed exterior but a rather garish interior. However, the rooms are of a good price, size and quality; a good and plentiful breakfast is included and staff are very friendly.

SZENTENDRE Aktiv Danubius Szentendre

Ady Endre u. 28, 2000 **Tel** *(26) 312 511* **Rooms** *50* **Map** *D3*

Something of a box from the outside, this hotel is a good option for those wanting to spend the night in Szentendre. It offers unfussy and clean rooms which do have excellent bathrooms and oversized televisions. Breakfast is included, as is access to the small gymnasium. It is located a short walk from the railway station.

SZENTENDRE Hotel Panzió 100

Ady Endre utca 100, 2000 **Tel** *(26) 310 661* **Rooms** *10* **Map** *D3*

This family house has eight double rooms and two three-bed rooms on a peaceful road. There's a pool, sauna and spa in the lovely garden and a terrace for barbecues, making it the perfect spot for relaxation. For the price, it's a bargain. **www.panzio100.hu**

VISEGRÁD Honti

Fő utca 66, 2025 **Tel** *(26) 398 120* **Rooms** *30* **Map** *C3*

A villa with a sloping roof and large balconies, the Honti is a good choice for budget travellers. The price for a room is really low, and the much smaller rooms in the separate pension are even better value. Almost every room has a terrific view, and note this is one of Hungary's few pet-friendly hostelries. **www.hotelhonti.hu**

VISEGRÁD Visegrád

Rév utca 15, 2025 **Tel** *(26) 397 034* **Rooms** *73* **Map** *C3*

A little too modern with an unattractive exterior for some tastes, the interior of the Visegrád, and its fair prices, more than make up for the lack in architectural beauty. The duplex rooms – with raised sleeping areas – are superb. There is a swimming pool and fitness centre in this value-for-money hotel. **www.hotelvisegrad.hu**

NORTHERN TRANSDANUBIA

BÜK Pension Bajor
Bükfürdő, Gyurácz utca 6/A, 9737 **Tel/Fax** *(94) 358 324* **Rooms** *10* **Map** *A3*

In the centre of Bükfürdő, this is a truly great little pension where rooms are simple but spotlessly clean. Visitors should not expect luxury, but will be able to enjoy the highest standards of service and some great local deliciacies in the restaurant. Children are especially welcome here. No credit cards. **www.bayerischpension.hu**

BÜK Greenfield Hotel Golf and Spa
Bükfürdő, Golf út 4, 9740 **Tel** *(94) 801 600* **Fax** *(94) 801 601* **Rooms** *207* **Map** *A3*

Situated in the heart of the thermal spring region of Western Hungary, this superb, four-star hotel offers excellent wellness facilities, superb restaurants and an 18-hole championship golf course. The service is exemplary and visitors arrive from all over Europe for high-class pampering and leisure. **http://greenfieldhotel.net**

BÜK Danubius Health Spa Resort
Bükfürdő, Thermal krt. 27, 9740 **Tel** *(94) 889 400* **Fax** *(94) 889 499* **Rooms** *200* **Map** *A3*

This lush and luxurious spa resort is one of the jewels in the crown of the Danubius hotel chain. With its great swimming pools, both indoor and out, health services and large, bright and modern rooms, it is a good choice all year round. It is located close to the Bük Medicinal Baths. **www.danubiushotels.com/buk**

BÜK Piroska
Bükfürdő, Kossuth Lajos utca 60, 9737 **Tel** *(94) 558 200* **Fax** *(94) 359 269* **Rooms** *83* **Map** *A3*

In a quiet location away from the bustle of the main part of Bükfürdo, the Piroska is a pleasant hotel where a reasonable price and decent levels of comfort combine to ensure value for money. Rooms are by no means luxurious, but they are a good size and all have great bathrooms. **www.hotelpiroska.hu**

DUNAKILITI Princess Palace
Kossuth Lajos utca 117, 9225 **Tel** *(96) 671 071* **Fax** *(96) 671 072* **Rooms** *22* **Map** *B2*

Although this hotel is not a genuine Princess's palace, it looks as though it might have been. Very few new-build hotels have this kind of opulence, elegance and wonderful taste, and staying here is a real pleasure. There is a golf club and spa on site. **www.princesspalace.hu**

FERTŐD Esterházy Palace
Joseph Haydn u. 2, 9431 **Tel** *(99) 537 649* **Rooms** *21* **Map** *A3*

Staying at such a wonderful place as the Esterházy Palace is a rare treat. Although the surroundings of the palace are second to none, the rooms are not furnished with period pieces, which may come as a disappointment. Simply being able to come back here after a day's sightseeing is reason enough. It is a budget hotel and booking is advised.

GYŐR Fehér Hajó Panzió
Kiss Ernő utca 4, 9025 **Tel** *(96) 317 608* **Rooms** *14* **Map** *B3*

Inauspicious-looking pension close to the centre of Győr painted in bright baroque yellow and with a super little portico. Rooms are big and bright but simply furnished and the breakfast is buffet-style featuring locally-made cheese. There's a sauna and solarium, and the staff are exceptionally friendly. **www.feherhajopanzio.hu**

GYŐR Golden Ball
Szent István út 4, 9022 **Tel** *(96) 618 100* **Fax** *(96) 618 109* **Rooms** *32* **Map** *B3*

In a decent location five minutes west of Győr's railway station is this decent hotel, where a huge gym and health spa and reasonable prices attract a mixed crowd of business travellers and sightseers. For a slightly higher rate, visitors can stay in one of the sensational split-level rooms with a raised sleeping area. **www.goldenball.hu**

GYŐR Kalvaria
Kálvária utca 22/d, 9024 **Tel** *(96) 510 800* **Fax** *(96) 510 801* **Rooms** *38* **Map** *B3*

South of the railway station and some distance from the city centre, amenities and services at this hotel are of a high standard. Rooms are surprisingly elegant for such a modern hotel, and superbly furnished. There is a decent restaurant, and if guests do not mind being a drive from the city centre then it is an economical option. **www.hotel-kalvaria.hu**

GYŐR Klastrom
Zechmeister utca 1, 9021 **Tel** *(96) 516 910* **Fax** *(96) 327 030* **Rooms** *40* **Map** *B3*

Located in the heart of Old Győr, this former monastery has been wonderfully renovated – monks' cells have been converted into rather spartan (as befitting their former purpose) but elegant and comfortable rooms. The Baroque former library, now the most amazing conference room in Hungary, is also worth seeing. **www.klastrom.hu**

GYŐR Raba
Árpád utca 34, 9021 **Tel** *(96) 889 400* **Fax** *(96) 889 414* **Rooms** *155* **Map** *B3*

This imposing hotel stands in a splendid location close to most of the city's sights. Prices seem a little steep considering the interior is tired-looking, and single rooms are tiny. However, breakfast is good and included in the price. There is also a small leisure complex and a Belgian Beer Café. **www.danubiushotels.com/raba**

Key to Price Guide *see p260* **Key to Symbols** *see back cover flap*

KŐSZEG Arany Strucc

🍴 📶 🅿️ 〓

Várkör utca 124, 9730 **Tel** *(94) 360 323* **Fax** *(94) 563 330* **Rooms** *15* **Map** *A3*

Inside a gorgeous Baroque house dating from the late 17th century is one of Hungary's oldest hotels. Though the exterior is offset by some rather garish interior design, rooms are superb value and have glorious high ceilings. Guests are advised to reserve well ahead in high summer. No credit cards. **www.aranystrucc.hu**

KŐSZEG Irottko

🍴 📶 〓〓

Fő tér 4, 9730 **Tel/Fax** *(94) 360 373* **Rooms** *52* **Map** *A3*

Looking not unlike a school, the least attractive building on Kőszeg's main square is, in fact, one of the best hotels in the city. Rooms are set around a pleasant central atrium, and all are decent-sized and some air-conditioned. Some bathrooms only have showers. The breakfast is good and the staff are friendly. **www.hotelirottko.hu**

MOSONMAGYARÓVÁR Thermal Hotel

🍴 ♨ 🛶 📶 〓 🅿️ ♿ 〓〓〓

Kolbai utca 10, 9200 **Tel** *(96) 206 871* **Fax** *(96) 206 872* **Rooms** *50* **Map** *B3*

In a quiet and secluded part of Mosonmagyaróvár, this hotel offers a wide range of thermal spa treatments and grooming services in a wonderful setting. The rooms are large and all have great views of the grounds. Day rates can be expensive but booking a week-long break here can be an unexpected bargain. **www.thermal-movar.hu**

ÖTTEVÉNY Földváry Kastélyszálloda

🍴 🅿️ 〓

Fő út 173, 9153 **Tel/Fax** *(96) 485 688* **Rooms** *18* **Map** *B3*

Built in 1870, the rooms at this former stately home are simply but smartly furnished, and all boast original wooden floors. The bathrooms are big and the wonderful buffet breakfast is included in the price. The excellent restaurant has an impressive wine cellar. **www.foldvarykastely.hu**

PANNONHALMA Pannon Pansio

🍴 ⚏ 〓 🅿️ ♿ 〓

Hunyadi út 7C, 9050 **Tel** *(96) 470 041* **Rooms** *20* **Map** *B3*

Positively Alpine in appearance, this gorgeous little pension on a central Pannonhalma square is popular with German visitors. Most of the rooms are a touch on the small side but all have private bath or shower facilities. Some rooms are suitable for four sharers. A super bistro and terrace only add to the charm. **www.hotelpannon.hu**

PÁPA Vero-Hotel Arany Griff

🍴 🅿️ 〓

Fő tér 15, 8500 **Tel** *(89) 312 000* **Fax** *(89) 312 005* **Rooms** *25* **Map** *B3*

Set in a historic house in the heart of Pápa, this is one of the best places to stay in town. The rooms are not plush, but they are large, clean and have high ceilings. Visitors are advised to stipulate whether they wish to book a double or a twin when they make their reservation. The hotel also boasts a good restaurant. **www.verohotel.hu**

RÖJTÖKMUZSAJ Szidonia Manor House

🍴 ♨ 🛶 📶 〓 🅿️ ♿ 〓〓

Röjtöki út 37, 9451 **Tel** *(99) 544 810* **Fax** *(99) 380 013* **Rooms** *51* **Map** *A3*

The Szidonia Manor House is a lush private home with superb, extensive gardens that provides large, well furnished bedrooms for a reasonable price. The suites are more expensive but offer great views of the grounds. The hotel is very popular as a wedding venue in summer and is often fully booked at weekends. **www.szidonia.hu**

SÁRVÁR Danubius Health Spa Resortl

🍴 ♨ 📶 〓 🅿️ ♿ 〓〓〓

Rákóczi utca 1, 9600 **Tel** *(95) 888 400* **Fax** *(95) 888 499* **Rooms** *136* **Map** *A3*

Looking like a block of flats from the outside, the Danubius is, in fact, a fine four-star hotel whose services make it good value. There are indoor and outdoor swimming pools, and a good restaurant. The rooms are simply furnished, though large, and all have air conditioning and splendid bathrooms. **www.danubiushotels.com/sarvar**

SÁRVÁR Vitalmed

🍴 ♨ 🛶 📶 〓 🅿️ ♿ 〓〓〓

Vadkert utca 1, 9600 **Tel** *(95) 523 700* **Fax** *(95) 523 707* **Rooms** *26* **Map** *A3*

Southwest of the city centre, the Vitalmed is a great hotel whose slightly out-of-the-way location means that visitors can expect to enjoy luxury at a terrific price. The rooms are spacious and the beds are extremely comfortable. The breakfast is excellent. Guests also have free access to the spa facilities next door. **www.vitalmedhotel.hu**

SOBOR Sobori Kastélyszálló

🍴 ♨ 🛶 📶 🅿️ 〓〓〓

Kossuth Lajos utca 9, 9315 **Tel** *(96) 287 260* **Fax** *(96) 287 260* **Rooms** *26* **Map** *B3*

This hotel is well-priced and only 40 km (25 miles) from Győr. The large swimming pool at the back is refreshing on hot summer afternoons, and the surroundings offer great fishing and hunting opportunities. Bikes can be hired from reception. **www.duditshotels.hu**

SOKORÓPÁTKA Sokoró Fogadó

🍴 🛶 📶 🅿️ ♿ 〓

Főmajor, 9112 **Tel** *(96) 549 002* **Fax** *(96) 549 003* **Rooms** *18* **Map** *B3*

This pension and riding centre in the Pannonhalma hills is close to the Pannonhalma Abbey. The rooms are decent if unspectacular, and the on-site restaurant serves a wide range of local dishes. The riding centre is open year-round and offers a choice of holidays to riders of all ages and abilities, from novices to experts. **www.sokorofogado.hu**

SOPRON Pension Jagermeister

〓 🅿️ 〓

Bécsi utca 81, 9400 **Tel/Fax** *(99) 349 045* **Rooms** *9* **Map** *A3*

Although the singles at this charming pension really are tiny, it is lovable for its genuine character and charming staff. Most rooms have bathrooms with a bath, and the breakfast is truly memorable. The decoration – much of which has a zebra theme – is as eclectic as one could hope for. **www.jagermeister-panzio.hu**

SOPRON Best Western Pannonia

Várkerület 75, 9400 **Tel** *(99) 312 180* **Fax** *(99) 340 766* **Rooms** *62*

Map *A3*

The oldest hotel in Sopron, the Pannonia was opened in 1893, having been built to a design by architect Móric Hintertraeger. Its superb Neo-Classical façade is matched by a wonderful colonnaded dining room and stunning common areas. The bedrooms, however, fall short of genuine luxury. **www.pannoniahotel.com**

SOPRON Hotel Lővér

Várisi út 4, 9400 **Tel** *(99) 888 400* **Fax** *(99) 888 499* **Rooms** *185*

Map *A3*

In a wooded location just a short drive from central Sopron, this hotel has well-furnished and well-sized rooms, if lacking in character. There is a wide range of activities on offer, from aqua therapy to spa treatments, giving visitors the opportunity to combine sightseeing with a health-retreat getaway. **www.danubiushotels.com/lover**

SOPRON Sopron

Fövényverem utca 7, 9400 **Tel** *(99) 512 261* **Fax** *(99) 311 090* **Rooms** *102*

Map *A3*

This sprawling, rather unsightly hotel offers slightly overpriced rooms in a stunning location. The rooms at the front all offer terrific views of the old town, although those set around the swimming pool are the quietest. The hotel also features a good fitness and health centre with sauna and Jacuzzi. **www.hotelsopron.hu**

SOPRON Wollner

Templom utca 20, 9400 **Tel** *(99) 524 400* **Fax** *(99) 524 401* **Rooms** *18*

Map *A3*

For a decent-priced hotel in Old Sopron, the Wollner is ideal. Originally a Baroque house, dating from 1715, it was remodelled in Neo-Classical style in the 19th century, and given its current façade after the end of World War II. The rooms are wonderful: large and furnished with antiques and fine art. **www.wollner.hu**

SZÉKESFEHÉRVÁR Budai

Budai út 286, 8000 **Tel** *(22) 302 686* **Rooms** *19*

Map *C4*

A great pension in a quiet location a little way from the town centre, the Budai's rooms are large and furnished in a homely style, creating a welcoming ambience. What is more, the double rooms truly are doubles, with plenty of space to walk around despite the enormous, comfortable beds. Breakfast is great too. **www.hotels.hu/budai**

SZÉKESFEHÉRVÁR Novotel

Ady Endre 19–21, 8000 **Tel** *(22) 534 300* **Fax** *(22) 534 350* **Rooms** *96*

Map *C4*

Located on the outskirts of the historic part of Székesfehérvár, the Novotel is a gem where everything is modern and convenient. The Novotel-standard orange and blue rooms are generously large, there is a vast fitness complex with both adult and children's pools, and the restaurant is bright and well-priced. **www.accor.hu**

SZÉKESFEHÉRVÁR Szent Gellert

Mátyás király krt. 1, 8000 **Tel** *(22) 510 810* **Fax** *(22) 510 811* **Rooms** *40*

Map *C4*

The Szent Gellert offers simple and reasonably priced accommodation in a decent location. The double rooms are austerely decorated. Almost all have their own bathrooms, although these are charged at a higher rate, while the lowest-priced rooms are dormitories, with shared facilities. **www.hotels.hu/szentgellert**

SZOMBATHELY Amphora

Dózsa György út 9, 9700 **Tel** *(94) 512 712* **Fax** *(94) 512 714* **Rooms** *19*

Map *A3*

A short walk west of the city centre, on the opposite side of the Perint River, the rooms at this hotel are relatively small, but they do all have wonderful, high ceilings. There are a couple of rooms that take four and five guests, making it a good choice for larger groups. There is also a pleasant café. **www.amphorahotel.hu**

SZOMBATHELY Wagner

Kossuth Lajos utca 15, 9700 **Tel/Fax** *(94) 322 208* **Rooms** *12*

Map *A3*

The Wagner Guest House, a short walk from the centre of Szombathely, is a great pension offering superb-value rooms of a reasonable size, all with air conditioning and wonderful bathrooms. The restaurant is great and the staff are friendly, multilingual and immensely helpful with children. **www.hotelwagner.hu**

ZALAEGERSZEG Balaton

Balatoni út 2/a., 8900 **Tel** *(92) 550 870* **Fax** *(92) 550 871* **Rooms** *50*

Map *A4*

The Balaton is one of the best hotels in the city and is located in a good part of town. Its interiors are all high-quality and the rooms are little short of luxurious. It has the Semira Day Spa, offering guests a full range of health treatments. There's also a good restaurant. **www.balatonhotel.hu**

SOUTHERN TRANSDANUBIA

BALATONALMÁDI Ramada Resort

Bajcsy-Zsilinszky u. 14, 8220 **Tel** *(88) 620 623* **Fax** *(88) 620 641* **Rooms** *210*

Map *B4*

Everything at this hotel is large. From the spacious rooms with their wide windows and super-sized beds, to the huge breakfast buffet that is included in the price – visitors can expect only the biggest and the best here. The swimming pools are superb and there is a full range of facilities from squash to saunas. **www.ramadabalaton.hu**

Key to Price Guide *see p260* **Key to Symbols** *see back cover flap*

BALATONFÜRED Hotel Margaréta 🛏 🏊 📺 🗐 🅿 🏧

Széchenyi utca 53, 8230 **Tel** *(87) 343 824* **Fax** *(87) 341 088* **Rooms** *51* **Map** *B4*

Hotel Margaréta is a large, anonymous tower block but has all the facilities for a restful holiday by the lake. The location is superb and guests can rent a bike, relax on jade stone massage beds or chill out by the pool. Children are well catered for and the restaurant offers hearty Hungarian dishes. **www.hotelmargareta.hu**

BALATONFÜRED Blaha Lujza 🛏 📺 🅿 🏧🏧

Blaha utca 4, 8230 **Tel** *(87) 581 210* **Fax** *(87) 581 219* **Rooms** *22* **Map** *B4*

From the front this stunning Neo-Classical villa appears to be the best bargain in Hungary. Alas, only the excellent restaurant is housed in the original building, dating from 1893 – the bedrooms are in a modern building at the rear. However, the rooms are very small and some of the bathrooms miniscule. No credit cards. **www.hotelblaha.hu**

BALATONFÜRED Annabella 🛏 🏊 📺 🅿 🏧🏧🏧🏧

Deák Ferenc utca 25, 8230 **Tel** *(87) 889 400* **Fax** *(87) 889 412* **Rooms** *388* **Map** *B4*

Close to the lake shore in the centre of Balatonfüred, the Annabella enjoys its own private beach. It also offers a number of smaller than standard double rooms, a bargain in a resort where these are hard to find. Pets are accepted at no extra cost, though not in the restaurants. Open only May–October. **www.danubiushotels.com/annabella**

BALATONFÜRED Marina 🛏 🏊 ♿ 🏧🏧🏧🏧

Széchenyi utca 26, 8230 **Tel** *(87) 889 500* **Fax** *(87) 889 512* **Rooms** *349* **Map** *B4*

Located in a park a short way from Lake Balaton and one of its few genuine sandy beaches, this is a decent high-rise hotel with semi-luxurious rooms of a good size, all with baths, showers and balconies. Almost every room has a great view of the lake. The buffet breakfast is excellent. Open only May–October. **www.danubiushotels.com/marina**

BALATONLELLE Francoise 🛏 🏊 🗐 🅿 🏧

Köztársaság utca 31, 8638 **Tel** *(85) 354 482* **Fax** *(85) 352 233* **Rooms** *22* **Map** *B4*

This is a gorgeous place, set in a glade a short walk from Lake Balaton. Views across the fields are lovely from all of the rooms, which are large, well-appointed and impeccably presented. The owners, who run the place themselves, are friendly and always on hand. Staying here is a joy. Open only March–October. **www.lellehotel.hu**

BALATONLELLE Napfény 🛏 🧗 🅿 🏧🏧

Honvéd utca 72, 8638 **Tel/Fax** *(85) 351 043* **Rooms** *94* **Map** *B4*

Despite the uninspiring exterior, the Napfeny is a decent budget option. It has a superb location on one of the grass beaches, a children's play area, and clean rooms, with those at the front enjoying great views of the lake. Stays of five nights or more attract huge discounts. Open only May–October. **www.napfenyhotel-balatonlelle.hu**

BALATONLELLE Viktoria 🛏 📺 🅿 🏧🏧

Szt. István út 13, 8638 **Tel** *(85) 554 233* **Fax** *(85) 554 234* **Rooms** *20* **Map** *B4*

Close to Balatonlelle's railway halt this is a classy pension where most rooms are bordering on genuine luxury. The majority have comfortable beds, big-screen televisions and spacious bathrooms. In the attic there are cheaper, less luxurious rooms. The pension has its own sailing boat which can be hired out by guests.

BALATONMÁRIAFÜRDŐ Janette 🛏 🧗 📺 🅿 🏧

Ady Endre utca 93, 8647 **Tel** *(85) 575 011* **Fax** *(85) 575 012* **Rooms** *36* **Map** *B4*

Modern but charming hotel about 150 m (165 yds) from the beach. Set in immaculate surroundings, the Janette offers well-appointed rooms in the main building as well as superb little cottages in the gardens. The hotel is open March–October, with barbecues and live music on most evenings in summer. **www.janette.hotel.hu**

FONYÓD Balaton 📺 🅿 🏧

Szent István utca 1, 8640 **Tel** *(20) 967 4511* **Fax** *(85) 560 335* **Rooms** *19* **Map** *B4*

Bright though somewhat small rooms (indeed, some bathrooms are larger than the sleeping areas) in a less-than-quiet setting close to the lake. The friendly staff and the great prices make this hotel a great choice – it is one of the cheapest yet clean places to stay on the whole of Lake Balaton.

FONYÓD Boros Castle 🛏 🏊 🧗 🅿 🏧

Csisztai utca 10, 8640 **Tel** *(30) 546 9673* **Fax** *(1) 318 96 65* **Rooms** *12* **Map** *B4*

Looking like it has been brought here direct from Disneyland, this folly of a palace offers apartments in gorgeous garden surroundings. A small, shallow pool is perfect for children, making it a great choice for families, especially as most of the rooms are large enough to accommodate extra beds. No credit cards. **www.boroskastely.hu**

HÉVÍZ Hunguest Helios 🛏 🏊 📺 🗐 🅿 ♿ 🏧

Vörösmarty utca 91, 8380 **Tel** *(83) 342 895* **Fax** *(83) 340 525* **Rooms** *162* **Map** *B4*

The Hunguest Helios is situated in the middle of a large park, a short walk from the Hévíz thermal lake. The hotel is split into two buildings, called Anna and Benjamin, connected by a covered walkway. Although the double rooms are a little bit on the small side, the hotel offers great value for money. **www.hunguesthotels.hu**

HÉVÍZ Napsugár 📺 🅿 🏧

Tavirózsa utca 3, 8380 **Tel** *(83) 340 472* **Fax** *(83) 343 284* **Rooms** *53* **Map** *B4*

The Hotel Sunshine (for this is what Napsugar means in English) is a decent three-star hotel close to Lake Hévíz. Bizarrely designed, it has an attractive entrance flanked by two less interesting wings, but it boasts value-for-money rooms. Some rooms also have kitchenettes and basic cooking facilities. **www.napsugarhotel.hu**

HÉVÍZ Danubius Health Spa Resort Aqua

Kossuth Lajos utca 13–15, 8380 **Tel** *(83) 889 500* **Fax** *(83) 889 509* **Rooms** *224* **Map** *B4*

Featuring luxurious rooms with giant beds, great swimming pools and a good location close to the centre of busy Héviz, what really attracts visitors to the Aqua Spa Resort is the endless range of health treatments on offer, including aquagym, hydromassage, mud treatment, drinking cures and special diets. **www.danubiushotels.com/aqua**

HÉVÍZ Danubius Health Spa Resort Hévíz

Kossuth Lajos utca 9–11, 8380 **Tel** *(83) 889 400* **Fax** *(83) 889 402* **Rooms** *210* **Map** *B4*

Though the Héviz offers all the spa treatments one would expect of a hotel in this class in a health resort, the emphasis here is more on good living than getting fit. Guests come to indulge in the fine food of the three restaurants, or simply to relax in the many pools, sauna, Jacuzzis and solaria. **www.danubiushotels.com/heviz**

HÉVÍZ Europa Fit

Jókai utca 3, 8380 **Tel** *(83) 501 100* **Fax** *(83) 501 101* **Rooms** *236* **Map** *B4*

A modern, attractive hotel close to the centre of Héviz, the rooms in the Europa Fit are large and comfortable. All have bath tubs as well as showers. The hotel also has an excellent swimming pool, with plenty of shallow areas that make it very suitable for children. Numerous fitness activities are also on offer. **www.europafit.hu**

HÉVÍZ Naturmed Carbona

Attila utca 1, 8380 **Tel** *(83) 501 500* **Fax** *(83) 340 468* **Rooms** *261* **Map** *B4*

One of the most original and modern hotels in Héviz, the crowning glory of this hotel is its superb swimming pool complex: part indoor, part outdoor. Catering both to those looking for a relaxing holiday as well as to the more energetic wanting to boost their fitness, this is one of the best hotels in the resort. **www.carbona.hu**

HÉVÍZ Rogner Lotus Therme

Lótuszvirág utca 1, 8380 **Tel** *(83) 500 500* **Fax** *(83) 500 591* **Rooms** *230* **Map** *B4*

This spa hotel is located in its own 16-hectare (40-acre) park and is based in a low-rise building in a landscaped garden with a range of swimming pools. The hotel restaurants are excellent, and the buffet breakfast a real pleasure. There are tennis courts, health treatments and even a golf course. **www.lotustherme.com**

KESZTHELY Pension Barbara

Zámor utca 2, 8360 **Tel** *(83) 319 865* **Fax** *(83) 319 865* **Rooms** *12* **Map** *B4*

In this friendly pension in a quiet part of the town a short walk from the lake, visitors will find a wide variety of bright and simply furnished rooms. There is a host of spa treatments on offer, and the breakfast is excellent. Its large garden and small yet refreshing swimming pool make it a good choice for families. **www.barbara-pension.hu**

KESZTHELY Bacchus

Erzsébet királyné utca 18, 8360 **Tel** *(83) 510 450* **Fax** *(83) 314 097* **Rooms** *26* **Map** *B4*

Stylish and refined, the Bacchus Hotel shares the building with a restaurant and a wonderful wine cellar – hence the name. Located between the centre of Keszthely and the lake, this is good value and has a friendly atmosphere. Its lovely garden is a great place to spend time enjoying the fine wines from the cellar. **www.bacchushotel.hu**

KESZTHELY City Hotel Éden

Kisfaludy utca 11, 8360 **Tel** *(83) 312 213* **Fax** *(83) 311 556* **Rooms** *21* **Map** *B4*

Built in what may pejoratively become known as "Mock-Secession" style, this hotel offers good accommodation a mere stone's throw from the Festetics Palace. The rooms are a little on the small side, but all have en suite facilities and free Wi-Fi Internet connections. The hotel also has a garden with a small swimming pool. **www.hoteleden.hu**

KESZTHELY Kakadu

Pázmány Péter utca 14, 8360 **Tel** *(83) 312 042* **Fax** *(83) 510 736* **Rooms** *34* **Map** *B4*

The elegant, well-furnished rooms of the Kakadu are set in two connected buildings close to the lake. There is a small but pleasant swimming pool and a rooftop sunbathing terrace. The hotel also offers a full range of health services, including mud treatments and specialist massage. **www.castrum-group.hu**

KESZTHELY Helikon

Balatonpart 5, 8360 **Tel** *(83) 889 600* **Fax** *(83) 889 609* **Rooms** *232* **Map** *B4*

For a hotel on the lake shore, this is the place to come. Not much to look at from the outside, the Helikon Hotel is, in fact, an excellent hotel, with plush rooms offering fantastic views either across the lake or of the town. There is a little jetty at the end of a pier, from where guests can hire sailing boats and pedaloes. **www.hotelhelikon.hu**

PÉCS Patria

Rákóczi út 3, 7626 **Tel** *(72) 889 500* **Fax** *(2) 889 506* **Rooms** *116* **Map** *C5*

If a little expensive, this wonderfully designed hotel is a Modernist masterpiece. The rooms are large and bright, and all have air conditioning and decent-sized bathrooms. There is a fine terrace and café on the first floor, overlooking the hotel's courtyard. **www.danubiushotels.com/patria**

PÉCS Palatinus

Király utca 5, 7621 **Tel** *(72) 889 400* **Fax** *(72) 889 438* **Rooms** *94* **Map** *C5*

A mix of Secession and Art Deco styles, the façade and lobby of this hotel are tourist attractions in themselves. In addition, the hotel boasts sumptuous rooms and a first-class location on the elegant Király utca. Sauna, solarium and steam bath are located in the basement. **www.danubiushotels.com/palatinus**

Key to Price Guide *see p260* **Key to Symbols** *see back cover flap*

PÉCS Fenyves   🍴 📺 🗐 🅿️   💳💳

Szőlő utca 64, 7625 **Tel** *(72) 211 429* **Fax** *(72) 315 996* **Rooms** *23*   **Map** *C5*

North of the city on Mecsekoldal, the views of Pécs from the hotel balconies are simply stunning. The rooms are modern, clean and unfussy, and there is a good on-site restaurant, as well as sauna and massage. It is, however, quite a trek from central Pécs and ideally visitors will need a car if they are staying here. **www.hotelfenyves.hu**

PÉCS Kikelet   🍴 📺 🅿️   💳💳

Károlyi Mihály utca 1, 7635 **Tel** *(72) 512 900* **Fax** *(72) 512 901* **Rooms** *33*   **Map** *C5*

Located up in the Mecsek hills, the terrace of this hotel offers great views of the city below. Alas not all the rooms offer the same view, so ask for one when making your reservation. The rooms are of an acceptable standard, and there is a small Jacuzzi and a fitness centre. A car is required by those staying here. **www.hotelkikelet.hu**

SIÓFOK Aranypart   🍴 📺 🅿️ ♿   💳

Beszédes József sétány 82, 8600 **Tel** *(84) 519 450* **Fax** *(84) 519 460* **Rooms** *198*   **Map** *C4*

A location right on the beach makes up for the lack of swimming pool at this decent three-star hotel. The pyramid design reminiscent of hotels all over Eastern Europe is less than attractive, but the rooms have good views and are clean. Children's activities and a lovely garden make it a good choice for families. **www.aranypart.hu**

SIÓFOK Fortuna   🍴 🅿️   💳

Erkel F. utca 51, 8600 **Tel** *(84) 313 933* **Fax** *(84) 311 087* **Rooms** *51*   **Map** *C4*

Simple, cheap accommodation close to the lake and its western beach, all rooms have bathrooms but only some are air-conditioned and these are charged at a higher rate. The Fortuna's low room rates make it particularly popular with young people and students, so it can be a bit noisy late in the evening. **www.hotelfortuna-siofok.hu**

SIÓFOK Ezüstpart   🍴 🏊 📺 🅿️ ♿   💳💳

Liszt Ferenc sétány 2–4, 8609 **Tel** *(84) 350 236* **Fax** *(84) 350 237* **Rooms** *344*   **Map** *C4*

This tall hotel, which is set back from the lake, has an enormous indoor swimming pool. The rooms here are larger than in most of the resort's package-oriented hotels; if booked as part of a five-night package, prices drop. Rooms with a balcony cost slightly more than those without. Open March–November.

SIÓFOK Janus Atrium   📺 🗐 🅿️   💳💳

Fő utca 93–95, 8600 **Tel** *(84) 312 546* **Fax** *(84) 312 432* **Rooms** *26*   **Map** *C4*

One of the value-for money hotels in Siófok, the Janus Atrium boutique hotel is situated in the centre of the resort. Each room is individually designed and themes range from Japanese style to Gothic to Gustav Klimt but the "1001 Nights Suite" is the best and most over-the-top. Its café serves cakes and sandwiches. **www.janushotel.hu**

SIÓFOK Magistern   🍴 🏊 👫 📺 🗐 🅿️ ♿   💳💳

Beszédes József sétány 72, 8600 **Tel** *(84) 519 600* **Fax** *(84) 519 601* **Rooms** *115*   **Map** *C4*

Right on the seafront and close to the centre of the resort, this is a good-value hotel with views from the upper floors that are quite superb. The rooms are a bit old-fashioned in their decoration, but they are all clean and a good size. A large indoor swimming pool makes this hotel a good choice at all times of year. **www.hotelmagistern.hu**

SIÓFOK Park   🍴 📺 🗐 🅿️   💳💳

Batthyány utca 7, 8600 **Tel** *(84) 310 539* **Fax** *(84) 310 539* **Rooms** *60*   **Map** *C4*

This hotel is the perfect choice for all those looking for something a bit different in Siófok. Set back from the lake, in a garden setting, the hotel is peaceful and quiet. The rooms are large but somewhat bare and there is a good outdoor restaurant with a barbecue most evenings. Wi-Fi Internet connection is available. **www.parkhotel.hu**

TIHANY Club Tihany   🍴 🏊 👫 📺 🗐 🅿️ ♿   💳💳

Rév utca 3, 8237 **Tel** *(87) 538 500* **Fax** *(87) 448 083* **Rooms** *330*   **Map** *B4*

Although the design of the main hotel building has done nothing to enhance the natural beauty of the Tihany Peninsula, this holiday complex offers great little bungalows alongside its standard hotel rooms. There is also a wide range of sporting activities here, from windsurfing, sailing and tennis to horse riding. **www.clubtihany.hu**

TIHANY Panoráma   👫 📺 🗐   💳💳

Lepke sor 9–11, 8237 **Tel** *(87) 538 220* **Fax** *(87) 538 221* **Rooms** *35*   **Map** *B4*

On the northeastern part of the peninsula, close to the village of Diós, stands this stunning villa. Built in 1933, the Panoráma is a quiet retreat. Everything is nice, from the rooms to the exquisite terrace, from where the views out to Lake Balaton are worth seeing. Open April–November. **www.panoramaht.com**

TIHANY Tihany Atrium   🍴 👫 📺 🗐 🅿️ ♿   💳💳💳

Kenderföld utca 19, 8237 **Tel** *(87) 538 100* **Fax** *(87) 538 101* **Rooms** *27*   **Map** *B4*

This is a super four-star hotel, located in the middle of a nature reserve and right by Lake Balaton. Elegance and style come at a decent price. The bathrooms are enormous, the breakfast is delicious, and there is a sauna, Jacuzzi and solarium. Visitors are advised to specify type of room when booking. Open May–mid-Oct. **www.hoteltihany.com**

VESZPRÉM Pension Éllő   🗐 🅿️ ♿   💳

József Attila utca 25, 8200 **Tel** *(88) 420 097* **Fax** *(88) 561 445* **Rooms** *18*   **Map** *B4*

A friendly pension with attentive and helpful staff. The rooms at the pension are huge, as are the bathrooms. The beds are terrific: fluffy pillows and huge duvets abound. The out-of-town location keeps the prices down, and visitors should ideally have a car when staying here. **www.ellopanzio.hu**

VESZPRÉM Gizella

Jókai M. utca 48, 8200 **Tel** *(88) 579 490* **Fax** *(88) 579 491* **Rooms** *22*   **Map** *B4*

This place is a real bargain. For relatively little money guests are given a simple but superb room, of which those in the attic – all white walls, sloping roofs and wooden beams – are the best. There is a superb on-site cellar restaurant, and the location, underneath the gaze of the Castle District, is great too. **www.hotelgizella.hu**

VESZPRÉM Oliva

Buhim u. 14–16, 8200 **Tel** *(36) 88 403 875* **Rooms** *11*   **Map** *B4*

Great value is on offer at the legendary Oliva Pension, which is as renowned for its restaurant as for its rooms. Guests can expect spacious and luxurious accommodation, modern and brightly furnished rooms, including Wi-Fi Internet connections. A good breakfast is included in the price. **www.oliva.hu**

VESZPRÉM Villa Medici

Kittenberger K. utca 11, 8200 **Tel/Fax** *(88) 590 070* **Rooms** *26*   **Map** *B4*

Some of the rooms at the Villa Medici have to be seen to be believed, and the suites especially are well worth the extra cost. The hotel is located close to Veszprém's famous viaduct and is exquisite in every detail. The swimming pool and vividly tiled Turkish bath are delightful, and the restaurant is one of the city's best. **www.villamedici.hu**

THE NORTHERN HIGHLANDS

BÉLAPÁTFALVA Pension Bélkő

IV. Béla út 1, 3346 **Tel** *(36) 554 111* **Fax** *(36) 354 175* **Rooms** *13*   **Map** *E2*

Five minutes' walk from the centre of Bélapátfalva, this is just about the only decent place in the village to stay. Each room is well equipped, with television and en suite facilities, although there is no air conditioning. It has a sauna, for which there is an extra charge. Guests can also hire bikes. No credit cards. **www.belko-panzio.hu**

EGER Eger

Szálloda utca 1–3, 3300 **Tel** *(36) 522 200* **Fax** *(36) 413 114* **Rooms** *209*   **Map** *E3*

Originally built in the 1980s, today Eger is a modern and bright hotel, in pleasant surroundings and only a short walk from the city centre. The rooms are well-furnished, although a bit overpriced. Nevertheless, the breakfast is good. **www.hotelegerpark.hu**

EGER Korona

Tündérpart 5, 3300 **Tel** *(36) 313 670* **Fax** *(36) 310 261* **Rooms** *54*   **Map** *E3*

Sober yet striking from outside, the interiors of the Korona are far more gentle and homely. The rooms are large and have high ceilings. There is an outstanding pool and spa centre, while the cellar houses a wine museum where some of Eger's finest wines can be sampled. The courtyard has a children's play area. **www.koronahotel.hu**

EGER Panorama Garnihotel

Dr. Hibay K. utca 2, 3300 **Tel** *(36) 412 886* **Fax** *(36) 410 136* **Rooms** *38*   **Map** *E3*

This elegant four-star hotel is set halfway between the castle and the city centre. Modern and bright interiors, large rooms and a good restaurant with a sun terrace make it a fine place to stay. There is also a spa centre with sauna, whirlpool, steam cabin, spa bath, as well as billiards and Internet connection. **www.panoramahotels.hu**

EGER Senator-ház

Dobó tér 11, 3300 **Tel/Fax** *(36) 320 466* **Rooms** *14*   **Map** *E3*

One of the oldest buildings in Eger, dating from 1753, the Senator-ház has a fantastic location on Dobó square in the shadow of Eger Castle. The rooms are on the small side but most have views of the castle. There is a good restaurant, a café and terrace. Guests have free admission to Eger's thermal baths at weekends. **www.senatorhaz.hu**

GYÖNGYÖS Opal

Könyves Kálmán tér, 3200 **Tel** *(37) 505 400* **Fax** *(37) 300 455* **Rooms** *16*   **Map** *D3*

Close to the centre of town in a quiet courtyard a rather dull façade hides an elegant hotel where you can expect comfort – if not luxury – at every turn. The rooms are a good size and well-furnished and offer excellent value for money. Staff are multilingual, helpful and very knowledgeable about the surrounding area. **www.opalhotel.hu**

LILLAFÜRED Hunguest Palota

Erzsébet sétány 1, 3517 **Tel** *(46) 331 411* **Fax** *(46) 533 203* **Rooms** *129*   **Map** *E2*

Part of the Hunguest chain, this exquisite hotel – set in a fairytale castle – is one of the most attractive places to stay in Hungary. The rooms fall a little short of complete luxury, but everything else here is superb. There is an underground swimming pool, galleried Baroque-style dining room and magnificent grounds. **www.hunguesthotels.hu**

MISKOLC Pannonia

Kossuth L. utca 2, 3525 **Tel** *(46) 504 980* **Fax** *(46) 504 984* **Rooms** *41*   **Map** *E2*

In a tall, elegant town house on pedestrian Szechenyi utca, the Pannonia is a three-star hotel that is fairly priced. The rooms, even the singles, are spacious and well-furnished, and most of the bathrooms have baths as well as showers. Breakfast is included. A sauna, and underground parking are available too. **www.hotelpannonia-miskolc.hu**

MISKOLC Pension Talizman

🍽 🍷 🅿   ⊕

Vár utca 14, 3534 **Tel** *(46) 378 627* **Fax** *(46) 370 660* **Rooms** *9*   **Map** *E2*

A quite superb guesthouse set in wonderful surroundings close to Diósgyőr Castle that is tremendous value. The garden is one of the best features, along with its popular pub and restaurant. The rooms are fine, with en suite facilities and TVs, although some are rather small. No credit cards.

MISKOLC City

🍽 🗖 🅿 ♿   ⊕⊕

Csabai kapu utca 6, 3529 **Tel** *(46) 555 100* **Fax** *(46) 555 105* **Rooms** *23*   **Map** *E3*

A short walk south of the city centre, the City Hotel is undoubtedly one of the least attractive-looking places in Miskolc, but it is also one of the best. The bedrooms have comfortable beds, well-stocked mini-bars and TVs and the bathrooms are large and modern. There is also a sauna, a steam room, a Jacuzzi and secure parking. **www.cityhotelmiskolc.hu**

MISKOLC Székelykert Panzió

🍽 🗖 🅿 ♿   ⊕⊕

Földes Ferenc utca 4, 3530 **Tel** *(46) 411 222* **Fax** *(46) 411 222* **Rooms** *7*   **Map** *E2*

A charming little pension with just seven bedrooms – none of them all that big. The friendliness of the staff, the quality of the food served in the restaurant and the thoroughly good-value prices make it a great place to stay for a stopover in Miskolc. Book ahead. **www.szekelykertvendeglo.hu**

PARÁD, PARÁDFÜRDŐ Erzsébet Park

🍽 🌡 🍷 🅿 ♿   ⊕⊕⊕

Kossuth út 372, 3244 **Tel** *(36) 444 044* **Fax** *(36) 544 170* **Rooms** *42*   **Map** *E3*

Built in 1893 to the designs of the legendary Hungarian architect Miklós Ybl, the building has been transformed into a semi-luxurious but affordable establishment. The rooms are too small to be truly five-star, but are elegantly furnished. The restaurant is known for its local specialities. **www.erzsebetparkhotel.hu**

PARÁDSASVÁR Kastélyhotel Sasvár Resort

🍽 🌡 🏋 🍷 🗖 🅿 ♿   ⊕⊕⊕⊕

Kossuth utca 1, 3240 **Tel** *(36) 444 444* **Fax** *(36) 544 010* **Rooms** *58*   **Map** *E3*

This hotel, once a former castle belonging to the Károlyi family, was built in the early 19th century. Each of the three wings, Renaissance, Romantic and Rendezvous, are luxurious, with huge rooms and antique furniture. The hotel also has some fine restaurants and an equestrian centre, and the surrounding parkland is perfect for walks.

SZILVÁSVÁRAD Gasthaus

🍽 🍷 🅿   ⊕

Egri úti parkoló 27/1, 3348 **Tel/Fax** *(36) 355 185* **Rooms** *7*   **Map** *E2*

In the centre of Szilvásvárad is this charming, simple little pension offering basic twin or double rooms for a relatively low rate. Luxuries are few but all rooms have en suite facilities and TVs. The pension has a good restaurant serving local specialities. No credit cards.

SZILVÁSVÁRAD Villa Park

🍽 🍷 🅿   ⊕

Park utca 11/B, 3348 **Tel** *(36) 564 044* **Fax** *(36) 564 045* **Rooms** *15*   **Map** *E2*

Situated a short drive or a pleasant walk from the village centre, the quiet surroundings guarantee peace and quiet. Rooms are all large with en suite facilities. The bistro and bar are very good and a great buffet breakfast is included in the excellent room price. **www.silabt.hu**

TOKAJ Makk Marci

🍽 🅿   ⊕

Liget köz 1, 3910 **Tel** *(47) 352 336* **Fax** *(47) 353 088* **Rooms** *5*   **Map** *F2*

Cottage-like and welcoming, the Makk Marci is a wonderful place to stay if you are lucky enough to get a room. (It gets fully booked during high summer, so visitors are advised to reserve well ahead). The charming rooms have little extras, such as the quirky lampshades or the pack of bathroom goodies. **www.hotels.hu/makk_marci**

TOKAJ Millennium

🍽 🍷 🅿   ⊕

Bajcsy-Zsilinszky utca 34, 3910 **Tel** *(47) 352 247* **Fax** *(47) 552 091* **Rooms** *18*   **Map** *F2*

Built in the year 2000, the outside of this charmless but decent hotel appears to be far older than it is. Inside, each room looks almost exactly the same as every other, feeling clinically clean. But its location at the head of the bridge over the Tisza, however, makes it a good choice while touring the area. **www.tokajmillennium.hu**

THE GREAT PLAIN

BAJA Kolibri Panzió

🍽 🅿   ⊕

Batthyány Lajos utca 18 **Tel** *(79) 321 628* **Rooms** *34*   **Map** *C5*

A cheap and cheerful pension a short walk from the centre of Baja. Indeed, it is the only place to stay anywhere near Szent Imre tér. The rooms are large, if simply furnished, and most but not all, have private facilities. Some rooms sleep four people. The staff are friendly and there is a great breakfast (at extra cost).

DEBRECEN Nádix Panzió

🍽 🏋 🍷 🗖 🅿 ♿   ⊕

Bessenyei utca 6, 4032 **Tel** *(52) 532 104* **Rooms** *28*   **Map** *F3*

Large and unusual pension in the north of the city, close to the thermal bath complexes. Rooms are far from being luxurious but all are well furnished and all have bags of character, be it a sloping ceiling or protruding wooden beams. All rooms have private facilities but not all have baths. Breakfast costs extra. **www.nadixpanzio.hu**

DEBRECEN Pension Stop
Batthyány utca 18, 4024 **Tel** (52) 420 301 **Rooms** 14

Map F3

Good value pension on Debrecen's charming little pedestrian side-street. Run by the owner – a friendly polyglot who looks after his customers – rooms are small and slightly stuffy, but fine for those on a budget. Breakfast is sometimes included, although it depends on what room you have and how long you stay. No credit cards. **www.stop.at.tf**

DEBRECEN Centrum Hotel
Kálvin tér 4, 4026 **Tel/Fax** (52) 418 522 **Rooms** 67

Map F3

Most rooms here resemble mini-apartments, with baths as well as showers, making it very popular in Debrecen. Many of the rooms have great views of the Great Calvinist Church and Kalvin tér. Guests may use the swimming pool and sauna of the Aranybika Hotel across the square free of charge. **www.centrumhotel.hu**

DEBRECEN Civis Aranybika
Piac utca 11–15, 4025 **Tel** (52) 508 600 **Fax** (52) 421 834 **Rooms** 205

Map F3

Behind the exquisite Secession-era façade is a hotel that was once one of the best in the country. It still offers reasonable value today and large, if now less than luxurious, rooms. There is a large swimming pool, a good ice-cream parlour on the ground floor, and the buffet breakfast is outstanding. **www.hotelaranybika.com**

DEBRECEN Hunguest Hotel Nagyerdő
Pallagi út 5, 4032 **Tel** (20) 410 588 **Fax** (52) 319 739 **Rooms** 106

Map F3

Overlooking the lake next to the thermal bath complex, the price of a room here (not cheap) includes free entry to the thermal baths. The rooms are spacious and quiet, those on upper floors have some good views; not all have air conditioning. There is free private parking and a restaurant. **www.hunguesthotels.hu**

DEBRECEN Aquaticum
Nagyerdei park 1, 4032 **Tel** (52) 514 111 **Fax** (52) 311 730 **Rooms** 96

Map F3

The best hotel in the thermal-waters zone of Debrecen, the rooms in this modern place are a little clinical, all steel and glass, but large and luxurious. However, what attracts visitors is the wide variety of aqua treatments available. Guests also have free access to the huge Aquaticum spa and pool complex next door. **www.aquaticum.hu**

GYULA Cívis Hotel Park
Part utca 15, 5700 **Tel** (66) 463 711 **Fax** (66) 463 124 **Rooms** 56

Map F4

An excellent value, three-star hotel on the opposite bank to the castle baths, the Park also has its own outdoor swimming pool and sauna, while rooms come in three sizes and price ranges. The best – and most expensive – are in the comfort wing, which can also take an extra bed. **www.civishotels.hu**

GYULA Corvin
Jókai utca 9–11, 5700 **Tel** (66) 362 044 **Fax** (66) 362 158 **Rooms** 27

Map F4

This hotel in the centre of Gyula is modern but a little lacking in charm. Prices are very good, however, and rooms are large. It also has a fantastic wine cellar, a superb terrace for barbecues on summer evenings, a garden with jazz music and guarded parking. Dogs are welcome. **www.corvin-hotel.hu**

KALOCSA Vigado Inn
Bátyai út 40, 6300 **Tel** (78) 461 038 **Fax** (78) 461 010 **Rooms** 6

Map C5

Small, cheap and cheerful motel ideal for those on a tight budget. All rooms have en suite facilities, though they are minute and less than salubriously furnished. Breakfast costs extra but there is no charge to park your car. Not ideal for young families as it can be a little noisy. **www.vigadofogado.com**

KECSKEMÉT Aranyhomok
Kossuth tér 3, 6000 **Tel** (76) 503 730 **Fax** (76) 503 731 **Rooms** 111

Map D4

While it looks no different from the other dreary blocks that surround this part of Kossuth tér, inside the Aranyhomok is a wonderful hotel. The rooms are spacious, the beds comfortable and the bathrooms all have a bath and a shower. Use of the hotel's health centre, steam bath and fitness room is included in the price. **www.hotelaranyhomok.hu**

KECSKEMÉT Central
Kisfaludy utca 10, 6000 **Tel** (76) 502 710 **Fax** (76) 502 713 **Rooms** 26

Map D4

"Central" may be a misnomer, as this hotel is in fact five minutes' walk from Kossuth tér, on the street behind the Town Hall. The rooms are well sized (even the singles in the loft), but are perhaps a little overpriced. Nevertheless the buffet breakfast is memorable, and the staff are among the friendliest in the city. **www.hotelc.hu**

KISKÖRE Ezüst Horgony
Tisza II LTP 7/A, 3384 **Tel** (36) 358 589 **Fax** (36) 358 130 **Rooms** 19

Map E3

Modern hotel offering good-value rooms in a quiet location on the southwestern shore of Lake Tisza. The best and biggest rooms are those in the tower, although the attic-style rooms are also attractive. The large garden has a good children's playground, and the staff will arrange water sports or trips on the lake. **www.hotelezusthorgony.hu**

KISKÖRE Tisza Park
Tisza II, 3384 **Tel** (59) 358 303 **Fax** (59) 558 080 **Rooms** 11

Map E3

A large and spacious hotel in quiet surroundings close to the shore of Lake Tisza. Visitors get a real sense of the Great Plain staying here, and it is a good base from which to explore further. Amenities include good-sized rooms and a superb Hungarian restaurant where the chef cooks goulash to order. **www.tisza-park-hotel.hu**

Key to Price Guide see p260 **Key to Symbols** see back cover flap

NYÍRBÁTOR Hódi

Báthory út 11, 4300 **Tel/Fax** *(42) 281 012*   **Map** *G3*

Nyírbátor's best hotel is a wonderful old house, set in a garden close to the centre of town. This Baroque mansion was built for the Báthory family in the 18th century, and has been fully restored. The restaurant is perhaps more famous – and better – than the hotel, but rooms are fine, spacious and good value. **www.hotelhodi.com**

NYÍREGYHÁZA Ózon

Csaló köz 2, 4400 **Tel** *(42) 595 448* **Fax** *(42) 402 001* **Rooms** *25*   **Map** *F3*

What looks more like a mountain retreat than an urban hotel is a slightly expensive pension in a quiet part of town. Rooms are large and have superb wooden beams running through the ceilings. The restaurant here is famous for its barbeque dishes, and the garden gets busy and raucous in high summer. **www.ozonpanzio.hu**

NYÍREGYHÁZA Fürdőház Panzio

Sóstófürdő, 4400 **Tel** *(42) 411 194*   **Rooms** *8*   **Map** *F3*

Away from the bustle of central Nyíregyháza, close to the Village Museum and thermal baths at Sóstófürdő is this divine hotel and restaurant. The rooms offer a decent level of comfort, but there are no proper double beds: just singles pushed together. Other than that it is a splendid place, and great for children. **www.furdohaz.hu**

NYÍREGYHÁZA Central

Nyár utca 2, 4400 **Tel** *(42) 411 330* **Fax** *(42) 408 710* **Rooms** *33*   **Map** *F3*

Situated a short walk north of the city centre, this unattractive, modern hotel is clean and relatively cheap. The rooms are well furnished, with baths and showers in all bathrooms. There is a small indoor swimming pool, with a fantastic stained-glass window. A good buffet breakfast is served in the small restaurant. **www.centralhotel.hu**

NYÍREGYHÁZA Continent

Sóstói út 52, 4400 **Tel** *(42) 501 500* **Fax** *(42) 402 865* **Rooms** *10*   **Map** *F3*

A short drive from the city centre, the sumptuous rooms with leather armchairs and huge beds at this hotel are worth every penny it costs to stay here. There's a sauna, 24-hour room service, a pretty garden and terrace and a wonderful Neo-Classical dining room. The hotel is invariably fully booked, so reserve early.

SZEGED Novotel

Maros utca 1, 6721 **Tel** *(62) 562 200* **Fax** *(62) 562 221* **Rooms** *136*   **Map** *E5*

While staying at a Novotel may not be original, at least visitors can be sure of what they will find. The Szeged version has large, bright rooms, lots of extras, a swimming pool, good restaurants and helpful staff. Brilliantly located on the river bank, almost all of the rooms have cracking views of the Tisza. **www.novotel-szeged.hu**

SZEGED Forrás

Szent-Györgyi Albert utca 16–24, 6721 **Tel** *(62) 566 466* **Fax** *(62) 566 468* **Rooms** *177*   **Map** *E5*

This is a good-value hotel where the vast range of services on offer to guests makes up for the average rooms. There is a great indoor swimming pool, a good restaurant, sublime gardens and guests have free entrance to Szeged's main thermal bath complex, which has some of the best water slides in Hungary. **www.hunguest.hu**

SZEGED Tisza

Széchenyi tér 3, 6720 **Tel/Fax** *(62) 478 278* **Rooms** *53*   **Map** *E5*

This distinguished, Neo-Classical building on Szechenyi tér has been taking paying guests since the 19th century. While the lobby, staircase and dining rooms are exquisite, the actual bedrooms are very spacious and have wonderful high ceilings but usually with musty blankets, and can seem a bit of a disappointment. **www.tiszahotel.hu**

SZEGED Dóm

Bajza utca 3–6, 6720 **Tel/Fax** *(62) 423 750* **Rooms** *17*   **Map** *E5*

Just about close enough to the cathedral to warrant the name Dóm, this modern hotel offers comfortable rooms, which are let down by tiny bathrooms. The hotel's restaurant is notable for its rather out-of-place stained-glass window, while in the basement there is a sauna. **www.domhotel.hu**

TISZAFÜRED Pension Nadas

Kismuhi utca 2, 5350 **Tel** *(59) 511 401* **Fax** *(59) 511 402* **Rooms** *10*   **Map** *E3*

This high-class pension close to the lake has its own celebrated wine cellar, a kidney-shaped swimming pool, a sauna, a crazy-golf course and an excellent children's play area. Accommodation is either in the thatched main building, or in one of five bungalows. Open all year round. **www.nadaspanzio.hu**

TISZAFÜRED Szőke Tisza

Hajnalköz 1, 5350 **Tel/fax** *(59) 353 169* **Rooms** *3*   **Map** *E3*

Cheap, rural accommodation that is perfect for those who prefer the luxuries of nature to 24-hour room service. That said, the hosts make you feel welcome, the rooms are clean and homely, and there is a garden for children to play in. Like much of Tiszafüred, it is open only in May–October. No credit cards.

TISZAFÜRED Mani

Szabadság utca 20–22, 5350 **Tel** *(20) 390 5545* **Fax** *(59) 350 484* **Rooms** *19*   **Map** *E3*

This small collection of self-catering thatched apartments (which sleep four comfortably) is in a quiet location, set back from the lake (a car is necessary if staying here). There is a tiny swimming pool and a small children's play area, but no breakfast. Open only during the summer season, from March to October.

WHERE TO EAT

ungary has a long tradition of hospitality and culinary excellence. Budapest especially is full of exquisite, luxurious restaurants fit for the emperors of old – this city is, in fact, home to some of central Europe's best and most historic restaurants. Yet visitors do not need a large budget to eat well here. Eating out remains a relatively low-cost experience because an ever-increasing number of restaurants make a special effort to ensure that visitors to any Hungarian city will be able to enjoy local delicacies. These are usually served in enormous portions at low prices, offering excellent value for money. Visitors on the move or in a hurry can avail themselves of an array of snacks too, usually at outlets that are open non-stop. And, of course, there are some excellent cafés and patisseries.

Sign in front of a restaurant

The outdoor terrace of the Pest-Buda Vendéglő (see p282)

EATING OUT

Even during the Soviet period Hungary retained a relatively good selection of restaurants serving excellent local cuisine. Today the choice is literally endless, although the best selection remains in the capital, where restaurants with names such as Robinson, Kacsa, Alarbardos and 1894 Borvendéglő resonate worldwide. The country has seen the arrival of foreign chefs bringing their own cuisine and know-how from all over the world. Among the ethnic cuisine options available are Italian – which was always popular in Hungary – Chinese, French, Greek and Thai. US-style fast-food chains are also popular, and ubiquitous.

Besides restaurants a great place to eat a light snack in Hungary is in a wine bar (*borozó*). Typically, such snacks consist of a slice of bread and dripping with raw onion, sprinkled with paprika, or *pogácsa* (a scone with crackling, cheese, caraway seeds or paprika). Wine bars with tables sometimes serve frankfurters or pork knuckle with cabbage. Beer houses, called *söröző*, serve an even wider range of moderately priced snacks and hot dishes.

Café culture was invented in this part of the world, and Hungarians love meeting and chatting with friends while enjoying coffee and cakes in a café. Hungary has one of the oldest coffee-drinking traditions in Europe. Introduced to Hungary by the Turks during their occupation (see pp40–41), the coffee culture blossomed towards the end of the Habsburg era (see p43), when there were almost 600 *kávéház* in Budapest alone.

Hungarians also love to eat and drink outside as long as it isn't raining. Locals can often be seen enjoying food and drink on a terrace even in freezing conditions. During the summer alfresco dining is an absolute must, and almost every restaurant and café will place tables outside. Restaurants and bars are now all non-smoking by law.

CHOOSING A RESTAURANT

Hungary offers a variety of places to eat for a range of prices that suit all budgets. Fashionable restaurants, notably in the capital, attract a trendy, young crowd, for whom money is often little object, and who do not mind loud music and a boisterous ambience. For a more relaxed atmosphere, try a more established restaurant, or one of the many excellent restaurants located in Budapest's luxurious five-star hotels.

As a general rule, Hungarian restaurants carry a name tag that indicates what kind of eatery it will be. *Étterem* simply means restaurant, and any type of cuisine may be served. A *csárda* comes in various forms – most are folksy restaurants offering

Dining-room of the Nautilius Étterem restaurant-boat, Budapest

Centrál Kávéház Café *(see p284)*, one of Budapest's historic cafés

interesting local dishes. A fisherman's *csárda*, known as a *halázscsárda*, will offer mainly fish dishes and soups. There are two types of inn: a *vendéglő*, which has an informal ambience, and a *kisvendéglő* (literally "small inn") which is similar to a bistro.

DINING HOURS

Most restaurants open for lunch at 11:30am and close around 11pm. It is unusual for them to close during the afternoon, though many, especially outside Budapest, close on Sundays and/or Mondays. Almost all of the restaurants in the Balaton area are open only during the season from May to September.

Prices for lunch do not usually vary from those for supper, though the set lunch menu may only be on offer at lunchtimes. Restaurants with terraces may charge a little more for sitting outside.

For eating late at night, visitors may have to make do with fast food, as Hungarian restaurants rarely stay open late, and even those which offer entertainment, music or a disco usually close their kitchens long before they close their doors.

VEGETARIAN FOOD

Vegetarian cuisine is not really found in any abundance in Hungary. There are very few vegetarian restaurants, though as interest in vegetarian food increases, more are appearing. Restaurants and shops can be found on the website of the Hungarian branch of the International Vegetarian Union, www.vegetarian.hu.

Vegetarians will usually find some meat-free dishes on the menu. *Főzelék*, a vegetable dish that often accompanies steak, can be ordered on its own or with egg. *Lecsó*, a tomato and pepper casserole, is a popular side dish that is a substantial meal in itself. Other meat-free specialities include *túrós csusza*, a pasta dish served with cottage cheese and sour cream. Ethnic restaurants often offer a wider range of vegetarian dishes.

RESERVATIONS

In Hungary it is customary to join other guests at a table, especially during the busy lunchtime. To secure a private table in advance, it is advisable to reserve it. This applies equally to Hungary's exclusive restaurants as well as to budget establishments.

CHILDREN

Children are welcomed in all restaurants without exception. If children's portions do not appear on the menu, then the chef will prepare suitable dishes and portions to order, usually at half price. The only exception is dessert, but this can often be shared. However, the desserts in Hungarian restaurants are so delicious (and sweet) that most children will happily eat a whole portion.

MENUS

By law, all Hungarian restaurants display a menu with prices by the entrance, and generally this is translated into English, or more commonly, German. The name of the dish is followed by a brief description. The day's "special" – a set menu consisting of a soup, a main course and a dessert – is listed at the top of the menu. Set menus are often very good value and provide an ideal opportunity to sample specialities.

The prices should also be displayed. If they are not, it is wise to go elsewhere. The introduction of printed and itemized bills has made it increasingly difficult for hidden extras to be added to the final bill.

In most restaurants the waiters tend to round up the bill. This led to a scandal in the late 1990s when a list of establishments doing this to excess was published on the internet. The government closed the offending establishments, and the practice has now stopped. Visitors should still be cautious, however, and note how much everything they order should cost. By selecting a restaurant from those we recommend *(see pp282–93)*, such problems should be avoided.

TIPPING

In some restaurants a service charge is included in the final bill, but this is not common practice. If a service charge has been included, it should say so on the bill. If such a charge has not been levied, it is customary to leave your waiter a generous tip of at least 10 per cent. Note that even if a service charge is included, a smaller additional tip will still be expected.

Tigris restaurant *(see p283)*, Budapest

The Flavours of Hungary

The fusion of Magyar, Turkish, Balkan and even French influences has made Hungarian cuisine one of the most interesting and flavourful in central Europe. Hungary is a country where cooking know-how has always been a key aspect of the national culture. The improvised stews of nomadic Asiatic settlers survive as a delicacy to this day. Although noted for its game, *foie gras* and rich meaty preparations, such as goulash and the legendary Debreceni sausages, it is also a good place to enjoy freshwater fish and an array of delicious cakes and pastries.

Hungarian peppers

Sausages and meats on sale at the Central Market Hall, Budapest

MEAT

Beef is Hungary's favourite meat and, as a result, is produced in large quantities, usually to a very high standard. Cuts of beef are a regular feature on Hungarian tables and menus, especially in Budapest, and veal is becoming increasingly

popular too. Steak is widely dished up with a rich sauce as in *Belszín Budapest módra* (chicken livers, mushrooms and peas). Beef is also used to make the many types of goulash, although pork is another key ingredient in this dish, especially in *gulyásleves* (goulash soup). Pork is found in a wide range of other stews and sausages, and is eaten as bacon.

POULTRY AND GAME

Geese are a large part of Hungary's culinary tradition, which is the world's second biggest producer of *foie gras* (after France). *Foie gras* is almost the national dish, usually cooked in its own fat and served warm. It is also found in pâtés and *confits*. Goose skin is widely enjoyed too, fried in its own fat and served with pickles.

Chestnut slice
Chocolate marzipan cake
Chocolate wafer cake
"Domino" cake
Apple slice
Cheesecake
Poppy seed slice

Selection of typical Hungarian cakes and pastries

LOCAL DISHES AND SPECIALITIES

Despite strong foreign influences, the classic dishes of Hungary dominate menus in the country's restaurants and cafés. Many show their roots in one of Hungary's three historical regions. Goulash and its many variants, for example, is a dish of the Great Plain, the traditional method of cooking it in a kettle reflecting the nomadic past of the Plain's inhabitants. *Foie gras* may have been introduced into the country by the Austrian Habsburgs, but has become so popular that it is key to the cuisine of the Northern Highlands, where most geese are now bred.

White asparagus

Transdanubia, and the area around Budapest, have always had the sweetest tooth and nearly all the nation's favourite cakes and desserts originate from here.

Lángos *Crisp and golden, deep-fried potato flour doughnuts make a popular, filling snack, served with soured cream.*

Market stall, laden with root vegetables and strings of dried peppers

Duck is another regular on Hungarian menus, frequently roasted with chestnuts or berries and served with red cabbage. Partridge may also be on offer, roasted with bacon and herbs. Rabbit, hare and venison are common as well, usually dished-up in spicy, goulash-style sauces.

FISH

Trout is probably the most widely eaten fish, although carp, perch, roach, zander and even eels can be found on most menus. A popular soup is *halászlé*, made with trout and carp and seasoned with a generous dash of paprika. Another favourite is *csuka tejfölös tormával* (pike in horseradish sauce). Many Budapest restaurants offer a variety of imported fish, but these are usually expensive.

VEGETABLES

Potatoes, parsnips and cabbage are usually the main vegetables. But from May to July, fine white asparagus appears on market stalls, with many restaurants

Roasting chestnuts, a common sight on Budapest's winter streets

serving *spárgaleves*, a rich creamy soup made from asparagus and veal stock.

Paprika peppers are a culinary staple. They are either cooked as part of a dish – *töltött paprika* (peppers stuffed with meat and rice) are served up everywhere – or dried and ground up to be used as a spice. There are hundreds of different types of ground paprika, which vary in flavour and strength, but they all fit into seven broad categories: "special" (sweet and very mild); "mild" (faintly spicy); "delicatesse" (slightly hot); "sweet" (mild but fairly aromatic); "semi-sweet" (medium hot); "rose" (hot); and "hot" (fiery).

BEST LOCAL SNACKS

Sausages Street vendors everywhere offer the lightly smoked Debreceni sausage, made from beef, pork, paprika and garlic. It is generally eaten with bread and mustard.

Chestnuts In winter, Budapest is crammed with stalls selling freshly roasted chestnuts.

Pancakes, fritters and doughnuts Snack bars all over the country serve tasty, fried, doughy snacks all day long. Try *alma pongyolában* (apple fritters).

Gingerbread Shops devoted to selling gingerbread are everywhere. At Christmas it is often highly decorated and given as a present.

Belszín Budapest Módra *Slices of fine sirloin steak served in a mushroom, pea and chicken liver sauce.*

Gulyásleves *A type of goulash, this pork, beef and vegetable soup is flavoured with onion, caraway and paprika.*

Dobos Torta *Fine slices of sponge cake layered with chocolate cream and topped with chocolate icing.*

What to Drink in Hungary

Hungary is famous for its excellent wines and, although it is not a big country, it has over 20 wine regions *(see pp28–9)*. These regions produce all the characteristic wine styles, from *pezsgő* (sparkling wine) and light whites that come from Mátra, near Lake Balaton, to dry reds from Villány or Eger, as well as Tokaji, a distinctive sweet dessert wine from Tokaj. Many wines from different vineyards are matured in the maze of underground cellars in Budafok. They are all widely available in Budapest's restaurants, wine bars and wine shops. As well as being a prominent wine producer, Hungary also makes beer, *pálinka* (a drink distilled from different orchard fruits), several types of brandy and a bitter herb liqueur called Unicum.

American-style drinks cabinet

Light Hungarian beers

PÁLINKA

Kecskemét is the largest region that produces the alcoholic drink *pálinka,* which is distilled from fruit grown in the orchards situated on the Great Hungarian Plain, some 100 km (60 miles) southeast of Budapest. *Pálinka* is a spirit native to Hungary and comes in a variety of flavours including *barack* (apricot) and *cseresznye* (cherry). The best of them, however, is *szilva* (plum) which comes from the Szatmár district and is much favoured by the Hungarians.

Pálinka is not the only spirit indigenous to Hungary. Other examples include Törköly, a spirit distilled from rape, which possesses a very delicate flavour, and Vilmos, a brandy made from Williams pears.

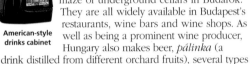

Barack pálinka

SPARKLING WINES

Sparkling wine, called *pezsgő* (the Hungarian word for "sparkling"), enjoys a good reputation in Hungary. The classic method of producing these wines was introduced to Hungary from France by József Törley, in 1881. It was Törley who

Pezsgő and Hungaria by Törley

built the first production plant in Budafok, which continues to produce excellent sparkling wines.

Today, Hungary has several other vineyards producing *pezsgő*, mainly concentrated around Budapest, in the Pannónia and Balatonboglár regions. As well as Törley, Hungaria is another good label to look out for.

HUNGARIAN BEERS

Hungarians have been turning increasingly to beer as their chosen drink as it goes exceptionally well with many traditional, paprika-flavoured Hungarian dishes, goulash among them. There are three remaining authentic Hungarian breweries. These are Arany Ászok, Kőbányai (which was established in the Kőbánya district of Budapest in 1854) and the excellent Dreher brewery. Unfortunately, many other formerly Hungarian breweries have now been taken over by large foreign corporations. However, many of these brands are also well known and all are widely available in Budapest.

HUNGARIAN WINES

The choice of good wine available in Hungary has increased dramatically over the past few years. This is thanks to the ever-improving wines being matured in private cellars. The styles currently

One of Budafok's cellars, where wines are aged in barrels

Egri Bikavér, "Bull's Blood", a full-bodied red wine

A dry white wine from the Badacsony vineyards

favoured by the producers include dry white Chardonnay and Riesling, medium-dry Zödszilváni, Hárslevelü and Szürkebarát, medium-sweet Tramini and the aromatic Muskotály, which is produced in Badacsony, Balatonboglár, Csopak and Somló.

Among red wines, the dry Kékfrankos, Burgundi, Oportó, Cabernet and Pinot Noir are popular, as is the medium-dry Merlot, which is produced in Siklós, Sopron, Szekszárd, Tihany and Villány.

Another vine-growing district is Eger, which is famous for its aromatic, robust red Egri Leányka and the dry red Egri Bikavér, or "Bull's Blood", which is produced from a combination of three grape varieties. Other Hungarian wines take their names from their place of origin or the variety of grape from which they are produced.

TOKAJI

The dessert wine Tokaji has a very different style. Its bouquet and flavour come from a mould that grows only in the fork of the Bodrog and Tisza rivers and the volcanic soil in which the vines grow *(see p228)*. Tokaji ranges from sweet to dry and is full-bodied and rich. Worth sampling is Aszú, which is made with the addition of overripe grapes harvested after the first frost. The proportion of these grapes added to the must (grape juice) determines the body and sweetness. The more grapes used, the richer and sweeter the Aszú.

Although cheap varieties of Tokaji do exist, they lack the quality of the genuine article.

UNICUM

Invented in 1790 to subdue indigestion, Unicum is made from a blend of 40 Hungarian herbs. The herbs, which are gathered in three separate areas, are combined to produce this bitter liqueur. Unicum can be drunk either as an apéritif before a meal or afterwards as a *digestif* with coffee.

The recipe has been held by the Zwack family, and remained a secret, since the reign of Austrian Emperor Joseph II.

Originally, Unicum was prescribed as a remedy for the king by the court physician, who was himself a member of the Zwack family.

Unicum herb liqueur

Sweet Tokaji Szamorodni

Dry Tokaji Szamorodni

Tokaji Aszú, a renowned golden dessert wine

Pear-flavoured Vilmos liqueur

Sisi, an apricot liqueur

Choosing a Restaurant

The restaurants in this guide have been selected across a wide price range for their exceptional food, good value and location. The chart lists restaurants by region, starting in the capital, Budapest. Map references refer to the Street Finder Budapest and the Road Map (*see pp118–23 and inside back cover*).

PRICE CATEGORIES
For a three-course meal for one with half a bottle of wine and including service:

Ⓕ Under 4,000 HUF
ⒻⒻ 4,000–5,500 HUF
ⒻⒻⒻ 5,500–7,000 HUF
ⒻⒻⒻⒻ 7,000–8,500 HUF
ⒻⒻⒻⒻⒻ Over 8,500 HUF

BUDAPEST

CASTLE DISTRICT Pest Buda Vendéglő
Fortuna utca 3 **Tel** *(1) 212 58 80*   **Map** 1 B4

A small, elegant restaurant with arcaded walls in a listed building, part of the former underground cave system gives space to its popular and extensive Hungarian and international wine cellar. The menu itself is not all that long but it is interesting nevertheless, and all the dishes are excellently prepared.

CASTLE DISTRICT Alabárdos Étterem
Országház utca 2 **Tel** *(1) 356 08 51*   **Map** 1 A4

A truly exclusive place in an outstanding Gothic building, serving Hungarian specialities from old, pre-paprika times made to please today's tastebuds. Everything from the service to the atmosphere exudes class, and the prices are as expensive as anywhere in the city. Evening guitar music adds to the candle-lit ambience.

CASTLE DISTRICT Fekete Holló
Országház utca 10 **Tel** *(1) 356 23 67*   **Map** 1 A4

In a terrific location up on Castle Hill this little gem is a super, traditional Hungarian restaurant where the kitsch medieval decor does little to detract from the excellent food. All the Hungarian favourites are on the menu, though there is little for vegetarians. Service can be slow, because the place is always full of happy diners.

CASTLE DISTRICT Pierrot Café Restaurant
Fortuna utca 14 **Tel** *(1) 375 69 71*   **Map** 1 B4

This place opened as a private café during Communist times, when it was one of a kind. It holds its own against stiff competition and its super atmosphere keeps a loyal crowd coming. It has been redesigned, but the original, elegant interior still has a cosy café feel. Live piano music in the evening, and all day at weekends. Highly recommended.

CASTLE DISTRICT Rivalda Café & Restaurant
Színház utca 5–9 **Tel** *(1) 489 02 36*   **Map** 1 B5

Next to the Castle Theatre, the Rivalda's decor is theatre-inspired yet not over-the-top. Its contemporary international cuisine with a frequently changing menu reflects the seasons, with most dishes based on local, fresh ingredients. Many dishes are inventive, and all are superbly presented. There is agreeable jazz piano music in the evenings.

GELLÉRT HILL AND TABÁN Búsuló Juhász Étterem
Kelenhegyi út 58 **Tel** *(1) 209 16 49*   **Map** 3 C3

Spectacular views can be enjoyed from this traditional Hungarian restaurant on the western slopes of Gellért Hill. Lighter versions of a wide choice of Hungarian specialities are a nod to current trends and satisfy those not always mad on paprika.

GELLÉRT HILL AND TABÁN Márványmenyasszony Étterem
Márvány utca 6 **Tel** *(1) 487 30 90*   **Map** 3 A1

An old-style Hungarian restaurant with a fine Gypsy band playing every night, this place is hidden away, yet it is not hard to find as its fine food, great prices and lively atmosphere are legendary. There are several rooms of various sizes that make it a great choice for groups, families or those wanting some peace away from the music.

GELLÉRT HILL AND TABÁN Tabáni Kakas Vendéglő
Attila út 27 **Tel** *(1) 225 04 78*   **Map** 3 B1

Poultry dishes are a speciality at this small restaurant with a family atmosphere. Goose and duck feature in soups and main courses, including the excellent goose breast with bread dumplings and vegetable sauce. There is no shortage of *foie gras* on offer, and a good selection of after-dinner ports to wash it all down with, at low prices.

AROUND PARLIAMENT Govinda
Vigyázó Ferenc utca 4 **Tel** *(1) 269 16 25*   **Map** 2 D5

Popular at lunchtimes, this is a vegetarian fast-food Indian restaurant where meatless cooking does not mean flavourless food. Diners are advised to choose with care – some of the dishes are extremely spicy! The adjacent shop sells Far Eastern-style gifts and krishna literature, and there is even a meditation room.

Key to Symbols *see back cover flap*

AROUND PARLIAMENT Kadar Étkezde

Klauzal tér 9 **Tel** *(1) 321 36 22*   **Map** *7 A2*

Gloriously rough and ready lunchtime place where you can pretend that Hungary is still in the dark ages of Communism. The food is great value, with huge portions of stew and goulash for around 1,000 forints. The red and white checked tablecloths are so kitsch you will love them and want to bring them home with you.

AROUND PARLIAMENT Picasso Point

Hajós utca 31 **Tel** *(20) 342 14 46*   **Map** *2 E4*

Just a short way from the Opera House *(see pp88–9)*, Picasso Point is a café and restaurant serving good bistro food, pizzas, strong coffee and superb cakes. Food is served all day, but the Picasso Point is especially popular in the evenings as a bar and café. There is a nightclub in the cellar, so guests can stay all day if they wish!

AROUND PARLIAMENT Regős Vendéglő

Szófia utca 33 **Tel** *(1) 321 19 21*   **Map** *2 F4*

The decor and ambience of this small, welcoming restaurant is reminiscent of 1970s Hungary. The cuisine here is traditional Hungarian and portions are hearty. The lunchtime buffet provides good value for money and there is also a daily changing menu.

AROUND PARLIAMENT Belvárosi Lugas Étterem

Bajcsy-Zsilinszky út 15/a **Tel** *(1) 302 53 93*   **Map** *2 D4*

Well-made, hearty dishes served in a simple, appealing atmosphere make this place a favourite with locals. Informal and relaxed, it offers tremendous value, especially the daily specials that are chalked up on a blackboard. Great soups. In summer tables are set up on the pavement, although the constant traffic may disturb any conversation.

AROUND PARLIAMENT Buena Vista Étterem

Liszt Ferenc tér 4–5 **Tel** *(1) 344 63 03*   **Map** *2 F4*

Providing a welcome retreat from busy Liszt Ferenc tér, Buena Vista Étterem is one of the oldest restaurants on the square. The international and Hungarian dishes are all beautifully presented, the service is excellent and there is an impressive wine list. Grab a table outside and watch the world go by.

AROUND PARLIAMENT Café Kör

Sas utca 17 **Tel** *(1) 311 00 53*   **Map** *2 D5*

Booking is recommended at this popular bistro that serves good salad plates and Hungarian/European-inspired dishes, none of which will win prizes but all offering great value. Vegetarian food is made to order. A good selection of Hungarian wines to sample by the glass betrays the fact that this café started off as a wine bar.

AROUND PARLIAMENT Marquis de Salade

Hajós utca 43 **Tel** *(1) 302 40 86*   **Map** *2 E4*

An extensive menu from around the world, including interesting lamb dishes from Azerbaijan and Georgia, as well as basic Hungarian fare, such as goulash, is on offer here. Vegetarians have plenty to choose from, and the restaurant's name usually puts a smile on the face of diners. The Marquis offers good value too, rare for this part of the city.

AROUND PARLIAMENT Sir Lancelot lovagi étterem

Podmaniczky utca 14 **Tel** *(1) 302 44 56*   **Map** *2 E3*

At this excellent restaurant, Renaissance-inspired dishes are served by people in period costumes. Only knives and spoons are provided for the substantial portions, which the diners can rarely manage to finish. Renaissance music is played in the evenings. Booking is recommended, especially for weekends.

AROUND PARLIAMENT Pomo D'Oro Restaurant

Arany János utca 9 **Tel** *(1) 302 64 73*   **Map** *2 D5*

As well as traditional Italian meals, many of the dishes served are from the head chef's own collection of recipes. The menu changes daily and often includes different varieties of mushroom, fresh fish specialities and the use of seasonal vegetables. The dishes prepared at the table side are popular with guests.

AROUND PARLIAMENT Tigris

Mérleg utca 10 **Tel** *(1) 317 37 15*   **Map** *2 D5*

This turn-of-the-century style restaurant serves traditional and modern Hungarian cuisine using fresh local ingredients. The beautifully presented dishes include such choices as crawfish in a spicy garlic and white wine sauce or rabbit served with dumplings. Good selection of Hungarian wines and delicious smoked meats prepared in-house.

AROUND PARLIAMENT Fausto's

Székely Mihály 2 **Tel** *(1) 877 62 10*   **Map** *2 E5*

Following the success of his London, New York and Valence restaurants, Fausto Di Vora's Budapest venue receives the same acclaim as its counterparts. Specialising in Medediterrean and international cuisine, Fausto's also offers an excellent selection of Hungarian and Italian wines. You'll experience a truly gastronomic delight while dining here.

AROUND PARLIAMENT Klassz

Andrássy út 41   **Map** *2 E4*

With a shopfront looking onto Budapest's grandest avenue and a floral wallpaper-lined interior, Klassz is indeed a classy place to eat. Light international dishes are accompanied by fine Hungarian wines, and the adjoining shop sells bottles to take home.

CENTRAL PEST Hanna Ortodoxkóser Étterem
Dob utca 35 **Tel** *(1) 342 10 72* Map 2 E5

This simple, orthodox kosher eatery in the courtyard of the Orthodox Synagogue on Kazinczy utca serves traditional Jewish dishes and kosher wines. Opening hours are from 8am to 4pm, except on Friday and the Sabbath, when the restaurant also opens in the evenings. Sabbath meals need to be paid for the day before or after.

CENTRAL PEST BohémTanya
Paulay Ede utca 6 **Tel** *(1) 268 14 53* Map 2 E5

For all those looking for reasonably priced, hearty Hungarian food and not too fussy about their surroundings, the BohémTanya (meaning Bohemian Farm) is a good choice. Guests take their places in wooden alcoves large enough for eight, and when the restaurant is busy they may be asked to share their table with other diners.

CENTRAL PEST Vak Varjú
Paulay Ede utca 7 **Tel** *(1) 268 08 88* Map 2 E5

With large windows overlooking one of Budapest's busiest streets, at the "Blind Crow" guests enjoy a range of meaty dishes. There's a lively atmosphere and a wonderful raised section, as well as live jazz performances several evenings a week.

CENTRAL PEST Haxen Király
Király utca 100 **Tel** *(1) 351 67 93* Map 2 F4

For the classic Germanic experience of lederhosen-wearing gents playing accordion music as cheerful waitresses serve up bratwurst, sauerkraut and huge mugs of beer to Budapest's friendliest patrons, visitors can do no better than this restaurant. The atmosphere is raucous and not for the fainthearted, but hard to beat for all-round good times.

CENTRAL PEST Károlyi Étterem és Kávéház
Károlyi Mihály utca 16 **Tel** *(1) 328 02 40* Map 4 E1

In the lovely courtyard of the Károlyi Palace is this elegant, sophisticated restaurant. Worth trying is the *borjúpaprikás lángosban* (veal paprika stew with potato pancakes). Its attractive gardens are uncommon in the city centre. At weekends it is worth booking – the restaurant is often closed for weddings in summer.

CENTRAL PEST Noir et L'Or
Király utca 17 **Tel** *(1) 413 02 36* Map 2 F4

This elegant restaurant has, as the name suggests, a slick black and gold interior. On the menu is colonial French cuisine seasoned with exotic spices, as well as some Hungarian specialities. The menu is accompanied by an excellent wine list. Half-price cocktails are available between 3 and 6pm and there are reduced-price menu options every Sunday.

CENTRAL PEST Soul Café & Restaurant
Ráday utca 11–13 **Tel** *(1) 217 69 86* Map 4 F3

This intimate restaurant is located on the once gloomy but now thriving Ráday utca, which is filled with cafés, restaurants and shops. The atmosphere is pleasant and easy, and the well-prepared and tasty international cuisine vies for space on the menu with Hungarian standards. All taste delicious, and there is plenty for vegetarians.

CENTRAL PEST Carmel Étterem
Kazinczy utca 31 **Tel** *(1) 342 45 85* Map 2 E5

This legendary, non-kosher Hungarian-Jewish cellar restaurant is always crowded with locals and tourists enjoying its famed *sólet* (cholent) with smoked goose. The food may not be entirely kosher but there are some super kosher wines available. Reservation is recommended, especially at the weekend.

CENTRAL PEST Centrál Kávéház és Étterem
Károlyi Mihály utca 9 **Tel** *(1) 266 21 10* Map 4 E1

This old-time café-restaurant with its authentic, relaxed pre-war central-European feel is open for breakfast and late-night dinner, serving good Hungarian and international cuisine. It also does excellent cakes, and in fact this place is as popular for coffee and cakes as it is for lunch and dinner.

CENTRAL PEST Mátyás Pince
Március 15 tér 7 **Tel** *(1) 318 16 93* Map 4 D1

While this restaurant is unquestionably touristy, and incredibly popular with tour groups who make getting a table a challenge, it is deservedly popular. The food is super – huge portions of Hungarian classics are served up by friendly waiters – and there is usually a Gypsy band on hand to create a rollicking atmosphere. Recommended.

CENTRAL PEST Baraka
Andrássy út 111 **Tel** *(1) 462 21 89* Map 4 E1

At Baraka fine French-inspired food is served, much of it genuinely inventive. This trendy restaurant has moved to the Hotel Andrássy and is a popular place – booking is recommended. The wine list is excellent and tempting, but as long as imported wines are avoided, meals work out (relatively) cheaply.

CENTRAL PEST Buddha-Bar
Váci utca 34 **Tel** *(1) 799 73 01* Map 4 D1

Spread over two levels, the Buddha-Bar's stylish and sophisticated interior is an exquisite fusion of both Western and Oriental styles, with mahogany furniture, Chinese artwork and elegant carvings. The food is Asia-Pacific coastal cuisine, including the special Buddha-Bar sushi. Live DJs and great cocktails.

Key to Price Guide *see p282* **Key to Symbols** *see back cover flap*

CENTRAL PEST Kárpátia Étterem és Söröző

Ferenciek tere 7–8 **Tel** *(1) 317 35 96*

Map *4 E1*

First opened in 1877, this is Hungarian cuisine, hospitality and imperial elegance at its best, set in an understated, beautifully ornamented interior. The beer hall, which shares the premises, serves the same dishes, but at lower prices in a less formal atmosphere. Gypsy music in the evenings. Reservation is advised.

CENTRAL PEST Kispipa Étterem

Akácfa utca 38 **Tel** *(1) 342 25 87*

Map *2 F5*

This excellent restaurant serves a wide choice of international and Hungarian dishes. Rezső Seres, who composed "Gloomy Sunday", no longer sits at the piano, but many of his songs are still played. He would be delighted to learn that the service and the food are as good as they were in his day.

CENTRAL PEST Százéves Étterem

Pesti Barnabás utca 2 **Tel** *(1) 267 02 88*

Map *4 D1*

Apparently the oldest restaurant in Budapest, first opened in 1831, and housed in a beautiful Baroque building furnished with antique pieces, Százéves Étterem offers Hungarian and international cuisine plus Gypsy music. Desserts here are outstanding – guests should leave enough room to try one. Expensive, but recommended.

FURTHER AFIELD Maharaja Restaurant

Csengery utca 24 **Tel** *(1) 351 12 89*

Map *2 F4*

In a quiet basement location, just off busy Király utca, Maharaja was the first Indian restaurant to open in Budapest. Its authentic curries, subtly flavoured with herbs and spices, have earned the restaurant a loyal following. The mainly North Indian cuisine includes meat, fish and vegetarian choices and there is a wide range of delicious desserts.

FURTHER AFIELD Bajai Halászcsárda

Buda Hills, Hollós út 2 **Tel** *(1) 275 52 45*

This eatery, by the Svábhegy cog-rail stop serves traditional Hungarian dishes. The speciality is fresh river fish – a real treat is the Baja fish soup with a huge portion of carp fillets served on the side. The menu also features goulash, and for dessert the fried doughnuts are worth trying. Bus number 21 from Moskva tér runs close by.

FURTHER AFIELD Firkász Étterem

Tátra utca 18 **Tel** *(1) 450 11 18*

Map *2 D2*

As the name "scribbler" might suggest, Firkász is popular with a literary crowd. The walls of the rustic dining room are decorated with old maps and photographs and the fare is simple Hungarian. Enjoy a meal and a glass of wine alongside charming live piano music. Good service and lovely ambience. Reservations are recommended.

FURTHER AFIELD Jókai Étterem

Buda Hills, Hollós út 5 **Tel** *(1) 395 36 58*

A relaxed restaurant in a lovely 19th-century villa in the hills near the Svábhegy cog-rail station, it excels with attentive service and well-prepared classic Hungarian dishes at low prices. The terrace is pleasant in the summer. Visitors not wishing to do the journey on the cog railway can take bus number 21 from Moskva tér which runs close by.

FURTHER AFIELD Jorgosz

Térezváros, Csengery utca 24 **Tel** *(1) 351 12 89*

Map *2 F4*

The Jorgosz is a terrific choice for all those wanting a change from Hungarian cuisine, as well as for vegetarians who may be short-changed by what is generally on offer in Budapest. A whole array of outstanding meze are served, main courses based on meat, fish, cheese or beans, and probably the best salads in town. The prices represent great value.

FURTHER AFIELD Bagolyvár Étterem

Városliget, Állatkerti út 2 **Tel** *(1) 468 31 10*

In the heart of Városliget (City Park), this enchanting restaurant (whose name means "Owl's Castle") offers home-style cooking of a high standard – the chef and waiting staff are all female. A Gypsy cimbalom player provides music in the evenings. The restaurant also organizes regular cookery courses.

FURTHER AFIELD Baross Étterem

Istvánmező, Baross tér 11/A **Tel** *(1) 343 62 38*

A beautifully restored restaurant in Budapest's late-19th-century Eastern Railway Station, Keleti pu, serving excellent food. The whole experience leaves guests feeling that they are about to board the Orient Express, which did once stop here. There is live piano music in the evenings.

FURTHER AFIELD Rosenstein Restaurant

Mosonyi utca 3 **Tel** *(1) 333 34 92*

This welcoming, family-run restaurant is located close to Keleti railway station. The multilingual menu features international and Hungarian cuisine, as well as a selection of traditional Jewish dishes. Friendly service, a wide selection of wines and excellent homemade desserts.

FURTHER AFIELD Csalogány 26 Étterem és Kávézó

Víziváros, Csalogány utca 26 **Tel** *(1) 201 78 92*

Map *1 B3*

This popular and trendy restaurant/café has a bright and breezy, modern Mediterranean interior. Excellent poultry, fish and meat dishes are all grilled on lava stones for a real burst of flavour. For such a meat-oriented place there is also a surprisingly good selection of vegetarian dishes and salads. Good wines, though not a large selection.

FURTHER AFIELD Gundel Étterem

Városliget, Állatkerti út 2 **Tel** *(1) 468 40 40*

Probably Hungary's most famous restaurant, the Gundel, while not cheap, is no longer the most expensive. The menu has innovative Hungarian and international dishes, including goose liver prepared in many different ways. In the evenings, Gypsy music livens up the atmosphere. The Sunday brunch buffet is excellent value. Lovely gardens.

FURTHER AFIELD Kacsa

Víziváros, Fő utca 75 **Tel** *(1) 201 99 92*

Map *1 B4*

The Kacsa serves some of the finest food in the country. The service is as ostentatious as the food is splendid, with dishes presented under silver serving domes, whisked away with great ceremony. Although duck dominates the menu, there is far more on offer, including inventive vegetarian options. Outstanding, but dreadfully expensive.

FURTHER AFIELD Pavillon de Paris

Víziváros, Fő utca 20 **Tel** *(1) 225 0174*

Map *1 B4*

This outstanding French restaurant scores highly in every field. The building itself is a protected national treasure. The main dining room is sparsely yet tastefully decorated. The service is efficient and friendly without being pretentious, and live jazz softens the mood most evenings. The food is international-French, and there is a garden in the rear.

FURTHER AFIELD Robinson

Városliget, Városligeti-tó **Tel** *(1) 422 02 22*

Robinson is justly renowned for having one of the most memorable outdoor dining areas in Budapest, a platform in the middle of Városliget (City Park). Indoors, the setting is equally exquisite, and the food is tremendous anywhere – modern Hungarian dishes prepared by one of the country's best teams of chefs. Highly recommended.

FURTHER AFIELD Vadrózsa Étterem

Rózsadomb, Pentelei Molnár utca 15 **Tel** *(1) 326 58 17*

Map *1 A1*

This exclusive and luxurious restaurant in a beautiful Neo-Baroque villa has been run by one family for decades. Soft piano music plays in the evenings, and lovely gardens appeal in summer. It's a taxi ride from central Budapest; the restaurant will happily book one. The food is outstanding, adventurous and expensive, but worth every penny.

AROUND BUDAPEST

ESZTERGOM Csülök Csárda

Batthyány utca 9 **Tel** *(33) 412 420*

Map *C3*

Popular with those who have been turned away from Prímás Pince *(see below)* – which is often booked up – the Csülök Csárda, a short walk down Majer utca, is worth seeking out in its own right. Good though unadventurous Hungarian cuisine is served here at decent prices, and the wine list is, in fact, better than that of its more famous neighbour.

ESZTERGOM Prímás Pince

Szent István tér 4 **Tel** *(33) 313 495*

Map *C3*

What has long been an Esztergom favourite has become an international one thanks to countless happy diners who come here year after year. While the cuisine is standard Hungarian and the wine list less than worthy, the setting in the cellars of the castle is legendary. Disappointingly, it closes at 10pm, with last kitchen orders a little before.

GÖDÖLLŐ Galéria

Szabadság tér 8 **Tel** *(28) 418 691*

Map *D3*

Plenty of choice on an extensive menu, featuring 60 Hungarian and international dishes (although not much for vegetarians), is on offer at this simple, cheap and hearty Galéria pension. A lack of elegance is more than compensated in charm, and the food is terrific value for money. The service is unmatched in town.

RÁCKEVE Savoyai

Kossuth L. utca 95 **Tel** *(24) 424 189*

Map *C4*

The menu at this outstanding restaurant in the elegant setting of the Savoy Castle is dominated by game and fish dishes, and there is a fine selection of Hungarian wines in the cellar too. Outside, the garden and terrace are very popular during summer. Prices are surprisingly reasonable given the opulence of the surroundings.

SZENTENDRE Dixie Csirke

Dumtsa Jeno utca 16 **Tel** *(26) 311 008*

Map *D3*

The wonderful Dixie Csirke (Dixie Chicken), a fast-food eatery near Fő tér, is ideal for busy sightseers visiting Szentendre and needing a lunch on the go. As it's open from 8am, visitors can take breakfast here too before setting off to explore the town centre. In the evening, the Dixie closes early at 7pm.

SZENTENDRE Rab Ráby

Kucsera Ferenc utca 1 **Tel** *(26) 310 819*

Map *D3*

While the decor is a little touristy for some tastes, the quality that comes out of the kitchen will be to everyone's liking in this enjoyably eclectic eatery. The usual Hungarian favourites all make an appearance on the menu, although there are some vegetarian and fish dishes too. The sweets are memorable.

Key to Price Guide *see p282* **Key to Symbols** *see back cover flap*

SZENTENDRE Aranysárkány

Alkotmány utca 1/a **Tel** *(26) 301 479*

Map D3

The Golden Dragon may suggest Chinese in any other country, but in Hungary it means high-quality local dishes, with game taking pride of place. There is goose, venison and even fried pigeon on the menu, all cooked in an open kitchen. The prices are good, but patrons are advised to choose their wine carefully if they are on a budget.

SZENTENDRE Nemzeti Bormuzeum es Labirintus Étterem

Bogdányi utca 10 **Tel** *(26) 317 054*

Map D3

This outstanding restaurant, in the cellars of Szentendre's National Wine Museum, offers a great selection of traditional Hungarian food, including venison, all served with equally worthy wines. Besides the cellars there is a small room on the ground floor for larger groups, and a small but sublime terrace.

VÁC Halászkert

Liszt Ferenc sétány 9 **Tel** *(27) 315 985*

Map D3

Located on the banks of the Danube, Halászkert offers an extensive menu of grilled or roasted meat and fish dishes, as well as a good selection of vegetarian options. For river views, dine on the terrace, or sit inside during the cooler months. A good wine list and live music on weekends.

VISEGRÁD Renaissance

Fő tér 11 **Tel** *(26) 398 081*

Map C3

There are few good restaurants in Visegrád, but this touristy but reliable Renaissance place is one of the better establishments. It's a medieval-themed restaurant, so all diners sit at huge long or round tables and wear a paper crown. The meat portions are huge, wine is served from great jugs, and there is jousting in the courtyard.

NORTHERN TRANSDANUBIA

BÜK Bajor (Bavaria)

Gyurácz utca 6/A **Tel** *(94) 358 324*

Map A3

Located in the centre of the village of Bük, a short distance from the thermal bath complex, this pension and restaurant is famous for its great selection of genuine Bavarian beers. Food is simple Hungarian and German cooking, with great homemade sausages and spicy hot goulash especially recommended. Excellent garden and terrace.

FERTŐD Gránátos

Joseph Haydn utca 2 **Tel** *(99) 370 944*

Map A3

Though a little rough around the edges, there are few places better in Fertőd to enjoy a good meal than the colonnaded terrace at Gránátos. The menu is simple but portions are large and the quality of the food is decent enough. A coffee on the terrace, in the shadow of the Esterhazy Castle, is equally enjoyable *(see p167)*.

FERTŐD Dóri

Pomogyi út 1 **Tel** *(99) 370 838*

Map A3

This restaurant enjoys a wonderful setting within the UNESCO World Heritage Fertó-Hanság National Park. Adjacent to the bicycle path encircling lake Fertó, Dóri is an ideal spot to stop for lunch before heading to Esterházy Castle. The restaurant offers a broad range of international and Hungarian dishes.

GYŐR Belgian Beer Café

Árpád utca 34 **Tel** *(96) 889 460*

Map B3

The Royal Belgian Beer Café on the ground floor of the Raba hotel is a great place to eat, drink and be merry. Guests will find long wooden tables, a fine selection of Belgian beers, good food and a terrific atmosphere in the evenings. A small street terrace fills up quickly on summer evenings – booking is advisable.

GYŐR Fonte

Schweidel utca 17/Kisfaludy utca 38 **Tel** *(96) 513 810*

Map B3

This marvellous restaurant, in the elegant Fonte hotel, has a fine interior dining room, all vaults and high ceilings, well-dressed waiters and large, round tables, and the outside terrace on Kisfaludy utca is a great place for people-watching. The restaurant has a superb wine cellar and a wine waiter is on hand to help select the best.

GYŐR John Bull Pub

Aradi Vértanúk utca 3 **Tel** *(96) 618 320*

Map B3

While the English pub abroad-type name may be off-putting, this is a genuinely good restaurant, serving great simple and hearty food. The Secessionist building is worth seeing in itself. In summer, on the pedestrian street, a terrace extends the full length of the pub. It is the perfect place to spend an evening in Győr.

GYŐR La Maréda

Apáca utca 4 **Tel** *(96) 510 980*

Map B3

Plush and opulent, dining in this restaurant is like stepping into a scene from the 19th century (the building in fact dates from far earlier – 1617). Imperial charm lines the walls in the form of stucco reliefs, while fine cigars and fine wines complement the often adventurous Hungarian cuisine. Worth every penny.

KŐSZEG Taverna Florian

Várkör 59 **Tel** *(94) 563 072*   **Map** *A3*

Elegant and refined dining on various levels of a splendidly bright red house is set in a quiet location just a short walk from the heart of Kőszeg. Four venues in one, there is a wine cellar, a dining cellar, an elegant ground-floor restaurant and a fine garden and street cafe. Diners can expect only the best Italian-influenced food and friendly service.

KŐSZEG Portré Panzió

Fő tér 7 **Tel** *(94) 363 170*   **Map** *A3*

A lively bar and bistro at the Portré pension serving light meals and a great selection of beers. The terrace out on the square is a great place to watch the people of Kőszeg go by, while the courtyard at the back is a quieter option. The special children's menu is a bonus for any parent and a commendable rarity in Hungary.

LAKE VELENCE, AGÁRD Nádas Csárda

Balatoni út 60 **Tel** *(22) 370 006*   **Map** *C4*

Open from noon to 10pm, this is on first appearance the quintessential Hungarian tourist restaurant as it caters mainly to local tourists, however, the food is surprisingly good. There is live music most summer evenings (it is best not to tip the band or they will continue to play at the same table), and prices are reasonable.

PÁPA Vero-Hotel Arany Griff

Fő tér 15 **Tel** *(89) 312 000*   **Map** *B3*

The delightful, sheltered courtyard terrace is the best place to enjoy the decent Hungarian or international food, including a couple of vegetarian options, served up from the kitchen of the Vero-Hotel Arany Griff Hotel. Prices are not cheap but value for money is good. Tables on the terrace in high summer need to be booked.

SÁRVÁR Várkapu

Várkerület 5 **Tel** *(95) 320 475*   **Map** *A3*

This yellow pension is a great place to try high-quality and ground-breaking Hungarian cuisine. Every month a gala evening is held where the restaurant's chef is given the freedom to create new masterpieces. At other times there is a good selection of classic dishes, all of which are best enjoyed on the little terrace, complete with picket fence.

SOPRON Vadászkurt Vendéglő

Udvarnoki utca 6 **Tel** *(99) 314 385*   **Map** *A3*

At this truly outstanding restaurant diners will find one of the best wine lists in the country (it has its own wine cellar). Everything about this place exudes luxury, from the polished parquet floors to the small but superb garden terrace, a riot of colourful blooms in summer. The fine dishes include goats' cheese from Őrség served with olives and garlic on toast.

SOPRON Lővér Pince

Ady Ede utca 31/b , **Tel** *(99) 313 175*   **Map** *A3*

This historic wine cellar serves a variety of delicious light snacks and showcases some of the greatest wines of Northern Transdanubia. Any number of these wines can be sampled by the glass, and then bought by the bottle or the crate. It closes at 6pm, but is open by pre-arrangement.

SOPRON Wollner

Templom utca 20 **Tel** *(99) 524 400*   **Map** *A3*

In a gorgeous Neo-Baroque house in the heart of Old Sopron, the Wollner hotel is home to some of the city's best food. There are two dining locations: the wine cellar downstairs and the courtyard terrace at the back. Both have the same menu of excellent value, traditional Hungarian dishes. It also holds wine-tasting events.

SOPRON Mediterrano Complex

Lackner Kristóf utca 33/b **Tel** *(99) 508 300*   **Map** *A3*

This is a vast complex of four excellent restaurants in a large shopping and entertainment centre about ten minutes from Old Sopron. Guests dine at Novo restaurant before moving on to the Gino patisserie for coffee and cakes. It is all a bit modern and lacking in atmosphere, but the food – in any of the eateries – cannot be faulted.

SÜMEG Vár Csárda (Castle Inn)

Várkert (Sümegi vár tövében) **Tel** *(87) 350 924*   **Map** *B4*

Next to Sümeg Castle *(see p158)* is this super restaurant, whose covered terrace is a great place to enjoy traditional Hungarian food. There is also a large garden and a delightful indoor dining room, complete with huge, centuries-old wooden beams. The wine cellar is excellent, and the castle's theatrical events can be enjoyed from the restaurant.

SZÉKESFEHÉRVÁR Belgian Beer Café

Szent Istvan 14 **Tel** *(22) 507 585*   **Map** *C4*

Besides the outstanding selection of Belgian beers, the long menu at this eatery offers a good number of traditional Belgian dishes, including mussels, of course, and Belgian sausages. Many are based on high-quality meat cooked in beer and served in rich sauces.

SZÉKESFEHÉRVÁR Kiskulacs Vendéglő

Budai út 26 **Tel** *(22) 502 920*   **Map** *C4*

This is the best – and most expensive – place in the city, a short walk from the heart of the old town. Upmarket Hungarian dishes are served in a refined setting to Székesfehérvár's beautiful set. As a result the presentation of dishes can be overwhelming, although the quality of the food never falters.

Key to Price Guide *see p282* **Key to Symbols** *see back cover flap*

SZOMBATHELY Gödör

Hollán Ernő utca 10–12 **Tel** *(94) 510 078*

Map *A3*

Founded by a group of students, Gödör, "The restaurant of Gourmands", is an inexpensive eatery serving Hungarian fare in an authentic wine cellar. The red-squared tablecloths, granite tableware and excellent food are the restaurant's trademarks. Not to be missed if you are in the area.

SZOMBATHELY Hotel Wagner

Kossuth Lajos utca 15 **Tel** *(94) 322 208*

Map *A3*

Just a short walk from central Fő tér, the restaurant of the Hotel Wagner serves up Hungarian and international dishes in either a cellar, banqueting hall – complete with giant mural – or garden terrace setting. The wine cellar is popular with connoisseurs who flock to its collection of Hungarian wines, all available by the glass.

ZALAEGERSZEG Belgian Beer Café

Kossuth Lajos utca 5 **Tel** *(92) 511 140*

Map *A4*

Another Belgian Beer Café (there are six in Hungary) but the consistent quality of these places makes them a good choice in any city. In Zalaegerszeg it is one of the best places to eat. It also boasts outstanding beers (far better than the local variety), a great vegetarian menu, super service and a classy ambience.

ZIRC Csalogány Étterem

Kardosrét Győri út 16 **Tel** *(88) 416 788*

Map *B3*

Just over 2 km (1 mile) outside Zirc, a town that does not have very many eating options, the Csalogány, which serves up decent if undistinguished Hungarian food that does not cost a fortune, is about the best bet. The goulash is very spicy in this part of Hungary, so visitors who don't like hot food need to exercise caution.

SOUTHERN TRANSDANUBIA

BADACSONY Kisfaludy Haz

Szegedy Róza utca 87 **Tel** *(87) 431 016*

Map *B4*

The best view of Lake Balaton is from the raised terrace of Kisfaludy House. As it's a bit of a hike from the town of Badacsony, jeeps shuttle guests from outside the post office. The food is great value, with the wild poultry spread a real treat. The wine list at this restaurant, set almost in the middle of a vineyard, is exemplary. Open April–November.

BALATONFÜRED Aranykorona

Kossuth utca 11 **Tel** *(87) 580 550*

Map *B4*

Balatonfüred's best-value restaurant is some distance from the lake shore, but well worth the short taxi ride (or brisk, 15-minute walk). Set over two levels, the once-derelict 19th-century house has been renovated and now houses a pub and beer garden besides the restaurant. English is spoken – a bonus in this resort.

BALATONFÜRED Stefánia Vitorlás

Tagore sétány 1 **Tel** *(87) 343 407*

Map *B4*

On the shore of Lake Balaton with views out to Tihany Peninsula, this restaurant is situated in the refurbished clubhouse of the Balatonfüred Rowing and Sailing Club. Serving fish and game dishes to a buzzing crowd from morning until late, it is also the perfect spot to sample great local wine.

BALATONFÜRED Annabella

Deák Ferenc utca 25 **Tel** *(87) 889 450*

Map *B4*

The restaurant at the Annabella hotel, just yards from the lake shore, offers a good-value buffet dinner, as well as Hungarian and international specialities. With excellent views of the swimming pool or the lake, a beer garden and a great selection of wines, it is a good – if not cheap – place to dine. Open May–mid-October.

BALATONFÜRED Borcsa

Tagore sétány **Tel** *(87) 580 070*

Map *B4*

Some of Hungary's finest vegetarian food can be sampled at this distinguished but expensive restaurant. In an enviable location on the Tagore Promenade the views out to the lake are fantastic. There are plenty of options for meat-eaters too, and a tasty children's menu. The pizzas offer the best value.

HÉVÍZ Magyar Csárda

Tavirózsa utca 1 **Tel** *(83) 343 271*

Map *B4*

One of the best restaurants on Tavirózsa utca, a short distance from the centre of Hévíz, this eatery serves decent traditional Hungarian food in a refined but friendly and unstuffy setting. A local legend, the prices are reasonable enough, though not cheap.

HÉVÍZ Öreg Harang Borozo

Dombföldi út 2880 **Tel** *(30) 927 9011*

Map *B4*

Located in the vineyards, slightly outside the town, this family-run tavern and restaurant serves delicious local food and has a great atmosphere. Barbeque evenings, held every Thursday and Friday, feature traditional Hungarian dishes prepared on the open fire. Note: no credit cards accepted.

KESZTHELY Margaréta

Bercsényi utca 60 **Tel** *(83) 314 882*   **Map** *B4*

Small, family-run and really quite cheap, this is a good option for those on a budget. The food comes in giant portions, with plenty of German sausages on the menu besides the more traditional Hungarian fare. There's a good terrace for dining on in warm weather.

KESZTHELY Bacchus

Erzsébet királyné st 18 **Tel** *(83) 510 450*   **Map** *B4*

Serving a wide range of dishes, it is fish from Lake Balaton that takes pride of place on the menu at Bacchus. The setting is great too, with the indoor dining room all dark wooden beams and original, heavy dining tables. Outside is an equally enjoyable small courtyard and covered terrace. Great selection of local wines.

KESZTHELY Hungaria Gösser

Kossuth Lajos utca 35 **Tel** *(83) 312 265*   **Map** *B4*

Not far from Festetics Castle, on the pedestrianized part of Kossuth Lajos utca and the corner of Fő tér, this superb restaurant is in a wonderful, renovated Secession-era house, complete with stained-glass windows. The reasonably priced food is traditional Hungarian with a modern twist. Booking is advisable at this popular place.

MOHÁCS Hálászcsárda

Szent Mihály tér 5 **Tel** *(69) 322 542*   **Map** *C5*

The Fish Soup Tavern serves, unsurprisingly, fish soup in a superb setting where many tables have fine views across the river. The grilled trout (a speciality of this part of Hungary) and carp are particularly good, but there is very little choice for vegetarians on the menu.

PAKS Dunakömlődi Halászcsárda

Csárda utca 1–3 **Tel** *(75) 311 413*   **Map** *C4*

A little rough round the edges, this place nevertheless serves the best fish soup in town, and is the perfect place for a quick lunch while exploring, or passing through Paks. Besides the soup and large juicy steaks, enjoyable but often incomprehensible conversation with locals is all part of the experience.

PÉCS Aranykacsa

Teréz utca 4 **Tel** *(72) 518 860*   **Map** *C5*

The Aranykacsa (meaning Golden Duck) serves delicious Hungarian food in a traditional setting on the ground floor and outside on the pleasant terrace, while downstairs a lively bar and music venue is open until the very early hours. As you may expect from the name, local game is the speciality.

PÉCS Cellárium

Hunyadi János utca 2 **Tel** *(72) 314 596*   **Map** *C5*

In catacombs that allegedly provided shelter from attacking Turks, the Cellárium restaurant is today a refuge from the many tourist traps that dot much of Pécs. The food is great, with local specialities served alongside the classics, and a couple of choices for vegetarians too. There is live music most weekend evenings – reservation is essential.

PÉCS Szent György Fogado

Nagyvárad utca 23 **Tel** *(72) 310 126*   **Map** *C5*

Sharing a building with the Finnish Consulate, the Szent György Fogado offers a good range of local and international dishes at reasonable prices. Service is brisk and friendly, but for a decent but cheap meal in Pécs this place is just about the best option.

SIÓFOK Balaton Restaurant

Kinizsi utca 3 **Tel** *(84) 311 313*   **Map** *C4*

This family-run restaurant is located just a short walk from Lake Balaton. The fare here is traditional Hungarian and there is a lovely sunny garden and terrace for diners during the summer months. Specialities include goose-liver with Mako onion, and Balaton's excellent beef and red wine stew.

SIÓFOK Fogas

Fő utca 184 **Tel** *(84) 311 405*   **Map** *C4*

Housed in Siófok's former post office, the Fogas (perch) unsurprisingly specializes in fish freshly caught in Lake Balaton. There is also a selection of meat dishes and a very good children's menu. All of the very tempting pastries are made daily on the premises.

SIÓFOK Camelot

Vécsey Károly utca 2 **Tel** *(84) 350 698*   **Map** *C4*

Diners are greeted by a court jester at this enjoyable, medieval-themed restaurant, and waiters in period costume serve up enormous platefuls of favourite Hungarian dishes, cooked in an open kitchen. This popular place has been around for decades.

SIÓFOK Hintaló

Vécsey utca 6 **Tel** *(84) 350 494*   **Map** *C4*

Standing in front of Hintaló is a life-sized figure of a jovial bartender beckoning punters in to enjoy traditional Hungarian cuisine and draught beer. Dine outside in the lovely, flower-filled garden during the summer months while the children make the most of the playground area. Closed October–mid-May.

Key to Price Guide *see p282* **Key to Symbols** *see back cover flap*

SIÓFOK Piroska Csárda
Balatonszéplak-felső 7 **Tel** *(84) 350 683* **Map** *C4*

This superb traditional Hungarian restaurant, away from the bustle of central Siófok, is decorated with much folk art. Many tables are set around a vast open hearth, and instead of windows it has painted scenes of Siófok's past. The extra-hot goulash is worth trying. An outstanding wine list features Balaton wines. Open March–December.

TIHANY Don Pietro
Rév utca 4 **Tel** *(87) 348 647* **Map** *B4*

In a tremendous setting on the Tihany Peninsula, Don Pietro serves up delicious pizzas, unusual this far from the capital. There are more than 40 toppings, including vegetarian ones, plus a number of pasta dishes to choose from. Bargain prices and a warm, friendly atmosphere make this a perfect eating choice.

TIHANY Ferenc Pince
Cserhegy 9 **Tel** *(87) 448 575* **Map** *B4*

At this memorable place, the best eatery of the Tihany Peninsula, they claim to serve the fieriest goulash in the region. There is also lamb – unusually good for Hungary – and a fine selection of fish dishes. Originally a wine cellar, there is always a superb selection of wines. The views from the outdoor tables are sensational. Open Easter–October.

VESZPRÉM Oliva
Buhim utca 14–16 **Tel** *(88) 403 875* **Map** *B4*

It is this kind of building that makes Veszprém such a wonderful place to visit. This high-class restaurant serves an international melange of dishes from far and wide – New Zealand green clams, for example. In summer there is a barbecue in the garden, and regular jazz evenings. This is the best place in the city.

VESZPRÉM Villa Medici
Kittenberger K. utca 11 **Tel** *(88) 590 070* **Map** *B4*

From the outside, this place on the outskirts of town is thoroughly modern and unappealing. Inside both the hotel *(see p272)* and restaurant are well worth checking out. The restaurant serves classic Hungarian fare in an elegant dining room, and outside is a large garden where a barbecue is set up most evenings in the summer.

VILLÁNY Oportó Panzió
Baross G. utca 33 **Tel** *(72) 492 582* **Map** *C6*

Quite the finest place to eat and drink on the Villány–Síklos wine route; the food is modern Hungarian, beautifully presented and created to complement the outstanding range of wines on offer in the cellar below. The imperial decor sets a standard many other restaurants in Hungary can only aspire to. A foodie's and wine-lover's treat.

THE NORTHERN HIGHLANDS

EGER Fehérszarvas
Klapka út 8 **Tel** *(36) 411 129* **Map** *E3*

This hunting-themed restaurant is not a place for vegetarians, nor those with a faint heart. The patrons tend to show off their trophies, and the implements that helped in their capture. The food is hearty, good value and there is some kind of folklore show some evenings, often with a band going from table to table. It is touristy but very enjoyable.

EGER Imola Udvarház
Dózsa Gy tér 4 **Tel** *(36) 414 825* **Map** *E3*

Looking traditional from the outside, yet modern and vibrant on the inside, Imola is the home of modern, adventurous and outstandingly presented Hungarian cuisine. It is unusual to see chefs outside of Budapest brave enough to try new things with traditional flavours: veal with citrus fruits and a hint of chilli is just one such example.

EGER Senator Ház Étterem
Dobó tér 11 **Tel** *(36) 411 711* **Map** *E3*

Located in Dobó square, in the centre of Eger, Senator Ház Étterem sits below the walls of Eger Castle. The hotel and restaurant is built out of the 17th-century stone that once formed the castle's outside wall. Enjoy traditional Hungarian cuisine, or choose from a wide range of international gourmet dishes.

GYÖNGYÖS Kékes Étterem
Fő tér 7 **Tel** *(37) 311 915* **Map** *D3*

A large canopy dominates this superbly designed Secessionist house in the centre of Gyöngyös. The terrace is busy from noon to midnight in summer, as diners enjoy the excellent if a little expensive Hungarian dishes while people-watching. There are good regional wines to savour too.

HOLLÓKŐ Muskátli Vendéglő
Kossuth út 61 **Tel** *(32) 379 262* **Map** *D2*

In one of Hollókő's original UNESCO-protected houses, this tiny restaurant has been serving great food since 1987. Like much of the village, it seems a little touristy, and it is certainly not cheap, but the experience of eating here surpasses all that. The garden is a veritable star sight it its own right, with a superb show of flowers in summer.

LILLAFÜRED Mátyás

Erzsébet sétány 1 **Tel** *(46) 331 411*   **Map** *E2*

Part of the Palota hotel, the Mátyás restaurant is a luxurious but reasonably priced place to enjoy Hungarian and international dishes. Service is formal, but complements the string quartet and antique lighting. There are two other restaurants on site: the medieval-themed Hunyadi and the Nagy Lajos, which serves international fare.

MISKOLC Rákóczi Pince

Rákóczi utca 23 **Tel** *(46) 343 916*   **Map** *E2*

One of the best eateries close to the town centre of Miskolc, this restaurant and wine bar is an old favourite with locals, serving decent Hungarian food in a boisterous atmosphere. There are vegetarian options on the menu and although it is in a cellar, smoking is permitted but there is a no-smoking section and it does have air conditioning.

MISKOLC Székelykert

Földes Ferenc utca 4 **Tel** *(46) 411 222*   **Map** *E2*

What looks like the tiniest house in Miskolc from the outside is the best little pub in town. The food is meaty, hearty and cooked with flair by a chef who really tries to make standard Hungarian dishes more interesting. The menu also has German dishes, with plenty of sausages and cabbage. Great garden and terrace at the back. Not cheap.

PARÁDFÜRDŐ Erzsébet Park Hotel

Kossuth L. utca 221 **Tel** *(36) 444 044*   **Map** *E3*

Designed and built by Miklós Ybl *(see p89)* and opened in 1893, this hotel-restaurant makes a great place to stop for lunch or dinner when touring through the Matra Hills. Besides the fine cuisine, both modern European and Hungarian, the vistas from the dining room windows and from the terrace are divine.

SÁROSPATAK V András

Béla király tér 3 **Tel** *(47) 312 415*   **Map** *F2*

Opposite Sárospatak's Castle Church, this restaurant offers great value. Giant portions of Hungarian food – including a memorable fish soup, big enough to have as a main course – are served with a smile by friendly young waiting staff. The list of Tokaj wines on offer runs to three pages.

SZILVÁSVÁRAD Fenyő Vendéglő

Szalajka-völgy út **Tel** *(36) 564 015*   **Map** *E2*

This eatery is located close to the Szalajka river in the picturesque mountain village of Szilvásvárad. The family-run restaurant serves traditional Hungarian cuisine in a relaxed setting and is an ideal place to stop for food in between excursions to the Bükk mountains. Grab a table outside and enjoy the views.

THE GREAT PLAIN

BAJA Véndió

Petőfi-sziget 1 **Tel** *(79) 424 709*   **Map** *C5*

Baja is a city where at certain times of year the streets can quite literally run with *halazse* (fish soup). As a result, restaurants are judged by the quality of their own *halazse*, and one of the best in town is served at this classy place on Petőfi-sziget. There is also a number of other fish dishes on offer.

BUGAC Karikás Csárda

Nagybugac 135 **Tel** *(30) 416 64 39*   **Map** *D4*

This restaurant is housed in a converted stables at the gateway to the Bugac National Park. Specialities include Puszta dishes, such as *bogrács gulyás*, a traditional Hungarian stew prepared slowly over an open fire in a kettle, and goose dishes for which the region is famous, as well as whole pigs roasted over a spit. Regular folklore shows and live music.

DEBRECEN Flaska Vendéglő

Miklós utca 4 **Tel** *(52) 414 582*   **Map** *F3*

Located in the heart of the city but away from the main tourist areas is this country-style restaurant serving good traditional Hungarian cuisine. Vegetarians are well catered for and there is an excellent selection of Hungarian wines. Head for the Apollo cinema and you will find Flaska Étterem next door.

DEBRECEN Belgian Beer Café

Piac utca 29 **Tel** *(52) 536 373*   **Map** *F3*

This Belgian Beer Café, on Debrecen's main street, has a huge garden out back, with a children's play area and a barbecue every evening. At weekends, when the diners have gone home, the cafe becomes one of the city's liveliest nightclubs, staying open until late the next morning.

DEBRECEN Csokonai Söröző és Étterem

Kossuth utca 21 **Tel** *(52) 410 802*   **Map** *F3*

This legendary Debrecen establishment is in a cavernous cellar where only the best Hungarian delicacies are served up to visitors and locals who throng here night after night. Diners may have to share one of the large tables with a passing group of tourists, but everyone is friendly and tucks into the vast portions of great food.

GYULA Kisködmön

Városház utca 15 **Tel** *(66) 463 934* **Map** *F4*

Under a sublime wooden ceiling is this folklore-fest of an establishment where the walls are all covered with lace, cloth and murals – a little tacky maybe, but it all adds to a great atmosphere. The food is good but unadventurous, including tasty salads. The service is friendly. The place fills up in the summer season so diners are advised to book.

HAJDÚSZOBOSZLÓ Kemences Csárda

Daru–Zug 1 **Tel** *(52) 362 221* **Map** *F3*

The oom-pah band is too loud to ignore, so it is best to go with the flow and tap your feet and try to enjoy everything as much as possible. The food is certainly delicious, including great local specials, such as many types of goulash and bread, and all at very moderate prices. There are fish dishes on the menu, but little for vegetarians.

KECSKEMÉT Géniusz Étterem

Kisfaludy utca 5 **Tel** *(76) 497 668* **Map** *D4*

This restaurant is headed by one of the youngest Hungarian master chefs in the country. Select one of the excellent, beautifully-presented culinary dishes and sit back and enjoy the experience along with one of their top quality wines. Reservations recommended.

KECSKEMÉT Kecskeméti Csárda és Borház

Kölcsey utca 7 **Tel** *(76) 488 686* **Map** *D4*

A short walk from the central square, this is one of the best traditional Hungarian restaurants in the country, and certainly the best on the southern Great Plain. The food is outstanding, produce is sourced from the best suppliers, and the team of chefs is always keen to push the boundaries of Puszta cuisine. Game is a speciality, but expensive.

KISKUNFÉLEGYHÁZA Kulacs Vendéglő

Széchenyi utca 39 **Tel** *(76) 575 112* **Map** *D4*

The town does not have many outstanding restaurants, but this place serves cheap and cheerful Hungarian food, including passable soups, steaks and river-fish dishes (including trout). A small terrace makes outdoor dining in warm weather a pleasant experience here and there is sometimes live music.

NYÍRBÁTOR Hódi

Báthory út 11 **Tel** *(42) 281 012* **Map** *G3*

Nyírbátor's best hotel is also its best restaurant. Close to the town centre, it is set in a stunning Baroque mansion with a large garden. There is high-class (and expensive) modern European food and a couple of traditional Hungarian dishes to choose from too. Service is informal and unobtrusive.

NYÍREGYHÁZA 424 Irish Pub

Blaha Lujza setany 1 **Tel** *(42) 424 000* **Map** *F3*

Despite the name, the cuisine on offer here is more traditional Hungarian than Irish. The terrace of this pavilion-type building is huge, leafy and fills up with the town's smart set on summer evenings. Although the Guinness served is expensive, the food is reasonable value, and there is plenty of acceptable local beer to drink too.

NYÍREGYHÁZA Svájci Lak

Sóstófürdő, Sóstói **Tel** *(42) 414 444* **Map** *F3*

Away from the bustle of central Nyíregyháza, close to the Village Museum at Sóstófürdő, this hotel and restaurant is an excellent place to sample local cuisine and fish from the lake at reasonable prices. Children are well catered for, and families can enjoy a good meal after a day visiting the museum and nearby zoo.

SZEGED Fehértói Halázscsárda

Budapesti út 4 **Tel** *(62) 555 960* **Map** *E5*

Although a short distance out of town, this place warrants a special trip. The interior is bright and atmospheric, the speciality is fish soup, but there are many other regional specialities on offer too. The restaurant is set around a vast attractive courtyard, and its wine cellar has a great selection of wines from the Villany region.

SZEGED Matuzsálem

Kölcsey utca 1–3 **Tel** *(62) 420 435* **Map** *E5*

Far better value than almost anywhere else on central Szechenyi tér, a real bonus is that most of the square can be seen from the terrace of this nice little restaurant. The food is simple but cheap, and the waiters are friendly, if a little rushed. Booking is advisable in high summer.

SZOLNOK Galéria

Szapáry utca 1 **Tel** *(56) 513 053* **Map** *E4*

Despite the expense, a visit to this first-class establishment is worth it. The fish is all locally caught, much of it from Lake Tisza, with the Szilvásvárad trout a favourite. There are platters for two, four or for families, and given its great location overlooking the river, this is probably the best restaurant in Szolnok.

TISZAFÜRED Molnár Vendéglő

Húszöles út 31/B **Tel** *(59) 352 705* **Map** *E3*

The Molnar Vendéglő has a loyal clientele. Locals come here to enjoy the wonderful selection of fish dishes, including catfish, carp and pike-perch, as well as traditional Puszta stews. There is also a wide range of meat and game dishes, as well as options for vegetarians and children.

SHOPPING IN HUNGARY

Some people complain that the explosion of shopping malls has taken much of the charm out of shopping in Hungary, yet visitors with a little patience and the right inside knowledge can still find some of the most wonderful, unique shops in Europe. The city centres bustle with small, family-owned shops selling inimitable trinkets, crafts and luxuries – *foie gras* is one of the nation's biggest exports. Then there are the flea markets, packed with the

Folk ceramics from Pécs

bizarre and the beautiful, the useful and the quirky.

Souvenir hunters are spoilt for choice too. Those looking for something typically Hungarian could buy Zsolnay porcelain, handmade textiles from the Folkart shops, vintage Tokaji wine, paprika or spicy Debreceni sausages. Horse-lovers will find the craft shops in the towns of the Great Plain a delight, where saddles, riding boots, crops and hats are of the highest standard and great value.

OPENING TIMES

Most small shops usually open at 9am and close at 7pm; some stay open later, until 9pm or 10pm, especially in modern, purpose-built shopping centres. Most shops open all day on Saturday, and an increasing number of outlets also open their doors on Sundays. Markets are set up seven days a week. Large supermarkets also open seven days a week, until at least 8pm. Shops also usually open on public holidays, with the exception of Christmas Day and New Year's Day. Many small kiosks selling bus tickets, cigarettes, alcohol, groceries and household essentials open 24 hours a day.

PAYMENT

Most shops now have to accept credit and debit cards, though producing one from

Westend City Center shopping mall in Budapest

Dried paprika and handmade wicker baskets in the market in Tihany

your wallet may elicit groans from the vendor. If you are using a debit card you may be asked for further identification, so carry your passport with you while shopping.

Visitors are advised to have a fair amount of cash with

them at all times, however, as the law on accepting credit cards is not particularly well enforced, and some smaller shops will simply refuse to take payment with a card.

VAT AND TAX-FREE SHOPPING

The price of all goods in Hungary includes a Value Added Tax (ÁFA) of 25 per cent. With the exception of works of art and antiques, it is possible for non-EU residents to claim back the ÁFA on any purchase costing more than 45,000 forints (€175) when leaving the country.

If you wish to reclaim the tax, you must make sure when purchasing the item that you ask for a special ÁFA refund receipt. You then have to present the receipt and the goods at a customs post within 90 days of purchase in order to receive a customs certification and a refund claim form. To apply for the refund your sales receipt and currency exchange or credit card receipt are also required. The money can then be claimed within 183 days of returning home. Payment is usually made direct to a bank account, minus a small service charge.

DEPARTMENT STORES AND SHOPPING MALLS

There are a number of department stores in Hungary, many of which are housed in spectacular old buildings. Besides

Typical goods for sale at the Central Market Hall in Budapest

the enormous shopping centres in Budapest, Debrecen, Pécs and Szeged all have large shopping centres, called *plazas*, within walking distance of the city centre. Open until late, and with a vast variety of food outlets, as well as multi-screen cinemas, these all-purpose malls are very popular. In all, there are 15 plazas in 14 cities around the country. There are also 21 popular Tesco hypermarkets, selling a wide range of food and non-food items. With the exception of Debrecen, however, all Tesco stores are on the outskirts of cities, and difficult to reach without a car.

MARKETS

Markets of all sorts are an essential part of everyday life all over Hungary. Apart from good, fresh produce, they offer a delightfully traditional shopping experience to visitors. Many cities also organize open-air craft and folk markets. The best is in Hollókő, and though some of the wares are kitsch by most standards, prices are good and souvenir ideas limitless. Debrecen city

council also organizes an excellent craft fair during August in Kossuth tér.

HANDICRAFTS AND FOLK ART

Hungary has a long tradition of producing high-quality porcelain and pottery, with the Herend and Zsolnay names carrying a worldwide reputation. Herend porcelain is famous for its decorative and highly colourful designs, and the factory shop in the small town of Herend *(see p203)*, north of Lake Balaton, stocks a small selection of recent productions. The Zsolnay porcelain factory in Pécs *(see pp186–9)* also has a shop. Bright colours are also characteristic of Ajka crystal, which has been recognized as Hungary's finest for more than 150 years. It is made in the small town of Ajka, close to Veszprém. There are two stores selling Ajka crystal in the village itself, and many more throughout Hungary.

For best examples of the finest Hungarian embroidery (found on dresses, tablecloths, place mats and cushion covers), the village museum of Hollókő is a great outlet. Prices are high, but the quality is outstanding. Lower-priced examples can be found in the many stalls and small shops

Paste made from Hungarian paprika

that line the busy pedestrian streets of Szentendre. Other local goods worth looking out for include carpets (especially rugs with plain, naive designs), and wooden toys (especially toy soldiers in Habsburg-era uniforms). Hungary is also renowned for its wonderful, handmade teddy bears, which although expensive make superb presents.

DELICACIES

Hungary exports more *foie gras* than any other country in the world with the exception of France. It is available from delicatessens all over the country, and prices are far lower than abroad. Look out for the distinctive black and gold labels and packaging of the Rex Ciborum brand: a guarantee of quality.

Paprika – as a condiment – can be bought in all colours, shapes, varieties and degrees of heat in Hungary. Alternatively there are many products containing paprika as an ingredient, from paprika pastes to spicy Hungarian salamis or sausages (try *gyulai kolbász* or *Debreceni*, for example). The best cheeses are smoked: *sonkás* is flavoured with ham, a popular and excellent cheese.

Markets all over the country will also sell their own regional specialities.

EQUESTRIAN GOODS

Given the pedigree of its horsemen, such as the famous Puszta Fivers *(see p247)*, it comes as no surprise to discover that Hungary is a great place to purchase tack. Finely crafted saddles made from the best leather, boots, bridles, crops and even polo mallets are made to the highest specifications at a great number of workshops throughout the country. The best are those from the Great Plain – Hungary's pre-eminent equestrian region – and there is no shortage of excellent sporting goods shops in Debrecen, Hortobágy and Szeged.

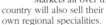

Traditional folk crafts in a Szentendre market

ENTERTAINMENT IN HUNGARY

The range of cultural events and entertainment in Hungary is wide and richly varied. It is a vibrant country where people have always known how to have a good time, and both mainstream and more eclectic forms of entertainment have always been encouraged. Music festivals – from opera in Miskolc, Baroque music in Sopron and

Poster pillar advertising events

jazz in Debrecen – feature regularly on the international arts calendar. Yet even the smallest Hungarian town usually has its own orchestra, dance company and theatre, while during the summer central squares and plazas are abuzz with outdoor concerts, plays and other artistic happenings. For entertainment in Budapest *see pp116–17*.

MUSIC, OPERA, DANCE AND CINEMA

While Budapest is home to one of Europe's finest opera houses, it does not hold a monopoly on Hungarian opera and music. In **Miskolc**, for example, the sublime **Grand National Theatre** often hosts excellent operatic performances. During the **Miskolc Opera Festival**, held over two weeks in June, some of the world's best performers can be seen here.

Pécs also has a rich cultural heritage. The city has both opera and dance companies of world renown, performing at the **National Theatre**, which is also home to the Pannon Philharmonic Orchestra. Summer festivals in Pécs take place in a spectacular setting: the ruins of the Renaissance Summer Palace, to the north of the city. Veszprém, likewise, is known as a musical city, and small-scale chamber concerts in the Castle district courtyard are a highlight of all

summer visits here. For details of music festivals throughout Hungary, including the annual **Debrecen Jazz Days**, or the **Baroque and Early Music Days** of **Sopron**, *see pp30–33*.

Most major Hungarian cities have a multiplex cinema, usually housed within the city's shopping centre. They show a wide range of films, some in the original language. Most foreign films in Hungary are both dubbed and subtitled into Hungarian, leaving cinemagoers free to choose which version they prefer. Non-Hungarian speakers should opt for the *angol nyelvű* (English soundtrack) version. Films may even be shown in English with no subtitles at all – these are advertised as *angol nyelvű, felirat nélkül* (English language, no subtitles). The cinemas also show Hungarian films, both the latest releases and repertory films from a time of cinematic glory, when Miklós Jancsó and István Szabó received international awards as directors.

Palace Disco, a lively nightspot outside Siófok

NIGHTLIFE

While for nightlife nowhere in Hungary compares to Budapest, there are plenty of nightspots in the regions to keep disco dancers and night owls happy. The university cities of Szeged, Miskolc and Győr are among the liveliest, with a wide range of pubs, clubs and nightclubs. Győr's **Vigadó Pince Pub** has live bands most nights, while the **Mister Bigg Pub**, always crowded, stays open until the early hours. Veszprém too gets lively in the evenings, with the **Expresszó Club** its buzziest venue. The **Mythos Music Club** has either live acts or top international DJs at weekends. During the summer almost all of Lake Balaton's resorts thump to the universal beat of Euro-pop. Siófok especially can be loud and really quite boisterous of an evening. The **Palace Disco** is one of the country's largest, though it is a 15-minute walk out of the town centre. A little more sophisticated is the north Balaton resort of

A performance at the Miskolc Opera Festival, held each year in June

Balatonfüred, where the **Macho Pub** and **Atrium Music Club** attract the crowds.

Casinos are now ubiquitous, and can be found in most of Hungary's major tourist spots. The venues in Győr and Sopron are both housed in glorious historical buildings. At any of Hungary's casinos – most of which are operated by one Austrian company – players can try their hand at roulette, blackjack, poker and the wheel of fortune. Most stay open 24 hours a day, and require visitors to dress smartly. Presentation of a passport is also required.

Pony-riding in Budapest, one of many activities for children

INFORMATION

The best listings magazines in Hungary are published by *Pesti Est*, the famous Budapest weekly. Though published almost entirely in Hungarian, the colourful ads should be decipherable to most people. As it is published weekly in 22 Hungarian cities visitors can find local *Ests* distributed for free in many bars, restaurants, hotels and shops. Hotel reception desks and TourInform offices will also usually be happy to help visitors with information about concerts and nightlife.

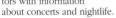

Veszprémi Est Magazine

CHILDREN

Hungarians of all ages love puppets, and most cities in the country have excellent puppet theatres. The best are those at Szeged and Kecskemét, which also has a toy museum and workshop that is very popular with children. Kids of all ages enjoy narrow-gauge and steam railways such as those at Bugac, Balaton, Nyíregyháza and Kecskemét. Horse-riding is another great way of entertaining children, and you are never far from an equestrian centre in Hungary *(see p300)*. Swimming pools, too,

are found across the country, although children often prefer modern aquaparks such as those in Debrecen and Zalaegerszeg *(see p298)*.

SPECTATOR SPORTS

Football (soccer) is the most popular spectator sport in Hungary. The domestic league is highly competitive, and crowds can be large. The country's best sides include Újpest, Honvéd and Ferencváros of Budapest; Videoton Székesfehérvár; Zalaegerszeg; and Debrecen. The season runs Aug–Dec and Mar–Jun. Tickets can be purchased from stadium ticket offices on the day. Handball is also popular, and both the male and female teams are world-class. Water polo, rowing, basketball, gymnastics tournaments and international swimming competitions also attract crowds. For details of the Hungarian Formula 1 Grand Prix, *see p31*.

Flatwater Rowing Championship in Szeged 2006

DIRECTORY

THEATRES & OPERA HOUSES

Miskolc Grand Theatre (Miskolci Nemzeti Színház)
Déryné utca 1, Miskolc.
Tel (46) 51 67 35. www.mnsz.eu

Pécs National Theatre (Pécsi Nemzeti Színház)
Perczel Miklós utca 17, Pécs.
Tel (72) 51 26 60. www.pnsz.hu

FESTIVALS

Debrecen Jazz Days
www.iranydebrecen.hu

Miskolc Opera Festival
www.operafesztival.hu

Sopron Early Music Days
www.filharmoniabp.hu

PUBS, CLUBS & DISCOS

Atrium Music Club
Blaha utca 7–9, Balatonfüred.
Tel (87) 34 32 29.

Expresszo Club
Brusznyai utca 2, Veszprém.
Tel (20) 940 27 72.

Macho Pub
Vasút utca 4, Balatonfüred.
Tel (30) 620 35 22.

Mister Bigg Pub
Fehérvári út 11, Győr.
Tel (96) 41 36 22.

Mythos Music Club
Szabadsag tér 1, Veszprém.

Palace Dance Club
Deák Ferenc sétány 2, Siófok.
Tel (84) 35 06 98. www.palace.hu

CASINOS

Casino Győr
Baross Gábor utca 33, Győr.
Tel (96) 31 94 49.

Casino Sopron
Liszt Ferenc utca 1, Sopron.
Tel (99) 51 23 50.

CHILDREN

Aquaticum Debrecen
Nagyerdei park 1, Debrecen.
Tel (52) 51 41 00.

AquaCity Zalaegerszeg
Fürdő sétány 2, Zalaegerszeg.
Tel (92) 59 91 01.

Aquaréna Mogyoród
Vízipark út 1.
Tel (28) 54 11 00.

SPORTS AND ACTIVITIES IN HUNGARY

Hungarians adore the great outdoors, and spend a great deal of their leisure time finding new ways of enjoying nature, both in winter and summer. Most Hungarians, at some stage, partake in the national ritual that is bathing, and since virtually all towns and cities feature at least one thermal baths visitors should take the opportunity to join in. On the Great Plain, horses are a hugely important part of everyday life, and there are a number of equestrian centres in and around the region's larger towns. They offer riding courses at all levels, as well as putting on displays of Hungarian horsemanship.

Tourist Information Office sign

GENERAL INFORMATION

Tourinform offices are an excellent source of information on sports and outdoor activities in Hungary. Most stock special publications outlining activities in the surrounding area, and will provide addresses, telephone numbers and directions to nearby thermal bath complexes, swimming pools and equestrian centres. Two helpful brochures in a number of languages, "Spas and Wellness Packages" and "On Horseback", can be downloaded for free from Tourinform's excellent website (www.tourinform.hu).

SWIMMING POOLS AND THERMAL BATHS

Most Hungarians view public bathing as a birthright, and with more than 300 operating thermal bath complexes in the country, most of which have larger swimming pools attached, it is not difficult to see why. Hungarians need no excuse at all to strip off and head for a steam bath, even in the outdoors in the middle of winter. Old men playing chess in the outdoor pool at Budapest's Széchenyi baths, steam rising from the water and snow on all sides, is one of Hungary's defining sights. With the exception of the football team of the 1950s, all of Hungary's most successful and best-known athletes have been swimmers, including Alfréd Hajós, who won the first-ever Olympic swimming gold medal in 1896, and after whom a swimming pool on Margaret Island, Budapest, has since been named.

It is no great surprise then that Hungary has made an industry out of its thermal baths. Visitors have for centuries flocked to this country from all over Europe to take to the waters, and to swim in its outdoor pools. The modern aqua-parks, including the super Aquaticum complex at Debrecen, which has slides, water jets, jacuzzis and artificial waves, make sure that children catch the swimming bug early. In summer, Lake Balaton is a popular swimming venue, and while most Balaton resorts do not restrict water access to swimmers, some parts of the lake are reserved for water sports. The water quality in Hungary is usually good. People even sometimes swim in the Danube, especially around the Danube bend towns of Esztergom and Szentendre.

For more information on Hungary's thermal bath complexes *see pp22–3*.

Slides at the Aquaticum thermal baths complex in Debrecen

Boats in the marina at Balatonföldvár, Lake Balaton

WATER SPORTS

Lake Balaton is a major water sports centre. Among the activities available here are water-skiing, wind-surfing, rowing, canoeing and water polo, the latter being a popular spectator sport. Ever since the Siófok Balaton Company opened its doors to paying customers in 1893, however, Hungary's favourite water sport has been sailing. In fair weather Lake Balaton can look like a floating forest of sailing boats.

Siófok is the main sailing resort, although there are also now yachting centres at Balatonföldvár, Badacsony, Szigliget and Balatonlelle. All offer sailing lessons to novices, and will hire out boats of various sizes to the more experienced. Visitors wishing to lease a boat require an International Sailing Licence, or need to be able to explain (in best pidgin Hungarian) that they know what they are doing. Usually, a driving licence, passport or credit card need to be deposited with the boatyard. For information contact the **Balaton Regional Tourist Office**.

To learn how to water-ski, visitors are advised to head for Siófok or Balatonfüred or contact the **Hungarian Water Ski Federation**.

HIKING

In summer trains heading for the hills are packed with hikers. The northeast of the country is home to some superb, challenging hiking trails, and there are easier, flat trails on the Great Plain and along parts of the Danube. In all, Hungary has more than 11,000 km (6,835 miles) of trails, marked with a coloured stripe according to the length of the trail (blue for a long-distance trail, yellow for a short, local trail). All the national parks have well signposted trails.

One of the best trails for good amateur walkers is the Balaton-felvidék trail in the southern Bakony Hills. The 94-km (58-mile) blue trail starts at Pétfürdő station in Várpalota, and goes through the most spectacular part of the Balaton-felvidék before ending at the railway station in Badacsony.

Tourinform have an excellent free brochure on hiking in Hungary, giving details of routes and accommodation.

Road sign aimed at walkers

CYCLING

Cycling became popular in Hungary post Communist times as in that era roads were never really good enough to make cycling attractive. Today, however, pedal power is one of the best ways to explore the Hungarian countryside. In Budapest, the city council has invested heavily in creating a city-wide cycle path network. It extends to over 200 km (124 miles). Nationwide there are more than 2,000 km (1,243 miles) of cycle paths, though not all of these are paved. Two EuroVelo routes traverse Hungary, one following the eastern bank of the Danube, one hugging the eastern bank of the River Tisza. In Northern Transdanubia, some of Europe's best cycle routes are around Lake Fertő. There are superb routes in the Northern Highlands.

Visitors can hire bikes from a number of rental centres in Siófok and most of the resorts on Lake Balaton – where the sport is especially popular – as well as at Bikebase in the capital. Cyclists may take their bikes on trains within Hungary for a fee (around 25 per cent of the ticket price), but only on specially designated trains identified by the bicycle icon on the timetable.

Cyclists pausing in front of the Millennium Monument, Városliget, Budapest

Steeplechase, a popular equestrian pursuit

HORSE-RIDING

Hungary and the Hungarians are invariably linked to horses and horsemanship, and riding is a one of the most popular activities among people of all backgrounds. Basically, if an activity or sport involves horses, it will almost certainly be pursued somewhere in Hungary. From simple pony-trekking rides to carriage driving and show jumping, it is all on offer here. Even polo has made a comeback. The sport was popular here before World War II – Hungary had 76 polo clubs competing in 19 leagues in 1936 – but the Communists condemned the activity as bourgeois. There are now two polo clubs in Hungary, and the Hungarian Open Championship held each May at the La Estancia Polo Club at Etyek, outside Budapest, attracts professional players from as far away as Brazil and Argentina.

There are more than 1,000 riding centres in the country, and just as there seems to be a thermal spa in every town in Hungary, riding centres

also abound. The **Hungarian Equestrian Tourism Association** (MLTKSZ) rates all equine centres using a five-horseshoe system, similar to the star ratings awarded to hotels. As a rule, the wider the range of activities that are on offer at an equestrian centre, the more horse-shoes it will have in its rating. Many riding centres also offer over-night accommodation. All offer gentle pony-trekking trails for children or beginners, as well as riding lessons for all abilities. Some riding centres offer special children's riding camps in summer.

The MLTKSZ is helpful and provides information about all the equestrian centres it rates. It also has details of shows, races, riding holidays and travelling with gypsy caravans, as well as riding facilities for the disabled. Local tourist centres also have brochures of riding centres in their area.

FISHING

Almost half a million Hungarians fish at one time or another during the year; indeed, after swimming, fishing is the nation's favourite participation sport. Lakes Tisza, Balaton and Velence are superb and popular fishing grounds, while a stretch of the Danube near Ráckeve is also renowned for the richness of species and quality of fish. Anglers are able to land carp, pike, pike-perch, bream, razor fish and even eels in Hungarian waters.

Anglers can fish in just about any stretch of water in the country, more or less at any time of year, but they do require a Hungarian National Fishing Licence to do so; this is available from angling shops or from the **National Federation of Hungarian Anglers** (Mohosz). The licence is valid for a year and costs around 2,000 forints. In addition to this national licence, fishing enthusiasts may also need to buy a local licence, depending on the stretch of water where they plan to fish. Local licences can usually be bought at the entrances to major fishing areas. Local tourist offices will have a list of sales points.

Waiting for river fish to bite in the Danube, near Esztergom

HUNTING

Hungary is a nation of huntsmen but hunting is now strictly controlled. After years of free-for-all shooting, great emphasis is now placed on conservation and sustainability. Depending on the time of year, the hunter can shoot stags, fallow deer, roebuck, wild boar, fox, rabbit and pheasant. The biggest prize is a stag, but the season is short – September and October – and interested visitors will need to join an organized shoot.

Anyone wishing to join a hunt in Hungary must hold a valid hunting licence, and there are strict regulations on the import of firearms for hunting purposes. Trophy fees are charged for almost all game; these are calculated according to the size of the bagged catch. There are a number of companies who organize hunting holidays and tours, and who will take care

Fishing in Lake Balaton, a popular participation sport

Skating at the ice rink in Varosliget Park, Budapest

of all the paperwork. OMVK, the **Hungarian National Chamber of Hunters**, offers advice on all hunting matters.

WINTER SPORTS

Hungarians love skiing, but they are more likely to ski in Austrian or Slovakian resorts, many of which are no more than a couple of hours' drive away. Hungary does have one small downhill ski resort of its own, however, the **Mátraszentistván Sípark** in the Mátra Mountains. It offers pleasant but rather tame skiing. In all there are five ski lifts giving access to seven short ski runs, none of which is more than a kilometre (half a mile) in length. There is, however, a good ski school, and children and beginners especially will love the quiet, gentle slopes here. Flood-lit skiing is possible at night.

Mátraszentistván is 96 km (60 miles) away from Budapest, and can be reached by a daily bus service departing from Stadion Buszpályaudvar at 7:45am and arriving at the ski resort at 10:20am. The return bus leaves at 4pm, arriving in Budapest at 6:30pm. Drivers should take the M3 motorway from Budapest to Gyöngyös, then the H24 passing through Mátrafüred, Mátraháza, Galyatető and Mátraszentlászló. Although the highest point of the resort is just 834 m (2,736 ft), there is usually enough snow for skiing from November to April.

Ice-skating is also popular, and the best place to do this is at the superb outdoor skating rink in Városliget park in Budapest (*see p107*).

GOLF

A sport gaining in popularity in the country, Hungary has seven full 18-hole golf courses, virtually all located in or around the capital. Golfing remains an expensive and exclusive sport in Hungary, however, and green fees at most courses are high: around 17,500 forints at weekends, slightly less during the week. The best course in the country is at the **Greenfield Hotel Golf and Spa**, close to Bükfürdő, about 50 km (31 miles) from Budapest. It is the only course in Hungary to have hosted an international golf tour event.

Visitors can find out more about golfing in Hungary at the excellent website www.golfhungary.hu.

DIRECTORY

WATER SPORTS

Balaton Regional Tourist Office
Blaha Lujza utca 2, Balatonfüred.
Tel (87) 34 28 71. **www**.bis.hu

Hungarian Water Ski Federation
1033 Hajógyári Sziget 108, Budapest.
Tel (30) 243 07 96.

HORSE-RIDING

Hungarian Equestrian Tourism Association (MLTKSZ)
Ráday utca 8, Budapest.
Tel (1) 456 04 44.

FISHING AND HUNTING

National Federation of Hungarian Anglers (MOHOSZ)
Korompai utca 17, Budapest.
Tel (1) 248 25 90.
www.mohosz.hu

Hungarian National Chamber of Hunters (OMVK)
Medve utca 34–40, Budapest.
Tel (1) 355 61 80.
www.omvk.hu

WINTER SPORTS

Hungarian Ski Federation (MSSZ)
Dózsa György út 1–3, Budapest.
Tel (1) 460 68 93.

Mátraszentistván Sípark
Tel (37) 37 66 85.

GOLF

Hungarian Golf Federation (MGSZ)
Istvánmezei út 1–3, Budapest.
Tel (1) 460 68 59.
www.hungolf.hu

Greenfield Hotel Golf and Spa
Golf utca 4, Bükfürdő.
Tel (94) 801 600.
http://greenfieldhotel.net

Teeing off at the Greenfield Hotel Golf and Spa, Bükfürdő

SURVIVAL
GUIDE

PRACTICAL INFORMATION

Hungary is not a large country, but it is highly centralized, and almost all roads and railways lead to Budapest. Any visit beyond the capital is well worth organizing in advance. Most visitors also find the Hungarian language hard to learn, remember and pronounce, and there is little or no English spoken outside the capital. Fortunately, Tourinform, the Hungarian National Tourist Office,

Tourist information sign

is one of the best and most efficient information services in Europe. Most Hungarian towns have modern facilities for the traveller, including good banking services and emergency medical care, and public telephone and transport systems are good. Customs and border controls now apply mainly to travellers from countries outside the EU. For EU and EEA citizens the entry procedure is a formality.

One of many tourist information offices, run by Tourinform

TOURIST INFORMATION

Hungary operates tourist offices abroad in 26 countries, all run by **Tourinform**. Visitors can find a list of these offices at Tourinform's international website. This also has a wide variety of useful information, brochures and maps, all of which can be downloaded for free in various formats. Holiday brochures can also be sent by post, free of charge. Once in Hungary, travellers can make use of the services of more than 150 Tourinform offices nationwide. In most of these offices young, friendly and multilingual staff will do everything to make visitors feel welcome in their country.

PASSPORTS AND CUSTOMS

Citizens of the European Union (EU), the European Economic Area (EEA), countries that are signatories of the Schengen agreement,

the USA, Canada, Australia and New Zealand – and a few other countries – are free to enter Hungary as tourists without requiring a visa. Almost everybody else – including South Africans – needs a visa, which must be obtained from a Hungarian Consulate outside Hungary before travel. Visitors should keep their passports (or at least a copy) on them at all times. A valid passport needs to be shown when registering at a hotel.

Visitors returning to EU countries may export unlimited quantities of alcohol and tobacco, provided these are for personal use. However, while Hungarian customs officers will not bother you, note that some EU countries have imposed their own limits on imports from countries such as Hungary where cigarettes and alcohol are cheap. Though these unilateral limits are illegal under EU law, they are strictly enforced. The UK, for example, limits cigarette imports from Hungary to just 800. Check before leaving home.

OPENING HOURS

Museums and galleries are open all year round, though there are some exceptions (Aquincum, Gödöllő Royal Palace, for example). Opening

times for specific venues are given under their individual entries. Typically, museums open from 10am to 6pm from April until October, and a couple of hours less in winter, from November to March. Most museums are closed on Mondays. Almost all charge an entrance fee, but many offer discounts.

Most small shops open from 9am to 7pm; some stay open until 9pm or 10pm, especially in modern shopping centres. Shops usually open all day on Saturdays, and an increasing number open their doors on Sundays too. Markets operate seven days a week from early morning to around 3pm. Large supermarkets also open seven days a week, until at least 8pm. Shops also usually open on public holidays, with the exception of Christmas Day and New Year's Day. Many of the small kiosks selling bus tickets, cigarettes, food and alcohol open 24 hours a day. Restaurants open at 11:30am and rarely close during the afternoon. Hungarians generally lunch early, between noon and 1pm.

Signs indicating local amenities and attractions

ETIQUETTE

Bans on smoking in public places are increasingly common throughout Hungary. The transformation this has led to is astonishing. All bars, cafés and restaurants are now

Staircase especially adapted for disabled use

non-smoking, and all museums, public transport, stations, airports and other public buildings are also entirely non-smoking.

Hungarians are usually very friendly towards visitors. They queue patiently, except when getting on and off any form of public transport. The only stumbling block is the language barrier – many older Hungarians speak no western languages.

Casual clothing is acceptable everywhere, even in the restaurants of Budapest's most expensive hotels. At business meetings, too, suits and ties are much less common than elsewhere in Europe. The one exception is Budapest Opera: you are expected to dress up, black tie if possible.

If invited to the home of a Hungarian, ensure you bring something: flowers or a bottle of good whisky are favourites.

In hospitals, it is common practice to tip doctors, nurses and domestic staff to make things happen just that little bit faster. The same is true of any Hungarian public official, a legacy of Communist-era bureaucracy.

DISABLED TRAVELLERS

Hungary has made giant strides towards improving life for its disabled citizens and visitors, a major plus point of the country's entry into the EU in 2004. That said, it can be tough for all but the very fittest to get on and off some forms of public transport: trains and trams are especially troublesome. In Budapest, the metro is adapted for disabled travellers.

Most hotels can accommodate disabled visitors, often in specially adapted rooms. As a rule of thumb, the better the hotel, the more likely disabled visitors are to find rooms that are adapted for them.

For advice and help, contact the **National Federation of Disabled Persons' Association**. They publish on their excellent website lists of hotels, restaurants, museums and other public buildings as well as transport links which are accessible to the disabled.

PUBLIC TOILETS

Unfortunately, when it comes to the provision of decent public toilets, Hungary remains in the dark ages. Public conveniences are rare, and those that one does come across can be very unappealing. Most are free; the modern, cubicle-style toilets, however, increasingly common in parks and public squares, are sometimes coin-operated. In cafés, restaurants and hotel public areas there is usually a toilet attendant, whom it is courteous to tip on your way out. Most railway stations have toilets, although they can be unhygienic.

Apart from the generally understood picture symbols, the toilets are signed in Hungarian: *Hölgyek* (ladies) and *Urak* (gentlemen) or *Nők* (women) and *Férfiak* (men).

ELECTRICAL AND GAS APPLIANCES

The Hungarian electricity supply is 220 V; the plugs are the standard continental Europe type, with two round pins. Sockets are generally earthed, and the plugs are most commonly of the flat type. Adapters are widely available.

Gas cookers have a bimetallic safety device – after lighting the knob should be held down until the burner warms up.

Street sign for Váci utca, not to be confused with Váci út

HUNGARIAN TIME

Hungary adheres to Central European time in keeping with most of mainland Europe – it is two hours ahead of Greenwich Mean Time (GMT) in summer and one hour ahead in winter.

If it is noon in Budapest it is 11am in London, 6am in New York, 5am in Dallas, 3am in Los Angeles, 1pm in Bucharest, 2pm in Moscow, 7pm in Perth, 8pm in Tokyo, 9pm in Sydney and 11pm in Auckland.

HUNGARIAN ADDRESSES AND STREET NAMES

Most famous Hungarians have squares *(tér)*, streets *(utca)* and avenues *(út)* named after them in every large city and town, which it is easy to confuse. Many first-time visitors to Budapest thus confuse Váci utca (the pedestrian street in the city centre) with Váci út (the wide avenue north of the city centre).

Hungarian addresses are written with the postcode first, followed by the street name and building number. In Budapest the district code is added to the city name, using Roman numerals. The floors of tall buildings are numbered from the ground floor up, exactly as in the UK.

DIRECTORY

TOURIST INFORMATION

Tourinform
1052 Deák tér (Sütő utca 2), Budapest.
Tel (680) 630 800 or (1) 438 80 80 (from abroad).
www.tourinform.hu
www.hungary.com

INFORMATION FOR DISABLED VISITORS

National Federation of Disabled Persons' Associations (MEOSZ)
San Marco utca 76, Budapest.
Tel (1) 388 5529 or (1) 250 9013 (international).
www.meoszinfo.hu

Safety and Health

Budapest police badge

Hungary has a relatively low crime rate, although pickpocketing can be a problem on public transport and in crowded sightseeing areas. The healthcare system is well-funded, efficient and most emergency treatment is free for visitors. Visitors are still advised, however, to take out a good health insurance policy before they depart. Most towns have modern facilities for the traveller, including good emergency medical care. The Tourist Police or the Hungarian National Tourist Office can help with language problems.

Hungarian police officers, on foot patrol in the streets

PERSONAL SECURITY

Although Hungary is a comparatively safe place, it is wise to take care. Popular outdoor events attract bag-snatchers and pickpockets. In Budapest and in crowded public areas visitors should be particularly careful to keep an eye on their property, especially handbags and cameras. Public transport in Budapest (especially the buses) is notorious for the gangs of pickpockets that operate there.

Visitors should make sure they lock valuables and personal documents in a hotel safe. It is equally important not to leave valuables in a car. Ideally, a hotel's car parking facilities should be used (parking space may be available at a small supplement – it is worth it).

There is no need to carry large amounts of cash around, because most credit and debit cards are widely accepted, and cash machines (ATMs) are also widely found, even in the countryside.

PERSONAL SAFETY

The Hungarian word for police is *rendőrség*. Hungarian police officers are frequently seen patrolling the streets on motorbikes, on foot or in cars. They may also be seen on horseback. Even the smallest village has its own police station. In the event of any loss or theft of property, a report should be made immediately to the

Fire department sign

police, as a number will be required for any insurance claim. This, however, is easier said than done as some police stations may not have anyone around who speaks the relevant language. In this case your embassy or consulate (see directory) may be able to help out.

Another possible route is the Tourist Police. Visitors who are arrested, for whatever reason, should try to contact their embassy and consular representative immediately. Random ID checks are rare, but visitors and locals alike are required to have some form of identification with them at all times. A photocopy of your passport will suffice.

CCTV is now common in Hungary's cities and towns, and has been installed on the Budapest Metro, on some buses, in department stores and in shopping centres.

Hungary also has one of the most modern speed-camera systems in Europe, and speeding warrants heavy on-the-spot fines, even imprisonment in extreme cases. Drink-driving is strictly forbidden in Hungary – the permissible blood alcohol level is 0.0 mg! Even a first drink-driving offence can lead to imprisonment.

The possession of all drugs is illegal. Prostitution is illegal, though tolerated in most big cities if practised discreetly. In any case, contact with street

Police car

Ambulance

prostitutes (of which there are many in and around railway stations at night) should be avoided as they are often run by criminals. In general, all of Hungary's railway stations can be rather unsafe places at night, as they are popular places for drunks and petty criminals to hang out.

All visitors must take care not to overstay their welcome – most tourists are permitted to stay in the country for up to 90 days without having a temporary residence permit. Visitors who extend their stay beyond the 90 days and then attempt to leave the country may be hit with a large fine, or prevented from leaving.

Ornately decorated interior of a pharmacy, Budapest

EMERGENCIES

The emergency telephone number for police, fire or ambulance is 112, and all operators speak English, French and German. There is also an English-language Tourist Police Information Service, run by Tourinform, which can provide information on English-speaking police stations, and give general advice if visitors are lost or need other kinds of assistance. The telephone number is (1) 438 80 80; it operates around the clock. Visitors who believe they have been over-charged by a restaurant, or a taxi driver, should report the incident to the Tourist Police. Officers can be approached in the street or at the headquarters at Vigadó utca 6, Budapest V.

Sign for a pharmacy

HEALTHCARE

Even during Communist times Hungary was a world leader in medical research and development. Hungarian doctors are superb though underpaid, and standards in hospitals and even local clinics in small towns and villages are generally high. Emergency treatment is in theory free for all, although visitors should always make sure to take out a good health insurance policy before travelling abroad. Any treatment (and all medicines) need to be paid for, as do hospital stays. The actual cost incurred by a visitor will depend on Hungary's reciprocal agreement with the relevant country. EU citizens are entitled to free treatment and hospital stays, although they will usually be asked to pay for medicines. Keep any receipts for treatments or prescriptions, and ask for a signed, stamped doctor's report if an insurance claim is to be made. Visitors should also note that tipping doctors and nurses is still widespread (a relic of the Communist system).

The Hungarian word for pharmacy or chemist is *Patika*, although the German word *Apotheke* is also widely in use. Hungary's pharmacies are strictly regulated and by law have to be owned by their pharmacists. There are therefore no pharmacy chains, and finding a 24-hour pharmacy can be difficult. If the nearest pharmacy is closed, there should be a list displayed – either on the door or in the window – of all local chemists, including those who will be open for 24-hour emergency duty. In practice, however, the list is often missing. The Tourist Police should be able to help in such situations.

Most dental treatment is relatively cheap in Hungary, and, in fact, "dental tourism" from other countries is a growing industry.

Visitors do not need any special vaccinations to travel to Hungary, and there are no specific health risks associated with the country. Tap water is perfectly safe to drink, but as bottled waters are cheap and of a high quality this is the preferred option. Food poisoning is a more common problem, and the ubiquitous street kebab *(gyros)* stands are best avoided for this very reason. Mosquitoes can be a problem in high summer, especially around Lake Tisza.

DIRECTORY

EMERGENCIES

General Emergencies
Tel 112
English Language Emergency Hotline (Tourinform)
Tel (1) 438 80 80.

EMBASSIES

British Embassy
Harmincad utca 6, Budapest.
Tel (1) 266 28 88.
www.britishembassy.hu

Australian Embassy
Királyhágó tér 8–9, Budapest.
Tel (1) 457 97 77.
www.hungary.embassy.gov.au

Canadian Embassy
Ganz utca 12–14, Budapest.
Tel (1) 392 33 60.
www.canadaeuropa.gc.ca/hungary

US Embassy
Szabadság tér 12, Budapest.
Tel (1) 475 44 00.
www.usembassy.hu

Banking and Currency

K&H Bank logo

Although a member of the European Union (EU) since 2004, Hungary has not yet joined the Eurozone. Hungary still uses its own currency, the forint (although many places will also accept dollars and euros). The banking system is generally excellent, and there are cash machines (ATMs) everywhere, as well as foreign exchange bureaux. It is advisable to change money in a bank as exchange rates are better, and the commission is far lower. The use of credit and debit cards is widespread, and most banks will advance cash on Visa cards and MasterCards.

BANKS

There are plenty of banks in all cities and towns, all providing a good service. Many of the branches have been modernized and the staff are all courteous and helpful. Their opening times vary, but the normal hours are 9am–5pm. Banks do not close for lunch. All banks are closed at weekends and on public holidays. The largest banks, with branches in all towns, are **UniCredit Bank**, **Erste Bank**, **Raiffeisen** and **OTP**.

CURRENCY EXCHANGE

Since Hungary joined the EU there have been no limits on the amount of foreign or local currency that can be brought in or taken out of the country. Visitors arriving with foreign

Logo of branches of the CIB Bank

currency should change this at a bank. Although independent exchange bureaux may appear to offer better rates of exchange, or lower commission, they usually advertise only their rates for buying local currency, not for selling. Most also charge additional fees which are not clearly signposted.

The easiest way to procure local cash is with a card in a cash machine. ATM machines are found everywhere and although the card issuers usually charge a small fee for every transaction, the rate of exchange is always the same as that of the National Bank of Hungary at the time of the transaction. This method of obtaining cash therefore works out far cheaper than using a bureau de change.

Credit and debit cards are almost universally accepted in Budapest. Traveller's cheques can usually only be changed at a bank, and then at high commission rates – they are best avoided. American Express cashes its own traveller's cheques free of charge.

There is also an increasing number of Automatic Currency Exchange Machines, where foreign currency is inserted to obtain forints in exchange.

Visitors may occasionally be approached by locals, offering to exchange currency at a better rate than the banks. This is to be avoided in all circumstances – it is illegal and likely to involve faked bank notes or other kinds of fraud and deception.

Entrance to a branch of the K&H Bank, in Budapest

An ATM cash dispenser, typically found all over the country

Visitors should try to spend all their Hungarian coins before leaving the country.

DIRECTORY

BANKS

Erste Bank
Népfürdő utca 24–6, Budapest.
Tel (40) 22 22 21 or (1) 298 02 21 (from abroad).
www.erstebank.hu

OTP
Nádor utca 6, Budapest.
Tel (1) 366 63 88 (from abroad).
www.otpbank.hu

Raiffeisen Bank
Akadémia utca 6, Budapest.
Tel (1) 48 44 400 (from abroad).
www.raiffeisen.hu

UniCredit Bank
Szabadság tér 5–6, Budapest.
Tel (1) 301 12 71 or (1) 325 32 00 (from abroad).
www.unicreditbank.hu

CREDIT CARDS AND TRAVELLER'S CHEQUES

American Express
Deák Ferenc utca 10, Budapest.
Tel (1) 235 43 00.

Discover Card
(lost/stolen cards and customer service)
Tel 00-1-801-902-3100 (toll-free in US).

MasterCard
(lost/stolen cards and customer service)
Tel (06) 80 01 25 17.

Visa
(lost/stolen cards and customer service)
Tel (06) 80 01 76 82.

Bank Notes

Hungary's currency is the forint (Ft). Banknotes come in denominations of 500, 1,000, 2,000, 5,000, 10,000 and 20,000. It can be difficult to pay using Ft 10,000 and 20,000 banknotes, especially in small stores or taxis.

1,000 forints

2,000 forints

5,000 forints

10,000 forints

20,000 forints

500 forints

Coins

The forint is available in seven coin denominations: 1, 2, 5, 10, 20, 50, 100 and 200 forints. A forint is equal to 100 fillér, but there have been no fillér coins in circulation since 1999. The international currency code for the forint is HUF.

5 forints

10 forints

20 forints

50 forints

100 forints

200 forints

Communications and Media

Internet access point sign

The Hungarian landline telephone system, operated by Magyar Telekom, part of Deutsche Telekom, is first class. Public telephones are almost all operated by phone card, although a few older, coin-operated phones do still exist. Phone boxes no longer contain telephone directories. However, the telephone information system provides a directory enquiry service *(see Directory)*. In recent years, Hungary's landlines have been joined by three nationwide GSM mobile telephone networks. All mobile telephone operators offer foreign-language information services. The country's postal service is less efficient, and even sending a letter from one district of Budapest to another can sometimes still take days.

Public telephone boxes mostly operated by phone card

MAKING A PHONE CALL

To make a call from one of the green public phone kiosks marked *Telefon*, phone cards are the best option. They can be obtained in units of 800, 1,800 or 5,000 forints and are widely available from tobacconist shops, post offices, street vendors and most newspaper kiosks. The few coin-operated phone boxes take 10, 20, 50 and 100 forint coins. To make an international call dial 00 and wait for the dialling tone, then dial the country code followed by the rest of the number. To phone a Hungarian number from abroad, the international access code is 36. To call long distance within Hungary, dial 06 followed by the city code. The area code for Budapest is 1. If you have dialled an out-of-date number, you will hear a message first in Hungarian, then in English, advising you of the correct new number.

MOBILE PHONES

Most Hungarians are mobile-phone crazy, and almost everyone has at least one. Coverage of the country is almost total, with only a few remote areas of the Northern Highlands not benefiting from the presence of at least one of the networks. Most European visitors can use their mobile phones in Hungary, though US and Australian visitors who do not have a GSM phone may not.

To make sure you can use your mobile phone while in Hungary you will need to ensure that you have roaming access enabled before you leave home. Once in Hungary most phones automatically search for the network with the strongest signal. If you want to use a particular network, which may have an agreement with your home network, thus offering reduced roaming charges, you should change your phone setting from automatic searching for networks to manual.

Mobile phone roaming charges are, of course, notoriously high, even on partner networks, and if you will be spending longer periods in Hungary it may be worthwhile buying a local SIM card for your phone. All of the local networks sell them, and you can obtain them in tobacconist shops, post offices and most newspaper kiosks, as well as specialist GSM stores.

INTERNET, WI-FI AND FAX

The majority of hotels, airports, train stations and large shopping centres offer internet services. There are cheap internet cafés dotted around the country, and even the smallest village usually has at least one internet access point. In larger towns and cities there are also Wi-Fi hotspots providing wireless internet connections for those with laptops or other enabled devices, although you will need to make sure your laptop is compatible before leaving home. Ask at the tourist office or at your hotel for information about how to access the public, and often free, Wi-Fi network with your device. Alternatively, visit a café such as **Farger** in Budapest with its free Wi-Fi service, or look online for **Wi-Fi hotspots**.

If you need to send a fax, any post office will be able to help, or your hotel, though it may charge you a high fee.

An internet café, now to be found even in the smallest village

POSTAL SERVICES

The Hungarian postal service is as bureaucratic and inefficient today as it was during Communist times. If you need to use a post office, therefore, set some time aside. Postage stamps can also often be purchased from tobacconists, newspaper kiosks and souvenir shops. Sending a postcard costs 235–300 forints depending on the destination. Most post offices are open Monday to Friday from 8am to 6pm and 8am to 2pm on Saturday. For urgent parcels, a courier service, such as **DHL** or **Federal Express**, will be more reliable.

Addresses in Hungary, written with the postcode first, can be confusing. See p305 for more information.

Newspaper kiosk, selling newspapers, magazines and phone cards

A Hungarian postbox, Budapest

TV AND RADIO

Almost every hotel room in Hungary – even in budget hotels – now has a television equipped to receive a variety of domestic, national, cable or satellite channels. The most popular Hungarian television station is the state-run MTV (not to be confused with the music channel), which operates two channels, while TV2 and RTL Klub are the largest and most popular private station. All imported programmes in Hungary are dubbed into Hungarian, so visitors are more likely to be interested in BBC World, CNN and EuroNews, the three English-language news channels invariably carried by all cable and satellite operators. There is also usually a variety of German-language news and entertainment channels.

There are literally hundreds of radio stations in Hungary. Most play a mix of international and local pop and rock music, but there are also stations dedicated to classical, jazz, folk music and more.

NEWSPAPERS AND MAGAZINES

Hungary's leading newspapers are the quality broadsheets *Népszabadság* and *Magyar Hírlap*, and the *Magyar Nemzet*, though there are hundreds of other newspapers published around the country, many regional.

There is one English-language Hungarian publication, the bi-weekly *Budapest Business Journal (BBJ)*, which provides financial and business news for Hungary. The Budapest *Timeout* guide is a monthly entertainments listing magazine. Major foreign publications can be bought at central newspaper kiosks, railway stations, the airport and at **World Press House** in Budapest. **Relay Székes-fehérvár** and **Relay Debrecen** are two other suppliers. Foreign papers are less widely available outside the capital, apart from German newspapers and magazines, sometimes found in the Lake Balaton resorts during the high season summer holidays.

DIRECTORY

COMMUNICATIONS

International Directory Enquiries
Tel 199.

POSTAL SERVICES

Post Office (Magyar Posta)
Krisztina krt. 6–8, Budapest.
Customer Service
Tel (1) 487 11 00.
www.posta.hu

COURIER SERVICES

DHL
Tel (6) 40 454 545.
www.dhl.hu

Federal Express
Tel (6) 40 980 980.
www.fedex.com/hu

INTERNET AND WI-FI

Farger
1054 Budapest
Zoltan utca 18.
Map 2 C4

Wi-Fi hotspots
www.hotspotter.hu

FOREIGN NEWSPAPERS

Relay Debrecen
Debrecen Station, Petőfi tér 12, Debrecen.

Relay Székesfehérvár
Székesfehérvár Station, Béke tér 3, Székesfehérvár.

World Press House
Városház utca 3–5, Budapest.
Tel (1) 317 13 11.

TRAVEL INFORMATION

Most visitors arrive in Hungary by air, at Budapest's only major airport Ferenc Liszt International. A second international airport, known as Hévíz-Balaton, is located near Keszthely, and a third has opened in Debrecen. Hungary has borders with no less than seven countries, so there are numerous road and rail entry points. As a

A railway conductor

rule of thumb, crossing the border from EU countries (Austria, Romania, Slovakia and Slovenia) and Croatia is quick and problem-free, while crossing from the Ukraine or Serbia can often involve long queues. Visitors can also travel into Hungary along the Danube, on scheduled summer ferry services from Bratislava and Vienna or hydrofoils from Vienna.

ARRIVAL BY AIR

Budapest's Ferenc Liszt International airport is served by a large number of international airlines, including **British Airways**, Delta, KLM/Northwest Airlines, Lufthansa, and several low-cost carriers. For travellers from the northern hemisphere, there are direct flights into Budapest from over 70 cities, including most European capitals.

Ferenc Liszt International has two terminals but Terminal 1 is closed indefinitely. Terminal 2 serves both low-cost airlines and scheduled carriers, including **easyJet**, German Wings and **Wizzair**.

Hévíz-Balaton at Sármellék near Keszthely, is served by **Ryanair** from London Stansted and German Wings from Berlin. Another way to get to Budapest and northwestern Hungary is via a flight to neighbouring Vienna or Bratislava. Northeastern Hungary can be accessed via Wizzair, which flies from London Luton to Debrecen.

Taxi at Ferenc Liszt airport, Budapest

GETTING FROM AND TO THE AIRPORT

Ferenc Liszt International is located 16 km (10 miles) southeast of Budapest city centre and is served by a public bus to Kőbánya-Kispest metro station, the last stop of metro line 3. Tickets costing about 320 forints can be bought from newspaper stands at the airport. An **Airport Minibus Service** takes passengers to and from any address in the city centre for about 3,200 forints (one way). There may be a wait until there are enough passengers heading in the same direction. There is a flat fee for taxi trans-

fers to each of Budapest's districts – to the city centre (Budapest V) is 4,000–6,000 forints. Take a receipt from the dispatcher and pay the driver on arrival. The official airport taxi company is called Zónataxi.

At Hévíz-Balaton airport, Fly-Car minibuses and Zala Volán buses run to Keszthely and other villages in the region. There are also hire cars and cheap taxis.

ARRIVAL BY TRAIN

Budapest has direct rail links with more than 25 other European cities, and several trains a day arrive here from Paris, Vienna, Bratislava, Munich, Bucharest and Sofia. The rail journey from London to Budapest is easy and takes just 24 hours, via Eurostar to Paris, Orient Express to Vienna and InterCity "Avala" to Budapest. There are also daily trains from Krakow, Warsaw, Minsk, Moscow and Kiev. Trains for most other cities in Hungary, such as Pécs, Debrecen, Győr and Miskolc, depart from Budapest. InterRail and **Eurail Passes** are valid in Hungary.

BUDAPEST'S RAILWAY STATIONS

There are three main railway stations in Budapest – Keleti pu (east), Nyugati pu (west) and Déli pu (west). Most international trains operate to and from Keleti pu, the exception being rail traffic to and from Croatia (Déli pu).

Ferenc Liszt International airport, Budapest

Nyugati pu, Budapest, serving the west of the country

All three stations are on the Budapest metro system, and just a couple of stops from the city centre. The buildings are grand from the outside but unwelcoming inside, and potentially dangerous for lone travellers late at night.

ARRIVAL BY COACH

Volánbusz and **Eurolines Coach Services** travel to Budapest from 13 countries (including Great Britain, Belgium, France, Germany and Austria). They arrive at Népliget, Budapest's international coach station, from where the M3 metro line can be accessed. The international routes are served by luxury coaches with facilities such as air conditioning.

ARRIVAL BY CAR

The driving distance from London to Budapest, using motorways, is 1,834 km (1,140 miles). The fastest route, via France, Brussels, Germany and Austria, would take about 17 hours if driving non-stop. Apart from petrol,

motorists need to budget for road tolls, overnight stops and motorway tax disks for Austria and Hungary.

Hungary has more than 100 road border crossings, although in practice many of these are unstaffed and not always open. The main and most frequently used border crossing is Nickelsdorf/Hegyeshalom from Vienna; Vienna also has the only direct motorway link to Budapest. Other major border points are at Schachendorf/Búcsú from Graz in Austria and Rusovce/Rajka from Bratislava in Slovakia.

To drive in Hungary, a valid driving licence with a photo or an international driving licence and adequate insurance are required *(see also pp318–19)*.

ARRIVAL BY FERRY

Perhaps the most exotic way to arrive in Hungary is by boat, on the Danube: **Mahart PassNave** operates daily hydrofoil services from Vienna to Budapest (Apr–Oct). The downstream journey takes 5 hours 20 minutes; it's a little longer heading the other way.

The trip is fairly expensive: tickets cost €125 return for adults. The hydrofoil arrives and departs in Budapest from the jetty at Belgrad rakpart, on the Pest side of the river, halfway between Szabadság and Erzsébet bridges.

DIRECTORY

AIRPORTS

Ferenc Liszt International
Tel (1) 296 19 00.
(flight information)
www.bud.hu

Hévíz-Balaton Airport
Tel (83) 55 42 00.
(flight information)
www.heviz.hu/heviz-airport

Debrecen Airport
Tel (52) 51 88 00.
www.airportdebrecen.hu

AIRLINES

Air Berlin
www.airberlin.com

British Airways
www.ba.com

easyJet
www.easyjet.com

Ryanair
www.ryanair.com

Wizzair
www.wizzair.com

Low-cost airlines (all)
www.flycheapo.com

RAIL TRAVEL

European Rail (Eurail) Passes
www.raileurope.com

Hungarian Railways (MÁV)
Andrássy út 35.
Tel (1) 371 94 49.
www.mav.hu
(general information)
www.elvira.hu
(timetable)

COACH TRAVEL

Eurolines
www.eurolines.com

FERRIES

Mahart PassNave
Belgrád rakpart, Budapest.
Tel (1) 484 40 13.
www.mahartpassnave.hu

Luxury coaches serve international destinations

Travelling Around Hungary

Hungary's excellent railway network makes it relatively easy to travel around. The train is probably the easiest mode of transport for longer distances as the fares are also fairly low. However, the road infrastructure is also rapidly expanding and improving (for information on driving in Hungary, *see pp316–17*). There are intercity buses, but these are often slow and crowded, though undeniably cheap. During the summer many of the towns on the Danube bend, north of Budapest, can be reached by ferry, a most enjoyable way of travelling. There are no internal flights in Hungary.

TRAVELLING BY TRAIN

Virtually all trains in Hungary are operated by **MÁV** (Magyar Államvasutak), a state-owned company which has a monopoly on passenger traffic on Hungary's 8,000 km (5,000 miles) of tracks. MÁV usually runs a very good, reliable service, which offers excellent value for money. Almost all of the country's major cities and towns are connected by train services, as are a surprisingly large number of smaller towns and villages. The one problem is that the network is very much focused on Budapest, and so often the quickest route from A to B involves a detour to Budapest.

There are five different types of train in Hungary, offering varying degrees of speed and comfort. The fastest and most luxurious trains are the international Express services (Ex), requiring a seat reservation, which run to all corners of Europe. The best domestic

Ticket office at Deli Station, Budapest

trains are the InterCity (IC) services for which a supplement is levied. They are very quick and comfortable, but currently only serve a limited number of cities to and from Budapest and stop at few – if any – places in between. Next in line are *sebesvonat* services, which are less comfortable and stop at more stations, while *gyorsvonat* (literally "fast" trains) services stop even more frequently. The "slow trains", *személyvonat*, stop at every single town, village and hamlet, and – if the passenger knows the conductor well enough – just about anywhere. Painfully slow, they should be avoided unless the destination is not served by a faster train.

Tickets are priced according to distance travelled, and the type of train used. InterCity trains are the most expensive, *személyvonat* the cheapest. In addition to the ticket, a seat reservation is required whenever a service is marked with an R, as well as busy services (otherwise you will travel standing up). For InterCity services reservations are usually included in the ticket price.

Buying tickets and making reservations can be difficult outside of Budapest, as little English is spoken. It is therefore advisable to learn in advance how to pronounce the desired destination correctly. Almost all tickets are singles (*egy útra*), as the system of charging per kilometre makes the notion of returns redundant. Returns (*retúr*) can be bought to be sure of a reservation in advance, but the price will almost always be exactly double that of a single.

A good way of ensuring that you get the ticket and train service you require is to buy all tickets in advance in Budapest, at the main MÁV office. Here, English and German are spoken and you can buy tickets for every destination in Hungary, and make reservations for up to 60 days before departure. A useful service is also provided by **Wasteels**, the international rail ticketing agent, which has an office at Keleti Station *(see Directory)*.

At the stations it is important to know that *indulás* means departures and *érkezés* arrivals. The Hungarian word for platform is *vágány*. The entire railway timetable for all routes in Hungary is also posted on the internet, in English, with full pricing and routing information.

An Express train in Nyugati Station, Budapest

TRAVELLING BY BUS

The state-owned **Volánbusz** company operates an extensive network of buses serving every corner of Hungary. Its fleet of 1,000 buses reach parts of the country even *személyvonat* trains do not get to, and visitors intending to visit the more remote areas of the Great Plain or the Northern High lands can be certain that one of these buses will take them there.

Volánbusz services are usually prompt and reliable, but single-carriageway roads may, of course, slow them down. Though most of the fleet is modern and relatively comfortable, the buses themselves are often crowded. On longer journeys a refreshment stop of around 15 minutes will be scheduled. As with the train network, almost all services begin and end in Budapest at Népliget, Stadion or Árpád Bridge bus stations. These are easily reached on the metro network, but note that in some towns the coach station may be some distance outside the city centre.

Tickets generally cost less than the second-class train fare equivalent and can be obtained from the ticket offices at the bus stations. These are usually open 6am–8pm daily. Volánbusz also has a central agency in Budapest, where

A Volánbusz coach in the bus terminal at Székesfehérvár

advance tickets can be purchased for any bus or coach journey in Hungary, as well as for Eurolines services. The Volánbusz timetable is available on the Internet.

TRAVELLING BY BOAT

One of the most enjoyable way of travelling around Hungary is by boat. During the summer **Mahart PassNave** runs daily services from Vigadó ter in Budapest to Szentendre, Vác, Visegrád, Esztergom and Százhalombatta, with additional services at weekends. Tickets are not cheap (from around 1,600–2,100 forints one-way for adults, children are half-price) but they do include the services of a guide, who will point out any sights on the

route, in several languages. There are additional cruises to popular places, such as Mohács, Solt-Révbérpuszta and Kalocsa. A commuter boat also operates between Újpest Központ and Rákóczi.

DIRECTORY

TRAINS

MÁV (Hungarian Railways)
Andrássy út 35.
Tel (1) 371 94 49 (general information).
www.mav.hu (timetable)
www.elvira.hu

MÁV Nostalgia Tours
www.mavnosztalgia.hu

Buda Hills Children's Railway
Széchenyi-hegyi, Budapest.
Tel (1) 395 54 20.
www.gyermekvasut.com

Wasteels
Kerepesi utca 2–6, Keleti Station (Platform 9), Budapest.
Tel (1) 210 28 02, 343 34 92.
www.wasteels.hu

INTER-CITY BUSES

Volánbusz/Eurolines
Üllői út 131, Budapest.
Tel (1) 382 08 88 (general information); (1) 219 80 63 (reservations).
www.volanbusz.hu

FERRIES

Mahart PassNave
Belgrád rakpart, Budapest.
Tel (1) 484 40 00.
www.mahartpassnave.hu

River boat in Budapest, passing the Royal Palace

Travelling by Car

Hungary is a small country: north to south the greatest distance is 268 km (167 miles), east to west it is 528 km (328 miles). Although the government has heavily invested in the motorway network, many towns remain connected by single-lane highways. Driving on these can be frustratingly slow, yet road surfaces are generally good, and traffic is not too heavy, except for the rush hour in Budapest. The capital is a very difficult city for a visitor to navigate as there are numerous one-way systems, making it easy to get lost. There are also few places to park, so exploring the city on foot and by public transport are better ideas.

Clear directions to European and national roads, and a motorway

ROAD STANDARDS

Hungary's road network is extensive, with more than 30,000 km (18,641 miles) of paved roads, of which 1,200 km (746 miles) are motorways. Hungary in all has five motorways (prefixed M), all of which lead to and from Budapest, and are currently being extended. The M0 ring-road circumnavigates the southern and eastern parts of Budapest; M1 goes to Vienna via Győr; M3 goes to Miskolc, with branches extending to Debrecen (M35) and to Nyíregy-háza (M30); M5 goes to Szeged; M7 goes to Lake Balaton (South). Five more

motorways are also currently planned.

To drive on Hungary's motorways visitors need to purchase an e-card or e-vignette (*'matrica'*) from a major petrol station (MOL, Shell or OMV). These are available for periods of 4 days, 10 days, one month and one year. A 10-day e-card for a family car costs around 3,000 forints. Visitors caught driving on a motorway without an e-card can expect a fine of 70,000 forints. The system is policed by effective cameras that randomly select licence plate numbers for inspection.

All of Hungary's other roads – prefixed by an E for European roads or an H for national roads – are toll-free.

Signposting in Hungary is generally of a high standard, with town names and road numbers clearly marked.

One of the more unusual traffic signs

RULES OF THE ROAD

Visitors need to be 17 years old to drive in Hungary, and have a full photographic licence issued by their home country. If you have a driving licence without a photo you will need an International Driving Licence.

Road safety is good, despite occasional severe weather conditions. During the winter, visitors may be prevented from entering Hungary unless their car is equipped with snow chains. Útinform advises on current road conditions. The law also obliges drivers to keep a first-aid kit and a warning triangle in the car.

There are still relatively few speed cameras, but for serious or repeat offences the driving licence may be withdrawn. The maximum permitted speed on motorways is 130 km/h (81 mph), 110 km/h (68 mph) on European roads, and 90 km/h (56 mph) on national roads. In built-up areas the limit is 50 km/h (30 mph). By law, all passengers must wear seatbelts, and children under the age of 12 are not allowed to ride in the front. Using a hand-held mobile phone while driving is illegal.

To drive legally the alcohol level in the bloodstream must be zero mg – which means no drinking at all. The law is very strictly enforced and even first offenders risk prison for breaking it.

Hungarians drive on the right, like the rest of mainland Europe, and at roundabouts vehicles already on the roundabout have priority. Many junctions in the countryside do not have traffic lights so always stop when joining a main road, even if there is not a sign telling you to do so. Where two minor roads meet and there are no signs or traffic lights, the car approaching from the right has priority. This rule also applies in cities when traffic lights are flashing amber continuously (as they often do late at night).

The M7 motorway from Nagykanizsa to Budapest

ROAD SIGNS

Hungarian road signs follow the European standard, and there are no solely Hungarian signs. All visitors should be aware of signs they may not be familiar with, however.

As in the rest of Europe, brown signs indicate recommended tourist areas, heritage sites, tourist areas and attractions along the road, such as national parks, leisure centres or historic buildings.

PARKING

In most cities and towns there is a charge for parking anywhere near the city centre. Tickets must be bought from the vending machines and displayed behind the windscreen. The vending machines usually only accept 100-forint coins, so it is best to keep a good number to hand. There are few traffic wardens, but alert locals will often berate drivers who do not pay and display. Parking on streets where there are no public car parking spaces is free but risky – locals may sometimes damage unfamiliar cars that are parked in their favourite spot.

Parking offences may result in being towed

Parking at large supermarkets as well as all larger shopping centres is free, but only for a limited period.

A petrol station operated by MOL, the state-run company

FUEL AND SERVICES

There are plenty of service stations in Hungary on major roads and in towns and cities, but they can be few and far between in rural areas. The biggest chain is operated by MOL, the state petrol company. OMV and Shell also have a major presence. All stations offer unleaded petrol and diesel, and most stay open 24 hours. There are emergency telephones on the motorways, connected to the emergency services. If you break down elsewhere, call the **Magyar Autóklub** for assistance. You will have to pay but may be able to recover this from your insurance.

RENTING A CAR

All major international car hire firms have offices in Hungary, but car hire here is relatively expensive. Drivers must be aged 21 or over, and have held a valid driving licence for at least one year. A deposit is usually required. Most major companies include unlimited mileage, though check that this is the case before signing a rental agreement. As well as the international companies there are smaller, local firms. While they at first seem to be cheaper, hidden costs can hike up the price. They may also not be so reliable in case of accident or breakdown.

Cars can be pre-booked at airports and major hotels, although dropping them off at a different point incurs a surcharge. Cars are always delivered with a full tank of petrol, and should be returned in the same condition.

DIRECTORY

VEHICLE RECOVERY

Magyar Autóklub (MAK)
Tel 188.

ROAD CONDITIONS

Útinform
Tel (1) 366 24 00/01/02/03.
http://internet.kozut.hu

CAR RENTAL

Avis
Arany János utca 26–28, Budapest. *Tel* (1) 318 42 40.
www.avis.hu

Budget
Krisztina krt. 41–43, Budapest.
Tel (1) 214 04 20.
www.budget.hu

Europcar
Erzsébet tér 9–10, Budapest.
Tel (1) 505 44 00.
www.europcar.com

Hertz
Tel (1) 296 09 99 or 235 60 08.
www.hertz.hu

USING A PARKING METER

2 When the display panel shows the time you require, press the green button to request a ticket.

1 Insert coins for the required time, or insert a parking card. The parking meter indicates the maximum and minimum parking charges.

3 To cancel and terminate your transaction press the red button.

4 Your ticket appears here.

Travel in the Cities

Metro line sign at
Oktogon tér station

Most of Hungary's cities have good public transport networks, making use of modern buses, trolleybuses, trams and – in Budapest – a metro system and a suburban railway network. Most city centres are also very pedestrian-friendly, with a growing number of streets in the city centres now being declared car-free. Budapest aside, most city centres are small, with many sights within easy walking distance of each other. Even in Budapest the excellent public transport makes getting around quick and easy.

PUBLIC TRANSPORT IN BUDAPEST

Budapest has three metro lines (see Streetfinder pp120–23) which intersect only at Deák tér station. A fourth is in the process of being built. The oldest line is the M1 line, which is also known as the Millennium line, as it was built for the Hungarian Millennium celebrations in 1894. The Budapest Metro was the first electric underground railway system in continental Europe. Its original stations, all wood and wrought iron, as well as its small trains, make it a sight in itself. The line serves central Buda, Andrássy út and Városliget. The other two metro lines (M2 and M3) were built in the 1970s and serve the rest of Pest. The M2 crosses the river and serves three stations in Buda. Two important words

Signs for the M2 and
M3 metro lines

to remember when using the metro are *bejárat*, meaning entrance, and *kijárat*, meaning exit. All metro stations display maps of the local area, and the route of each line hangs above the doors in each carriage. A recorded voice announces the name of the next station. The metro service runs from around 4:30am until 11:30pm.

Besides the metro lines there are also 30 tram lines and over 200 bus routes in Budapest. Trams are yellow, buses blue. Trams are a particularly efficient way of traversing the city as they avoid road traffic and run very frequently.

One ticket is valid on all forms of public transport in Budapest. Tickets can be purchased from the metro stations, tobacconists and newspaper kiosks. They cannot, however, be bought on board trams or buses. A

single journey ticket costs 320 forints. The ticket must be validated in the machines located at the entrance to metro lines or on board buses and trams. For each new journey, a new ticket has to be stamped. You do not need to stamp another ticket when you change lines on the metro. Children under six travel free. Season tickets for 1, 3 or 7 days travel are sold at metro stations, as are books of ten tickets for 2,800 forints. The Budapest Card (Ft 6,900 for 48 hours or Ft 7,900 for 72 hours) allows free use of public transport as well as giving various discounts in museums and at tourist sights.

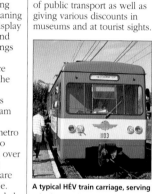

A typical HÉV train carriage, serving suburban stations

THE HÉV

Budapest and its suburbs also benefit from HÉV trains, an efficient and reliable – if sometimes slow – suburban rail service. Trains serve all of Budapest's suburbs, as well as a number of towns further afield, including Szentendre, Gödöllő and Ráckeve. HÉV trains are green, and depart from Batthyány tér for Szentendre, from Örs vezér tere for Gödöllő and the Hungaroring Formula One circuit, and from Közvágóhíd for Ráckeve. Standard Budapest transport tickets are valid for journeys on HÉV trains within Budapest, but for journeys beyond the city limits tickets costing from 155 forints can be purchased at station entrances or automated kiosks. Information and timetables for travel on Budapest's metro and HÉV trains as well as buses can be obtained from **BKV** who run Budapest's transport system.

A typical station on the original M1 metro line, the first in Europe

Tram in Debrecen, with the Great Reformed Church in the background

PUBLIC TRANSPORT IN OTHER CITIES

While Budapest has the only metro network in Hungary, most large towns, including Debrecen, Győr, Pécs and Szeged have tram systems. Every town (and even some smaller villages) has bus services. As a rule, all tickets need to be purchased before boarding the means of transport, and then franked or validated once on board. Tickets can usually be bought from tobacconists and newspaper kiosks, and sometimes from ticket machines.

It is important to validate tickets as there are many ticket inspectors, both in uniform and plain clothes, who may stop travellers and demand to see their tickets even after they have got off their trains or buses.

In many towns trams can double as cut-price city tours. In Debrecen, for instance, the only tram line runs from the railway station to the city's large thermal bath complex, passing through the centre

and past most important sights on the way. In Miskolc trams No 1 and 2 run from the train station to the city centre, and on to Diósgyőr Castle (see p227). In Pécs there is a sightseeing tourist train which departs from opposite the Csontváry Museum (see p186), while Szeged's tram No. 1 runs from the station into the town centre.

In Hungary passengers are allowed to carry one piece of luggage and a children's buggy on buses and trams, but the bag must not be too large. Ticket inspectors may demand an additional payment if a bag is too large, or more than one bag is carried.

TAXIS

As elsewhere in the world, visitors should be wary when getting into a taxi anywhere in Hungary, but especially in Budapest and at popular tourist places. While most taxis are safe, cheap and a

good way of getting around cities, many turn out to be far more expensive than expected, and they have been known to prey on bewildered visitors.

Most, but not all taxis are yellow, and all should have a licence number issued by the city council clearly displayed. They should also post their tariffs on the windscreen or side of the passenger door.

Taxis can be booked over the phone, which is slightly cheaper, or hailed in the street. The best place to find a cab is in the taxi ranks near major bus stations, squares, markets or railway stations.

Most taxis are operated by authorized taxi companies, and will display the company name and telephone number prominently. These are the taxis that should always be

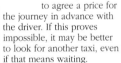

Sign denoting a taxi rank

used. Private taxis are often more expensive. Visitors are advised to take extra care when getting into a taxi outside a railway station. If a private taxi is the only one available, it is best to agree a price for the journey in advance with the driver. If this proves impossible, it may be better to look for another taxi, even if that means waiting.

Most hotels and restaurants will phone for a taxi for their guests. In fact, this may be cheaper than hailing one.

DIRECTORY

TAXIS

6x6 Taxi (1) 666 66 66.

Budapest Taxi (1) 433 33 33.

Budataxi (1) 233 33 33.

City Taxi (1) 211 11 11.

Fötaxi (1) 222 22 22.

Rádiotaxi (1) 777 77 77.

Taxi 2000 (1) 200 00 00.

Taxi4 (1) 444 44 44.

Tele5 (1) 555 55 55.

LOCAL TRANSPORT

BKV www.bkv.hu

A licensed Hungarian taxi

General Index

Acknowledgments

HACHETTE LIVRE POLSKA would like to thank the following staff at Dorling Kindersley:

Publisher
Douglas Amrine

Publishing Managers
Anna Streiffert, Christine Stroyan

Managing Art Editor
Jane Ewart

Editors
Sylvia Goulding, Jacky Jackson, Michelle Crane

Designer
Kate Leonard

Translator
Magda Hannay

Map Co-Ordinator
Casper Morris

DTP Manager
Natasha Lu

Additional Picture Research
Rachel Barber, Ellen Root

Production Controller
Shane Higgins

DORLING KINDERSLEY would like to thank all those whose contributions and assistance have made the preparation of this book possible:

Main Contributor
Craig Turp is a linguist by training, and has spent most of his adult life studying and writing about the languages and peoples of Central and Eastern Europe. He has written a number of guide books to the region, and lives in Bucharest, Romania.

Additional Text
Steve Fallon

Factcheckers
Szilvia Szőke, Judit Mihalcsik

Proofreader
Stewart J Wild

Indexer
Helen Peters

Additional Photography
Demetrio Carrasco, Eddie Gerald, Ian O'Leary, Piotr Ostrowski, Mirek Osip

Additional Illustrations
ichapel.co.uk

Cartography
Base mapping supplied by Cartographia Ltd., Budapest.

Revisions Editorial and Design
Caroline Elliker, Rhiannon Furbear, Claire Jones, Hayley Maher, Lucy Mallows, Agnes Ordog, Marianne Petrou, Susana Smith, Conrad Van Dyk

Special Assistance
The Publishers would like to thank the staff at shops, museums, hotels, restaurants and other organizations in Hungary for their invaluable help. Particular thanks go to: the Ambassador for the Republic of Hungary in Warsaw; the Ambassador for the Republic of Poland in Budapest; Peter Hajnal at Europress; Csilla Pataky at Cartographia Ltd., Budapest; Vanda Tódor at the Budapest Festival Centre.

Photography Permissions
The Publishers would like to thank all those who gave permission to photograph at musuems, palaces, churches, restaurants, hotels, shops and other sights too numerous to list individually. Particular thanks go to: the Aquaticum Thermal Baths in Debrecen; Bacchus Borkereskedés; the Christian Museum in Esztergom; staff at Festetics Palace and Helikon Palace Museum, Keszthely; Loránd Bereczky at the Hungarian National Gallery; Gyula Fülöp at the Szent István Király Museum, Székesfehérvár; Ágnes Langer at the Zettl-Langer Collection, Sopron.

Library/Graham Salter 26tl; mediacolor's 124–5; Melba Photo Agency 231b; Ball Miwako 10cla; Gianni Muratore 23bc, 116tr; nagelestock.com 60cr; Luke Peters 247cr; Pictorial Press Ltd 44cb; PjrFoto.com/Phil Robinson 191c; Simon Reddy 22clb; roughguidespictures.com 191cr; Stephen Photography Saks 39br; Norman West 310br; Stephen Wilson Photography 311cl. ARDEA: Chris Knights 21br; Jens-Peter Laub 21clb; Ake Lindau 20tl; Duncan Usher 21bc, 21tr. THE ART ARCHIVE: National Gallery Budapest/Dagli Orti 38bl.

BAGLIONI HOTEL & RÁCZ THERMAL SPA: 75cl. GÁBOR BARKA: 49c, 62cb, 63tl, 63br, 80cl, 80br, 81 all, 87tl, 87cr, 87crb, 87bc, 88cb, 88c, 88br, 89 all, 92cl, 97tl, 106cl, 258tc, 276b, 312tc, 318bl. BUDAPEST AIRPORT: 312bl. BUDAPEST FESTIVAL CENTRE: 30b. BUDAPEST HISTORY MUSEUM: 56tl. BUDAPEST SPA LLC: 105tr. BUDAPESTI TURISZTIKAI HIVATAL: 73t, 84tl, 110bc. BUDDHA-BAR HOTEL: 96cl.

CEPHAS PICTURE LIBRARY:Herbert Lehmann 28br. CORBIS: Atlantide Phototravel 301t; Bettmann 9c, 42bl, 43cbl; Bernard Bisson 47t; Astakhov Dmitry/ITAR-TASS 47br; Rose Hartman 23cra; Kit Houghton 300tl; Hulton-Deutsch Collection 45c, 46bl; Wolfgang Kaehler 136–7; Barry Lewis 32b, 71tl, 279tl; Ira Nowinski 26c; Schlegelmilch 31b; Attal Serge 191bl; Swim Ink 2, LLC 23crb; David Turnley 46crb; Peter Turnley 191tr; Sandro Vannini 24br, 25tl; Uwe Walz 220tl; Zefa/Klaus Hackenberg 27bl.

DANUBIUS HOTEL GROUP: 258cr.

EUROPRESS FOTOUGYNOKSEG: Koltai Andor 33bl; Robert Bacsi 191clb, 310bl; Laszlo Beliczay 32cr; Ilovsky Bela 296b; Janos Bugany 247tl; Katalin Darnay 73tr, 92bl; Marian Reismann 46t, 63cr; Tibor Rigo 244-5, 247cl; Vereb Simon 297b; Tibor Szabó 93crb; Bela Szandelszky 30cr, 47crb.

GETTY IMAGES: Oliver Benn 15b. GRAND PHOTO AGENCY: 111t; Koltai Andor 24cl; Molnar V. Attila 21cb, 22br; Zoltan Bagosi 20c, 20bl, 21cla; Béla Budai 28bc; Katalin Darnay 29cr; Anita Huszti 20clb; Diósi Imre 20cb; György Kallus 27c; Kata Kovács 29br; Szabolcs László 45tc; Tibor Rigo 25cra, 28clb, 28tr; Tibor Szabó 29bl.

HEMISPHERE IMAGES: Giuglio Gil 256-7; Wysocki Pawel 48–9; Frilet Patrick 222–3; Torrione Stefano 319tr; Emilio Suetone 19tr. HOUSE OF TERROR: 101br. HUNGARIAN NATIONAL GALLERY: 34, 38bcl, 38tr, 40cb, 58–9 all, 185br. HUNGARIAN NATIONAL MUSEUM: 8–9, 35crb, 36cb, 36bl, 36br, 39cla, 39cb, 39bl, 40tl, 40cr, 41crb, 41br, 41tr, 98–9 all, 183br.

JON ARNOLD IMAGES: Doug Pearson 14.

THE KOBAL COLLECTION: Paramount 26cra.

LONELY PLANET IMAGES: Martin Moos 22tl; Jonathan Smith 25cr.

MAGYAR NEMZETI BNK: 309 all. MARY EVANS PICTURES LIBRARY: 43bl; 44tl. MUSEUM OF APPLIED ARTS: Ágnes Kolozs 83clb. MUSEUM OF FINE ARTS: 106cr.

NATIONAL OFFICE OF CULTURAL HERITAGE: 38–9.

PA PHOTOS: AP 26bc; AP/Arpad Hazafi 45crb; S&G 27tr. PHOTOLIBRARY: Jon Arnold Images/Jon Arnold 20tr. PHOTOSHOT: NHPA/Bill Coster 20bc; Andy Rouse 21cl.

REX FEATURES: Bela Szandelszky 30ct; Laszlo Toth 33cr. ROBERT HARDING PICTURE LIBRARY: Gavin Hellier 11tl.

SZAMOS MARZIPAN MUSEUM: 138tr. SZÉCHENYI NATIONAL GALLERY: 78tr. SZÉCHENYI NATIONAL LIBRARY: 37ca, 38cl, 39tc, 56bc. ÁGNES SZEL: 78bc, 280br.

TOPFOTO.CO.UK: Topham Picturepoint 44bc. TOURINFORM SZEGED: 242cr.

ZSOLNAY MUSEUM: István Füzi 186cr.

JACKET: Front – GETTY IMAGES: Sylvain Sonnet. Back – 4CORNERS: Huber/Reinhard Schmid tl, bl; ALAMY IMAGES: JTB MEDIA CREATION, Inc. clb. Spine – GETTY IMAGES: Sylvain Sonnet, t.

All other images © Dorling Kindersley.

For further information see: www.dkimages. com

SPECIAL EDITIONS OF DK TRAVEL GUIDES

Phrase Book

Pronunciation

When reading the literal pronunciation given in the right-hand column of this phrase book, pronounce each syllable as if it formed part of an English word. Remember the points below, and your pronunciation will be even closer to correct Hungarian. The first syllable of each word should be stressed (and is shown in bold). When asking a question the pitch should be raised on the penultimate syllable. "R"s in Hungarian words are rolled.

a	as the long 'a' in father
ay	as in 'pay'
e	as in 'Ted'
ew	similar to the sound in 'hew'
g	always as in 'goat'
i	as in 'bit'
o	as in the 'ou' in 'ought'
u	as in 'tuck'
y	always as in 'yes' (except as in *ay* above)
yuh	as the 'yo' in 'canyon'
zh	like the 's' in leisure

In Emergency

Help!	Segítség!	sh**eg**eetshayg
Stop!	Stop!	shtop
Look out!	Tessék vigyázni!	teshayk **vid**yahzni
Call a doctor	Hívjon orvost!	**heev**yon **or**vosht
Call an ambulance!	Hívjon mentőt!	**heev**yon **ment**urt
Call the police!	Hívja a rendőrséget!	**heev**ya a **ren**dur shayget
Call the fire department!	Hívja a tűzoltókat!	**heev**ya a **tewz**oltowkot
Where is the nearest telephone?	Hol van a legközelebbi telefon?	hol von a **leg**kurze-lebbi **tel**efon
Where is the nearest hospital?	Hol van a legközelebbi kórház?	hol von a **leg**kurze-bbi **koor**hahz

Communications Essentials

Yes/No	Igen/Nem	**ig**en/nem
Please (offering)	Tessék	**tesh**ayk
Please (asking)	Kérem	**kay**rem
Thank you	Köszönöm	**kurss**urnurm
No, thank you	Köszönöm nem	**kurss**urnurm nem
Excuse me, please	Bocsánatot kérek	**boch**anutot **kay**rek
Hello	Jó napot	yow **nop**ot
Goodbye	Viszontlátásra	**viss**ontlatashruh
Good night	Jó éjszakát/jó éjt	yaw-**ayss**ukat/yaw-ayt
morning (4–9 am)	reggel	**reg**gel
morning (9am–noon)	délelőtt	**day**lelurt
morning (midnight–4am)	éjjel	**ay**-yel
afternoon	délután	**day**lootan
evening	este	**esh**teh
yesterday	tegnap	**teg**nup
today	ma	muh
tomorrow	holnap	**hol**nup
here	itt	it
there	ott	ot
What?	mi?	mi
When?	mikor?	**mik**or
Why?	miért?	**mi**ayrt
Where?	hol?	hol

Useful Phrases

How are you?	Hogy van?	**hod**-yuh vun
Very well, thank you	köszönöm nagyon jól	**kurss**urnurm **noj**jon yowl
Pleased to meet you	Örülök hogy megismerhettem	ur-**rewl**urk **hod**-yuh **meg**ishmerhettem
See you soon!	Szia!	**see**yuh
Excellent!	Nagyszerű!	**nud**-yusserew
Is there ... here?	Van itt ... ?	vun itt
Where can I get ...?	Hol kaphatok ...-t?	hol **kup**hutok ...-t
How do you get to?	Hogy lehet ...-ba eljutni?	**hod**-yuh **leh**et ...-buh **el**-yootni
How far is ...?	milyen messze van ...?	**mee**yen **mess**eh van ...
Do you speak English?	Beszél angolul?	**bess**ayl **ung**olool
I can't speak Hungarian	Nem beszélek magyarul	nem **bess**aylek **mud**-yarool
I don't understand	Nem értem	nem **ayr**tem
Can you help me?	Kérhetem a segítségét?	**kayr**hetem uh sh**eg**eechaygayt
Please speak slowly	Tessék lassabban beszélni	**tesh**ayk **lush**ubbun **bess**aylni
Sorry!	Elnézést!	**el**nayzaysht

Useful Words

big	nagy	noj
small	kicsi	**kich**i
hot	forró	**mel**eg
cold	hideg	**hid**eg
good	jó	yow
bad	rossz	ross
enough	elég	**el**ayg
well	jól	yowl
open	nyitva	**nyit**va
closed	zárva	**zar**va
left	bal	bol
right	jobb	yob
straight on	egyenesen	**ej**eneshen
near	közel	**kurz**el
far	messze	**mess**eh
up	fel	fel
down	le	leh
early	korán	**kor**an
late	késő	**kaysh**ur
entrance	bejárat	**beh**-yarut
exit	kijárat	**ki**-yarut
toilet	WC	**vayt**say
free/unoccupied	szabad	**sobb**od
free/no charge	ingyen	**in**jen

Making a Telephone Call

Can I call abroad from here?	Telefonálhatok innen külföldre?	**tel**efonalhutok **in**en **kewl**furldreh
I would like to call collect	Szeretnék egy R-beszélgetést lebonyolítani	s**er**etnayk ed-yuh er-**bess**aylgetaysht **leb**on-yoleetuni
local call	helyi beszélgetés	**hay**ee **bess**aylgetaysht
I'll ring back later	Visszahívom később	**viss**uh-heevom **kaysh**urb
Could I leave a message?	Hagyhatnék egy üzenetet?	**hud**-yuhutnayk ed-yuh **ewz**enetet
Hold on!	Várjon!	**vahr**-yon
Could you speak up a little, please?	kicsit hangosabban, kérem!	**kich**it hungosh-shob-bon **kay**rem

Shopping

How much is this?	Ez mennyibe kerül?	ez **menn**-yibeh **ker**ewl
I would like ...	Szeretnék egy ...-t	s**er**etnayk ed-yuh ...-t
Do you have ...?	Kapható önöknél ...?	**kup**hutaw **urn**urknayl
I'm just looking	Csak körülnézek	chuk **kur**-rewlnayzek
Do you take credit cards?	Elfogadják a hitelkártyákat?	**el**fogud-yak uh **hit**elkart-yakut
What time do you open?	Hánykor nyitnak?	**Hahn**kor **nyit**nak
What time do you close?	Hánykor zárnak?	**Hahn**kor **zár**nak
this one	ez	ez
that one	az	oz
expensive	drága	**drah**ga
cheap	olcsó	**ol**chow
size	méret	**may**ret
white	fehér	**feh**eer
black	fekete	**fek**eteh
red	piros	**pi**rosh
yellow	sárga	**shar**ga
green	zöld	zurld
blue	kék	cake
brown	barna	**bor**na

Types of Shop

antique dealer	antikvárius	**on**tikvahrioosh
baker's	pékség	**payk**shayg
bank	bank	bonk
bookshop	könyvesbolt	**kurn**-yuveshbolt
cake shop	cukrászda	**tsook**rassduh
chemist	patika	**put**ikuh
department store	áruház	**aro**o-haz
florist	virágüzlet	**vi** rag-ewzlet
greengrocer	zöldséges	**zurld**-shaygesh
market	piac	**pi**-uts
newsagent	újságos	**oo**-yushagosh
post office	postahivatal	**posh**ta-hivatal
shoe shop	cipőbolt	**tsi**purbolt
souvenir shop	ajándékbolt	**uy**-yandaykbolt
supermarket	ábécé/ABC	**a**baytsay
travel agent	utazási iroda	**oot**uzashi iroduh

Staying in a Hotel

Have you any vacancies?	Van kiadó szobájuk?	vun ki-udaw soba-yook
double room with double bed	francia-ágyas szoba	frontsia-ahjosh sobuh
twin room	kétágyas szoba	kaytad-yush sobuh
single room	egyágyas szoba	ed-yad-yush sobuh
room with a bath/shower	fürdőszobás/ zuhanyzós szoba	fewrdur-sobahsh/ zoohonzahsh soba
porter	portás	portahsh
key	kulcs	koolch
I have a reservation	Foglaltam egy szobát	foglultum ed-yuh sobat

Sightseeing

bus	autóbusz/busz	owtawbooss/booss
tram	villamos	villumosh
trolley bus	troli(busz)	troli(booss)
train	vonat	vonut
underground	metró	metraw
bus stop	buszmegálló	boossmegallaw
tram stop	villamosmegálló	villomosh-megahllaw
art gallery	képcsarnok	kayp-chornok
palace	palota	polola
cathedral	székesegyház	saykesh-ejhajz
church	templom	templom
garden	kert	kert
library	könyvtár	kurnvtar
museum	múzeum	moozayoom
tourist information	turista információ	toorishta informatzeeo
closed for public holiday	ünnepnap zárva	ewn-nepnap zarva

Eating Out

A table for … please	Egy asztal szeretnék… személyre	ed-yuh usstult seretnayk … semayreh
I want to reserve a table	Szeretnék egy asztalt foglalni	seretnayk ed-yuh usstultfoglolni
The bill, please	Kérem a számlát	kayrem uh samlat
I am a vegetarian	Vegetáriánus vagyok	vegetari-ahnoosh vojok
I'd like …	Szeret nék egy …-t	seret nayk ed-yuh …-t
waiter/waitress	pincér/pincérnő	pintsayr/pintsayrnur
menu	étlap	aytlup
wine list	itallap	itullup
chef's special	konyhafőnök ajánlata	konha-furnurt oyahu-lotta
tip	borravaló	borovolo
glass	pohár	pohar
bottle	üveg	ewveg
knife	kés	kaysh
fork	villa	villuh
spoon	kanál	kunal
breakfast	reggeli	reg-geli
lunch	ebéd	ebayd
dinner	vacsora	vochora
main courses	főételek	fur-aytelek
starters	előételek	elur-aytelek
vegetables	zöldség	zurld-shayg
desserts	édességek	aydesh-shaydek
rare	angolosan	ongoloshan
well done	átsütve	ahtshewtveh

Menu Decoder

alma	olma	apple
ásványvíz	ahshvahnveez	mineral water
bab	bob	beans
banán	bonahn	banana
barack	borotsk	apricot
bárány	bahrahn	lamb
bors	borsh	pepper
csirke	cheerkeh	chicken
csokoládé	chokolahday	chocolate
cukor	tsookor	sugar
ecet	etset	vinegar
fagylalt	fodyuhloot	ice cream
fehérbor	feheerbor	white wine
fokhagyma	fokhodyuhma	garlic
főtt	furt	boiled
gomba	gomba	mushrooms
gulyás	gooyahsh	goulash
gyümölcs	dyewmurlch	fruit
gyümölcslé	dyewmurlch-lay	fruit juice
hagyma	hojma	onions
hal	hol	fish
hús	hoosh	meat
kávé	kavay	coffee

kenyér	ken-yeer	bread
krumpli	kroompli	potatoes
kolbász	kolbahss	sausage
leves	levesh	soup
máj	my	liver
marha	marha	beef
mustár	mooshtahr	mustard
narancs	noronch	orange
olaj	oloy	oil
paradicsom	porodichom	tomatoes
párolt	pahrolt	steamed
pite	pitch	pie
sertéshús	shertaysh-hoosh	pork
rántott	rahntsott	fried in batter
rizs	rizh	rice
rostélyos szelet	bifstek	steak
roston	roshton-	grilled
sajt	shoyt	cheese
saláta	sholahta	salad
só	shaw	salt
sonka	shonka	ham
sör	shur	beer
sült	shewlt	fried/roasted
sült burgonya	shewlt boorgonya	fried potatoes/chips
sütemény	shewtemayn-yuh	cake, pastry
szendvics	sendvich	sandwich
szósz	sowss	sauce
tea	tay-uh	tea
tej	tay	milk
tejszín	taysseen	cream
tengeri hal	tengeri hol	seafood
tojás	toyahsh	egg
töltött	turlturt	stuffed
vörösbor	vur-rurshbor	red wine
zsemle	zhemleh	roll
zsemlegombóc	zhemleh-gombowts	dumplings

Numbers

0	nulla	noolluh
1	egy	ed-yuh
2	kettő, két	kettur, kayt
3	három	harom
4	négy	nayd-yuh
5	öt	urt
6	hat	hut
7	hét	hayt
8	nyolc	n-yolts
9	kilenc	kilents
10	tíz	teez
11	tizenegy	tizened-yuh
12	tizenkettő	tizenkettur
13	tizenhárom	tizenharom
14	tizennégy	tizen-nayd-yuh
15	tizenöt	tizenurt
16	tizenhat	tizenhut
17	tizenhét	tizenhayt
18	tizennyolc	tizenn-yolts
19	tizenkilenc	tizenkilents
20	húsz	hooss
21	huszonegy	hoossoned-yuh
22	huszonkettő	hoossonkettur
30	harminc	hurmints
31	harmincegy	hurmintsed-yuh
32	harminckettő	hurmintskettur
40	negyven	ned-yuven
50	ötven	urtven
60	hatvan	hutvun
70	hetven	hetven
80	nyolcvan	n-yoltsvun
90	kilencven	kilentsven
100	száz	saz
110	száztíz	sazteez
200	kétszáz	kayt-saz
300	háromszáz	haromssaz
1000	ezer	ezer
10,000	tízezer	teezezer
1,000,000	millió	milliaw

Time

one minute	egy perc	ed-yuh perts
hour	óra	awruh
half an hour	félóra	faylawruh
Sunday	vasárnap	vusharnup
Monday	hétfő	haytfur
Tuesday	kedd	kedd
Wednesday	szerda	serduh
Thursday	csütörtök	chewturturk
Friday	péntek	payntek
Saturday	szombat	sombut

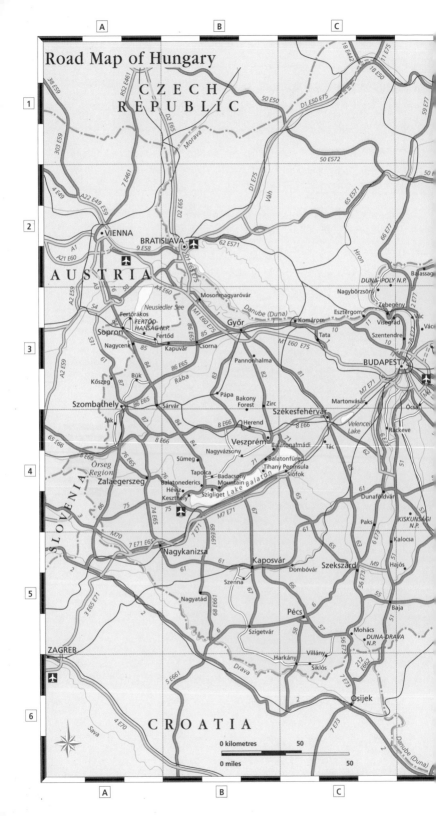